D1091959

Courtesy of Overland Journal Vol. 11, Number 1, Page 3. Oregon California Trails Association

EMIGRANT TRAILS TO THE OREGON TERRITORY BY 1846

- - - SOUTHERN ROAD TO OREGON
(the Applegate Trail)
——— OREGON AND CALIFORNIA
TRAILS
······· OTHER TRAILS AND ROADS

FROM THE OREGON-CALIFORNIA TRAILS ASSOCIATION'S
MAP, "WESTERN EMIGRANT TRAILS 1830 - 1870"

WYOMING

River

Fort Hall

Snake

R.

Fort Bridger

Great Salt Lake

HASTINGS CUTOFF (1846)

UTAH

OREGON TRAIL

Fort Boise

Boise R.

Three Island Crossing

IDAHO

Malheur R.

OREGON

River

Snake

Whitman Mission

Blue Mountains

Fort Walla Walla

River

Walla Walla

John Day River

Deschutes R.

Site of Applegate drownings of 1843

Cascades Portage

The Dalles

Fort Vancouver

Columbia

Oregon City

La Creole Creek

Champoeg

Lee's Old Mission

Calapooya
Umpqua Divide

Canyon Creek Canyon

Rogue R.

S. Fk.

Umpqua R. N. Fk.

SOUTHERN

Klamath R.

Emigrant Creek

Upper Klamath Lake

Lower Klamath lake

Tule Lake

Clear Lake

Blue Mtn.

Goose Lake

Fandango Pass

Surprise Valley

High Rock Canyon

Mud Lake

Black Rock

Rabbit Hole Springs

Thousand Springs Valley

NEVADA

CALIFORNIA TRAIL

Ruby Mountains

Humboldt River

Antelope Springs

Humboldt Sink

Pyramid L.

initial route to Humboldt River

ROAD TO

OREGON

CALIFORNIA

Mt. Shasta

Hat Creek

OLD CALIFORNIA PACK TRAIL (Siskiyou Trail)

Barlow Rd.

Mt. Hood

Cascade Range

Willamette R.

Pacific Ocean

Pacific

CHW

Beautiful McKenzie

To Glenn and Arlene,
for your birthdays,
With much love
Enjoy...
Richard & Lory

Leroy B. Inman

A History

Of Central Lane County

By Leroy B. Inman

-- A South Fork Press Publication --

ISBN   0-9655076-0-2

Library of Congress Catalog Card Number 96-95042

Other Books   by Leroy B. Inman
Early Days on the McKenzie

To order additional copies, contact:

South Fork Press
374 SE Ella Street
Roseburg, Oregon 97470

*Printed by * Maverick Publications, Inc.*
*P. O. Box 5007 * Bend, Oregon 97708*

Table of Contents

Acknowledgments

No history written today is the work of one person but a compilation of the works of many. Much has been written in bits and pieces, tucked away in closets or publications hidden in historical files in obscure corners of libraries not easily available for public perusal.

So we must rely upon those writings, diaries, newspaper files, vital statistics, census and court records to supply the information needed to tell the story of our ancestors who settled the great West. Our goal is to preserve as best we can in a concise form a history of the area. Special recognition must be given that source material.

We wish to acknowledge, first, that so-called bible of all contemporary historians, A. G. Walling's *History of Oregon* and his *History of Lane County*, published initially in 1884. Walling obtained first-hand information, interviewing many pioneer settlers and viewing the records which he included in his masterful presentation.

Second, we wish to acknowledge Lewis A. McArthur's *Oregon Geographical Names*, first published in 1928 and carried on in recent years by his son, Lewis L. McArthur of Portland.

We must give special recognition to Gerald W. Williams for his unpublished *McKenzie River Names*. Williams is Umpqua National Forest sociologist and historian, and chairman of Region-6 History Committee. Jerry, a personal friend, has granted permission for use of and reference to his material gathered over the years.

The Story of Eugene, authored by sisters Lucia Moore, Nina McCornack and Gladys McCready (1949), recently republished by the Lane County Historical Society, provides background material.

Lois Barton, Eugene author, has granted permission to use excerpts from her book, *One Woman's West*, the enthralling diary of Martha Gay Masterson.

Special thanks must also be given to Carl Stephens, Walterville historian, who is not only knowledgeable of McKenzie history but has been very cooperative in sharing this knowledge and pictures.

We have scoured the Oregon section of the University of Oregon Library for historical writings in the Lane County Historian and other publications in order to authenticate our information. We have picked the bare bones of "Historic Leaburg and Vicinity," of River Reflections, The Springfield News, Eugene Register-Guard and other newspapers.

We have interviewed many people and read their diaries to authenticate historical records. Most of these sources we have recognized within the pages of this book. If we are to be faulted for omissions, it is not by intent.

Last, but not least, I must give special recognition to my wife for her consideration and inspiration provided while I have spent countless hours at the computer putting this manuscript together. She has not only assisted with research but has also served as a copy editor.

TAMOLICH FALLS is one of three picturesque falls
on the upper reaches of the McKenzie River. They
are Sahalie, the upper; Koosah, the middle, and
Tamolich, the lower falls. Tamolich now is a part
of the Eugene Water and Electric District Carmen-
Smith hydroelectric system. The other falls can
be reached from the Clear Lake Highway.

SNOW CAPPED THREE SISTERS in Oregon's high Cascades dominate the landscape on the Lane-Deschutes County line.

BEAUTIFUL McKENZIE©

CHAPTER 1

Mt. Multnomah

What does our mind's eye see when we think of the McKenzie?

A beautiful valley, walled with high mountains, curtained with the green of Douglas fir trees and other species -- a swift-flowing river, its white caps glistening from the rays of a morning sun -- a paved highway wending its way up the valley offering easy access -- an hour or more drive from where the McKenzie River joins the Willamette River near Harrisburg to its source in Clear Lake high in Oregon's Cascades.

But what did the early pioneer see when he first came up the Willamette and looked eastward? Beautiful country, yes, but its access limited to a few Indian trails, otherwise a jungled mass of underbrush and tall trees that had to be cut through to negotiate, and rivers and streams that had to be crossed.

Let us go back a few million years, long before humans are known to have come on the scene. What do we see?

A towering mountain, snowcapped, massive -- Mt. Multnomah!

Just what and where was Mt. Multnomah? This mountain is believed to have risen in what is now the Three Sisters Wilderness in the high Cascades. The name was given to a suspected mountain by Dr. Edwin T. Hodge, University of Oregon geologist, in 1924.

Mt. Multnomah some ten million years ago blew its top. What remains is the Three Sisters "family" group of mountains -- the North, Middle and South Sisters, The Husband, The Wife, Little Brother and The Bachelor -- which dominate the area today that was once part of Mt. Multnomah. The mountain exploded and the family group is all that remains.

Mt. Multnomah rose a mile above the highest mountain in today's group -- perhaps 15,000 to 16,000 feet in elevation, making it the highest mountain in Oregon, possibly in the United States.

Indians spoke of the mountain that no longer exists. Lucy and Walter Miller, Warm Springs Indians, said they heard the story from their grandfathers who signed the treaty in 1855 establishing their reservation in Central Oregon. It is hardly conceivable they were referring to something that happened a few million years ago, but the implication is interesting.

"Multnomah is an old Indian name for that part of the Willamette River between Oregon City and the Columbia River. It is chosen for Oregon's highest prehistoric mountain because of the dignity and beauty of the name," Dr. Hodge wrote in 1925.

About 3,000 years ago, lava flowed from vents near Sand Mountain to dam the flow of water from the Cascade Mountains to create Clear Lake, which became the headwaters of the McKenzie River near its main source, the Great Spring.

Belknap Crater -- named for James Henry Belknap, pioneer of 1869 -- some 1,600 years ago, spewed lava over the earlier lava flows, forming the vast lava beds of the McKenzie Pass and plunging into the McKenzie Canyon. This caused parts of the river to be absorbed into the lava rock and disappear underground, to appear again at the base of Tamolitch Falls.

The McKenzie

The McKenzie River, named for Donald Mackenzie (note spelling), early-day explorer with the John Jacob Astor Pacific Fur Co., truly is one of the beautiful rivers of the world.

That statement might be rightfully challenged: What about the Umpqua? the Rogue? the Santiam? the Willamette itself? -- all beautiful rivers noted for fishing and favorites of such notables of the past as author Zane Gray, Ex-President Herbert Hoover, movie stars. But each has its own distinctive quality as to terrain, volume of water and nature of its flow. Which is the most beautiful is in the eye of the beholder.

Surely the McKenzie can hold its own for its beauty and clear, cold water flow through steep canyons curtained by Douglas green. It also is distinctive for available farm lands and recreational uses on either side of the river all the way to the high Cascades and the awesome beauty of snow-capped peaks and lava beds.

But this is not a treatise on the McKenzie's attributes, offered only to illustrate what attracted such early-day settlers as James Belknap, his father Rollin Simeon Belknap, who founded Belknap Springs in 1871, and James' father-in-law, Benjamin Franklin

"Huckleberry" Finn, who blazed the way, removing monoliths in his path. And there were the Cogswells, Storments, Millicans, John Craig, Martins, Foleys, Pepiots, Thomsons, Wycoffs, Sims.

The full power of the upper McKenzie River is seen in a short walk along a mist-covered trail to Sahalie Falls. Rushing water, moss-covered banks and tall trees illustrate the breath-taking beauty of this wilderness river.

The 90-mile-long McKenzie River has its source in Clear Lake, near the Santiam Pass in the Mt. Jefferson Wilderness. It picks up Smith River, Olallie Creek and other large tributaries -- Lost Creek, Horse Creek and the South Fork from the Three Sisters drainage.

Then Blue River, Quartz Creek, Gate Creek, Camp Creek, the Mohawk and lesser streams feed the river as it wends its way down the valley, narrowing here, widening there, slowing, then quickening its pace in scenic white water to converge with the Willamette River near Harrisburg -- thence to the mighty Columbia and Pacific Ocean.

Indians were first to traverse the mountains and valleys of Oregon. The Warm Springs tribes of north-central Oregon made annual sorties over the summit of the Cascades into the McKenzie Valley to pick huckleberries, catch and smoke salmon, and in later years pick hops, a practice continued well into the 1930's. Indian trails that crisscrossed the state were followed by pioneers wherever practical.

Spanish Mariners

A brief look into the history of Oregon opens the door to a better understanding of early days on the McKenzie and what pioneers were to find in their explorations and settlements.

The name Oregon was first applied to the river now known as the Columbia, later to the country drained by that river. The first known white men to sail along the coast were Spaniards. Bartolomi Perrelo, who accompanied Juan Rodriques Cabrillo on his expeditions up the California coast, continued northward after Cabrillo's death in January 1543. He claimed to have passed the mouth of what is now known as the Rogue River and reached the 43rd parallel.

Sir Francis Drake may have seen the cliffs along the coast in 1579, may even have put into port. Two centuries later, in 1774-75, other Spanish mariners, including Juan Perez and Bruno Heceta, made voyages along the entire Oregon Coast. It is certain the great British sea captain, James Cook, was in the Northwest in 1778. He discovered and named Cape Foulweather on March 7 that year. The weather was particularly inclement on the day of discovery.

Within another decade American and British ship captains were trading with the natives. From 1791 to 1793, ships made appearances along the coast from California to the Queen Charlotte River in Canada to trade with the Indians.

One of these American mariners, Capt. Robert Gray, May 19, 1792, discovered and entered the long-sought "River of the West." He named it the Columbia for the ship he commanded. Some reports say Gray only penetrated the Columbia about 12 miles into what is now Baker's Bay at the entrance of the river. Gray then proceeded north along the coast and revealed his discovery to other ships' captains at Vancouver Island.

After Gray's historic entrance of the Columbia, the Englishman Capt. George Vancouver, on a memorable voyage from 1790-92, during which he explored Puget Sound, approached the Columbia.

On Oct. 19, he anchored his flagship *H.M.S. Discovery* off the coast. On Oct. 20, under orders from Vancouver, his escort *H.M.S. Chatham*, commanded by Lt. W. R. Broughton, entered the river mouth to explore it more thoroughly.

This was the third vessel known to have entered the Columbia. When they rounded Cape Disappointment, they found the *Schooner Jenny*, under the command of Capt. James Baker, at anchor.

Research shows the *Jenny* may have visited the river more than once that year, an indication Capt. Baker knew the channel well. The three-masted schooner sailed out of Bristol, England. It carried slaves from Africa to Barbados before entering the Pacific fur trade.

Lt. Broughton took two small ships -- a cutter and a launch -- and ascended the Columbia to an island, now called Flagg Island, near present day Corbett. He went ashore and formally took possession of the river and country in the name of his British Majesty.

When he returned to the *Chatham* 12 days later and left the river, the lightweight schooner *Jenny* led the way across the Columbia bar on Nov. 12. They named several sites -- Baker Bay for the *Jenny's* captain; Walker Island for their surgeon; Youngs Bay for Sir George Young of the Royal Navy; Tongue Point, Mt. St. Helens and Mt. Hood for a diplomat in the British admiralty.

The *Jenny* reappeared on the Columbia briefly in 1792. It was one of numerous trading vessels that plied the northwest coast with increasing frequency at the end of the 18th Century, adding to the eventful year of 1792.

In 1805, the Lewis and Clark expedition, commissioned by President Thomas Jefferson, reached the upper Columbia and explored the river to the Pacific Ocean. They wintered on the coast south of the river's mouth during a period of incessant rain.

Added strength was given the United States' claim to the Oregon country in 1811, when the partners of John Jacob Astor established a trading post on the south bank of the Columbia River near its mouth. Active trading operations were cut short with the outbreak of the War of 1812. Discovery of the McKenzie River by Donald Mackenzie (note spelling), however, was an outgrowth of the Ft. Astoria establishment, and here is where our story begins.

CHAPTER 2

Donald Mackenzie

Much of the following account, with some modifications, was extracted by permission from Gerald W. Williams' unpublished manuscript, *McKenzie River Names*. Other portions are supplied.

Donald Mackenzie (1783-1851) was a huge man, often referred to as "Fat Mackenzie" and "Perpetual Motion" because he was always on the go. Skilled as a rifleman and in woodcraft, he was an able Indian trader before he joined John Jacob Astor's enterprise.

He was born in Ross-shire in the highlands of Scotland June 16, 1783. His father, Alexander, was killed in a duel six years later in 1789. This was the same year Donald's cousin, Sir Alexander Mackenzie, an old Northwester, became the first white person to discover the Mackenzie River in northwest Canada while on a coast to coast exploration.

Donald Mackenzie

(The Mackenzie family name has been variously spelled McKenzie, M'Kenzie and Mackenzie).

In 1801, Donald left Scotland for Canada. He was subsequently employed by the North West Fur Co. In April 1810, Mackenzie joined as a partner in the new Pacific Fur Co., organized and financed by Astor, a German immigrant, who acquired wealth in America.

Astor's ambition was to control the virtually untapped fur trade on the Columbia River basin, then the Russian sea otter trade, and finally the lucrative China market.

Astor's grand scheme, to quote from Alexander Ross' *Adventures of the First Settlers on the Oregon or Columbia River,* 1849: 5, ". . .

contemplated carrying off the furs of all the countries of the Rocky Mountains; at the same time forming a chain of trading posts across the continent, from the Atlantic to the Pacific, along the waters of the Great Missouri; connecting by this chain the operations of the South-West Co. (a major company in the eastern U. S. Astor formed by combining the American and Mackinaw Fur Companies in 1811) on the east, with that of the Pacific Fur Co. on the west side of the dividing ridge (Rocky Mountains). . .All the rich cargoes of furs and peltries thus to be collected annually over the vast expanse were to be shipped in American vessels for the great China Mart."

By July 1810, Astor's fledgling Pacific Fur Co. began gathering seasoned British fur traders and canoe men for the long and difficult journey to the Pacific Ocean. Astor's party was split into two groups, one traveling by sea, the other overland.

The ocean party, under the leadership of Alexander McKay, proceeded from New York Sept. 8, 1810, in the American ship Tonquin. The party consisted of 54 men, with Jonathan Thorn as the sea captain. They sailed around Cape Horn to the Hawaiian Islands.

Capt. Thorn turned out to be a psychopath. Through his madness, eight men were lost at sea before the Tonquin arrived at the mouth of the Columbia River March 22, 1811. On April 12, they began constructing a fort, which they called Ft. Astoria after their principal financial backer. The location, on the south side of the Columbia, was not far from Lewis and Clark's earlier Ft. Clatsop.

"At first glance it seemed most inviting. The weather was good," wrote Gabriel Franchere, one of the clerks. But the contingent met with many obstacles in clearing the land and contending with the Indians. Three of the men were killed by native Americans. Exploratory forays up the Columbia proved hazardous.

Tonquin Blown Up

In the spring of 1811, Capt. Thorn set off in the Tonquin for a trading expedition up the coast. On Vancouver Island, Thorn, acting with his usual intemperance, struck a native chief across the face with a roll of fur. A few days later, in retaliation, the natives massacred Thorn and his crew during which the ship blew up.

Astor's overland contingent of men also left New York in July 1810. They wintered in St. Louis, leaving that fledgling city on April 12, 1811. This party, which included Donald Mackenzie, was under the overall direction of William Price Hunt, personal representative and chief manager of Astor's business.

The overland route to the Pacific was still practically unknown, as the Louis and Clark expedition had returned less than five years before. The party split into two groups, one commanded by Mackenzie and the other by Hunt. After suffering indescribable hardships the Mackenzie party arrived at Ft. Astoria Jan. 18, 1812. The Hunt party arrived Feb. 15, 1812. (*History of the Northwest Coast;* 1864: Vol. 2).

In April 1812, Mackenzie led a party from Ft. Astoria to visit the interior valley known as the Willamette. They explored the valley for about 160 kilometers (100 miles), ascending the Willamette River well into the Indian country, and probably discovered what was later known as Mackenzie's Fork. Several writers including Mackenzie's grandson, Cecil McKenzie, felt the party had crossed over the Cascade Mountains at McKenzie Pass, but there is no evidence to support the claim.

Probably the best account was written by F. S. Perrine (1924: 19-30): "On April 1, 1812, Donald Mackenzie started with William Matthews and five or six men as hunters to man an excursion up the Willamette. How long this party remained is only a matter of conjecture, as we have no record of the trip, its duration, or the amount of territory covered. We only know Mackenzie went up the willamete (sic) till he reached its fork, which is now called the McKenzie River. He returned to Astoria, however, before June 29 or 30, for on one of those dates he set out for the Snake River. . ."

Mackenzie organized another party to explore eastward into the interior. While conferring with John Clark at the Pacific Fur Co.'s Spokane House in December, John George McTavish of the rival North West Fur Co. told Mackenzie of the declaration of war between the United States and Great Britain -- War of 1812. Mackenzie was told the armed British ship *Isaac Todd* was to arrive at Astoria the following March with orders to take possession of the fort for England. Mackenzie immediately cached his goods and raced for Ft. Astoria, arriving Jan. 15, 1813.

After much consideration, Mackenzie and Duncan McDougall agreed to abandon Astor's project, but they needed the other partners to agree. On the last day of March, Mackenzie, John Reed, Alfred Seton and seventeen men returned to the interior, where they conferred with partners David Stuart and John Clarke. They were opposed to selling the fort. They felt more time was needed before abandoning the company, especially the post in the interior.

On June 14, 1813, the partners arrived at Ft. Astoria and were confronted by McTavish with news an armed warship was due in the Columbia to take possession of Ft. Astoria by force. Reconsidering their precarious position they agreed to sell the company before it was taken in an act of war, in which they would receive nothing.

"On July 1, 1813, a resolution was passed by partners McDougall, Mackenzie, Stuart and Clarke to abandon Astoria. . .Owing to the terrible state of affairs, war and no possible way out, they decided it the best thing to do." (Cecil McKenzie, 1937:81).

Fort Astoria Sold

Fort Astoria, with most of its supplies, was sold to the British North West Fur Co. on Oct. 16, 1813. This company took possession of the fort, which they renamed Ft. George, on Nov. 22. In December the stars and stripes came down. The Union Jack went up. Astoria became Ft. George. Several members of the defunct Pacific Fur Co. joined the rival company and remained in the Pacific Northwest.

The following April, Mackenzie and others left Ft. George for Montreal via canoe, on horseback and again by canoe. After a five-month journey, the party reached Montreal Sept. 1, 1814. Shortly thereafter Mackenzie and Clarke left for New York to report the loss of the Columbia River venture to Astor.

On Nov. 12, Astor, Mackenzie and Clarke had published in New York newspapers the official notice of the dissolution of the Pacific Fur Co. Thus, Astor's dream of total control of the Pacific fur trade came to an abrupt end. Astor felt betrayed by the shareholders in their sale of Ft. Astoria. He refused to rehire Mackenzie in his other fur operations.

The Astorian enterprise had some benefits. The overland parties explored new territory. The fur collection stations established in various locales of the Pacific Northwest, including the Willamette Valley, provided a more extensive knowledge of the region.

Ft. Astoria was the first continuously occupied structure in the Pacific Northwest and, along with Capt. Gray and Lewis and Clark's activities, became the basis for later United States territorial claim to the Oregon Country. But the price was very high. All told the Astorian enterprise took the lives of 60 adventurers.

After a treaty in 1818 between the United States and Britain establishing joint occupancy of the territory, the name of Ft. George slowly reverted to Astoria.

Mackenzie rejoined the North West Fur Co. and was once again assigned to the Northwest, traveling back to Ft. George (his old Ft. Astoria) on the Columbia. He was appointed as the company's chief of the interior, an area consisting of eastern Washington and Idaho. Beginning in the spring of 1817, he organized an expedition to explore and trap in the unknown interior.

A year later he and 100 men erected Ft. Nez Perce, near the place called Walla Walla, Wa. The fort was intended to replace the Spokane House as the main trading center for the fur trade of the Snake River country. Mackenzie's efforts to trap in the Snake River Basin were a great success. Through his leadership much of the interior was opened to trade and eventual settlement.

In 1821, the North West Fur Co. merged with the Hudson's Bay Co. (HBC). On March 28, Donald Mackenzie was appointed Chief Factor for the HBC. He left the interior in 1822 for the Red River district in Canada, where he became acquainted with Dr. John McLoughlin. (McLoughlin, appointed Chief Factor for the HBC's Columbia District, didn't leave for Ft. George/Ft. Astoria until three years later).

Mackenzie's headquarters were at Ft. Garry, which is today called Winnipeg, Manitoba. In May 1822, Mackenzie was appointed Councilor of the Governors of the Company's Territories. In June of the following year, he was appointed Governor of the Red River Colony, the second highest post in the Hudson Bay Co. Thus, Ernest Cawcroft reported, ". . .at 42 years of age he became the commercial and semipolitical ruler of the region, now divided into three Canadian provinces (Manitoba, Saskatchewan and Alberta). . ." (Cecil McKenzie, 1937: 149).

Mackenzie held that position eight years and acquired a great amount of personal wealth. He retired from HBC in 1833 because of ill health. He left Canada for New York State and lived at Mayville on Lake

Chautauqua near Buffalo.

One summer night in 1850, one year after Oregon became a territory of the United States, Mackenzie, returning on horseback from Buffalo, was thrown from his horse. He never fully recovered from his injuries. He died Jan. 20, 1851.

Donald Mackenzie was reported to have married several times. Apparently his first common law marriage was at Ft. Astoria to Princess Choim (or Chowa), daughter of Chief Concomly (or Comcomly) of the Chinook Indian tribe (Corning, 1956, Montgomery, 1934, and Rees, 1880a and 1880b). It was common practice among the lower Chinook and nearby Clatsop Indian tribal leaders ". . .to offer their daughters (to the white traders) to secure material benefits for themselves and their people. Although company rules did not require its male employees to make permanent unions with Indian women, it did require them to accept responsibility for care and support of their dependents." (Ruby and Brown, 1976:169).

It is also recorded Mackenzie was married in 1821 to Marie McLoughlin at Ft. Garry, although records indicate he did not arrive at the fort until the following year. Sylva Van Kirk (1980:277) wrote, "Although absolute proof is lacking, evidence points to Mackenzie's country wife (a white fur trader and Indian or part-Indian woman living together without a religious ceremony) being Mary McKay, a daughter of Alexander McKay and Marguerite Wadin McKay."

Marguerite was the daughter of a Cree Indian woman and Jean-Etienne Wadin, one of the founders of the North West Co. Marguerite married Alexander McKay, who abandoned her in 1808. He was killed in June 1811 while aboard the Tonquin. In 1811, she "married" Dr. John McLoughlin, the formal marriage ceremony waiting until 1842.

Mackenzie's first actual church marriage was at Ft. Garry to Adelgonde Humbert Droz (sometimes spelled Drose) on Aug. 18, 1825. She ". . .initially entered Mackenzie's household as governess to his three mixed-blood children. Mackenzie had 'turned off' his native wife several years earlier. In his new bride, he felt he had a won a wife who possessed many more of the qualities esteemed in a wife.

"In describing Adelgonde, Mackenzie revealed (in a letter to William Price Hunt June 25, 1827) important clues to the qualities nineteenth-century officers sought in a marital partner. 'Strict and exemplary in conduct,' his wife was 'the acknowledged model of the sex in this quarter.' She was devout, 'never missing a sacrament by any chance,' and commendably industrious, being expert with her hands 'in all that females are accustomed to perform in continental Europe from the bonnet to the slippers.' Mackenzie did express some reservations about her beauty and intellect. His bride was hardly 'a muse for wit,' but this, he added, might not be a disadvantage: 'for my part, I esteem her also in consideration for her habit taciturnity for you may rely upon it that nothing can give greater comfort to a husband than the satisfaction of having a wife who is nearly mute." (Van Kirk, 1980:180). She and Donald remained married for 26 years until her death.

Corning (1956) reported Donald Mackenzie and Princess Choim had three children. However, Cecil McKenzie, (1937) a grandson of Donald and biographer, did not mention the Indian princess but did state three children were born to Donald and Marie: Rachel, Donald and Caroline. In reality Princess Choim or Chowa, Mary and Marie may have been the same Indian woman. Donald and Adelgonde had 13 children: Jerima, Catherine, Roderick, Noel, Fenella, Alexander, Alice, Henry, William, Celeste, Humbertson and Adelgonde.

Donald Mackenzie, as reported by biographers of his time, was said to have been quite a remarkable fellow. Washington Irving, (commissioned by Astor to write a history of his ill-fated venture) said: ". . .he had a frame seasoned to toils and hardships; a spirit not to be intimidated, and he was reputed to be a remarkable shot. Ross (with him at Ft. Astoria) said he was a 'corpulent, heavy man, weighing 312 lbs.'"

Another contemporary called him "fat Mackenzie." His physical energy was extraordinary. He didn't know the meaning of fear. Ross said, "to travel a day's journey on snowshoes was his delight -- when not asleep, he was always on foot, strolling backwards or forwards, full of plans and prospects: so peculiar was his pedestrian habit, he went by the name of 'Perpetual Motion'. . . His traveling notes were often kept on beaver skin, written hieroglyphically with a pencil or piece of coal. He complained of the drudgery of keeping records. When asked why he didn't like to write, he answered, 'we must leave something for others to do.'" (McKenzie, 1937:26).

John Jacob Astor

Although Mackenzie never published an autobiography, he began to write his life story before the accident.

"He is said to have hated book work of all kind and found difficulty in keeping even the slightest of records. . .He seems to have made an effort in retirement to prepare his memoirs, but it caused him so much distress his wife threw the records in the fire rather than see him unhappy in the attempt to record his achievements." (Stewart, 1968:238). (Disputed).

Thus, we are left with only secondhand and inaccurate accounts of Mackenzie's remarkable life and work in the Pacific Northwest.

CHAPTER 3

Disputed Claims

Following the War of 1812, the Oregon Country was claimed by both England and the United States on the basis of discovery, exploration and settlement. Spain and Russia also had claims, which were less founded. In 1818, when the boundary between the United States and the British possessions was established along the 49th parallel from the Lake of the Woods to the Rocky Mountains, the two countries agreed to a joint occupancy of the Oregon country.

In 1818, Spain conceded all claim to territory north of the 42nd parallel to the United States. In 1824 and 1825, in treaties with the United States and England, Russia agreed not to make settlements south of parallel 54 degrees, 40 minutes. The joint occupancy arrangement between the United States and England was extended in 1827, until in 1846 the 49th parallel was made the international boundary line west of the Rocky Mountains.

In 1821, the North West Fur Co. was absorbed by the Hudson's Bay Co., which established headquarters on the north bank of the Columbia opposite the mouth of the Willamette River at Fort Vancouver. Here under the leadership of Dr. John McLoughlin, the "Great Company" enjoyed a monopoly of the fur trade for 25 years and until the very end exercised government control.

Year 1834 marked the coming of the first missionaries. "Churches of the United States had long been interested in missionary work among the Indian tribes," wrote Dan Clark, University of Oregon historian in the 1949-1950 Oregon Blue Book. "Early in the decade of the thirties, this interest was directed toward the Indians in Oregon. The Methodist Church was first to translate this interest into action."

In 1834, Jason Lee with a small missionary party accompanied a trading expedition to the Pacific Coast. Arriving at Fort Vancouver, Lee was advised by Dr. McLoughlin to locate the mission in the Willamette Valley. Lee selected a spot a few miles north of the present town of Salem (then known as Chemekata). A building was erected and a school for Indian children was opened. Reinforcements brought women to the mission station. Agriculture activities and the raising of livestock were undertaken.

Gradually the nature of the missionary work came to be of service to the white population of the region. A manual training school was inaugurated, later moved to Salem, where it was known as the Oregon Institute, still later became Willamette University. Efforts were made to establish branch missions. A station was founded at The Dalles.

"The American Board of Commissioners and Foreign Missions decided in 1834 to send missionaries west of the Rocky Mountains," Clark wrote. "The result was the first journey of white women across the plains to the Oregon Country. In 1836, Mr. and Mrs. Marcus Whitman, Mr. and Mrs. Henry H. Spalding and a few associates came to the upper Columbia Region.

"They established a main station at Waiilatpu, near the present city of Walla Walla, another near where Lewiston now stands, and, a third, a short distance northwest of Spokane. They and later-arriving missionaries labored among the Indians until the tragic massacre at the Whitman Mission in 1847. During the last year the mission at Waiilatpu was a haven of refuge and a relief to numerous settlers on their weary journey over the Oregon Trail."

The Catholic Church was a few years later in entering the Oregon mission field because of a lack of priests qualified for the service. In 1838, Father Francis H. Blanchet and Father Modeste Demers journeyed across Canada to Ft. Vancouver. A mission was established at St. Paul. Reinforcements came in succeeding years and educational, as well as purely religious, activities were begun. Especially noted for his work among the Indians of the interior was Father P. J. DeSmet, known as the "Apostle of the Flatheads."

"The Oregon Country was so far away from border settlements in the United States that public interest in this region was slow in developing," Clark wrote. During the 20's "several bills were introduced and debated in Congress for the occupation of the Columbia region, but there were no immediate results. During the next decade, however, interest grew rapidly, and by 1840 it was quite certain American settlers would soon be coming to Oregon.

"The missionary activities attracted widespread attention. Then enthusiastic writings of Hall J. Kelly proclaimed the beauty and resources of the country. The trading expeditions by Nathaniel J. Wyeth in 1832 and 1834 gained considerable publicity. In the meantime a few Americans, some of the 'Mountain Men,' drifted into the upper Willamette Valley. They settled among French-Canadians, former employees of the Hudson's Bay Co., who laid out farms, especially in the region known as French Prairie, west of Woodburn.

"The migration that wore the deep rut of the Oregon Trail began in 1841, when the 'Oregon fever' was beginning to spread throughout the upper Mississippi Valley. The so-called Bidwell-Bartleson party of that year numbered nearly 70 when it left Independence, Mo. At Soda Springs the large party divided. About 30 came to the Willamette Valley. The remainder went to California.

"The emigration of 1842, led by Dr. Elijah White, numbered more than 100. In 1843 there came the 'Great Migration' when nearly 1,000 people traveled the trail to Oregon. Because of the importance of this accession to the population much attention has been paid to this migration. The large party left the Missouri River late in May and arrived at Ft. Walla Walla before mid-October."

There was no cessation of the annual influx of settlers into Oregon, although the number varied from year to year. In 1845, some 3,000 settlers arrived. In 1846, there was an estimated 1,350, in 1847, about 4,500. In 1848, it dropped to about 700.

Joint occupancy of the Oregon country with Great Britain ended in 1846, following settlement of the boundary question establishing as the dividing line between the United States and Canada the 49th parallel from the Rocky Mountains to the coast and a line along the mid-channel between Vancouver Island and the mainland to the Pacific Ocean.

Provisional Government

Even before the treaty of 1846 had recognized the undisputed jurisdiction of the United States, Willamette Valley settlers had in accordance with American Pioneer customs adopted a provisional government to administer their most urgent local affairs.

They chose a justice of the peace and other officials. In 1843, at the so-called "Wolf Meeting" held to devise protection of livestock against wild animals, steps were taken that led a few months later to adoption at Champoeg of a constitution and a definite provisional government. This was revised and improved in 1844 and 1845.

Meanwhile, Congress was petitioned urging the establishment of a regular territorial government. When the boundary question was settled, a favorable response to these petitions was confidently expected, but the Mexican War and the sectional controversy between the North and South delayed action. It required a tragedy to dramatize the need for more adequate government.

Late in November 1847, there occurred the terrible massacre by the Indians of Marcus and Narcissa Whitman and several of their associates at their mission in the Walla Walla region. There was alarm throughout the settlements when news of this massacre reached the Willamette Valley, for there was fear of a general Indian uprising. A regiment of volunteers hastened up the Columbia and succeeded in "punishing" the Indians.

Clark wrote: "John Meek was sent to Washington with news of the massacre and with a very insistent petition for the immediate establishment of a government 'capable of coping with the problems of the Oregon settlers'. . . . On Aug. 13, 1848, Congress passed a law, creating the territory of Oregon, embracing all the country from the Rocky Mountains to the Pacific and between the 42nd and 49th parallel. Early in March 1849, Joseph Lane, the governor, and Joseph Meek, United States marshal, arrived in Oregon City and the new territorial government was put into operation.

The discovery of gold in California diverted immigration from Oregon and attracted large numbers of settlers from this region. But after the subsidence of the gold excitement, and after the passage of the land law for Oregon the tide again turned in this direction.

"Considering the remoteness of Oregon, the territorial period was one of rapid development. Troops stationed at Vancouver and Oregon

City brought money into the country and gave the settlers in the Willamette Valley a feeling of security, although Indian uprisings in other sections of the territory kept the soldiers busy.

"The California gold rush, which at first caused a stampede from the Oregon country, later proved a boom to the new settlements. Not only did some Oregonians return to their new homes with bags of gold, but California offered a ready and lucrative market for the products of Oregon's farms and forests.

"By 1852, it is said some 15,000 people had settled in Oregon. The new state was credited with a population of 52,465 by the 1860 census. Settlements had spread to the head of the Willamette Valley and into the valleys of the Umpqua and Rogue. Towns had sprung up. Oregon City, begun by Dr. John McLoughlin in 1842, soon became a sizable village and was the first territorial capital. Portland, founded a few years later, rapidly forged to the lead and gave early evidence of becoming the metropolis of Oregon. Salem, Albany, Corvallis (first called Marysville) and Eugene were among the early towns that gave promise of permanence and prosperity."

A generous donation land law Congress enacted added to the attractiveness of the Oregon Country. The capital of the territory was first at Oregon City. In 1850, it was moved to Salem; in 1855 to Corvallis, later the same year back to Salem.

In 1853, due to the growing settlements along the Cowlitz River and the shores of Puget Sound the separate Territory of Washington was created, thus reducing the territory of Oregon to the area south of the Columbia River and the 45th parallel.

Meanwhile, a movement for statehood was in progress in Oregon. After three times voting against the proposal, the people in 1857 approved calling a constitutional convention, which met at Salem and drafted a constitution that was ratified by the people.

Without waiting for congressional action a state government was organized in 1858. John Whiteaker was first governor. On Valentine's Day, Feb. 14, 1859, Oregon was admitted to the union with its present boundaries.

Gen. Joseph Lane

CHAPTER 4

Pioneers

The ingenuity of early-day pioneers in getting from here to there almost boggles the mind. Waterways were used to full advantage. But there were floods and other hazards. Traveling over burning deserts, crossing raging rivers, cutting through jungled forests and transporting wagons, horses, oxen and other livestock over precipitous mountains, often facing hostile Indians, proved monumental tasks.

Logs lashed to wagons served as booms in crossing rivers that couldn't be forded. In descending mountains, such as Canyon Mountain where stream beds between steep canyon walls were the only route, trees were tied to wagons to prevent them overrunning draft animals.

There are tales of oxen bleeding at the nose or falling by the wayside as the travelers pushed on, fearful of being caught in winter snows on mountain passes, such as those which trapped the wagon train on Donner Pass, where many people starved and others resorted to cannibalism before spring thaws permitted survivors passage on to the valley floors. Oxen seemed to be the stronger -- hence the expression "strong as an ox." But horses seemed to better withstand the ordeal, especially when water was scarce.

Many people died on cross-country travel and countless livestock was lost. But a sufficient number of people survived to settle the West, and livestock was replaced. Stories of pioneer hardships are legend. But few turned back once they had reached the "promised land" as described by such stalwarts as Elijah Bristow, Eugene Skinner, Felix Scott, John Cogswell, Cornelius Hills, Lester Hulin and others.

With the coming of great wagon trains to the West, settlements were established in the Willamette Valley in the 1840's and 1850's. As early as 1845 trails of sorts, used by Indians and trappers, ran through central Lane County and were followed by pioneers.

What was referred to as the Old Trail or Hudson's Bay Trail ran southward from Yamhill and Polk counties along the foot of the Coast Range, some 20 miles west of present-day Eugene, through Lorane into southern Oregon. This was an old Indian trail trappers followed into California. Rivers flowing from the Coast Range on the west were smaller and shallower than the ones flowing westward from the Cascades. Canyon Mountain in southern Douglas County proved one of the greatest hazards faced by pioneers traversing this route.

Travel took time, endurance and determination.

The first Lane County settlers were Elijah Bristow, who put down his roots at Pleasant Hill; Eugene Skinner, co-founder of Eugene City; Felix Scott Sr., and William Dodson, who came west to California in 1845.

They wintered at the Mexican settlement of Sutter's Fort, now Sacramento, which was part of the Mexican land grant given to John Sutter, who figured in California gold discoveries.

In the spring they traveled north to Oregon to the vicinity of Dallas in Yamhill County. Soon after, they rode south, far beyond white settlements, to stake their claims in what became Lane County.

Reports vary on the western trek of these four men. Their backgrounds also differ, but they all had a "vision and dreams perhaps, but dreams fortified with action -- dogged, unremitting and occasionally fractured with danger -- sustained action over the days, weeks, months -- years," to quote Art Clough in *Lane County Historian.*

Clough tells of the arrival of Bristow and Skinner at Sutter's Fort but makes no mention of Scott and Dodson, who reportedly arrived in Sacramento the same year and also wintered at Sutter's Fort.

Olga Freeman, from Leah Menefee's research in Lane *County Historian,* wrote: "Here, supposedly, they (Scott and Dodson) met Eugene Skinner and Elijah Bristow. No doubt the latter talked of going to Oregon in the spring and influenced Scott and Dodson to accompany them."

ELIJAH BRISTOW

Elijah Bristow, eldest son of James and Delilah Bristow, was born in Tazewell County, Va., April 28, 1788. In his youth he moved to Tennessee, raw and sparsely settled. On March 7, 1812, he married Susannah Gobbert, who was born in 1791.

Bristow was about 57 when in 1845 he left his "numerous and mostly grown-up and married-off family in Missouri to take the Oregon trail. He proposed to seek a promised land for them all," wrote Clough. Bristow, at age 14, had been the champion rifle shot of Tennessee. "As a personal scout to Gen. Andrew Jackson, he had ridden a walking horse to New Orleans and helped him whip the British there in 1815."

His family "probably suspected as a young man he had been something of a hell-raiser, but by 1845 that was water under the bridge. . . so to his family Elijah Bristow, as he readied for that long journey, was probably an opinionated, stubborn old man. . ."

Alone, with only one wagon and a hired helper, this forceful, vigilant, determined man shortly was elected captain of the train. Bristow took the California trail, while most of the wagon train continued on to Oregon. California records show Bristow's wagon and possibly three others were the only wagons to use the trail that year.

In Bristow's wagon train were Eugene Skinner, a young farmer from New York state; his wife, Mary; Wesley Shannon, and, probably, Wesley's brother, Davis. They were welcomed at Sutter's Fort and they wintered there.

Wesley Shannon, wrote, "In the spring of 1845, we (he and his brother, Davis) left Knox County, Ill., for Oregon. On the third day out, we met Bristow who was leaving for the west." He also is quoted as saying that upon their arrival in California, Bristow wasn't satisfied with what he saw and came overland to Oregon the following spring.

Whether Bristow, Skinner, Scott and Dodson came north together or just how the four men got together in Oregon is in question. We have no evidence Scott and his family came north at the same time.

Clough, still making no mention of Scott, said the Bristow-Skinner party, five people in all (believed to include Mary Skinner, William Dodson, Wesley and Davis Shannon), followed the old Hudson's Bay trail, entering the Willamette Valley by way of Lorane. They continued northward along the west side of the valley until in the neighborhood of the present Dallas (Yamhill County) they came upon a single settler, at the far southern outskirts of the existing settlements. There they left Mrs. Skinner domiciled temporarily.

Elijah Bristow

Freeman wrote: "It was March 1846 when the 'Four Horsemen' set out for their journey north. They traveled the California-Oregon trail and, upon arriving at Yoncalla, decided to take the west-side trail along the foothills of the Coast Range. They traveled on through the pioneer settlement of Marysville (now Corvallis) to Rickreal.

"Here Mrs. Skinner left the party. Arriving in Yamhill County, Scott settled his wife and children with Joe Watts of whom no information is provided."

Not satisfied to settle permanently there, the men proceeded south along the west side of the valley to explore and help Bristow find his "promised land" and stake their claims. After passing the Luckiamute River, no white man's habitation was found.

Arriving at the upper Willamette Valley, at a point between the Coast Fork and Middle Fork of the Willamette on a rolling ridge, sparsely covered with oak, fir and pine timber, Bristow was struck with the beauty of the country. The land reminded him of his native Virginia.

"This is my claim. Here I will live, and when I die, here shall I be buried," he was quoted as saying.

The party camped at a spring nearby and cut the logs. Assisted by Skinner, Shannon and Dodson, Bristow built what was termed a "claim cabin" and began perfecting a settlement.

Dodson staked off his claim south and east adjoining Bristow's. Scott took one on the west. These claims, 640 acres each, were filed in Polk County since Lane County did not then exist.

As soon as claims were staked, the men returned to Mrs. Skinner's stopping place -- Bristow to get a message to his family. Early August found them all back up here (in Lane County) at work on cabins. In the fall of 1847, he sent for his family who joined him the following year.

An editor's note in the *Historian* said, "Felix Scott was one of the 'Four Horsemen' -- first white settlers in the present Lane County (1846) -- Elijah Bristow, William Dodson and Eugene Skinner, who rode up the Willamette River, south from the settlement of Dallas to locate claims. Bristow paced off his at Pleasant Hill. Dodson and Scott staked theirs adjoining, while Skinner built his cabin at the SW slope of Skinner's Butte -- to later establish Eugene City -- to which he brought his family in 1847."

Clough wrote: "That Bristow's accepted purpose was accomplished is evident, for several families of his relatives, including his wife, Susannah, arrived in 1848 and all were able to find land of their choice in the immediate area."

Capt. Scott soon abandoned his Pleasant Hill claim for one on the south bank of the McKenzie River opposite the mouth of the Mohawk and down river from present-day Hayden Bridge.

Immigration of 1847

In the summer of 1847 a party of immigrants arrived from the east coast. The wagon train turned off the Oregon Trail at Fort Hall, Ida., crossed the ridge into Humboldt Valley in Nevada, then through California to enter Oregon by way of Tule and Klamath lakes, over Green Springs mountain to the Rogue and Umpqua Valley on the Scott-Applegate Trail. It was a tedious journey and the people were so worn out they were content to stop at the embryo settlement at Pleasant Hill.

Among them were Isaac Briggs and his son, Elias, who founded Springfield; Prior Blair, who married Ellen Mulligan; Charles Martin and their families; also Charnel Mulligan, co-founder of Eugene, and Wickliff Gouley, single men, relatives of Blair. They took up claims initially near Bristow.

Of the same migration, Cornelius Hills, a single man, settled on the north side of the middle fork of the Willamette (Jasper area), across from the Bristows. A. Cargell and his son, Louis, located on the Coast Fork. Benjamin Davis, John Akin and H. Noble and their families settled near Skinner in Eugene and became welcome neighbors.

Lester Hulin, one of the train's leaders, a man named Fergueson, Thomas Hinton, John Brown and Benj. Richardson located along the Long Tom River west of Eugene.

Jacob Spores, John Diamond, William Stevens and Mitchell Wilkins, Coburg area settlers, arrived via Barlow Pass the same year.

Bristow's Family Arrives

Not until 1848 was Bristow joined by his wife, Mrs. Susannah Bristow, three of their sons -- Abel K., William Wilshire and Elijah Lafayette Bristow -- and Robert Callison and wife, the former Mary Bristow, who arrived from Illinois.

With them were James M. Hendricks, possibly Caswell Hendricks, Michael and Harrison Shelley, William Bowman and Calvin Hale, and their families, who first settled at Pleasant Hill.

The year 1849 brought many additions to the population,

including James and Richard Robinson, Milton and Rufus Riggs, who returned from the California mines and settled on Camas Swale, east of Spencers Butte. They brought with them a large band of cattle and became the first "cowboys" of Lane County.

Hilyard Shaw, Thomas Smith, James and Abraham Peek settled near Eugene, and James Chapin on the Coast Fork.

Indian Problems

Bristow was not without Indian problems. In the spring of 1848, Klamath Indians killed an ox of Cornelius Hills. Five or six men, led by Bristow, pursued as far as what became known as Butte Disappointment, above what is now Lowell. The butte was so named because of their disappointment in not being able to further pursue the Indians through the mountainous terrain.

Another time an Indian came and made threats. Bristow got his gun and fired as the man ran away. The Indian apparently was wounded and died, according to friendly Molalla Indians.

Bristow laid down the law. "His Illahe," that was the Indian name for a section of the Middle and East Forks of the Willamette. "No Klamath tolerated." Pleasant Hill was the central section, which Bristow claimed. "Beautiful hills, beautiful valley, sparkling water."

Bands of the Klikitat tribe from north of the Columbia River frequently passed through. In the spring of 1849, five of that tribe came to Bristow's claim and, finding no game, killed his fattest oxen. He pursued without avail. When a few weeks later another band came through, Bristow caught and whipped one of their party.

The next day his house was surrounded by 13 mounted, armed and painted Indians. During a short parley they demanded pay. He refused. Seizing a handspike, he struck at the nearest native, who ducked. The blow felled his pony. The "braves" broke rank and fled, pursued by Bristow. A Klikitat raised his gun to fire, but Bristow's son appeared with his own rifle. This put an end to the Klikitat war.

Elijah Bristow, Lane County's first permanent settler, gave land for a school, church and cemetery. In 1850, a log cabin was erected to serve as a school-house. This school, Lane County's first, became District No. 1. Bristow's son, William, was the teacher. That same year the Christian Church was organized. Services were held in the school. In 1850 or 1851, the first post office, called Pleasant Hill, was established with Elijah Bristow as postmaster. In 1854, it was moved to a new location but retained the name.

William Bristow, born in Kentucky July 19, 1826, moved with his parents to Illinois, then to Oregon. In 1849, he joined the rush to California gold, returning the following year to improve his land claim and teach school. In 1852-53, he was justice of the peace, then postmaster at Pleasant Hill. In 1857, he was elected a delegate to the constitutional convention which met in Salem Sept. 3. In 1858, he was elected state senator and served three terms. In 1865, he sold his farm and moved to Eugene as a partner in Bristow Mercantile business. He and his wife Elizabeth, age 30 in the 1860 census, had children John,

Edith and Adeline. He died Dec. 8, 1874.

Elijah LaFayette Bristow was born in McDonough County, Ill., Jan. 2, 1832. Arriving in Oregon with his family, he filed on a claim at Pleasant Hill, farmed the land and served as justice of the peace from 1857 to 1859. He sold his farm, moved to Eugene and clerked in the office of the surveyor general. In 1860, he engaged in a mercantile business, and erected the first brick building in Eugene in 1866.

In 1871, he was elected grand master of the Independent Order of Odd Fellows for Oregon, Washington and Idaho. In 1873, he was appointed one of the Capitol Building Commissioners. In 1874, he sold his business, moved to Salem and purchased the newspaper Mercury, which he edited and published for five years. In 1882, he served as grand patriarch of the I.O.O.F. Encampment.

Abel K. Bristow, a farmer, was listed as 41 in the 1860 census, and his wife, Elmira, 35. Children were Samuel, John, Alice and William.

Robert Callison, born in Adair County, Ky., June 5, 1818, married Mary Bristow in McDonough County, Ill. She was born in Cumberland County, Ky., Oct. 20, 1828. They came west with Mrs. Bristow in 1848. Children were Joseph, Josiah, Henrietta, Lucetta and Marietta.

Elijah Bristow lived on his claim until his death, Sept. 19, 1872. His wife, Susannah, died March 7, 1874, at age 83.

By 1880, Pleasant Hill, twelve miles southeast of Eugene, had two merchandise stores, a blacksmith shop, wagon shop, saddle and harness store. The post office was in the store of Samuel Handsaker.

"Much of the county's chronicles center around this spot, while its traditions make it hallowed ground," wrote A. G. Walling in 1884. "On the site of the original school-house, a handsome church edifice has been erected at a cost of twelve hundred dollars, while nearby stands a school-house, having a fair attendance." Pleasant Hill's growth, however, languished, as Eugene, Coburg and Springfield developed.

Dodson, a bachelor, stayed near Bristow. In 1853, he married Sarah Littreal of Linn County at Union Point. The couple had three children, but as their son, Joshua, never married the name has not been perpetuated in the annals of Lane County.

Wesley Shannon, born in McDonough County, Penn., Jan. 9, 1820, moved with his family to Knox County, Ill. He came to Oregon with Bristow and Skinner in 1846. He and his brother, Davis, settled eight miles north of Salem in the Champoeg district. On July 15, 1847, he married Elizabeth Simmons. Born in Randolph County, Ind., she came with her father, Samuel Simmons, in 1845, settling in Marion County. In 1848, Shannon helped Bristow, Dodson and Robert Callison build their homes at Pleasant Hill, after Bristow's family arrived.

Shannon was elected to the Territorial Council in 1849. He farmed until 1863, moved into Salem, then in 1872, came to Eugene, where he was highly regarded. Of Elijah Bristow, he eulogized:

"Among our pioneer friends whose memory I cherish."

CHAPTER 5

EUGENE SKINNER

Eugene Skinner was born in Essex County, New York, Sept. 11, 1809. A brother, St. John Skinner, was assistant postmaster general during the administration of President Johnson. At age 14, Eugene was taken by his father, John Joseph Skinner, to Green County, Wisc. He returned to New York, then came west again to Hennepin, Ill., where he furthered his education and farmed.

On Nov. 28, 1839, he married Mary Cook. She was born in Augusta, Oneida County, N. Y., Feb. 7, 1816. In Illinois, Skinner held several political offices, including sheriff of Putnam County. However, he did not have good health. In 1845, when he and Mary had been married seven years, they headed west. Their covered wagon joined those of Elijah Bristow and Wesley Shannon, bound for Oregon.

A businessman rather than a farmer, Skinner, not yet 37, sought a different location on which to settle. As the party rode through the bottom lands of the Willamette and McKenzie rivers, he saw possibilities near a butte (Skinner's Butte) along the Willamette.

Eugene Skinner, Founder
of Eugene City

The Story of Eugene, authored by sisters Lucia Moore, Nina McCornack and Gladys McCready (1949:1-2), related that as Skinner looked for a place to settle, "towards afternoon two Indians came bringing trout from the river. 'Build high up,' they said. 'Ya-po-ah.' They pointed to the hillside. He knew their (Chinook) jargon (trade language, a mixture of Indian, British, French and American words), and he asked, 'Why?' 'Big water come some day,' they told him."

Skinner selected a site at the base of the Indian-named butte, which now bears his name, and staked his claim. He constructed a crude log cabin on the west side of the butte before heading back north to his temporary home near Dallas.

Cogswell First Viewed Area

Although Bristow, Skinner, Scott and Dodson were first to stake their claims in Lane County in 1846, John Cogswell is reported to have climbed what became Skinner's Butte several weeks before the arrival of the "Four Horsemen." He settled along the McKenzie later.

Skinner's cabin -- one room, with skins hung across a door opening -- that winter sheltered a fourteen-year-old boy, a cattleman named Turnage from the Applegate Trail and a sailor named Stillwell. They were the first white men to live on the slope that would one day look down on the city of Eugene. They herded cattle below the hill, hunted bear and killed wolves in the wooded area to the south and east.

Early the following summer of 1847, Eugene and Mary Skinner, with baby daughter Mary Elizabeth, born that winter in Clackamas County, settled in the cabin at the base of the butte.

Another daughter, Lenora, was born the following year, 1848, the first white child born in the what became Lane County.

The cabin grew with two doors and a window looking out across the prairie. The only white woman in all the vast upper Willamette Country, Mrs. Skinner often was left alone with Indians and wild animals all around, while her husband made the long ten-day trek to Oregon City for supplies.

"In the high valley, the few Indians made very little serious trouble for the first white settlers," wrote Moore, McCornack and McCready. "However, before the days of the Hudson Bay Co. ended in the upper valley, one of their hunters, an Englishman named Spencer, lost his scalp to Indians upon the butte south of Eugene which bears his name." Spencer was a member of a party sent out by the company to hunt and trade with the Indians. The party, en route to California, camped near what is now Spencer Creek. Spencer left to climb the butte, which stands 1,500 feet above Eugene City. He never returned. His naked body was found mutilated, full of arrows. He is the only white man documented as killed by hostile Indians in Lane County. Dr. McLoughlin told this story to Elijah Bristow, Walling's history said.

Brags of Scalping

Tyee Tom, later chief of the Chifen tribe of Indians who inhabited that portion of the county adjacent to Spores Point and well known in the area, it is said, bragged happily of having, when he was a young man, scalped and otherwise mutilated Mr. Spencer.

"'He come Champ-a-te,' Chief Tom explained. Champ-a-te meant Rattlesnake Mountain, five miles distance to Ya-po-ah. Across the valley between these hills the Calapooia Indians roamed, most of the time harmlessly," wrote Moore, McCornack and McCready.

"There came a day, however, when Chief Tom was filled with resentment at the thought of three palefaces in the cabin by Ya-po-ah. The Skinners spoke enough jargon to know their danger. The Old Settler shouldered his musket. Through the night he walked around the cabin, while Mary Skinner bent above her fire to mold bullets and small Mary Elizabeth whimpered from the depths of her cradle. The sun was high before Chief Tom and the Old Settler smoked the pipe of peace."

Skinner established a ferry crossing the Willamette River in the vicinity of what is now the Ferry Street Bridge. He also established the first post office, bearing his name, Eugene, Jan. 8, 1850. The name was changed to Eugene City Sept. 3, 1853, and to Eugene May 19, 1889. (McArthur, 1982: 183.) The name of Eugene City post office was given by Mary Skinner to honor her husband.

In 1852, the Skinners donated the east part of their land claim for the new city government, and, in 1853, laid out the city of Eugene. With Charnel Mulligan, they donated land for a county seat.

Later the Skinners subdivided another portion of their land for settlers. The fledgling city carried the same name as the post office. Yet the site was unwisely chosen and soon was known as "Skinner's Mudhole," because of the heavy rains mixing with the dirt streets. Floods of 1861, 1881 and 1890 added to the problem.

The Skinners had three other children: Phoebe, born March 29, 1850; St. John B. L., born Nov. 7, 1851, and Amelia R., born April 16, 1855. The first child, Mary, died Oct. 4, 1860. Lenora died Aug. 29, 1862. Phoebe, on Aug. 30, 1868, married John D. Kinsey, a native of New York. He was born Oct. 12, 1835, and died March 13, 1881, leaving his wife and three daughters (Maggie, Clara and Mary Louis). St. John on Nov. 23, 1871, married Amanda J. Walton. Amelia, on Aug. 24, 1871, married Byron Van Houten. She later became Mrs. Combs.

Prophetic Prediction

Eugene Skinner did not live long enough to see his town grow. The Indian prediction, "Big water come some day," was more than prophetic. The greatest recorded flood of all times came in 1861. Much of the Willamette Valley became a lake. The Willamette and McKenzie Rivers ran together over present-day Springfield. Men rowed boats over fences. The river overflowed Eugene's city streets.

Not a robust man, Skinner suffered exposure in an attempt to save his cattle. He was ill the next two years. Meanwhile, he had moved his family into a large log house he purchased from James McClaren, at 260 Sixth St. at Lincoln. He was first to be initiated into the Masonic Lodge. His death in 1864 was the first to occur in the ranks of the lodge.

"He was our first citizen, first ferryman across the river; the 'proprietor' of our town, whose imagination, foresight and generosity put us forever in his debt," wrote Moore, McCornack and McCready.

Mary Skinner later married Capt. N. L. Packard. Born in Camden, Knox County, Maine, Packard at age fifteen began a seafaring life for sixteen years, rising to the rank of commander. In 1849, he sailed on the ship Empire City to the Isthmus of Panama, then took passage on the steamer Panama for San Francisco. He mined in California and Idaho. He came to Gardiner City in Douglas County in 1864, then to Eugene in 1865. He and Mary Skinner were married Feb. 7, 1867. Mary died June 4, 1881.

A replica of Skinner's cabin now stands on the north side of Skinner's Butte Park. The replica was built in 1970 by Lawrence Hills, Bud Pickens and Jim White. In 1996, it was relocated to a more favorable place for easier public viewing.

Mulligan   Co-founder

Charnel Mulligan, co-founder of Eugene, was born in Louisville, Ky., June 20, 1826. A descendant, Mrs. Orval Mulligan, is quoted as saying he crossed the plains by ox team in 1847. (Records spell his name variously as Charnal, Charnelton and Charnal Milligin). With Lester Hulin, he fought in the Cayuse Indian War in 1847/48, went to California in 1848 to search for gold, returned two years later on the ill-fated schooner Hackstaff, which grounded on the Rogue River bar. They and 30 others from Lane County walked home in 24 days.

On Oct. 15, 1851, he married Martha Jane Spores, daughter of Jacob Spores, pioneer Coburg settler of 1847. On Feb. 14, 1853, he and Martha settled on a claim adjoining Skinner's, where the Lane County Courthouse, Eugene City Hall and city park are located.

Charnel and Martha Jane helped found the county seat in Eugene City, after the Territorial Legislature in January, 1851, created Lane County, named for Territorial Governor Joseph Lane.

They donated forty acres of their land claim to the county, along with a like amount by Skinner. All deeds within the early town site still bear the names of Mulligan and Skinner. The courthouse park blocks are a memorial to the Mulligans. Charnelton Street is named for Charnel. He died in Springfield May 3, 1893, at age 72.

Martha Jane died the year before. They had seven children, including Jacob, 14 in the 1870 census; Amanda, 11, and Francis, 7.

THE METROPOLITAN AREA OF "SKINNER'S MUD-HOLE"
A view down Willamette Street in the early days

CHAPTER 6

FELIX SCOTT SR.

Captain Felix Scott Sr., less known in Lane County annals than Skinner and Bristow, nevertheless was a colorful figure. Born Dec. 13, 1776/1788 (reports vary), in Monongalia County, Va., near the Pennsylvania border, he moved in 1819 to St. Charles County, Mo.

He married Nancy Castlio, daughter of John Castlio and the "widow Dodson," who had moved to St. Charles County in 1806 from Tennessee, according to Olga Freeman in *Lane County Historian*. (William Dodson who came to Oregon with Scott may have been a relative of the "widow Dodson").

On Nancy's death, Scott married Ellen Castlio, perhaps a sister of his first wife, April 5, 1821. He had 22 or 24 children, including two pairs of twins. The *Pioneer Families of Missouri* lists: Taswell, George, Presley, Herma S., Nancy Ellen, Harriett, Julia, Felix Jr., Maria and Marion. Others were Lucinda, Lindian, Nimrod, Rodney, Harrison and Jane Linn, accounting for sixteen.

Educated and a lawyer and active in political affairs, Scott served many years as a justice of the peace, then served in both the lower house and state senate representing St. Charles County, Mo., between 1822 and 1830, according to the Sunday *Oregon Journal*.

He was a man of indomitable will and energy and of a fearless disposition. The story is told that a son-in-law challenged him to a duel. The agreement was Scott was not to fire his double-barreled shotgun until after his son-in-law discharged his. Although a great fighter himself, Scott waited patiently for his son-in-law to fire. When he did and missed, Scott laid down his gun and proceeded to give his son-in-law a good pounding with his fists.

In the spring of 1845 with his wife and seven of his children, he joined an immigrant party bound for California. A number of his children remained in Missouri. Because of his previous military experience, he was elected captain of the 50-wagon train. Arriving in California Scott, his family and William Dodson wintered at Sutter's Fort. Here, supposedly, they met Skinner and Bristow.

In the spring they traveled north to near Dallas in Polk County, Ore., where Scott left his family. Just when and where he teamed up with the Bristow-Skinner party we haven't been able to establish.

Scott very soon abandoned his Pleasant Hill claim (1847) for one on the south bank of the McKenzie River opposite the mouth of the

Mohawk and down river from present-day Hayden Bridge along the foothills of the Coburg Hills to the north. To this claim he brought his family and began improvements. He had brought with him on his trip west a train of saddle and pack horses.

William Stevens and Michael Wilkins, who had arrived in Oregon City in 1847, had come up the valley to stake their claims in Willamette Forks, then returned to their families near Salem. Stevens came back the same year to build his cabin. Meanwhile, Scott had settled further to the east. He and Stevens together owned a vast strip of fertile land between the Willamette and McKenzie rivers. In 1849, Stevens built a double log house for Scott. Eventually, it sheltered quite a family.

John Diamond and Jacob Spores had taken claims north of the McKenzie (Coburg area) in 1847. The following year Thomas Cady and David Chamberlain took land at West Point, and Michael Wilkins returned from Silverton to build on the hill slope.

When gold was discovered near Sutter's Fort in 1847, Capt. Scott with sons Felix Jr. and Marion joined the flight of others from the Willamette Valley to the gold fields of California. They came back to Oregon two years later with considerable capital.

In 1850, Felix Sr. sent his son, Felix Jr., then 33, to Missouri to purchase cattle and horses and drive them to Oregon. This was the first livestock transportation of any size across the plains. Felix Jr. settled far to the west in Willamette Forks.

Having practiced law in Missouri, Scott Sr. continued to practice in Oregon. He built a sawmill in Willamette Forks in the winter of 1851-52 about a mile further up the McKenzie River from Felix Jr.'s claim. He built another sawmill in Benton County near Marysville (Corvallis), which he leased in 1853 to John L. Kline. Litigation ensued for several years over the lease.

Scott, later a victim of the Indians himself, was appointed a sub-agent of Indian Affairs for Southern Oregon by H. A. G. Lee, superintendent of Indian Affairs. Early settlers were frequently disturbed by rumors of intended Indian hostilities. Scott had become increasingly concerned over the possibility of Rogue Indian raids in Southern Oregon. The Indians who on the whole had been peaceful in Western Oregon had shown more militancy after the Cayuses had murdered the Whitmans at Walla Walla.

Predatory incursions of Klamath Indians bands over trails leading into the settlements were especially troublesome at this time. Companies of volunteers had been hastily formed to rid the settlements of intruders. A battle occurred between one of the wandering bands and the whites on the banks of a small stream south of Salem. The rivulet still bears the name Battle Creek.

Up on his "pleasant hill" Elijah Bristow. . . fought and won two small wars, both over stolen stock. He accomplished this by brandishing anything at hand, from handspike to rifle.

Lee asked Scott to raise a company of rangers to watch the Indians and give protection to immigrants coming to Oregon over the southern route. When told there was no money available for the purpose, Scott raised 19 men on his own and became their captain. He was henceforth known as Captain Scott.

Several letters Scott wrote to Lee revealed considerable Indian activity. On May 5, 1848, he wrote from Salem that on a tour of the upper Willamette Valley he found few Indians, about 50. Most of them were in the Umpqua Valley. They promised to deliver to him some thieves who had taken cattle. On May 12, he wrote from Oregon City, after touring the upper valley, he found the residents greatly excited in consequence of thefts and forays by the Indians.

The settlers were acclaiming their intentions, in case of further forays, to "chastise them with death." Scott attempted to ease their concerns. In letters he mentioned thefts of clothing and horses from valley residents and attempts to recover the goods. He asked for more men, because, he said, he couldn't defend against an uprising.

Acquires Prominence

Scott acquired prominence from business dealings in Oregon and California. He divided his livestock between his sons, Felix Jr. and Presley, who moved them to northern California, near Crescent City.

A man of undoubted great will and energy, Scott, in 1857, returned to Kentucky by way of the Isthmus of Panama to purchase a band of blooded stock. He apparently returned to Oregon for the winter, as he made a will and signed it on Jan. 19, 1858. He would have been 70 years of age at the time. He then returned to Kentucky on an ill-fated trip to drive out his cattle.

His son reported he was at Ft. Laramie coming westward on June 17, 1858. Later, he was set upon and murdered by the Modoc Indians near the headwaters of the Pitt River at Goose Lake on the Oregon-California border. Two of his men also were killed, his wagons burned and the cattle were scattered or lost.

Scott was a man of considerable wealth. His will revealed he already had made advances of property to four of his sons and six daughters. It bequeathed to his wife, Ellen, considerable personal property, "as many cows as she may want," also her choice of "either my house on my claim or in the vicinity of Eugene City as a residence during her lifetime." The will also made bequeaths to other children.

Ellen, described as "a beloved woman and true pioneer," remained on their donation land claim until 1880. She died at Dallas in Polk County Dec. 9, 1882, at age 77.

Felix Scott Jr., who opened a wagon road over the McKenzie Pass in 1862, died at age 49 in Arizona Nov. 10, 1879.

At least two of Scott's other children achieved prominence. Rodney, born in Missouri in 1842, served as Oregon state senator and later as regent of the University of Oregon. It is known that in 1893 one of his daughters was a librarian at the University.

CHAPTER 7

Coburg and Willamette Forks

The Coburg story began in 1847 with the arrival of Jacob Spores and John Diamond. Spores took a 640-acres land claim on the north side of the McKenzie River near the present Armitage Bridge. Diamond, a bachelor, located nearby.

Jacob Collyar Spores was born in Montgomery County, N. Y., in 1795. His father, also named Jacob, came to this country from Germany and lived to be 115 years old. Jacob Jr. fought against the British in the War of 1812, under Gen. Winfield Scott. He was in several battles, including Lundy's Lane and Sackett Harbor.

In 1816, he married Eliza Hand. They had nine children: Cornelia, Catherine, twins John and Esther, Electra Ann, Jacob, Nancy, James Madison and Martha Jane. The couple lived near the main wagon route in New York State. Jacob was inspired to join the pioneers who were moving westward to conquer a new continent.

Stopping briefly in Ohio, then a virgin wilderness, the family journeyed on to Winnebago County, Ill. Here his wife Eliza died in 1838. In 1842, Jacob married Nancy Orndorf Trimmer, widow of Frederick Trimmer. She had a son, William Frederick. Jacob and Nancy had four children, Lewis, Henry, Mary E. and Arminda.

Three years later the family moved to St. Louis, Mo., where Jacob organized a wagon train. Because of his military experience, he was elected captain of the train. The Spores party consisted of his wife Nancy and children: Esther, Nancy, Martha Jane, James Madison, Lewis and Henry; also Nancy's son, William.

Born in Ireland

John Diamond, born in Londonderry, Ireland, in 1815, sailed from Belfast April 14, 1833, landing at Ogdensburg, N. Y. He went the following August to New York City. In 1835, he moved to Monroe County, Mich., then to Chicago. He dwelt there until 1847, when he joined Spores and his family en route to Oregon.

The party had a successful journey across the plains via the Oregon trail and Barlow Toll Road. They had no trouble with the Indians. A Flathead Indian acted as guide and interpreter for the company.

Spores and Diamond traveled together as far as Fort Hall, Ida. Diamond pushed on ahead with horses, arriving at Whitman's Station Aug. 3, continuing on to what became Lane County, arriving Sept. 20.

Spores arrived in Oregon with his family Sept. 5, 1847, said the *Eugene Register-Guard* (Nov. 20, 1959). Leaving his family in the northern part of the state, he came alone to the McKenzie, joining Diamond that fall. He staked his donation land claim along the future Coburg Road and set up his camp. The following spring, assisted by Diamond and his eldest son, James Madison, Jacob erected a log cabin and was joined by his family.

The only other white residents in the area were the Eugene Skinners at the west end of Skinner's Butte, Elijah Bristow and a couple of his neighbors at Pleasant Hill, awaiting arrival of their families. Mrs. Echo Spores Neal, a granddaughter, wrote that Spores was not aware of Skinner's presence, and it was by chance they met for the first time the following year, 1848.

Diamond took up his land claim on which the town of Coburg now stands. In April 1848, he commenced building a home for himself on the edge of the timber, where he lived until 1858.

Other Area Settlers

In November, after Spores and Diamond arrived, Mitchell Wilkins took up a claim three miles northwest at Willamette Forks.

William Stevens, the same year, left his family at Molalla and rode south to stake his claim north of Springfield on what is now Game Farm Road. He moved his family there the following spring.

Toward the end of the year 1847, Luther White commenced constructing a house three miles down river from where the present Coburg Bridge now stands. But he didn't take possession. In May 1848, a German, Peter Herb, settled on White's place. Still later, the house was occupied by Floyd Vaughn. Thomas and Walter Monteith and James Lemmon, en route to Sutter's Fort after the Whitman massacre, stopped at Spores' place, stayed and filed claims.

In April 1848, Thomas Cady and David Chamberlain, who settled in Linn County in 1847, relocated to West Point. Jess Haskett settled west of Wilkins. That spring, William Vaughn and his sons located on the Cady and Chamberlain place, in later years occupied by Enoch Coleman.

In the fall Charles Roth commenced building a house, later occupied by a Mr. Jones, due west from West Point. In the spring of 1849, a German began building a house, but was soon called by the California gold strike. The house was subsequently occupied by James Riley. There was no immigration to the area in 1850. In 1851, James Hunsaker settled on land adjoining that of Jacob Spores, later occupied by Henry Spores. Other early settlers were the Teals and Cawthornes, William Landreth, Frank Sutter and Frank Skinner.

Builds First Ferry

Spores first used a canoe to ferry passengers across the McKenzie River. Regarding the river from the standpoint of utility, in 1849, he acquired a ferry boat, which he operated until 1878, when the first bridge was built. This first ferry, about 12x25 feet in dimensions, was built along the lines of a skiff with a curved bottom and decking, guided with a rawhide cable strung across the river.

The origin of the name of two Lane County valleys -- Mohawk and Camp Creek -- is an interesting chapter in early Spores' history.

Mrs. Neal wrote: "A band of Indians rode into the Coburg Valley one night and stole a herd of Jacob's horses, then disappeared eastward over the mountains. Discovering the loss, he and a posse set out in hot pursuit. While trailing the Indians out of the mountains, the settlers discovered below them a beautiful valley.

"Because of its similarity to the Mohawk he had known as a boy in New York, Jacob named it the Mohawk Valley. Further pursuing, his posse finally overtook the Indians, who were camped along a creek. They recovered the horses. To this day the area is known as Camp Creek, deriving its name from the Indian encampment."

Diamond, more interested in exploring and road building than farming, spent the next few years helping build the Oregon Military Road over the Willamette Pass, the old Immigrant Pass.

Diamond Peak, a large mountain (8750 feet) north of the pass which he, along with another pioneer, William Macy, climbed in 1852, was named for him. Diamond Lake, "Jewel of the Cascades," in Douglas County, first viewed by Diamond from Diamond Peak, is also named for John. Nestled between 9200-foot Mt. Thielsen and 8363-foot Mt. Bailey, the lake is world famous for fishing.

In 1855, Spores and Diamond erected a sash sawmill.

After 1858, Diamond spent some time in California and visited the Eastern States. In 1861, the sawmill was purchased by Zack Pollard. That same year Isaac VanDuyn bought Diamond's donation land claim.

Born Aug. 17, 1810, in Somerset County, N. J., Van Duyne moved with his parents to Ohio, where his mother died. In 1827, his father moved to Vermillion County, Ind. Here Isaac on March 27, 1832, married Sarah Miles. She was born in Breckenridge, Ky., Sept. 5, 1815. They moved in 1840 to Mercer County, Mo., and crossed the plains by ox teams to Oregon in 1851. They settled at the Santiam forks, moving in 1852 to the Coburg area. Their children were Mary Ann, Isaac, Thomas, John, William, Cornelius, Marion and Ellen.

VanDuyn purchased the sawmill from Pollard, but the mill was swept away by the massive flood of 1861-62. In 1865, the site was purchased by J. L. Brumley and a new mill built with capacity of 15,000 board feet in 24 hours. In 1876, Brumley sold the mill to Horace Stone, who in turn sold to Hiram Smith. It was then sold to Coburg Milling.

Diamond eventually returned to Coburg and lived there until his death in 1902. He is buried in the I.O.O.F. Cemetery at Coburg.

Jacob Spores died in 1890. Nancy died the following year.

James Madison Spores, born in Winnebago County, Ill., in 1835, helped his father build the first cabin, break the sod, herd the stock and operate the ferry.

Jonathan and Jeanette Thomas -- Spores' neighbors in Illinois -- came west by ox team in 1852 and settled nearby. James Madison married their daughter, Mary Catherine (1832-1908), one of five children.

James and Mary had at least 10 children: Arminda, John H., George V., Mary S., Samuel A., Irene, James Frank, Charles, Daniel and Leila. (Chapman Publishing Co., 1903, and Clark, 1927).

In 1857, James moved to a farm in the lower Mohawk Valley. He served as a county commissioner. He eventually accumulated more than 1,000 acres. The house, built in 1866, served as the hub of community dances and parties. The place kept the family name under Manley Spores, and became a century farm after 102 years. The couple had 47 living descendants as of 1959.

Martha Jane married Charnel Mulligan, co-founder of Eugene.

Marvin Spores, a great-grandson of Jacob, was the last of his generation of this pioneer family. He was born in Springfield Feb. 15, 1901, to George Washington and Helen Josephine Clark Spores. He married Marie A. Norwood Aug. 29, 1927. She died in 1969. He later married Zelma Norwood in Springfield Feb. 27, 1977. He had lived on the Mohawk 74 years, farming for 40 years, and at Cottage Grove 20 years.

Marvin died Dec. 13, 1995, at age 94. Survivors were his wife, Zelma; daughters, Caroline Marie Spores, Springfield, and Jeanne Spores Wilder, Honolulu, Hawaii; sons, Ronald Marvin, Nashville, Tenn., George William, Depot Bay, and John Clark, Missoula, Mont.; stepson, Grant Edward, San Gabriel, Calif.; eight grandchildren and eleven great-grandchildren.

MITCHELL WILKINS

Mitchell Wilkins was born Sept. 28, 1818, in Orange County, N. Car. His father and mother both died when he was five years old. He was taken in charge by an uncle, then a brother until age 14, when he started out on his own. Learning the carpentry trade, he built flat boats for the Mississippi River and spent some time in St. Joseph, Mo., where he erected the first warehouse and built a house.

Moving to Weston, Mo., he married Permelia Ann Allen on Christmas day, 1844. The daughter of Robert and Elizabeth Allen, she was born in 1827 in Arkansas. When she was four years old, her parents moved to Missouri. She lived there until her marriage to Mitchell. The ceremony took place in an old schoolhouse in Platt County.

Their wedding journey was made on horseback through the snow to near Fort Leavenworth, where they lived until 1847. Her mother died in 1845. In May, Wilkins, 29, and Permelia, 20, accompanied by Permelia's father, started across the plains by ox team with the train of 95 wagons, headed by "Uncle Billy" Vaughn as wagon train captain.

"Uncle Billy" had come to Oregon in 1845 among the 3,000 emigrants who came west that year. He had liked what he saw so returned to Missouri to get his family.

The trip was difficult. Two people died on the journey. In the Blue Mountains, Wilkins became sick. Mrs. Wilkins drove the ox team. The oxen gave out in the Cascade Mountains. Leaving their wagons, they packed what they had left on a horse and started on foot, arriving at Barlow's Gate in September, going on to near Silverton in October.

In the spring of 1848, Wilkins took up a donation land claim in the foothills north of Coburg. He broke ten acres of ground. That October he moved his family to their new home. They ultimately developed this into a 3,000-acre ranch, one of the best stock farms in

Oregon, raising Devonshire and Hereford cattle and blooded sheep.

In January 1851, a post office was established at the Wilkins' home, known as Willamette Forks Post Office, the name for the only post office in this part of the valley until Sept. 18, 1884. Wilkins mined on the Trinity River in Northern California. Nominated for governor of Oregon, he lost, but served in the state legislature in 1862. He managed the State Fair and for many years was president of the Oregon State Agriculture Association. He was commissioner from Oregon to the Philadelphia Exposition in 1876, to New Orleans in 1884 and to the Chicago World's Fair in 1893. He died Jan. 31, 1904, at age 85.

WILLIAM STEVENS

Among the adventurous pioneers who headed west from Missouri in the spring of 1847 were William Stevens, his wife Hixey Villia (Jones) and their ten children. Stevens was born June 25, 1805, in Raleigh, N. Car. He and Hixey moved to Ray County, Tenn., in 1828. A son, Harrison Andrew, was born Jan. 1, 1829. They moved to Polk Co., Mo., in 1836.

Hearing tales of the West and the government's offer of 640-acre donation land claims, Stevens with wife, Hixey, and children left Bolivar, Polk County, Mo., May 7, 1847. After crossing the Missouri line headed for Oregon, they joined Capt. Billy Vaughn's wagon train.

Stevens, driving 120 head of stock, was first attracted to a farm near Molalla. Not satisfied, he left his family there and headed south. He came to where Jacob Spores was camped in a tent near the present Coburg bridge. He was ferried across the McKenzie by Indians, their horses swimming the stream. Finding an area nearby in what is now known as Gamebird Village on Game Farm Road, north of Springfield, he staked his claim and returned to Molalla.

Christmas day, 1847, Stevens, with sons Alvin and Isaac and 13-year-old daughter, Sarah Jane, arrived at their claim. Sarah Jane was the first white woman to cross the McKenzie, crossing in a covered wagon drawn by oxen. Three friendly Indians plunged into the deep, cold water and steadied the wagon bed as they crossed.

Stevens and his sons felled timber, the first cut in the area, for a log cabin, 16x18 feet, with a puncheon floor. In the fall of 1848, they broke 40 acres of land with a wooden plow. It is said Stevens and Eugene Skinner were unaware of each other's presence until some time later upon a chance meeting.

Mrs. Stevens and the other children joined them in the spring, the first family to settle down in the valley. Others built up in the hills, safe from floods. The family consisted of his wife, Hixey, and children: Harrison Andrew, Ashland Orlando, Alvin Burt, Sarah Jane, Isaac E., Mary Ann, James Anderson, Emmaline Matilda, William Henry, Charles Jefferson and Mandely Caroline.

There was a good sized Indian settlement in this area near the McKenzie. While not unfriendly, they were often a nuisance to the settlers by being ever present and taking whatever was attractive.

Stevens farmed his land. In 1849, he operated Briggs Ferry on the Willamette River at Springfield. For passenger service he used two canoes lashed together. Wagons were taken apart and thus ferried across. Livestock was forced to swim.

Stevens, at age 55, was killed by his horse in an accident on his farm, May 25, 1860. He is buried in the Gillespie Cemetery.

The Stevens house, northwest of Springfield at 3050 Game Farm Road, stood for many years as the oldest house in Lane County, one of about eight from the 1859's and the only two-story example.

GEORGE ARMITAGE

George Henry Armitage, born in Queens County, N. Y., Jan. 26, 1824, moved to St. Joseph, Mo., in 1845. (Walling's History). He had intended coming to Oregon earlier but was discouraged by two men who said the entire Willamette Valley was covered by water. He purchased a canoe and paddled 2,000 miles to New Orleans, where he was employed as a ship's carpenter during the war with Mexico.

In 1848, he bought passage on the steamer San Francisco that carried mail between Panama and Astoria. At San Francisco the steamer was ordered to abandon the Oregon route because of good business transporting gold miners to San Francisco. Armitage prospected for gold but soon gave up and came to Oregon, arriving in Oregon City Dec. 16, 1848. He spent the winter on the Calapooya, site of Brownsville. He helped build the first school east of Salem.

During the spring of 1850 he bought a saddle horse in Oregon City and started up the valley. The trail, from the McKenzie River near the future Coburg crossing to what later became Springfield, led past William Stevens' home. There he met Sarah Jane. He stopped briefly, then went on to California. After a short stay in the south, he came back to the valley and took up a claim where the Maughn place is today, not far from the old Coburg Bridge.

George and Sarah Jane Stevens were married Nov. 1, 1851. They had seven children of whom Sylvanus, James, Ella and Frank were living at the time of Armitage's death in 1893.

George and his brother-in-law, Harrison Stevens, built a ferry in Stevens' whip-saw, water-powered sawmill. He floated it down to the McKenzie River crossing, taking in as much as $100 daily from those going south to join the gold rush. For a time competing ferries were operated across the McKenzie by Spores and by Stevens and Armitage at the Coburg crossing a short distance from each other. Authorities, sensing future complications, sought a compromise.

When Joseph Lane took over as governor of the newly organized Territory of Oregon, ferry operators were required to qualify and be licensed. On the day assigned for appearance in Oregon City, Armitage and Stevens were prevented from going by raging currents. Spores being on the north bank had no difficulty in getting there, and thus obtained the desired license to operate the ferry. Spores then purchased Armitage and Stevens' ferry and continued operation until 1878, when it was replaced by the Coburg covered bridge.

Armitage Park was offered to the state of Oregon as a gift in 1935 by Sylvanus Armitage, son of George and Sarah. The 32.82-acre tract was accepted into the state park system in June 1938.

MAHLON H. HARLOW

Among settlers north and northeast of Eugene was Mahlon H. Harlow, a builder. He was born in Barnes County, Ky., in 1811, son of Anderson Harlow. With his wife, Frances (Tandy), and their family, he headed west May 16, 1850. They met Mormon troubles when crossing their "promised lands." He was fined and imprisoned by Mormons who coveted his oxen. They were forced to winter in Salt Lake City, Utah.

Arriving at The Dalles May 30, 1851, Harlow left their wagon and stock with their son and took the women and children by boat to Portland, thence to Yamhill County. Returning to The Dalles he brought the stock over the Barlow Pass in July. He came up the Willamette by mule and staked his claim between the Willamette and McKenzie rivers along what is now Harlow Road.

In 1852, he was elected Lane County's first clerk. That year the Baptist Church was organized in his home as Willamette Forks Baptist Church of Jesus Christ. Between 1860 and 1866, he worked on constructing the old military road over the Willamette Pass. He built a hotel where the Osborn Hotel stood for many years. He also built the original Lane County Courthouse and other buildings.

Gillespies and Youngs

Historically prominent in Lane County annals were Jacob Gillespie and his son-in-law, Charles Walker Young, who in 1852 settled a mile north of Eugene on what is today Cal Young Road.

Gillespie, born in Sumner County, Tenn., in November 1803, moved to LaFayette County, Mo., in 1831. He married Almyra Hannah Aug. 4, 1831. They had seven children. After her death he married Mrs. Amelia Martin in 1845.

Young, born in LaFayette County, Mo., May 12, 1830, was the youngest son of James Young. On Feb. 22, 1852, he married Mary B. Gillespie, Jacob's eldest daughter. In May of that year they joined a company of eight wagons of which Jacob Gillespie was captain. They crossed the plains by ox team from Independence, Mo., "enduring all the hardships attending that journey over unknown wilds of trackless prairies and rugged mountains." (Walling).

Arriving at The Dalles Aug. 27, they floated down the Columbia on a raft. At Oregon City, Gillespie and Young went on to Lane County, where Gillespie purchased the Abraham Peek donation land claim, a mile north of the Willamette River by the hill now called Gillespie Butte. He took up his residence there Oct. 6, 1852.

In 1854-55, Gillespie represented Lane County in the Territorial Assembly. He was elected to the county board of commissioners in 1857, serving until Oregon became a state in 1859. In July 1857, he married Mrs. Elizabeth Goodpasture, a Lane County pioneer who came west with her former husband in 1853.

Young was penniless when he arrived and had to borrow fifty cents from Gillespie to pay for a ferry crossing. He and his wife took up residence on the Gillespie farm a year later. After first working elsewhere, he began farming and became prosperous. He and Mary had three sons and eight daughters. A son, Cal Young, who became well known in the county, was born June 25, 1871.

Marcellus M. Gillespie, son of Jacob, was born in La Fayette County, Mo., Jan. 26, 1846. He came west with his father and married Selma Goodpasture Nov. 2, 1865. She died Nov. 5, 1869. He married, second, Damaris T. Benson Jan. 21, 1874. He had two children by his first wife and four by his second.

Nellie Gillespie, sister of Marcellus, married Robert M. Masterson, pioneer of 1854, born April 30, 1829, in Kentucky.

On his trip west, Masterson, a single man, his brother James Alfred Masterson, and wife, their two sisters, their husbands (one of them named Ward), ten children and hired help, totaling about twenty, formed a wagon train. They were harassed by Indians along the Snake River in Idaho. They camped on the Boise River at present-day Middleton. Next morning James, his wife and Robert went on ahead driving their cattle. The remainder of the party were set upon by Indians and all were killed, except two boys, children of the Wards, who escaped, and two who were taken captive. This is since known as the Ward Massacre. (See John Cogswell chapter).

Masterson fought in the Rogue Indian war, 1855-56, then settled near Springfield in 1862. He and Nellie had seven children.

The Youngs, Tandys and Harlows were neighbors in Missouri.

Another settler, Hulins Miller, a Quaker, crossed the plains from Indiana in 1852 with his wife; two sons, Cincinnatus Hiner and James, and a daughter, Ella. Their eldest son died in Pennsylvania. He had served as a surgeon in the Union Army.

They located on the north side of the McKenzie River near the Willamette Forks Post Office. Hulins was an early-day justice of the peace. He died Feb. 2, 1882, from injuries suffered earlier when he was thrown from his wagon, his team of horses having run away.

Cincinnatus was better known as "Joaquin" Miller. He became famous on the Pacific Coast and even in foreign countries as the Poet of the Sierras. Ella married John Luckey.

George Melvin Miller, born in May 1853 after the family arrived in Oregon, was educated in the public schools and taught one year. He moved into Eugene in 1882 and entered law practice. In the 1890's, he tampered with a small model flying machine. In 1901, he participated in the final decision on the boundary line between Canada and the United States. He spent years promoting the New York to Florence Highway.

Coburg's Community Life

Early Coburg area settlers were mainly interested in raising grain and cattle for food. Community life centered around church activity. First meetings were outside, presided over by Elder Perne, a Methodist circuit rider. Soon other denominations were organized.

The first store was operated by Ritz and Hovey about 1854. The partners bought a stock of goods and erected a shed where the school house later stood. Born in Londonderry, N. H., July 11, 1830, A. G. Hovey moved with his parents to Marietta, Ohio, crossed the plains to California in 1849, and dug for gold near Sacramento. In 1850, he came to Oregon, settling at Corvallis, where he taught the first school.

Isaac VanDuyn bought Ritz and Hovey's store in 1855 for $2,500. Two years later VanDuyn sold to William Landreth.

Returning to Benton County, Hovey was elected the first county clerk. He represented that county in the state senate from 1862 to 1866. He moved to Portland, then to Springfield in 1867. He was Springfield's first postmaster, was engaged in milling and merchandising until 1879, then moved to Eugene City. One of the founders of the Lane County Bank in 1882 and a delegate to the Republican National Convention in 1884, Hovey was involved in other business pursuits, including president of the McKenzie River toll road. He served as mayor of Eugene. He married Emily Humphrey. They had three children.

Frank Sutter opened a business in Coburg in 1878, and M. H. Skinner, in 1879. Being close to the McKenzie River, which furnished both logs and water power, the community became a sawmill center. During the McKenzie and Mohawk rivers log drives (1880-1912) large log booms caught the logs as they floated down the river. The logs then were diverted to the large sawmills near Coburg, including the J. C. Goodale and Booth-Kelly mills.

Isaac VanDuyn surveyed and platted the town in 1881 as a part of Lane County. Platting of the town was instigated by arrival from the north of a narrow-gauge railroad, which made this point its southern terminus. A "neat and commodious" station house, grain elevator and hand-powered turntable and other necessary equipment were built. James Steele, Portland, built a warehouse for $5,000. (Walling).

Coburg did not have its own post office until Dec. 18, 1884. Until then people had to go three miles to Willamette Forks Post Office at the Wilkins' residence, although all other activities were in town. A rival town, Willamette, on the railroad a mile and a half north of Coburg, was promoted. Buildings were erected to house certain lodges, but they were mysteriously burned, ending the city.

The period between 1898 and 1915 could be called "Golden Years" for the town with two sawmills, general merchandise stores, hotel, bakery, drug store, a weekly newspaper, the *Coburg Journal,* and four trains daily. A motor coach, known as The Skunk, took care of overflow passengers to Springfield and Eugene. Coburg probably was the leading sawmill city in the county and remained so until 1912, when river logging was ended by government authority.

Originally called Diamond, the name Coburg was bestowed on the settlement by blacksmith Charles Paine, who was very proud of a locally owned stallion named Coburg, from the famous horse breeding center, Coburg, Germany, wrote Stuart Hurd in *Lane County Historian* (1966: 64). For 50 years the town was noted for its horses.

CHAPTER 8

Central Lane Settlers

The migration of 1847, which entered Oregon via the southern route on the old Scott-Applegate Trail and arrived that fall at Pleasant Hill, proved a perilous and toilsome journey. The Oregon Trail by this time was pretty-well defined as far as The Dalles, although fire had blackened sections of the trail through the Blue Mountains. Travel on to Portland, via the Columbia River or over the Cascade Mountains on what became the Barlow Pass Toll Road, was hazardous and costly.

Jesse Applegate, Yoncalla settler who had lost two children to the turbulent Columbia, and Levi Scott, for whom Scottsburg and Scotts Valley in Douglas County are named, set out with a small party in 1846 to locate and establish a new route into Oregon from the south.

This route turned off the Oregon Trail onto the California Trail some 40 miles west of Ft. Hall, Ida. It followed the Humboldt River through northern Nevada to the vicinity of Imlah, west of present-day Winnemucca, thence northwesterly into California to Goose Lake. The trail entered Oregon via Tule Lake, proceeding on to Klamath Lake, over the Green Springs Mountains to the Rogue River Valley, and north to the Umpqua and Willamette valleys. This route was first used in 1846 by a wagon train which had to cut 500 miles of trail.

With the 1847 migration was Lester Hulin. Born in 1823 in Saratoga County, N. Y., he moved to Henry County, Iowa. In 1845 at St. Louis, Mo., he joined John C. Fremont and Col. Ebert on exploring expeditions through Kansas, Colorado, New Mexico, Texas and Indian Territories, experiencing many adventures and "hair breadth escapes," to quote from Walling's history. From St. Joseph, Hulin, who kept a journal, joined the Oskaloosa Company wagon train captained by David Donald Davis. Because of his experience Hulin served as "pilot."

Davis, born about 1807 in Pennsylvania to a Welsh family, Edward and Ann (Rees) Davis, moved to Dearborn County, Ind., where on Feb. 22, 1831, at Lawrenceburg, he married Hannah Donahoe, daughter of John and Elizabeth Donahoe. In 1839, he moved his family to Iowa. He became a well-to-do farmer but was lured to the West.

Davis, age 39, with Hannah, and their eight children, left Iowa in April of 1847 bound for Oregon. Davis had seven well-supplied wagons of his own, pulled by 14 yoke (28 oxen), along with cattle, milch cows, horses and sheep. The children were Jane, 15; Hannah Ann, 14; Rebecca, 12; Meshach, 10; Thomas, 8; Elizabeth, 5; Rachel, 3, and William, 1.

The Davises joined other families where they crossed the Des Moines River into Missouri. They probably met the large Belknap, Watts, Starr and Gilbert families near Keosauqua in Van Buren County, Iowa.

The train at times numbered as many as 80 wagons.

The Oskaloosa Company, as portrayed in his book by that name by Charles George Davis (Copyright 1996), was one of three or four wagon groups that turned off the Oregon Trail west of Ft. Hall, Ida., to follow the poorly-defined Scott-Applegate route. After crossing over Fandango Pass, east of Goose Lake in northern California, the travelers, believing they had crossed the Sierra Nevada Range, were rejoicing in a dance the night of Sept. 29, 1847. The train had been harassed from time to time by Indians, who that night shot arrows into the circle of wagons.

Hannah Ann Davis, age 14, kneeling beside a camp fire, baking bread, was struck by three arrows. One went through the calf of her leg, another through her arm into her side. She fell face down into the fire. Although she was rescued quickly, fire burned her hair and clothing. The right side of her face was badly burned and permanently scarred.

The arrows had to be removed to prevent infection. In the dead of night without the benefit of an anesthetic, several men held the girl down, while another cut the arrows out with a sharp knife. Her screams rent the air. Her pain was so great she had to be carried on a stretcher by men of the party for several days. Hulin's journal listed her as "Miss Ann Davis, who became the wife of Caswell Hendricks." Hendricks, in 1862, established a ferry on the McKenzie River at Walterville.

The Wagon train continued on into Oregon to Klamath Lake, over the Green Springs Mountains, thence along the Rogue River to the Grants Pass area and north over Sexton Mountain to the most hazardous part of the journey -- Canyon Pass. Here many of their wagons were broken up and much property lost. Trees had to be tied to wagons to keep them from overrunning draft animals. Prior to reaching this pass, Martha Leland Crowly died of Typhoid Fever. She was buried at what is known as Grave Creek near Leland north of Grants Pass.

The Oskaloosa Company had endured extreme hardships. Some families settled at Pleasant Hill. The Belknap and Starr families settled west of present-day Monroe. (See Chapter 21). The Davis family went on to Salem to obtain medical care for Hannah Ann. (See Chapter 12).

After arriving in Oregon, Hulin, Charnel Mulligan and others fought in the Cayuse war around Walla Walla, Wa., from January to July, 1848, then went to California to seek gold. They tried to come home by boat in 1849 but were stranded in a calm for sixteen days and grounded on the bar at the mouth of the Rogue River. They walked home.

In three weeks Hulin was off again to California. He returned in 1850 by ship to Portland and took up a claim on the Long Tom River three miles from Junction City. On Dec. 1, 1853, he married Abbey J. Craig, a native of Jackson County, Mich. They had four children, Charles, Anna (Tozer), Samuel and Lester.

Of the same 1847 migration, Cornelius J. Hills, born in Madison County, N. Y., in 1818, settled on the north side of the Willamette River (Jasper area). He went to California during the 1849 gold rush and came back to Oregon on the ill-fated ship with Hulin and Mulligan. Returning to Iowa, he married Sophrona P. Briggs Feb. 19, 1851. He brought her to his claim at Jasper. They had seven children: Henrietta, Jessie, Jasper B., John A., Sheridan P., Joel S. and Elijah.

Risdon Early Settler

Judge D. M. Risdon was quoted by A. G. Walling as saying, when he arrived in Eugene in 1851 there was no dwelling within the area later incorporated as Eugene City. Skinner's cabin was outside the area.

William Smith resided one and a half miles distant on the Springfield Road. Hilyard Shaw dwelt in a little house near where Deady Hall, the University's first, was later built. Shaw and Smith in 1851 dug the Eugene millrace, providing water power for the sawmill they erected and a grist mill. Shaw ran a newspaper briefly and contributed land to downtown Eugene. Hilyard Street is named for him.

Smith, born in Berkshire, England, March 11, 1826, came with his parents to Rochester, N. Y., then to Ohio and Indiana. He crossed the plains to Portland in 1847, visited California, then filed a claim a mile east of Eugene. He married Nancy A. Luckey. They had four children.

Prior Blair and family occupied a log cabin on the west side. Born in Henry County, Ky., Blair married Ellen Mulligan in 1837. Their children were Sarah, Eveline, Eleanor, Annie and Francis. Blair Boulevard was named for him.

Next to the Blairs, Lemuel Davis had a cabin. His father, Benjamin, lived two and a half miles beyond. Four miles down river dwelt the James Davis family. Below was James Peek. Then came John Vallaly. North of the Willamette River was Henry Peek. Abraham Peek occupied land later sold to Jacob Gillespie on what became Cal Young Road.

Risdon, born June 3, 1823, in Fairfield County, Vt., where he grew up and was educated, moved to Illinois, taught school, then studied law. First attracted to the California gold fields in 1850, he soon came to Oregon and filed a claim adjoining that of Skinner. He employed Hilyard Shaw to erect a twenty by fourteen-foot frame house, covered with split boards with puncheon floor, costing $76. He dug a well and cut a nearby pine tree from which he manufactured furniture.

He and Skinner established a meridian with the view to laying out a town. Risdon served in the Territorial Legislature, 1851-52, then was county judge. He married Pauline Gertrude Wright, daughter of Ezekial Wright, Oct. 8, 1853. Children were Augustus D. and Ella Pauline.

In the summer of 1851, James Huddleston opened a store on the river banks near where Skinner started his ferry. Several other families arrived later that year.

Schools of Eugene

Eugene's first schools, known as "select schools," were private. In the early 1850's, Sarah Ann Moore opened the first "select school" on a hill south of town in rattlesnake country near the present Masonic Cemetery. *The Story of Eugene,* by Lucia Moore, Nina McCornack and Gladys McCready, reported the house was of logs with puncheon floor. It closed in 1858 after a pupil was bitten by a rattlesnake.

With Lane County's incorporation in 1851, Robert Robe was appointed first county school superintendent, serving 1851-55. Others were: R. H. Parson, 1855-56; D. M. Risdon, 1856-57; J. H. D. Henderson, 1858-60; Daniel Locke, 1860-62; Ben Underwood, 1862-64; Nathan Hull, 1864-66; J. W. Skaggs, 1868-70; Thomas Hendricks, 1870-74; R. G. Callison, 1875, and A. W. Patterson, 1882-86.

The first public school was built of logs with dirt floor at the corner of Eleventh and Olive streets on land donated by Skinner in 1856. Eugene became Lane County School District 4. First teacher was J. H. Rogers or G. R. Caton. However, no less than ten private or select schools existed at various locations well into the 1870's. It was not until 1878 that Central School, Eugene's first permanent public structure, was built on Eleventh Street between Willamette and Olive, serving some 300 pupils.

The ill-fated and controversial Columbia College, begun in 1855, was Eugene's first effort at higher education. This was two years after Skinner had marked off his land in a town plat, and Eugene City had built a courthouse and laid out Hitching Post Square.

Rev. Enoch P. Henderson, 1855 graduate of Waynesburg College, Penn., was named president. Born in Calloway County, Mo., July 24, 1818, he married Elizabeth Schroyer March 25, 1850. They came via the Isthmus of Panama to California in 1856, moving on to Eugene City.

The first building of wood erected on College Hill, south of town, burned after four days of classes. Henderson moved his fifty-two students into a private dwelling near-by while a second wooden building was being built. The enrollment climbed to 100. Before the end of that year the second building burned. Arson was suspected.

Amidst controversy, a stone building was erected. Henderson resigned and returned to California. He was replaced at Columbia College by Professor Ryan, a rabid Southerner. Slavery and secession were on many people's minds. The Union League disapproved violently of Ryan.

One of his students, Harrison Kincaid, was a reporter for the Republican paper, *The People's Press,* edited by B. J. Pengra. When Ryan wrote an article for the *Democrat Herald* defending slavery and signed it Vindex, Kincaid answered in the *People's Press,* signing himself Anti-Vindex. One article followed another, until Ryan sought out Pengra at the Ellsworth and Belshaw drugstore and took a shot in his direction. Whether or not Pengra was hit, he survived.

Ryan immediately fled the country. The Columbia board of directors gave up. Eugene's population at the time was only about 900. However, a number of Columbia's students became prominent in city and state government and community business affairs. A later effort to open the Eugene Academy also failed.

After various pursuits with the ministry in the East, Henderson, in 1862, was back in Oregon, as principal of an academy at Harrisburg. In 1864, he was elected chief clerk of the Oregon State Senate. Settling in Eugene, he conducted an independent graded school for three years. He took the 1870 Lane County census and wrote articles on Oregon's resources for the *Oregonian.* He and Elizabeth had five children.

The first move to establish a state university at Eugene was begun in 1872. The federal government in 1803 had declared the granting of two townships of land in each state entering the Union for universities. Oregon Agricultural College, a land grant institution established at Corvallis in 1867, was the outgrowth of Corvallis Seminary, organized by the Methodist Episcopal Church South. Rev. Silas M. Stout, pioneer of 1845 who settled in Benton County and rode circuit throughout the valley, was one of the seminary's organizers.

The Union University Association was organized and capital stock of $50,000 subscribed. The association petitioned the state legislature for purchase of a site and erection of a building at Eugene. Opposition arose from other Oregon cities but the bill passed. Eugene citizens began a private subscription campaign. Enough money was raised to start construction in 1873 on the first building, old Deady Hall, named for Judge Matthew P. Deady. The building was completed in 1875.

The University of Oregon's first class was graduated in 1878. Villard Hall, named for Southern Pacific Railroad industrialist, Henry Villard, who contributed generously, was added ten years later.

Eugene's first newspaper, *The News*, printed in 1858 by John B. Alexander, soon folded. The second paper, the *Pacific Journal*, became *The People's Press*, published by Pengra. The paper did not soft pedal its stand against the confederacy and slavery, resulting in the incident when Ryan shot at Pengra. Joel Ware followed Pengra as editor. In 1859, the Democratic Herald, edited by Joaquin Miller who had attended Columbia College and supported the confederacy, was soon suppressed.

Hilyard Shaw published the *State Republican* in 1861. Harrison Kincaid, as printer, took his pay in land from Shaw. James Newton Gale arrived from Posey County, Ind., in 1852. He married Harrison's sister, Elizabeth, quit a mill business and joined his four brothers to learn the printing trade. He took over the *State Republican* and strongly expressed his abolitionist views. Threatened by secessionists, he later took his paper to Salem and published there as the *Argus Republican*.

During the Civil War years, the *Union Crusader and Copperhead Killer* was edited by the Rev. A. C. Edmunds. Pengra and Judge Stratton urged Kincaid to buy out Edmunds. Joel Ware, then publisher of *The People's Press*, joined Kincaid. They established the *Oregon State Journal*. Ware withdrew after a year to take other employment. Kincaid and family members continued to publish the paper for many years.

Harrison Rittenhouse Kincaid, born Jan. 3, 1836, in Madison County, Ind., was the eldest son of Thomas and Nancy Kincaid.

Thomas, of Scotch-Irish parentage, was born in Greenbrier County, Va., July 27, 1800. At age 17, he emigrated by canoe and flatboat down the Great Kanawha and Ohio Rivers to Indiana in 1817. On Jan. 9, 1831, he married Nancy Chodrick, age 15, born July 7, 1816, in Ohio. After traveling throughout the midwest seeking a better home, in 1853 with five children, they left Indiana with horse and ox-drawn wagons and came to Lane county in October, settling on a donation land claim southeast of Eugene. They moved into town in 1860. Thomas died in 1886.

Harrison, at age 17, had walked from Indiana, driving the ox team. He split rails and made fences for his parents, and helped Isaac and Elias Briggs dig the millrace at Springfield. In 1856, he mined in southern Oregon and California, worked at other jobs, then returned by steamer from San Francisco to Portland. Back in Eugene, he attended Columbia College. In between his newspaper activities, he mined in Eastern Oregon, returning in 1864 to found the *Oregon State Journal.*

Turning the newspaper's management over to family members in 1869, Harrison traveled extensively in the Midwest and East and became involved in numerous political activities. On Sept. 29, 1873, he married Augusta A. Lockwood in Macomb County, Mich. She was born Sept. 3, 1852. He made several trips back to Eugene, finally returning in 1881. Their first child, a son, was born in 1883 in the house where the Kincaid family had resided since 1860.

Thomas and Nancy Kincaid had nine children, all but two born in Indiana. Austin C., born Dec. 18, 1837, died Feb. 20, 1838. Rebecca Ann, born Feb. 8, 1840, married Horace E. Lawrence in 1858. She occasionally wrote for the press. She died Feb. 5, 1864, at age 24. Elizabeth Marie, born Feb. 16, 1842, married James Newton Gale in 1860. They were in newspaper work for many years. A son, John was born and died in 1844.

John Sandford Kincaid, born in Iowa May 14, 1845, worked for and published the *Oregon State Journal* from 1869 until his death in December 1873. Mary Alice, born June 28, 1848, died Jan. 27, 1870, on a visit to New York. Eliza Jane, born in 1850, died in 1851.

George Summerfield Kincaid, born March 4, 1858, in Oregon, worked for the *Oregon State Journal* and was publisher from 1878 to 1882, when he became a partner. On Sept. 10, 1876, he married Laura A., youngest child of James and Mary J. Watkins. She was born May 25, 1860.

In 1867, the *Guard*, a Democrat paper appeared in Eugene, with John B. Alexander as publisher. The *Journal* was Republican. Getting national news was extremely difficult, until telegraph service came to the area along with the railroad in 1871.

The *Eugene Register* was started in 1884 as a weekly paper by S. M. Yoran. Many changes took place in the ownerships of Eugene's newspapers. The *Guard*, after buying out *The Register*, a morning paper, in 1930, exists today as the *Eugene Register-Guard*, owned by the family of Alton Baker, originally from Cleveland, Ohio.

The Lane County Bank was opened Jan. 1, 1882, by Messrs. Hovey, Humphrey, Peet and Co. It closed ten years later. A second bank, opened by Messrs. T. G. Hendricks and S. B. Eakin in 1884, became Lane County's pioneering banking institution, owned by family heirs until 1947.

Eugene had only about 900 people in 1858 and about 3,000 in 1884. The population climbed to around 16,000 until the late 1930, when many new industries, geared to the timber industry, were spurred on by World War II. Today, Eugene's city limits extend north of the Willamette River and is expanding to the west and south. Its population exceeds 110,000.

JOAQUIN MILLER, Poet

Cincinnatus Hiner Miller was well known for his stand on slavery, liquor and kindred subjects, but better known for his poetry. A collection of his poems, *"Songs of the Sierras,"* was published in 1882.

His pseudonym, "Joaquin" Miller, was due to his defense of Joaquin Murietta, a Mexican bandit.

Joaquin was the controversial son of Hulins Miller, a Quaker, who with his wife, two sons and daughter crossed the plains in 1852. He became famous on the Pacific Coast and in foreign countries as the Poet of the Sierras. Born in Wabash District, Ind., Nov. 10, 1841, he was a small boy when his parents arrived in Oregon. He had little schooling. At age 14 with a neighbor boy, Will Willoughby, he ran away from home, cooked in mining camps and mined near Yreka. He reportedly got into trouble and shot at the sheriff of Siskiyou County.

He accompanied William Walker, American journalist, lawyer and adventurer, on his Mexico and Nicaragua filibustering expeditions in the late 1850's, when he took up the cause of the Mexican bandit. He lived familiarly with Indians and Spaniards of the Pacific slope.

Returning to Eugene he studied law, graduating from the ill-fated Columbia College. In 1859, he edited the *Democratic Herald*, which supported the confederacy. His paper was soon suppressed.

About 1860, he spent a year in Eastern Oregon and Idaho Territory running a pony express, carrying letters and messages two hundred miles over mountains through Indian country to the miners. Returning home, for a short time he edited the *Eugene City Review* which also was suppressed because of its "treasonable" character.

He married Miss Minnie Myrtle (a pseudonym), who had acquired a reputation as a writer of verses They met through correspondence. When he called at her home in Coos Bay, he found another suitor there. Whereupon, the impetuous Joaquin introduced himself by whipping out a revolver and driving his rival from the room.

Miller, about 1864, went east of the Cascades with his young wife and settled in the gold mining camp of Canyon City, Ore., on the John Day River. En route to Canyon City, they were ambushed by Indians on the McKenzie Pass and narrowly escaped.

He practiced law in Canyon City, became popular by his services against the war-like Snake Indians. Elected by the Democrats, he served as Grant County judge from 1866 to 1870 and accumulated a considerable sum of money. He published some of his poems in the local newspaper.

Returning to Eugene, he separated from his wife and, leaving her and two children alone and bitter, left the Willamette Valley. Before going, he published a farewell to his wife. She responded by publishing a reply in verse in which she criticized him severely.

Miller couldn't sell his writings, collected under the title "Songs of the Sierras," in the East. He visited London in 1873, and was a war correspondent for a leading New York newspaper during the Franco-German war. Eventually his poems were published in London and brought him fame. Two poems pertained to the revolutionary activities of Walker, who was captured and shot. He traveled around the world, lived in Washington, D. C., then in 1887, settled near Oakland, Cal.

CHAPTER 9

Gateway to McKenzie

Springfield -- Gateway to the McKenzie -- lays four miles east of Eugene on the banks of the Willamette River. Its name derived from ". . . a natural spring which sent up its water in a prairie or open field. In the early 1850's, the spring and land near it were fenced off. The place became known by its present name. Elias K. Briggs, the first settler there in 1849, for many years ran a ferry on the Willamette River." (McArthur, 1982:695).

The *Oregon State Journal*, Eugene, Jan. 31, 1891, points to both Elias and his father, Isaac, as the original settlers. It said Isaac and Elizabeth "Betsy" Briggs and their son, Elias, crossed the plains in 1847, first settling in Pleasant Hill. "Uncle" Isaac drove a band of sheep with the family, the first sheep in Lane county. In 1848, Isaac went to the California gold fields along the Feather River and reportedly made a considerable sum of money.

"In 1849, as nearly as we can ascertain, they (father and son) moved from Pleasant Hill and took up two sections, 1280 acres of land where Springfield is now located, extending two miles or more along the north bank of the Willamette River," *The Journal* said. "'Uncle' Isaac and 'Aunt' Betsy lived on the upper claim near a large spring, after which the town was named and where 'Uncle' Isaac resided at the time of his death. Elias lived on the lower claim."

Life-long Springfield resident the late Crystal Fogle, writing for the *Springfield News* Dec. 1, 1949, said:

Elias Briggs ". . .chose for the location of his home a place convenient to a spring of water that sent up little bubbles with ceaseless energy. A part of the prairie where this spring stood in due time was fenced in. The enclosure became known as Spring Field -- hence the name of the town. The Briggs family dwelt here for two years and conducted a ferry across the Willamette where a fine bridge later spanned the river. At the end of that time they moved to a farm about a mile and a half from that original location."

The spring lies about center within the block today bounded by North A and B streets between North Second and Mill. Ironically, an apartment house now sets astride the spring.

Congress, to encourage emigration to Oregon, passed the donation land claim law of 1850. It provided each person who came to Oregon before Dec. 1, 1850, up to 320 acres of land from the government.

Suffers Scalding

On their trip west, "old Uncle Isaac Briggs, now a resident of Springfield, suffered a severe scalding by falling through an active mud spring at Black Rock," to quote from Walling's 1884 *History of Lane County's* biographical sketch of Lester Hulin, one of the train's leaders.

Believed by early Lane County settlers to be the site of future industrial activity, Springfield was known as the "handle" of the forks of the Willamette River.

Walling wrote, "Around it the mountain ranges are bold and grand, while the water power is extensive and valuable. At Springfield there are sites and falls for at least ten more factories."

The volume of water available in the Willamette, and the indication this source of power would be unlimited, led planners to visualize a great future for Springfield, expected to have manufacturing industries "second to none in the state."

In October 1853, Elias Briggs gave bond and received a license for a ferry across the Middle Fork of the Willamette opposite his house at Springfield. It was operated for a time by William Stevens, pioneer of 1847. The ferry was just upstream from the present mouth of the millrace in the vicinity of South B Street.

A 3.5-mile-long canal called the Millrace, dug by the Briggs in 1852, taps the Willamette two miles above Springfield, giving a fall at that place of about 20 feet and following more or less the course of an old flood channel. The work was done by spade, shovel, oxen and plow. Power derived ran the old grist mill the Briggs built in 1854.

Springfield's first two mills, the grist and the sawmill, were erected in 1853 and 1854 by an experienced millwright from the East. Briggs, Thomas Monteith, one of Albany's founders, and Jeremiah Driggs, a Linn County banker, supervised the construction.

None but the latest, best and most improved machinery of the time was used. These two mills cost the builders $10,000. The sawmill, the first erected, was started in the fall or winter of 1853-54. Both mills were located on the river approximately two blocks south of Main and Mill streets, an area early known as "Millers' City."

The millrace water not only ran the waterwheels for the sawmill and grist mill, but it was used to float and store logs cut upstream. The sawmill was replaced twice due to fire and the need to upgrade equipment and technology.

PENGRA EARLY DEVELOPER

Little importance was attached to Springfield, beyond the mills located there, until 1865, when the Briggs' claim passed into the hands of pioneer developer Byron J. Pengra. When Pengra, age 30, came to this section in 1853, there was but one place of business -- a trading post kept by J. N. Donald. This was Springfield's first store, located near Mill and Main streets. Donald owned what is known as Douglas Gardens. There was only one other house, that of Elias Briggs.

The original plan of Springfield, laid out for two blocks, was recorded Dec. 24, 1853. Descriptions of distances and locations were all measured as so many chains from Donald's store.

Pengra was born in Genesse County, N. Y., Feb. 11, 1823. His family moved to Erie County, Pa., where he lived eight years, then emigrated to Green County, Wisc., afterwards to Winnebago County, Ill., wrote Josephine Evans Harpham in *Lane County Historian.*

On May 1, 1849, Pengra married Charlotte Stearns in Winnebago County. She was born in Panten, Vt., May 1, 1827, to the Rev. and Mrs. John Stearns. Educated in public schools of New York and Ohio, she also attended Hampton Academy. She entered into educational work then moved to Illinois.

In 1853, the Pengras with their three-year-old daughter and Pengra's 19-year-old brother, William B., joined a wagon train for Oregon. Their first home was in the foothills east of the present town of Springfield where Pengra farmed and raised stock.

The first private school was started in the early 1850's. However, Springfield School District 19, was not established until 1854. The school building was located near the present-day Southern Pacific tracks at South Seventh and B streets. Agnes Stewart, first teacher, lived with the Pengras during the school term. She later married and was the mother of C. E. Warner, long-time resident. This school operated along with Bogart's and Gages, or Smith's, as it was called. (Walling).

In 1855, Pengra established the first Republican newspaper in Oregon at Eugene City, named the "People's Press." On the staff was young Harrison Kincaid. The paper later became the *Oregon State Journal* with Kincaid as editor. Joel Ware also was briefly involved.

The story is told that Pengra came home one day with a new pair of trousers that were too long. He asked his wife to cut them off and hem them in time for church on Sunday. Church time came and the trousers were not ready. The first of the week Mrs. Pengra proceeded to fix the trousers without any family comment. The last of the week Pengra, wishing the trousers were ready, without saying a word to anyone, cut and hemmed them to his satisfaction.

Pengra was appointed surveyor-general of Oregon by President Lincoln in 1862. He was superintendent of construction for the Oregon Central Military Road up the middle fork of the Willamette from Eugene to Owyhee. His dreams of a railroad over the Willamette Pass became a reality in 1925. Pengra railroad station above Jasper was named for him.

In 1865, the Pengras moved to the site of present-day Springfield. With partners R. E. Stratford and J. B. Underwood, Pengra purchased the town site. Joined by A. G. Hovey, Norris Humphrey, M. Blanding, Joseph W. Stewart, B. F. Powers, A. D. Burton, M. H. Harlow, Wm. H. Haley and T. D. Edwards, they incorporated the Springfield Manufacturing Co. This company owned all of what became Springfield and some distance north, with all mills and water rights.

The town was first platted Dec. 4, 1866, as recorded in Lane County Deed Records, Book A. The plat shows the location of J. N. Donald's "Storehouse." A grist mill and sawmill operated at that time near the platted town site.

As pioneer developers the new company established flour and sawmills to promote the area. The old sawmill was torn down and a new one erected, considered the best in the county. It operated two circular saws. The Springfield Flour Mill, a continuation of the grist mill put in by Isaac and Elias Briggs in 1854, was owned by the Springfield Manufacturing Co. After this company ceased to exist, the mill became the property of Pengra in 1873.

William Pengra, who came west with his brother, Byron, was born in New York May 5, 1834. He first settled on his brother's farm. In 1854, he moved to Phoenix in Jackson County and assisted in the erection of the first sawmill there. He moved to Yreka, Cal., where he was engaged in mining until 1858, returning then to Springfield. He became one of the owners of the large flour mill and sawmill.

The Springfield post office, established May 15, 1868, was located on the south side of Main Street in William Laird's Drug Store. Albert. G. Hovey was postmaster (McArthur, 1982). Hovey later established Eugene's first bank and served as that city's mayor.

Mail in the 1880's was carried on horseback from the Southern Pacific station, half a mile southeast of Glenwood. Ira Young later carried the mail for 25 years with his horse and buggy. The Baptist Church, erected in 1871 at a cost of $1,600, was Springfield's first.

The sawmill, Springfield's mainstay, was destroyed by fire the night of May 29, 1882. This proved a temporary catastrophe for the community, as it was the best sawmill in the county. Loss was estimated at $5,000. The mill was replaced with a building three stories high and containing all the best and newest machinery. It had a capacity of thirty thousand board feet of sawed and five thousand board feet of dressed lumber. In 1891, the sawmill was purchased by Albert S. Walker.

City Incorporated

Springfield, incorporated Feb. 25, 1885, received its first charter March 17, 1893. Albert Walker was the first mayor. Other officials were Joseph W. Stewart, treasurer; W. E. Walker, recorder, and T. O. Maxwell and William B. Pengra, councilmen.

Albert Walker was born in Greene County, Mo., Jan. 11, 1846. His father, Wm. W. Walker, a pioneer of 1853, crossed the plains by ox team. The family settled on 360 acres of land near Creswell and in 1856 moved into Eugene, where William entered the drug business. Albert, a graduate of Columbia College, moved to Springfield in 1881 and opened a blacksmith shop. In 1891 he bought the sawmill and in 1903 he went into the real estate and insurance business. He had sons Herbert E. and Wm. F. Walker.

The Springfield Flour Mill changed hands several times until taken over in 1890 by B. A. Washburn and son, C. W. Washburn. It operated as Washburn and Son, Proprietors. B. A. Washburn, pioneer of 1849, was manager. His son was a Junction City banker. They made many improvements. A fire at the Eugene flour mill in 1892 proved a boon for the Springfield mill, which produced the well-known Snowball brand of flour and other grain products with daily capacity of 100 barrels.

The mill burned in 1930 and was not replaced. The site today is the home of the Borden Company, producer of glues for secondary wood processing. An old wooden grain storage house on South Second Street north of the Southern Pacific Railroad line is the sole remaining structure associated with the flour mill.

Springfield early on was head of navigation on the Willamette. Steamboats came up the river. On Dec. 29, 1861, the steamer *Relief*, captained by Mr. Cochran, made a trip from Eugene to Springfield, a distance of five miles in 26 minutes.

But the flood of 1861-62 -- the worst in history -- changed the river's course, ending this mode of transport. Four feet of water covered the town. Three other disastrous floods, the first in 1851-1852, then in 1881-1882 and again in 1890 hit the area.

Without reliable river transportation, markets were relatively inaccessible to Springfield, especially after Eugene received the main line of the Oregon and California Railroad in 1871. Springfield's population fluctuated. The first of four bridges, constructed across the Willamette River at Springfield in the late 1870's to replace Briggs' ferry, washed out in the flood of 1881. It was replaced with a covered bridge, which in turn was washed out in the flood of 1890.

S. K. George reported seeing three men on the bridge -- Jake Mulligan, Marvin Mulligan and Charlie Bowman -- who had to make a dash for the river bank when the bridge started to go out.

The third covered bridge built that year was one of the longest single-spans west of the Mississippi -- 402 feet long. The present bridge was built in 1929. The parallel bridge connecting South A Street with Glenwood was built in 1957.

Springfield I.O.O.F. Lodge No. 70, organized in 1881, met in the Odd Fellows Hall, northwest corner of South A and Mill. The building became very important in the community's early history. The first jail was located in the basement, the council chambers were upstairs, and the fire department occupied part of the building. The first band organized in 1880, with Tim Wheeler director, practiced in the council chambers.

The first fire department in the 1890's was a "hook and ladder and bucket brigade." The second was a fire engine, hand drawn and hand pumped by men. Next was a two-wheeled cart drawn by men. After city water was put in, the fire station was moved to F Street.

Springfield Manufacturing Co. deeded land between D and E streets on Mill to School District 19 for the second school. The one-story, one-room building later was cut in two and made into two houses, which were moved a little to the east. Board members were T. J. Brattain, John Kelly and M. H. Harlow.

The third school, erected before 1890 in this same location, was two-room, two-story. Later additions made this building into a high school. About 1921, it was replaced with a new high school, which served later as a junior high. The Lincoln School was built at Seventh and G. The Brattain school was built at Tenth and C as a grade school. The present high school was constructed in 1941-42.

There was one other school -- a cheese factory two blocks south of Mill and D. This building also was used for shows and lodges. Professor Hunt was principal in 1892. Mrs. Hunt and Miss Emma Dodd taught there. Merle Chessman, one-time mayor of Astoria, was a pupil.

As early as 1892, Springfield boasted a baseball team.

Dr. A. B. Van Valzah operated a drug store from about 1896 at Fourth and Main streets. Surgery was rarely performed. The story is told of a Springfield woman whose life depended on an operation. The doctor ordered one room in his house on B Street to be lined with sterile cloth. He performed the operation, removing a 50-pound tumor. The lady survived and lived in the community many years.

Booth-Kelly Mill

Booth-Kelly Lumber Co. in 1901 purchased the sawmill, millpond and millrace, and in 1902 relocated the millpond upstream to its present site. The company erected a steam-powered sawmill, the largest in the Willamette Valley with daily capacity of 150,000 board feet of lumber. The town's population between 1900 and 1910 grew from 353 to 2,000.

The mill burned in 1911. A large oil storage tank west of the mill by the railroad was threatened. The citizens helped fight the fire all through the night to prevent its spreading. They knew if the flames reached the oil tank the entire town was doomed.

The mill, replaced in 1912, for many years furnished employment for a large number of Springfield area residents. It was closed for three years during the depression '30's before reopening. It was eventually sold to Georgia Pacific Co. and operated until 1964.

Today, a modern facility, owned and operated by Springfield Forest Products Co. constructed on the northeast edge of the millpond, replaces the out-dated Booth-Kelly mill. The old Booth-Kelly site was converted to a shopping center in 1970 but was closed in the early 1980's. Georgia-Pacific in 1985 donated the old mill site and its buildings, about 75 acres of land, most of the millpond and millrace to the city of Springfield. The site is being developed for small businesses and secondary wood products firms.

Records show development of electricity and city water came when Booth-Kelly in December 1902 requested a franchise to furnish power. The request was granted with the provision the service should be supplied in 12 months. Lane County Electric Co. took over Nov. 23, 1903. The first electricity was early in 1904. On Jan. 15, 1906, the Willamette Valley Co. took over, then the Northwestern Co., and on Jan. 31, 1909, it was transferred to Oregon Power Co. In 1918 the name was changed to Mountain States Power Co.

Springfield has been served by two newspapers, The *Springfield Messenger* published about 1896, and the *Springfield News* begun Jan. 1, 1903. First telephone service came July 10, 1903, with 38 customers. The First Bank was established Jan. 1, 1904, with Elmer E. Kepner, president, and Henry Stewart, cashier. The first library was set up in 1908 at the old city hall site. Mayor Welby Stevens appointed the first library board in 1912.

Early travel to Eugene was by stage, which left Springfield in the morning and returned in the afternoon. A round trip cost 25 cents. Later, two round trips were made daily. If a party of eight or ten went to Eugene, the driver would wait until the entertainment was over, then bring the crowd home. Sometimes mud would be hub deep. The stage was covered and had side flaps to protect passengers from the rain.

In 1910, street car service was established between Springfield and Eugene. One trolley traveled on a high trestle through trees, over hop yards, past a ball park to reach Springfield. Later the street car used the Southern Pacific rails over a portion of its route. The street car was replaced by motor buses in the late 1920's.

The city's first paving was completed in October 1911, on Main Street to Tenth; North A, Fourth, Fifth and Sixth streets and some cross streets. Prior to paving, streets were described as "muddy in winter and knee deep in dust in summer." Citizens celebrated by putting candle wax on the paved streets and holding a mammoth dance. Badges worn by dancers read, "Springfield Paves the Way." Beyond Tenth Street, a graveled road continued four miles. "The long lane to Springfield" turned north through Thurston, continuing on up the McKenzie.

L. E. Thompson, a blacksmith, in 1907, built his own shop and did work for Booth-Kelly. He retired in 1930. The Thompsons came to Springfield in 1893. Four children were long-time Springfield residents -- Grace Stevens, Maude Bryan, Earl Thompson and Avis Barrett.

Maude and Joe Bryan opened a grocery store in 1904. Later, they owned the first, second and third theaters in Springfield, having bought out the first show house from Mr. Jordan. Mrs. Bryan sold tickets, while Joe ran the picture machine, with the help of a pianist, snare drum and trombone player in days of silent movies, wooden benches and Merry Widow hats. Admission was 5 and 10 cents.

John M. (Jack) Larson, who came west from New York state, operated the old Bell Theatre from 1922 until 1930 on Main Street.

A booklet "Springfield" published in 1915 listed services as: (1) Largest flour mill in Lane County. (2) Two banks. (3) A $45,000 ice and cold storage plant. (4) Forty-two blocks of pavement. (5) A good sewer system, six miles long. (6) A gas and electric light plant which furnished power and light for 11 towns. (7) Street car service. (8) A creamery. (9) Two newspapers. (10) Steam laundry. (11) Two hospitals.

Mrs. Pengra, mother of seven children, found time to write for the local papers. She was active in the Baptist Church and in cultural and charitable organizations. She died in August 1912, preceded by her husband's death Sept. 18, 1908.

The venerable Pengra house at 225 Mill Street dated back to 1866. The original site comprised the equivalent of one city block. On the lot were alder, oak and locust trees the Pengras planted. The two-story house was built of wood, put together with square-headed wooden pegs. There were wide planks throughout the house. The walls were plastered and hung with quaint wall paper. Black iron, hand-forged locks and bolts were used on some doors.

"On the gentle north slope of Willamette Heights at the end of South Third Street rests the mortal remains of Elias Briggs and his family in an old abandoned graveyard. A cluster of mounds is the historic reminder of this old pioneer, his wife and six children," wrote Crystal Fogle. "Many years ago there was discussion concerning the removal of the Briggs' bodies to another cemetery but so far as can be ascertained they were never exhumed. Elias Briggs donated the location for the First Christian Church, which for many years reposed upon the old burying ground. It was later moved to Fourth and A streets."

Among prominent early-day Springfield residents was Joseph Wilson Stewart, born in Macoupin County, Ill., Sept. 13, 1835. Early in his life his father took him to Missouri, then to Iowa in 1849 and across the plains to Oregon in 1852. The family settled on the Willamette near Eugene City, but in 1855, he moved into the city.

Stewart went to Idaho's Elk City gold mines, then to Boise. Returning to Lane County, he opened a general merchandising store Nov. 5, 1863, at Main and Mill streets in Springfield. He married, first, Julia Walker. They had children Henry and Hattie. He married, second, L. Elizabeth Evans. Children were James, Ethel and Harry.

Stewart, one of the Springfield Manufacturing Co. incorporators with Byron Pengra and others, served as first city treasurer in 1893. He was killed at the Springfield grist mill, when a lift gate fell on him, according to his grandson, Morris Stewart of Springfield.

Joseph Stewart had acquired land holdings within the city which included the springs for which the city was named. The city block bounded by Second Street, North A, Mill Street and North B was divided. The north portion, which contained the springs near the dividing line, was given to Stewart's daughter, Ethel, who married James Clark. They built a large house on the property in 1904.

The south portion was given to his son, Harry. Soon after Harry's marriage in 1905 to Elsie Boutin, he built a house similar in design to that of the Clarks. The same carpenter did the building.

Harry and Elsie Stewart had a daughter, Charlotte, and a son, Morris, who was born March 31, 1915. Harry handled slab wood sales for Booth-Kelly Lumber Co. for many years. After the Commercial State Bank in Springfield was closed in 1933 and its assets liquidated, he was instrumental in opening a new bank at the same location. In 1933, he was appointed postmaster by the Roosevelt administration, replacing Frank B. Hamlin. He remained in that position until his death in 1947.

Morris Stewart bought the house from his mother. He had a son, Curtis, by a prior marriage. He is now married to Katherine Soderstedt, born Oct. 1, 1918, near Cottage Grove. He sold the old house and moved to Emerald Heights. He was in auto and real estate sales until retiring.

The original Joseph Stewart home was located on South Second at South A Street. James, Harry and Ethel were born there. After Joseph's death, his wife, Elizabeth, occupied the house, which eventually was taken over by James. The house was in the way when South A Street was constructed and had to be moved. J. M. Larson bought the house and had it moved to North D Street east of North Second. Current Mayor Bill Morrisette and his family lived in the house for a time.

James Stewart's son, Lewis Evan, died in 1990 in Kennewick, Wa. His wife currently makes her home with Morris and his wife.

Ironically today, an apartment house sits astride the springs for which the city of Springfield was named, much to the chagrin of Mayor Morrisette and other civic leaders. The apartment complex was built after the old Clark home burned down. It had passed through several owners in recent years.

Paul Brattain, a prominent early Lane County settler, was born in North Carolina in 1803. He removed to Illinois, thence to Iowa. He assisted in forming the constitutions of those states. He came to Oregon prior to 1853 with six children, settling first at Willamette Forks. He was elected a member of the Oregon constitutional convention from Lane County. His brother, Johnathan, was a member from Linn County.

In 1854, he was elected Lane County auditor and combined the position with that of clerk until July 1, 1859. He held other responsible county positions. The 1860 census for Springfield precinct lists Brattain, 57, a farmer; William and May, both 23, born in Illinois; Martha, 19; Amelia, 17, Francis, 16, and James Chris, 15, all born in Iowa.

He died at his residence at Springfield Aug. 20, 1883, at age 83. The large Brattain land holdings were held in family ownership into the 1950's. Brattain Grade School, built on donated land, was named for the family. The Springfield school district offices were relocated to the large home of Paul Brattain Jr., a grandson, on East G Street.

Hazelnut Production

Oregon has become a major producer of hazelnuts, commonly called filberts. The Hazelnut Marketing Board in Tigard reports the Willamette Valley grows 99 per cent of the commercial hazelnut crop in the United States. Springfield and the McKenzie River valley account for a large share of that total.

Hazelnuts were introduced into Oregon in 1858, when Sam Strictland, a retired employee of the Hudson's Bay Co., planted a tree at Scottsburg on the Umpqua River. But it wasn't until George Dorris planted filbert trees on his property a mile south of Springfield along the Willamette that the crop became commercial.

George, born in Crescent City, Cal., in 1858, was the oldest son of Benjamin F. and Cecille Dorris.

Benjamin, born in Nashville, Tenn., Dec. 18, 1829, came via the Isthmus of Panama to California in 1852. He mined for gold at Jacksonville in Southern Oregon in 1853, then settled at Crescent City, Cal., in 1854. He married Cecille Pellet June 16, 1857. They had eight children: George, Edward P., Alice, Mary, Sue, Kate, Cecille and Benetta. They moved to Eugene in 1868. He was prominent in business and political circles. He served as the president of the Blue River Mining Co. in the 1890's and was the company's attorney.

George grew up on Pearl Street in Eugene, attended the University of Oregon and was admitted to the bar with the class of 1882.

He first practiced law in Astoria, then Eugene. Finding law boring, in 1892, he purchased his 277-acre ranch along the east bank of the Middle Fork of the Willamette River just below the Coast Fork confluence. He and his wife, Lulu, moved into a house built in 1880.

In 1898, he built a house that still stands. Hops and alfalfa were already successful crops when he bought the ranch. He began growing asparagus and other farm crops, later fruit and walnuts. In 1908, he joined in forming the Eugene Fruit Growers Association, now Agripac.

George Dorris

It wasn't until he started growing filberts that his farm really paid off.

He purchased several two-year-old trees of different varieties from Felix Gillet, a French nurseryman from Nevada City, Cal., in 1903, and set them out near his house. Today, the Barcelona variety accounts for 80 per cent of the state's filbert crop.

The first nuts were sold locally. Ben Dorris joined his uncle in the ranch operation in 1925. When the Fruit Growers Association acquired a drier in 1926, the nuts were marketed outside the area. By 1931 the farm had 30 acres of filberts, shortly increased to 75 acres. Before 1931, the Dorrises established a two-acre nursery. They added three more acres in 1935, and 70,000 trees were sold annually throughout the Northwest.

Ben Dorris and wife, Kay, took over full management in 1936 when George died. The nursery was operated at full scale until 1956, when four acres were turned into orchards.

Dorris Ranch, a 250-acre farm complete with historic buildings, the nation's first commercial filbert orchard, river frontage, meadows and forest, is now owned by Willamalane Park and Recreation District, which is developing it as a "living history farm." The ranch has eleven different filbert orchards, but orchards are also found in several outlying areas. The McKenzie Valley has proved to be a particularly good growing area, especially around Vida,

On July 7, 1942, the Dorrises donated land to the state of Oregon for a park, known as Ben and Kay Dorris State Park, four miles east of Vida on the McKenzie River.

Eugene and Springfield, once small river towns, now form a rapidly-growing metropolitan center, serving Lane County. Lying in the shadow of Eugene where the University of Oregon and county seat are located, Springfield, a center for local farming activity, was known primarily as a sawmill town with Booth-Kelly the principal employer. A flour or grist mill also was a mainstay of the community, with water power supplied by the canal from the Willamette River.

Hops were grown beginning in the late 1800's around

Springfield, Camp Creek, at the Frank Storment and Stephen Smeed ranches at Walterville, at the George Dorris Ranch, and well into the 1930's at the Jim and John Seavey ranches near Springfield, and the Anderson and Fish hop yards in Garden Way, west of Springfield. The Chase family developed greenhouses extensively in Garden Way.

After 1910, the town retained its population of around 2,000 up to the time of the great depression of the 1930's, when the Booth-Kelly mill was closed for three years. Growth began about 1939, prior to World War II, when the Rosboro Lumber Co. moved there from Arkansas, and the Springfield Plywood Co. plant was built. A flax plant and alcohol from wood plant also were operated for several years during the late 1930's. The war years brought other industries.

Springfield today with a population exceeding 44,000 (1990 census) is a major service center for the McKenzie, Mohawk and upper Willamette valleys. Numerous wood products operations and a wide variety of service industries cater to the needs of eastern Lane County. Its city limits extend from the Willamette River north almost to the McKenzie River and east into the Thurston vicinity.

The rapidly-expanding Eugene-Springfield areas are growing together, separated by the Willamette River and Interstate Highway 5. The metropolitan area, including Eugene, Springfield, River Road, Santa Clara, Bethel and Glenwood areas, approaches 300,000 population.

Today (1996) the old Springfield millrace dug by the Briggs flows from Clearwater Park to near Island Park. A major civic improvement project is under way to improve the canal's water quality threatened by urban development. In days gone by the millrace was a focal point for social life. It served for many baptisms, tugs of war, log rolling competitions and for baseball games nearby. It still provides water for irrigation, industrial uses and replenishes ground water supplies, and serves as a corridor for wild life. Water quality is substandard for fisheries. Long range plans call for developing wetlands within the mill pond area and other improvement of wildlife habitat and water quality.

In 1993, Willamalane Park and Recreation District acquired land between the Willamette River and South Second Street, including the millrace park site. The site is upstream from the metro area's only waterfall and a viewpoint developed years ago by architect John Amundson. The millrace drops 12 feet where it enters the Willamette River. The city and Willamalane secured a $20,000 grant through the National Park Service to develop a kiosk providing information on the millrace, its history and functions, wrote Phillip Farrington, one of Willamalane's planners, in Lane County Historian.

To the north of the park stands the relocated Springfield railroad depot. Listed in the National Register of Historic Places, the depot is the last surviving example of a two-story train depot in Oregon and the city's only Queen Anne/Stick style commercial structure. The building houses the Springfield Chamber of Commerce offices and the visitor's information center.

CHAPTER 10

John Cogswell, Man of Action

John Cogswell was a man of action. He knew what he wanted and how to get it. He wanted a new home in the West. He acquired it. He wanted gold. He sought and found it. He wanted Mary Gay!

So it is not surprising that this tall, handsome young man turned to his companion on his long trek west and said: "See that pretty girl standing by that stove? Well, she's the woman for me -- the girl I'm going to marry."

The year was 1851. They were out on the trail en route to Oregon. This was John's second trip west. It was while he was plodding along with his herd of selected stock from Michigan that the wagon train, which included the wagons of Martin Gay, caught up with John and his hired help.

But in the confusion of tending his stock, John not only failed to meet, let alone court, 19-year-old Mary Frances (Mamie) Gay (born in 1832). The young lady's train pushed on ahead and soon was hidden from sight by a cloud of prairie dust, leaving John and his cattle herd far behind. The train entered the Willamette Valley by way of the Barlow pass. John brought his stock to Oregon by way of California that fall.

John and Mary Cogswell

John, son of James and Mary (Stratton) Cogswell, was born in Whitehall, N. Y., on Valentine's Day, Feb. 14, 1814. When he was 10 years old, his family moved to Inkster, Mich., according to writings of Charlotte Mitchell in *Lane County Historian*, 1961, based on material compiled by sisters Celeste Campbell and Eva Frazer Johnson.

At age 16, John left home with only 75 cents and a jackknife in his pockets to seek his fortune. He found work on the Erie Canal. Later, while working in Missouri, 1840-45, he decided to take the trail to the Far West. Although starting out on foot, he met a man who was taking a herd of horses across. The man offered John a horse to ride for his assistance. John finished his long journey on horseback, arriving in California in 1845.

In the spring of 1846, John first came to Southern Oregon by wagon train via Mt. Shasta and the Rogue River Valley. Moving on to the Willamette Valley, he claimed to have climbed the Indian-named butte, Ya-po-ah, later known as Skinner's Butte, a few weeks before the Eugene Skinner, Elijah Bristow, Felix Scott Sr. and William Dodson party reached the present site of Eugene the same year.

Staring at the tall, waving grass that covered the valley below, he is quoted as saying, "I've found what I've been seeking -- a land that beats Heaven for having every thing a man needs."

John found work at the mouth of the Columbia River "whipping timber" (sawing oak) for ship building with "Hen" Owen. He owned a "whip saw," over which he had a law suit, the first such in Oregon.

In 1849, John and a companion embarked on a barge for California during the gold rush. On the Feather River he found much gold. In 1850, having enough for his needs, he gave his mine to a friend, packed his gold in saddle bags on horses, then crossed the plains for Pennsylvania, where he had his precious metal minted.

"John Cogswell now had a dream of a large ranch stocked with fine cattle, horses and sheep," wrote Charlotte Mitchell. "So for a year he stayed at his father's home in Michigan, selecting stock and outfitting for his second journey west."

Although this proved to be a long, tedious journey, it was while plodding along the trail that the wagon train -- and Mary Gay -- caught up with him and his slow-moving, blooded stock. John watched with a heavy heart as the wagon train moved out of sight, not knowing whether he would ever see Mary Gay again.

Cogswell brought his stock by way of California, and when he looked out into the Sacramento Valley, he saw the people were "as thick as bees." He wondered how so many could have crossed the plains so quickly. (This portion of the story differs from an account told in the diary of Martha Gay Masterson referred to later. The diary says he came into Oregon by way of the Barlow Pass).

"He came to Oregon through the Siskiyous, by the Rogue River and Table Rock, then into the Willamette Valley," wrote Mitchell. "He took his donation land claim on the north side of the McKenzie River four miles east of what is now Coburg Bridge at the mouth of the Mohawk River. This included the Coburg Hills, 'Old Baldy,' then known as 'Old Richey's Butte.' It was named for a demented man who lived in a shack and rolled rocks down on the road." The DLC was directly east across the river from that of Felix Scott Sr.

He stayed there only one winter, then moved to a farm on the south side of the McKenzie in the Thurston area, later owned by Isaac Stevens. John, 37, "worked for some time on his claim, sawing and splitting timber, for there were no mills then. He plowed and cultivated the virgin soil for his gardens and fields. He worked hard, while dreaming of the pretty girl he had met on the plains.

"When his house was completed (the first frame house in Lane County), he mounted his strongest horse to ride up and down the valley, questioning settlers as to the whereabouts of the Gay family."

John found Mary Gay near the center of the Willamette Valley, visiting the Jess Looney family. It was dinner time and he was invited to stay. Accepting the invitation, John lost no time courting Mary, who was promised to a man back East.

Gay Family Moves West

The story of John Cogswell and Mary Frances Gay (known as Mamie) would not be complete here without a look into the history of the Martin Gay family as told in the brilliant diary of Martha Gay Masterson, sister of Mary, presented by Lois Barton of Eugene in her fascinating book, *One Woman's West*. Martha prefaced her diary with an account of the Gay family's life.

Martin Baker Gay was born in Virginia in 1803. His foreparents were English and had settled near Jamestown in 1630. He often related his family history as handed down from one generation to another. He told about the early settlements, Captain John Smith, the story of Pocahontis and about Mount Vernon, home of George Washington.

A Virginia planter, Gay emigrated to McCreary County, Ky., where he met and married Johana (Ann) Evans Stewart March 7, 1827. She was born Feb. 23, 1808, in Kentucky, near the home of Abe Lincoln. Her parents were Southern people of Scotch descent, traceable to Mary Stuart of Scotland (note spellings, Stewart-Stuart).

Gay, an industrious man, was a farmer and cabinet maker. They moved to Tennessee, then to Boone County, Mo., and on to Arkansas, where Martha was born in 1837, the only family member born there. In 1838, Gay brought his rapidly growing family of six children to Greene County, in southwestern Missouri. They settled on a tract of land near Springfield and built a large log house. He enlarged the farm and had tenant farm laborers. He went into the furniture business extensively in 1846. The children attended school there.

Martha related childhood incidents when Mamie was chased by a wolf, a time when Mamie was struck by a rock thrown by a neighbor boy, leaving a permanent facial scar, and other near-tragic events.

As the westward movement began, Gay got the fever. He talked about Oregon and the Columbia River. His wife was very reluctant to leave their Missouri farm and make the long and dangerous trip to Oregon with eleven children and expecting a twelfth. There also was some dissension among family members, some of whom were now adults.

Gay's determination prevailed. His pregnant wife finally consented to go. After nearly a year of preparations the family, with three wagons and strong animals, left their happy home and many friends and headed west April 10, 1851.

The trip was full of hazards and encounters with Indians and buffalo herds. Mrs. Gay gave birth to a daughter, Sarah Julia (known as Pink), along the way. She later fell ill and was confined to bed in the wagon several weeks. After a five-month journey father, mother, twelve children and a young man who came with them arrived at the Barlow Pass and continued on into the Willamette Valley.

According to Martha Gay Masterson's diary, the incident on the trail where Cogswell first saw Mary occurred on the Barlow Pass Road. After an arduous trip over the Cascades, the family had camped on the Zig Zag River the night before and were ascending a long, tiresome hill. All who were able to walk did so, as the wagon was a load for the oxen.

"We were about half way up the road and someone said, 'See that big stove'," wrote Martha Gay. "We went to look at the stove left by an emigrant who was almost in sight of the valley. Mamie (Mary) was standing in front of the stove with her foot on the hearth, resting and waiting for our wagon to come up the hill. While we were looking and remarking about its size, two men came riding along and also noticed it. The gentlemen spoke to us and then rode on. They had a band of cattle they had brought across the plains.

"The older man said to the other. 'Did you notice the pretty, black-haired girl who had her foot on the stove? She's to be my wife.' His partner asked who she was. The man said he didn't know, but when he got settled he would find out. We looked after them and spoke about them. They were strangers to us and we thought they were from the valley and had been out to meet friends. They were weary emigrants like ourselves and were driving their own cattle. When we got up the hill they were gone. Their wagons were ahead of us. They had left their cattle to bring the wagons up and had gone back for them. We met those two men many times in after years."

Martin Gay first settled his family near Albany and built a house of lumber from a nearby sawmill. While they were there John Cogswell made his first, but unsuccessful, attempt to court Mary Gay, who was visiting at the Jess Looney place.

Not satisfied with the Albany area, Gay a year later took his family to Lane County and settled on a homestead eight miles south of Eugene, due south of Spencer's Butte and west of Camas Swale.

After John's first rejection by Mary Gay, he didn't give up. His persistence soon changed her mind and he finally won her consent, after an incident at the new home site of the Gay family.

Gay put up a camp, temporarily, for a kitchen by standing four posts in the ground to support the roof. The wagon boxes with their covers were set off the wagons onto wooden boxes to serve as bedrooms and protect from rattlesnakes, which were numerous in the area. They fixed up their utensils around the camp kitchen.

One afternoon just as they had finished dish washing and had the milk pans set up on a shelf and the buckets and cups hung about the eaves of the roof, a man came riding into their camp. He spoke and alighted, then tied his horse to one of the posts.

They recognized him as Mamie's "would-be beau," wrote Martha Gay in her diary. He said he had located on the McKenzie River. While he was talking with Mary his horse became frightened and tried to pull loose. To their dismay his horse pulled down the kitchen. Pots, kettles and pans all fell in a crash under the roof.

Chagrined, John assisted in rebuilding their temporary shelter. They all laughed. Mamie had given up her old lover and was becoming very fond of her new beau, Martha wrote.

Second Marriage License

John and Mary were married Oct. 28, 1852. Theirs was the second marriage license recorded in the Lane County Clerk's office. Martin Gay made a special trip by wagon to Portland to purchase supplies and a wedding dress for Mary.

The wedding at the Martin Gay family's large, comfortable log house, which he had built, drew friends from 50 miles away. After the ceremony the couple rode horseback to their new home on the McKenzie. They were ferried across the Willamette River by Charles Walker Young, father of Cal Young, an early settler north of Eugene.

On their DLC, John Cogswell raised sheep and cattle. In 1860, he imported new Oxfordshire and Hampshire Down sheep. The family lived on the farm for some time, where most of their eight children were born. They were: Mary Ann, b. 1853; Florilla, b. 1856; Elizabeth Maude (Lischen), b. 1858; DeEtta, b. 1861; Idaho, b. 1864; Bolivar, b. 1866; Clara, b. 1868, and Ivan Stratton, b. 1871.

Tragedy struck when Mary Ann and Florilla died in 1857, after they had contracted scarlet fever while visiting their grandparents, the Martin Gays. They were buried on a nearby hillside where they had played, their graves being the beginning of the Mary Gay Cogswell Pioneer Cemetery. Other graves of the Gay and Cogswell families and their neighbors are found in this old cemetery.

Included are graves of Martin Gay, who died on his homestead Nov. 17, 1867, and his wife, Johana, who died in January, 1874.

"Mary Gay Cogswell was heartbroken over their daughters' deaths. John decided to take her on a trip east," wrote Mitchell. "They traveled by ship down the coast, across the Isthmus of Panama by mule back, then up the Mississippi. Although it was a dangerous trip they made it there and back safely."

In 1862, Cogswell was with Felix Scott Jr. in the first cattle drive over the McKenzie Pass. He, Scott and others were associated in the McKenzie Wagon Road Co. Incorporation papers were filed in the Lane County Courthouse Dec. 20, 1862. This was to be a toll road but was later abandoned. Cogswell, Scott and John Craig in the late 1860's were associated with the McKenzie Salt Springs and Des Chutes Wagon Road.

John and Mary resided in Lane County, except for one year spent in Portland in 1870, where their eldest daughter attended school. At one time John owned a large part of the land where East Portland is now located. He exchanged this for Lane County property east of Thurston in 1871. He returned to the McKenzie and operated a sawmill.

Cogswell's Thurston ranch was heavily timbered with many springs and streams. John built a ten-room, four-gabled house at the foot of a timbered mountain. It was a comfortable home for those times with four fireplaces, halls and closets, a spacious yard, many fruit trees, flowers and shrubs. The children attended school in one of their father's tenant houses. Emma Guthrie was the teacher. Later, they attended a one-room school built by their father on his land.

John also owned property 25 miles up the river, past Leaburg, where he had a sheep ranch and the first pond stocked with fish. He called this the Fish Ranch.

"The Cogswell children, like other pioneer children, had to work, doing chores about the place and sometimes helping their father drive stock to the upper ranch, braving the dangers of wolves, panthers and bears. Their busy mother stayed at home, washing, carding and spinning wool for their clothing. In summer she did the family washing below the dam, under the maple trees, where she heated river water in a big black kettle over the fire," wrote Mitchell.

Although Mary Cogswell had nine children to care for, she was always ready and willing to care for a sick neighbor, for she was known as a "born nurse."

The Cogswells seldom were molested by Indians, although once while Mary was ill in bed, she was startled to see a "savage" Indian standing at her door. He demanded payment for the land. Though frightened, Mary was relieved when her sister, Martha, who was visiting, came into the house. The children followed the Indian outside, where he began sharpening a knife on a grindstone. But when he heard some men driving cattle down near the river, he only asked for some bread and left in haste.

On one of his many trips over the McKenzie Pass, John and his companion, John Diamond of Coburg, had a narrow escape from starvation. While traveling to Eastern Oregon they became lost.

"The men, on horseback, wandered around for several days until they came to an Indian camp. An old Indian squaw welcomed the men, helping them off their horses and leading them to her fire to rest. She fed them stew, made with meat, wild roots and vegetables seasoned with strong wild onions. On this diet they quickly regained their strength, although John Cogswell 'to his dying day' declared he could never stand the sight or smell of onions again," Mitchell wrote.

The Cogswells lived on their Thurston ranch for many years, raising and educating their children. Although a hard working family, they found time to entertain friends. John often talked of his youth and his work on the Erie Canal. He told this anecdote of the workmen there who had to eat pork on Friday. "It was then the Catholic priest would take the bacon and put it in the river, saying 'Go down, mammon, come up salmon,' then he would give it to them to eat."

After Mary's death Oct. 8, 1887, John moved to his Fish Ranch.

"John lived to see the country develop from a wilderness into a land of prosperity and plenty and was one of its most substantial and influential citizens. He seldom missed annual pioneer meetings. He traveled much by horseback, wagon train and by ship and steam trains. He lived to see man conquer the air," wrote Mitchell.

Cogswell Hill, named for John, was a local name for a highway grade between Thurston and Cedar Flat near the junction of the present Thurston Road with the McKenzie Highway. It was graded out when the new highway was built in the early 1930's. Cogswell Creek enters the Eugene Water and Electric Board (EWEB) Power Canal between Leaburg and the Leaburg dam at river mile 35.6.

John Cogswell died May 13, 1907, at age 93. He was buried in the Mary Gay Cogswell Pioneer Cemetery on the Martin Gay donation land claim, eight miles south of Eugene, established Oct. 4, 1857.

The Mastersons

Martha Gay Masterson's diary is primarily the story of her life after she, at age 33, married widower James Alfred Masterson, Aug. 27, 1871, and took on the raising of five of his nine children. Masterson, 44, a blacksmith, was a survivor of the Ward Massacre of 1854 in Idaho.

Born Oct. 4, 1827, in Logan County, Ky., Masterson came west first in 1850 from his home near Jefferson City, Mo. He and two other men, later joined by two more, left their wagon train domiciled for the winter at Salt Lake City and proceeded on.

After several narrow escapes from Indians, they arrived in California, according to his handwritten account now in the Lane County Historical Library. A copy is included in Lois Barton's book, *One Woman's West.*

Masterson worked in California. In 1851, he came to Eugene in fledgling Lane County and met a brother, probably M. A. Masterson but not further identified, and his family who had crossed the plains that year. However, he returned on a steamer, by way of San Francisco, the Isthmus and the Gulf of Mexico, to his Missouri home and was warmly greeted. After a time he became restless. On April 6, 1854, he married Vilinda H. Campbell and decided to go west again.

A company was organized. It consisted of Masterson and his wife; his brother, Robert; their two married sisters and their husbands, one of them named Ward, with nine children; the other sister's five year old son, and some hired men, about twenty in all. They had a small band of cattle, some horses and oxen they worked on the wagons.

While traveling down the Snake River in Idaho, they had several encounters with the Indians, who were further aggravated by pranks played on them by a young member, Tom Adams. Adams threw burning coals on the bare feet of an Indian who got too close to the fire. In a later encounter with this Indian, Adams shot and killed him. Infuriated, the Indians followed, awaiting their chance.

On Aug. 19, the party camped along the Boise River. Masterson, his wife and Robert left ahead of the others next morning, driving the cattle before them. At noon others in the party were set upon and massacred by the Indians.

All were killed, including the Mastersons' sisters, their husbands and all of their children, except for two Ward children, a boy and girl, who were taken captive, their fate never learned. Two other Ward boys, ages 12 and 15, were wounded and left for dead, but were rescued and revived. In all, fifteen were killed. This is known as the Ward massacre.

Arriving in Oregon, Alfred, as he was called, and his wife first settled in Eugene City. Both he and Robert fought in the Rogue Indian War of 1855-56. Alfred and Vilinda had nine children. Vilinda died of tuberculosis in 1870 near Salem.

Robert Masterson married Nellie Gillespie. In 1862, they settled on a farm near Springfield. They had seven children.

After his marriage to Martha Gay, Alfred Masterson, a drifter, moved twenty times in twenty years often under most difficult conditions. Martha, not only took on the raising of five of his nine children, but followed her husband by team and wagon into gold- rush towns, railroad camps and all over the Northwest, often in the dead of winter through drifting snows. She told of the deaths of her own two sons left buried in lonely graves along the way.

In 1891, Masterson decided to return to Oregon from where they were living in Centralia, Wa. He would go to Portland to visit cousins. Martha, with daughter, Hortense, would go to Eugene, where Hortense would enter school. As usual, Alfred took off alone, leaving his wife and daughter to pack up and follow. This was to be their last move. The couple separated after that. Hortense was married to Louis Vitus June 8, 1898, in Eugene.

Alfred died Sept. 11, 1908, in Couer d'Alene, Ida.

Martha, who spent much of her remaining years in the home of Hortense, died Dec. 12, 1916, at age 79.

Mary and John in later years

CHAPTER 11

Lost Wagon Train

"The McKenzie Pass Highway (Route 242) has a long and varied history. The apparent discoverer of the McKenzie River, Donald Mackenzie (or McKenzie) may have made a trail up the river and traveled over the Cascade Range in 1812, but there is no evidence.

"The route was well known to the Warm Springs Indians, but the first recorded trip by white men over the Cascades in this region was in 1853 by a group of immigrants on horseback who were lost in the mountainous area near the Three Sisters, eventually traveling down the river to Springfield." (Williams *McKenzie River Names).*

"These lost and weary travelers were part of the Elliott and McClure wagon train, the famous Lost Wagon Train of 1853 that came down the Willamette River. The McKenzie party consisted of two groups. The first, comprised of eight men on horseback, included Andrew S. McClure (1829-1898), Benjamin Franklin Owen (1828-1917), Calvin P. Nolan, Robert Tandy, Joe Denning, Charles Clark, Charles Long and James McFarland. Names of the second group are unknown."

Andrew S. McClure's diary of the wagon train of 1853 recorded he started west with relatives, Vincent Scott and Sarah Bruce McClure, James F. McClure (? -1862) and his family. They and the Bonds, Allens and Williams families made up the McClure wagon train. Vincent McClure was born in Knox County, Ind., Aug. 30, 1815. On Nov. 13, 1834, he married Sarah Bruce. They had two daughters and a son.

At Boise, Ida., the McClure, Elliott, Kinny and several other wagon trains, totaling about 67 wagons and perhaps as many as 1,000 persons, elected to follow Elijah Elliott on the old Meek Cutoff Trail. This route to the southern Willamette Valley was said to be many miles shorter than going north to the Columbia River and then south through the Willamette Valley.

To better understand the Lost Wagon Train story we refer to writings of Leah Collins Menefee in *Lane County Historian.* Mrs. Menefee, daughter of Rev. Dr. Henry C. and Fannie MacNab Collins, grew up on a northern Klamath County ranch near where the train camped. She and her husband, Don, devoted much time to research.

An editor's note states: "As the great covered wagon emigration to the west increased from 1843 to reach its peak in 1852 with hundreds of groups of wagon trains, using the Oregon Trail, it became obvious deviations and cutoffs would develop.

"Many immigrants were ill-equipped and more inexperienced than others, but all were urged on by the compelling desire to get to

Oregon before the best land was taken up and before winter snows would overtake them in the mountains. Oregon City was the main terminus at first. Later branches were developed from points in Idaho to reach various sections in Oregon more directly. These would save precious time and many weary days of travel.

"The Applegate Trail provided access through Southern Oregon. The early settlers in Lane County were interested in getting a shorter route into the upper Willamette Valley by way of Central Oregon. A project inspired in 1852 to establish a route (although not adequately carried out), and resulting in the near-disastrous 'Lost Wagon Train of 1853,' are subjects of the following story."

Excerpts from the Menefee article follow:

The story begins in the Mahlon Harlow home in March 1852. Men from Linn and Lane counties met and decided to do something about a new route across the Cascade Mountains into the Willamette Valley. Three men were commissioned to make a "road viewing" trip over the Middle Fork route and see if a way feasible for wagons could be found.

On Aug. 20, 1852, these three, with four others, started on horseback up the Middle Fork. The party consisted of William M. Macy, Joseph Meador, John Diamond, Alexander King, William T. Walker, J. Clark and William Tandy.

Traveling up the incline of the mountains, they reached a pass just south of the large mountain which John Diamond, along with Macy, then climbed and named for himself, Diamond Peak. They were the first recorded white men to climb the mountain. They called the peak to the south Macy's Peak. This latter name has been lost, but Johnny Diamond's mountain still bears his name.

The men reached the plains beyond the present city of Bend without incident but soon were attacked by Indians. Diamond, Clark and Macy were wounded. King, Tandy and Walker made repeated stands on ridge tops, while Meador hurried the men along under the protection of the three cracking rifles. The men finally reached the Oregon Trail near Vale and met an emigrant train.

Return was over the Barlow Pass. The report to the Territorial Legislature was made without any mention of the Indian trouble. However, the notes of the trip were lost during the battle. The report was therefore quite general and made from memory. In it the seven men stated the route was quite possible for wagons and set the sum of three thousand dollars as sufficient to open a wagon road up the Middle Fork and through to the Deschutes River.

Subscription lists were opened to raise this sum. Meetings were held and a contract for construction let for $12.00 a mile.

"Elijah Elliott, who was about to go east in 1853 to meet his family, was assured by the commissioner of the road, before he left over the Barlow Trail, that should he wish to return over the new route he would find it cut through to the Deschutes River by fall," wrote Menefee. "Followed by other parties, Elliott, who met his family near Ft. Boise, turned west over the new route. In all about 1,500 persons, with over two hundred wagons are said to have followed onto the supposedly shorter route to the Willamette Valley."

The wagon train actually was a series of groups of wagons, knit together in parties with ties of family, neighborhood or by chance meeting in Independence, Mo., or on the Oregon Trail. The story has been handed down for more than 100 years in families of those who traveled the Middle Fork route that fall of 1853.

Each party turned into the new route just west of Ft. Boise, went astray in the Harney-Malheur lakes country, suffered with thirst on the Eastern Oregon desert, lost oxen and wagons and discarded cherished possessions. Yet many of the travelers never saw each other on the trail or afterwards. Dozens never even knew the names of the other parties.

The train traveled too far south of the old Joseph L. Meek Trail of 1845. Three weeks of precious time were wasted around Harney and Malheur lakes. They wasted food and wore out their weary draft animals.

Finally, the train turned north, crossed Crooked River upstream from the present store at Post and reached the Deschutes River near Bend. Here they lost more time searching for the road, finally finding some trail blazes 30 miles south on that stream.

Bearing on the south shoulder of Diamond Peak, they followed the faint traces toward the Willamette Valley. In mid-September, parties of young men began to leave the train to attempt a quicker crossing of the Cascades to get help.

Andrew McClure (on Sept. 14) with Joe Denning and B. F. Owen from the McClure train and five men from other trains, left, attempting to reach the Willamette Valley and send back aid to the struggling emigrants. They went too far north and, confusing the Three Sisters with Diamond Peak, wandered in the wilderness of the Oregon Cascades, with great suffering to all the men. (Willamette National Forest report).

After crossing the Cascade Summit they found the western slopes almost impassable because of steep canyons, fallen timber and thick brush. On Oct. 3, Clark, Long and McFarland left their horses and proceeded on foot. The three remaining horses and men struggled westward and downward toward what they knew was civilization.

Suddenly they were overtaken by five men on horses from the same wagon train, who passed them and rode on to what is now the Thurston area and contacted Isaac Briggs, 1847 settler at what became Springfield. (McClure, 1853). Briggs, Charles Hardesty, James Wallis, James Sanders, Morris and Tanner succeeded in rescuing the McClure party on Oct. 20, 1853. The rescuers were paid $2 per day by Briggs. (B. F. Owen, 1853).

By the time the McKenzie contingent was rescued, the plight of the immigrants in the main wagon train had already become known to the settlers. A young schoolmaster, Martin Blanding, had been sent ahead over the Willamette Pass to carry word to the valley. Near Butte Disappointment, not far from present-day Lowell, he was cooking a piece of still-born colt when discovered by settlers attracted by the fire. He was cared for by them and lived to found the Cloverdale Academy.

October 1853 was dry and warm. The Middle Fork of the Willamette River was very low. It could easily be forded with ox teams in many places. To that fact many members of the Lost Wagon Train probably owe their lives. For in mid-October, they were making their way slowly and painfully down the Middle Fork after crossing over the Cascade Mountains summit through a pass just south of Diamond Peak. They crossed the river 27 times on their way to what is now Oakridge.

Within hours riders were speeding down the valley to tell the settlers of the emigrants toiling behind Blanding. Men gathered oxen. Women cooked and packed food. Men on horseback were the first to reach the train. They built campfires and piled up stacks of pancakes, apportioning them equally to the starving families. Laden wagons and beef cattle on the hoof followed these men in quick procession.

The list of rescuers reads like an early Who's Who of the Willamette: Abel and John Russell, Jacob Spores, Marion Scott, Squire Powers, John Bardell, W. W. Bristow, Hulings Miller, Dr. Cheshire, Presley Comegys, Adin McDowell, Daniel Hunsaker, Lester Hulin Sr., Mahlon and Henry Harlow, Walker Young, Cornelius Hills, James M. Hendricks and many others.

The first wagons apparently reached Fall Creek Oct. 24, fifty-four days after leaving Vale. Homes in the valley bulged during the next few weeks as settlers took in the travelers. Donation land claims were found for them whenever possible. By Nov. 9, W. W. Bristow was able to report to the *Salem Statesman* that all the immigrants were in Lane, Linn and Benton counties, richer by 615 men and 412 women and children who came with the Lost Wagon Train of 1853.

In spite of the very real hardships only one death occurred. Mrs. Joseph Petty, struck by a trunk during a river crossing, was killed. The baby in her lap escaped injury but died later. One young man reportedly died from over-eating after being rescued.

The McKenzie contingent of the McClure Party probably crossed the Cascade Summit south of the South Sister, traveled down Separation Creek to Horse Creek, thence to the McKenzie River and rescue.

Unconfirmed reports say some rescue party members may have traveled to Clear Lake, headwaters of the McKenzie River.

In a postscript to the Owen diary, it was noted B. F. Owen married Jane McClure, daughter of James McClure Sept. 1, 1859.

Vincent McClure first settled eight miles west of Eugene. His first wife, Sarah, died April 26, 1858. On Oct. 15 1859, Vincent married, second, Sarah Scott Benson, who arrived in Oregon in 1851. Her wagon train, which started out in 1849, was delayed by Mormons at Salt Lake City. Sarah's brother-in-law, M. H. Harlow, was taken prisoner. The Mormons threatened to kill him and all the men in the party and retain the women and children. They finally were allowed to proceed. Vincent and Sarah in 1862 moved two and a half miles north of Eugene. That year he was elected to the Oregon Legislature, serving one term. He died in 1893.

CHAPTER 12

River Transportation - Thurston

Discovery of gold at Sutter's Fort in California, which sparked the Gold Rush of 1849, had a profound effect upon the fledgling Oregon settlements. The magic word spread throughout the Willamette Valley. Men seeking fortunes left their farms, fields, shops and offices to head southward, facing difficult traveling and often unfriendly Indians.

Wives, children and cripples were left, often alone, to get along as best they could in a land where settlers were few and far between, and Indians and wild animals often were troublesome. To pioneer women that was a vivid, bitter summer. But it is said some women fared better than their husbands by growing crops which they sold to men traveling to the gold fields and by providing food and lodging.

While some men returned with bags of gold, many returned empty handed to take up where they had left off and begin to rebuild their farms and communities. Others never returned.

For many settlers the valley rivers were primary means of transporting goods and people. Many river boats plied the lower Willamette. But Eugene could be reached by boats only in high water periods. As crude roads were built, rivers and streams became a problem because they had to be crossed. Bridges still were a thing of the future. Rivers were forded where possible.

Ferries, like the one Skinner built at the present Ferry Street Bridge site and the Briggs Ferry at Springfield, begun in 1853, became important links in Lane County's pioneer road system. Spores Ferry crossing the McKenzie at Coburg, begun in 1848, was vital to north-south transportation. In 1878, it was replaced by a bridge. Other ferries operated in the area, most privately owned. The owners exacted tolls. An important ferry at what is now Hayden Bridge led into the Mohawk and Camp Creek valleys. An early-day ford crossed the McKenzie into Camp Creek. Hendricks Ferry near Walterville was begun in 1862.

Many years went by before people ventured far from these settlements, except for hunting, trapping and explorations.

Oregon's Territorial Legislature authorized extension into Lane County of the Eastside Territorial Road from Oregon City via Molalla, Silverton and Lebanon to Brownsville. The new road was to extend to Coburg and via Spores Ferry to Elijah Bristow's home at Pleasant Hill.

In 1854, Lane County assigned five road districts. Supervisors were warned "to keep the roads open." Six years later 37 road districts were formed. In 1857, construction began on two U. S. government and territorial roads. These were the Westside Road skirting the Coast Range, and the Eastside Road from Oregon City down the valley along the edge of the Cascades. Ferries continued to provide the principal means of crossing rivers.

Settlements developed in the Thurston, Mohawk, Camp Creek, Cedar Flat and Walterville areas in the 1850's and 1860's.

A wagon road extended east from Springfield. Known as the High Banks Road, it followed along the McKenzie River through Thurston, over Cogswell Hill to Cedar Flat, where the river was forded, and then on into what became Walterville.

THURSTON

"The alluvial soils of Thurston, tucked between a deep bend in the McKenzie River on the north and the rolling hills that slope into the Willamette River on the south, attracted eastern settlers as early as 1851," wrote Eric Jones in *Brief History of Thurston (1985: 29-36, Lane County Historian, Vol. 30 #2)*.

On Aug. 25, 1851, John McNutt, an Irish immigrant, came to Oregon at age 22 with his brother, David. John recorded the first donation land claim in what became Thurston, a 290-acre parcel, bounded roughly by what is now 58th Street on the west, 66th Street on the east, Main Street on the south and Thurston Road on the north. The area includes such landmarks as Thurston High School, the pillared Courtwright family home, where the first high school stood, the Thurston Grange Hall and site of the first store and post office.

The community of Thurston, however, was named for George H. Thurston, an early-day land surveyor of the county. George, born in Burlington, Ia., Dec. 2, 1846, was the son of Samuel R. (1816-1851) and Elizabeth F. (McClench) Thurston, pioneer Lane County settlers. Samuel was Oregon's first territorial delegate in Congress in 1849.

George was brought to Oregon in 1847, before he was a year old (McArthur, 1982:731). Educated at Willamette University, he became associated with W. H. Odell and B. J. Pengra, who surveyed the Oregon Central Military Road from Idaho across the Cascade Range at Willamette Pass (old Emigrant Pass) to Eugene.

In 1872, he married Marietta Henderson, daughter of Enoch Henderson, Eugene pioneer of 1856 and first president of ill-fated Columbia College. She was born in 1851. They had three children: Blandina Sybil, born in 1877; Samuel R., 1879, and Anita Elizabeth (Hines), 1893. George moved to Lake County in 1880 to raise sheep.

Samuel R. Thurston, son of George and Marietta, was a Department of Interior forest ranger in 1902-03 on the Cascade Range Forest Reserve. A Lane County native, Spanish War Veteran and University of Oregon graduate, he died at the Merrit Hospital in Oakland, Cal., Feb. 7, 1932. *The Oregonian*, Feb. 10, 1932, reported, "His ashes will be brought to Oregon and cast upon the water of Crescent Lake at the summit of the Cascade Mountains."

FREDERICK L. GRAY

Among early-day Thurston area settlers was Frederick L. Gray, who crossed the plains to Oregon in 1851 and first came to Lane County in 1855. It was not until 1861 that he bought 160 acres of ranch property seven miles east of Springfield and raised stock.

Gray was born in Washington County, Pa., Jan. 2, 1831, the son of Alexander and Lydia (Lutanner) Gray. The father of Irish extraction and mother of German descent were reared and married in Pennsylvania. In 1831, they moved to Ohio, but Lydia died five years later and was buried in Wooster. The father and four sons -- Frederick, John, Alexander and Jacob S. -- returned to Pennsylvania.

Alexander later married Mary Andrews. In 1844, they moved to Indiana, settling near Greencastle. Gray died there Dec. 26, 1866. Their five children were: Samuel R., Robert, Sarah M., Nancy Jane, and William J., who was accidentally killed in Idaho.

Frederick Gray, educated in district schools and trained to agricultural pursuits, left home at age 17, employed as a farm hand. In 1851, he came to Oregon, then worked in the Rogue River and California gold fields. In 1855, he gave up prospecting and came to Lane County. For a year he worked in the Deadwood mines and in 1855-56 participated in the Rogue Indian War, guarding Jacksonville.

He filed on a 160-acre claim and raised stock with good success. On receiving the deed four years later, he disposed of his claim and went to the Willow Springs mines and prospected two years. In 1861, he returned to Lane County and bought a 320-acre ranch, on the old stage road between Springfield and Walterville.

Soon after acquiring the property, he joined a party and headed for the Salmon River mines. It was a perilous journey fraught with many hardships and privations. There were heavy snows, high prices for food, and, on their arrival, it was too late to find work, so he returned to his Lane County ranch, where he farmed successfully.

In 1864, he married Olive Looney, widow of James C. Looney, who had filed on a donation land claim in Lane County in 1852. The claim included the present Gray Ranch. Olive was born in Iowa.

Her parents, Mr. and Mrs. Davis, also crossed the plains in 1851 and settled in the Thurston area. She had four children by her first marriage: Daniel, William, Sarah and Martha, who married William McKinney of Independence.

The Grays had eight children: (1) Alexander, b. Nov. 9, 1864; (2) Charles, b. Sept. 2, 1866; (3) Mary Jane, b. Oct. 22, 1868, m. Bert Mathews of Pleasant Hill; (4) Frederick, b. April 14, 1871; (5) Ira, b. June 24, 1873; (6) Margaret Ann, b. June 7, 1875; (7) John, b. in 1876, died in infancy; (8) Nellie, b. Sept. 20, 1879, died at age eleven.

Margaret Ann married Frank Campbell, who died in 1900. She and her son, Frank, lived on the homestead many years. Frederick also lived on a portion of the old homestead.

Ira Gray became a well-known and well-to-do farmer of the Thurston-Springfield area. Upon obtaining his majority he became a farmer, renting and operating land or working for agriculturists in his locality. He purchased 112 acres, while living on his father's place, which he later bought when his father retired at age 88.

Ira Gray, on Oct. 20, 1893, married Lizzie Kumm, a daughter of Jock and Frances (Hypt) Kumm, natives of Germany. She was the second of four children, the others being Annie, wife of Jake Houston; Frank and John, all of Tillamook.

The Grays had two children, Stanley, born Jan. 1, 1895, and Zola, born July 4, 1899. Gray was very active in community affairs.

Thurston Post Office

The Thurston Post Office and general store, corner of Russell Road (now 66th Street) and Thurston Road, was established March 16, 1877, by Dr. Ben F. Russell. Thomas H. Hunsaker was postmaster.

Russell and his wife, Margaret E. (Maggie), daughter of Orrin J. and Nancy Hull, were long-time Thurston area residents. A medical doctor and justice of the peace, he was sometimes in charge of the county home for the poor. Children were: Nancy E., b. Mar. 8, 1871; Georgiana F., b. Mar. 8, 1873; Benjamin F., b. July 4, 1875; James F., b. July 4, 1877; Mabel C., b. Oct. 18, 1881; Pearl I., b. Mar 8, 1884; John I., b. July 18, 1886, and William H., b. Feb. 18, 1889.

Dr. Russell is buried in Mt. Vernon Cemetery near Thurston.

"The general store became the hub of life in the community and early on was used as a stopping place for stages and freighters plying the route between Eugene and the mines and resorts to the east (on the McKenzie)," wrote Jones, 1985:34.

"Passengers would spend the night in rooms above the store, and horses were cared for at Charles Hastings' coach stop across the street from the elementary school. On occasions Alma Hastings rented rooms and served dinners in a house next to the coach stop. The general store served all the needs in the community. Groceries, dry goods, buggy whips and other notions and 'remedies' were sold. The gas station and garage helped fuel the changing, petroleum-based farming industry."

Frank and Opal (Taliaferro) Rennie operated the post office for 43 years, beginning in 1929. "Because the Thurston Post Office was allowed to accept heavier packages than the Springfield Post Office, many trappers and farmers came to Thurston to mail their products. One such customer, a Mr. Smiley, shipped mink hides in the 1930's from his ranch about one mile east of the store, recalled Opal Rennie, Thurston postmaster from 1950-1971." (Jones, 1985: 340). Mrs. Rennie descended from the old-time Taliaferro family of Natron.

The post office was changed to a rural branch July 1, 1973, but it still keeps its own zip code - 97482.

Names long associated with the Thurston and Cedar Flat areas were the Harbert, Ruth, Phetteplace and Jenkins families, the Hart families, Clements, Eastons and others too numerous to recall.

CAMP CREEK

A number of pioneers chose Camp Creek, known to the Indians as Chastin, as a place to settle. The stream rises in the foothills of the Cascade Mountains and, taking a southwesterly course, empties into the McKenzie seven miles east of Springfield. The valley through which it runs is about six miles long and one mile wide.

The first arrival was the Joseph McLean family, who crossed the plains in 1850. In 1852, McLean built a cabin along the stream in the area known as Upper Camp Creek, where Beth Mitten later lived. McLean is buried in the nearby Camp Creek Cemetery.

George Marshall also arrived in 1850 from Ohio and took up the claim later owned by the Harbin family. Alexander Storms settled on what became the McCabe place.

The Revs. Jeremiah M. Dick and James T. Worth arrived in 1853. Dick, born in 1818, and educated in Westmoreland County, Pa., was graduated from Western University, Pittsburgh in 1835. A theological student in Allegheny City, he entered the ministry in 1841.

Leaving New York Nov. 5, 1851, Dick sailed via the Isthmus of Panama to San Francisco and proceeded to Oregon in 1852. In 1853, he took up his donation land claim east of Camp Creek. He engaged in agricultural pursuits, while retaining his interest in the ministry. He conducted religious services in the area for many years. The Goddards, in 1875, purchased part of Dick's homestead. (See Goddard-Stephens chapter). Jeanette Bergsma more recently lived on the property.

Worth and Dick were followed shortly by William McMeeken and his nephew, who settled on a portion of land where Joseph McLean later resided.

About the same time R. B. Martin, Mrs. Eleanor Duff, David N. Hyde and M. D. "Dill" Ritchey took up claims.

Jeremiah Dick

Just where the Ritchey family settled, after crossing the plains in 1853, is in question. Some sources place the location along the Camp Creek stream. An early-day map shows the site much further east, extending north and west of where the Eugene Water and Electric Board's Walterville power plant is now located.

With them was Ritchey's wife's brother, John Templeton Craig who developed a road over the McKenzie Pass. The 1880 census for Camp Creek precinct lists the family as including Ritchey, 58; his wife, Mary, 55; James, 25; Melvin, 21; George, 19, and Annie, 17.

The dirt road from the then small community of Springfield into Camp Creek was only passable when dry. The river had to be forded near where Camp Creek empties into the McKenzie River.

The first school house, a log cabin, was built in 1854 on land donated by Joseph McLean in what was known as Upper Camp Creek.

This became District No. 5. The first church, Presbyterian, was erected with logs at the cemetery site in 1869. In 1893, the district was divided and another school built for lower Camp Creek. Chief industries were farming and hop growing. Fifty acres were devoted to hops.

Camp Creek's post office was established July 22, 1871. The simple building was situated on property where Oswald and Bernice Petersen later lived. Mail came from Walterville twice a week. It was closed to Springfield Sept. 15, 1921, when rural delivery was begun.

Later arrivals in Camp Creek were the Goddards and Stephens, the Trotters, Browns and Crabtree families.

Walling's *History of Lane County* reports the first Walterville settlers of record were Ross Pollock and his brother, who located on the banks of the McKenzie River in 1852, and John Jamieson. Other early settlers were James Wilson Storment and John Latta, 1852; George Millican, 1854; Robert Millican, 1859, and the James Davis Fountains, 1868. Up river at Gate Creek were Nicholas Oliver, William Allen and Thomas M. Martin, 1863; Regis Pepiot, 1868, and Fayette Thomson, 1870. Beyond Martin's there were no further settlers until James Belknap arrived in 1869. There will be more on these settlers in later chapters.

CASWELL HENDRICKS

A pioneer of note was Caswell Hendricks, who established Hendricks Ferry crossing the McKenzie River southwest of Walterville. Caswell, son of Abraham Hendricks, was born July 7, 1816, in Indiana. On Aug. 4, 1851, he married Hannah Ann Davis. She was born Jan. 12, 1833. There is some question as to whether Caswell came to Oregon with the migration of 1848, or with the David D. Davis wagon train of 1847.

The 1848 train, route not known, included Caswell's brother, James M. (Jim) Hendricks, Robert Callison, Michael and Harrison Shelly and family members of Elijah Bristow. They settled in Pleasant Hill.

If Caswell came with the Oskaloosa Company in 1847, he may have been one of the young men who helped carry Hannah Ann, age 14, on a stretcher after she was wounded by Indian arrows and fell face down into the camp fire the night of Sept. 29, 1847. The incident occurred after the Davis wagon train had crossed over Fandango Pass east of Goose lake as related in Lester Hulin's journal. Hulin served as "pilot."

The Davis family included David's wife, Hannah, and their children Jane, 15; Hannah Ann, 14; Rebecca, 12; Meshach, 10; Thomas, 8; Elizabeth, 5; Rachel, 3, and William, 1. They left Iowa in April. Davis was elected captain of the train which at times numbered as many as 80 wagons. The Oskaloosa Company was one of three or four wagon groups that turned onto the California Trail to follow the poorly-defined Scott-Applegate trail to enter Oregon via the southern route.

The Davises had been in constant turmoil with Hannah Ann, who needed medical care. North of Skinner's cabin at Eugene, David cut down a tree and chopped out a "dugout" canoe, in which he loaded his family and traveled downriver to Salem. Davis had traveled by dugout canoe on the Ohio River from Dearborn County, Ind., to the Mississippi with four children in 1839. Ann was treated at the mission of Jason Lee.

After living briefly in Salem, Davis built his cabin along Soap Creek in Benton County near what is now Adair, on May 15, 1848. He established the community known as Tampico, where he served as the first and only postmaster of the Soap Creek Post Office.

His wife, Hannah, died from measles June 15 of the year they moved to Soap Creek. Reports that she died on the trip west appear unfounded. A grave marker bearing her name is found in a cemetery one miles south of Monmouth along with those of her husband and daughters, Rebecca and Rachel. Rebecca, died in 1851 at age 16.

Hannah Ann married Caswell Hendricks Aug. 4, 1851. They moved to Lane County. In 1852, David Davis married Sarah Bowman, widow of William Bowman and mother of six. They had two more children.

The oldest Davis daughter, Jane, married John Withers Aug. 6, 1849. They had two children. She died Dec. 3, 1853, and was buried in Lane County. Rachel died in 1854 at age 10. David Davis died in September, 1860, age 54. With his death Tampico and the Soap Creek Post Office became memories. His second wife, Sarah, died in 1861 at age 48.

Although Caswell Hendricks and Hannah Ann first settled at Pleasant Hill, he moved his family after 1860 to Cedar Flat and acquired property on both sides of the McKenzie River. He obtained a license to operate a ferry from the Lane County Court in April 1863. However, a later application for license renewal said he began operating the ferry, just upstream from present-day Hendricks Bridge, in 1862.

The 1860 census, showing the family still living at Pleasant Hill, lists Caswell, 41, his wife, Hannah, 29. The census and family records list their children, all born in Oregon, as:

(1) Rufus Augustus, b. in 1852, m. Mary M. Page; son Claude.

(2) Hugh, b. in 1854.

(3) Melissa J., b. 1855, m. Thomas A. Fountain. Children were Arron and Mattie.

(4) Benjamin Franklin (Frank), b. 1857, m. Lizzie Reese; children were Leland, Pearl and Marie.

(5). Martha J., b. 1859, m. (1876) Eugene Finn, son of B. F. and Mary Finn, pioneers of 1871 who settled at Vida. Children were Loren, Herbert, Otis, Elmer and Isa.

(6) Isabelle, b. in 1861, m. Edward Fortner. Children were Pearl, Fred, Ethel, Frank and Archie.

(7) Filena, b. in 1864, m. William B. Tucker. Children were Vernon, Effie May, Lloyd and Hazel. (Effie, b. June 7, 1886, in Thurston, d. June 1919 in Lebanon).

(8) George L., b. in 1866, m. Fannie Russell; children were Howard, Mabel, Homer, Merle and Wilma.

(9) Ulysses Grant Hendricks, b. in 1868, m. Margaret N. (Nannie) Russell; children were Russell and Normal.

Caswell died in 1893. Hannah Ann died in 1904. They were buried in Mt. Vernon Cemetery, east of Springfield.

Fred Fortner, a son of Edward and Isabelle (Hendricks) Fortner and grandson of Caswell and Hannah, in a letter written July 22, 1947, to

Isa Finn Baldwin, a granddaughter from the Eugene Finn family line, tells some of the family history. He said Caswell, a captain in the U. S. Army, apparently was sent to Oregon to establish a command. His understanding was Caswell arrived in 1847.

Excerpts from the letter follow: Rhuane Hendricks Stroud wrote to Martha Hendricks Finn, mother of Isa, that Grandfather Hendricks, father of Caswell, leased out 160 acres of land, now in Des Moines, Iowa, for 99 years so that the family would have money to go west. She said the lease would terminate in 1949 and the property should go back to the heirs. Rhuane, a sister or half sister of Caswell, lived in Iowa.

Hannah Ann Hendricks

In July 1897, Fred, at age 14, ran away from home. Hendricks Ferry at Walterville was being operated then by Sol Dodson. When Fred told him he was leaving home, Dodson made him recross the McKenzie and stay all night with his Grandmother Hannah Ann Hendricks, who lived in the little house on the south side of the river.

That evening Grandmother Hendricks told Fred, as well as he could remember, that it seemed Caswell came west ahead of the wagon train that later settled in Pleasant Hill.

"Caswell was an officer in the U. S. troops. It appeared there was an army fort near Pleasant Hill or Oakridge where soldiers were stationed. His regiment was Indiana Regulars or Volunteers. The command was either in Lane County or preceded the wagon train of 1848," said Fred. (There is no record of such a military establishnment).

"Grandmother Hendricks came with the wagon train. On the way she was shot in the back with an arrow, and fell face down in the campfire. Perhaps you have seen the scar, as I have. Family photographs never showed that side of her face," he said.

"As I remember she was already married to Caswell, in a town called Hope, and his command got here in 1847," Fred wrote. (This seems unlikely since she was only 14. Fred could have confused the name Hope with Soap of Soap Creek, where the family settled).

"Grandmother Hendricks gave me his coat, cap and sword, but I never got them, although I dressed up in them whenever we visited on the McKenzie. Your (Isa's) father, Uncle Gene (Eugene Finn) made a butcher knife of the sword. The cap was misplaced and the coat was burned in a fire in the upstairs of what we called the 'big house.'

"Uncle Bill Davis, grandmother's brother, stayed with us a lot. He was quite young at the time and didn't remember much."

CHAPTER 13

The McClung Party

The first known route across the McKenzie Pass was one used by the Warm Springs Indians in annual migrations to the McKenzie Valley. They came to hunt, pick huckleberries, take salmon for smoking and (in later years) to pick hops. Following the Lost Wagon Train episode, routes were established. There are conflicting accounts of early travel and cattle drives over the Cascade Mountains from Lane and Linn counties.

"In 1857, Dr. James McBride of Yamhill County set out with a party from The Dalles to find the Bluebucket mine in Central Oregon. When they ran into hostile Indians, the men turned back and crossed the Cascades to descend the McKenzie River to the Willamette Valley." (Hubert Howe Bancroft, *History of the Northwest Coast*, 1888:479).

Note: The Bluebucket was applied to a mythical gold discovery in Eastern Oregon. Lewis McArthur (1982) reports Bluebucket Creek rises just west of Antelope Mountain in southeastern Grant County and after flowing through Antelope Swale in Harney County joins a tributary of the Malheur River.

Members of the Joe Meek Party in 1845 picked up yellow pebbles and hung them under the wagon in a blue wooden bucket. The bucket was either lost or abandoned later. It was not until some time elapsed that the emigrants realized they possibly had found gold.

It is generally thought the discovery must have been on a tributary of the John Day or Malheur River, though suggestions that the locality was near the Steens Mountains and also Tygh Valley have been advanced. The source of the gold was sought by many people over the years. There is no known connection between Bluebucket Creek and the gold discovery. The mystery of the location of the real Bluebucket Creek probably never will be solved.

George Millican, in an interview in 1919 shortly before his death, said: ". . .cattle had been taken across the Cascade Mountains prior to the opening of the Scott Road, from both Linn and Lane counties. (Henry Harmon) Spalding, the missionary (who arrived with Dr. Marcus Whitman in 1836), Jake Gullford, a man named Compton and another named Stafford crossed with cattle in 1859. Spalding went to Umatilla County and Compton and Stafford to Yakima."

In 1859, members of the McBride Party, according to Walling's *History of Oregon* (1884), were first "to seek for the headwaters of the McKenzie and discovered what later became Belknap Springs."

In the party were George Millican, who came in 1854; John Templeton Craig, pioneer of 1853, a Bible-totin' hermit, who did much toward building a road over the Cascade Summit; James Wilson Storment, Walterville settler in 1853, and Joseph Carter, who operated a ferry briefly on the upper McKenzie two miles east of Blue River about 1863.

Followed Indian Trail

What later became historically known as the Scott Trail was known prior to that time and described by J. H. McClung as an old Indian trail. He noted: "Indian ponies, which traveled down the mountainside, had plowed out the trail two or three feet in depth."

In August 1860, a group, referred to as the McClung Party, made a trip up the McKenzie to the Three Sisters area, "never having been in close proximity with the snow-capped mountains," wrote McClung. Other members of the party were A. S. Patterson, A. J. Welch, Dr. Alexander Renfrew, Joel Ware, C. H. Moses and Joseph Stevenson.

This trip was the forerunner of discoveries, many years later of gold on Gold Hill, above Blue River.

The outfit consisted of seven riding horses and two pack animals necessitated by the fact there was no wagon road beyond the John Latta place just east of what became Walterville. The first day out from Eugene they stopped at the Rev. Jeremiah M. Dick place in east Camp Creek to obtain a horse -- a gentle old mare with a colt at her side -- for Dr. Renfrew, who was not used to riding.

McClung, years later, wrote they followed an old Indian trail and camped the next day along the river at present-day Leaburg. "During the day we passed through a heavy forest, consisting principally of Douglas fir suitable for lumbering. At the present time this accessible timber has been cut and floated down the river to mills in the valley.

"The following day we camped at Gate Creek. Just before reaching here we entered the great burn of 1855. This destroyed billions of board feet of prime timber, the fire extending 15 miles up and leaving hardly a green tree standing. We found it difficult to go through the burn. Many trees six to eight feet in diameter had fallen across the trail. Where we could not go around the upper ends we had to bridge over them with smaller logs and bark."

The next day "we had our first experience with yellow jackets. Their nests were near the trail. They would light on the horses in great numbers. By the time the doctor (Renfrew) came along, they were furious and covered the mare and colt, and she would go bucking through the brush and over logs. The doctor rode on the mare, thus his silk hat, which he always wore, would disappear and next his wig. He then called for help and the party stopped and went to his assistance and got him back on the trail again," wrote McClung.

They traveled only three miles to Rock House, named for a large boulder which projected over the trail with an opening in the lower side large enough for several people to sleep comfortably, and in front plenty of room for a camp fire. They slept mostly in the open under blankets. Rock House today, along with famed Martin Rapids, is encompassed within Ben and Kay Dorris State Park.

"This being an ideal camping place and the fishing being so

good, we decided to stop here a day. Blackberries were plentiful in shady places. We soon got enough to have some nice pies, which our cook, Mr. Patterson, made and added to our menu. Our fruit, which we brought, consisted principally of dried apples and peaches.

"Stevenson shot at a bear across the river. It fell, struggled, then clambered up the bank into the bushes. The river was very swift here. The only means of crossing was to build a raft, which would have been difficult to manage, so we gave up trying to capture the bear."

They camped next day at what later became the Wycoff place, later Cook's Ranch, a popular fishing and hunting resort, now Heaven's Gate. Their next camp was at the mouth of Elk Creek, a mile west of Blue River, where an island made by the creek and river afforded a fine camping place with plenty of grass for the horses.

"Here we remained two days to allow Mr. Moses and Dr. Renfrew to prospect for gold in that vicinity. On the first day they reported small particles of gold found along the river at the mouth of Blue River, but above Blue River, no indications," McClung wrote.

"The following day they continued their explorations, going up Blue River where prospects improved. They thought gold in paying quantities would be found later. Dr. Renfrew was especially enthusiastic. He spent several seasons thereafter helping develop mines on Gold Hill, where a number of quartz ledges were discovered."

The party moved on to a point across from the mouth of the South Fork, trying to keep to the north side of the river, as they had been told a hot spring (Belknap) had been found a few miles above the big prairie (McKenzie Bridge). They came to a mountain which jutted out into the river. It was impossible to go around because of logs and underbrush.

This meant going back to the Indian crossing or trying to cross where they were. They decided to ford at a riffle. McClung took the lead, but some 20 feet out his horse slipped into a deep hole and had to swim. He was soaked, but finally made it across. The others found a less dangerous crossing downstream. One pack horse stumbled over a large boulder and soaked its load. They camped at a small prairie to dry their clothes and provisions.

"The next day we reached the big prairie, but just before making this place we heard much shooting to the south of us. When we reached the prairie we found it full of Indian ponies and squaws drying meat. And the shooting we heard was the Indians hunting. An old Indian came out and handed us a paper, which said, 'These are good Indians,' signed by the agent at Warm Springs, so we knew we were safe.

"The Indians were campers and drying their meat on the bank where the Log Cabin Inn now stands. Just before reaching the prairie, I caught a fine big redside trout about 18 inches long. A squaw wanted the trout. I made her understand I would trade it for elk meat. She brought out a large piece and we had it for supper, but the odor was anything but appetizing . . .

"After leaving the prairie we went about six miles to Lost Creek. Here we found a large log, partially submerged in the water. We walked the log, leading our horses. This log later was used as a support for a wagon bridge and served many years for this purpose.

"About a mile further on we should have found the hot spring. Unfortunately, we failed to find it because of brush obstructing our vision. Above this point a couple of miles the McKenzie comes from the north and takes a westerly course, which indicated this river rises at Mt. Jefferson, instead of the Three Sisters as many supposed. . .

"We leave the McKenzie and go easterly up a canyon with a stream of water now known as Scott Creek. The trail much of the way was in the stream bed and over very rough boulders. Following the stream a couple of miles we turned south and followed up a very steep mountain. The Indian ponies which had traveled down the mountain had plowed out the trail two or three feet in depth. It was so steep we could only lead our horses and walk beside the trail.

"At the top we came into a beautiful prairie, afterwards known as Finger Board. In this we camped, as the grass was good, and we found strawberries of small size, but good flavor. The altitude had greatly increased and it required all our bedding to keep comfortable."

The return trip was uneventful. McClung said he kept a diary, which was lost, so he wrote the account from memory after the other members of the party were long since dead.

"I have lived to see the McKenzie Valley settled from Walterville to Belknap Springs and all land suitable for settlement occupied. The upper portion is now in the forest reserve, which will probably prevent further settlement at least for many years to come.

"This probably is the end of the story, but I cannot refrain from adding some happenings of a later date. I've said nothing of the Foley Springs for they were not discovered for several years after a hunter and trapper found them. They soon became the property of Dr. Foley of Eugene and still retain his name. These, with Belknap Springs, which were improved about the same time (by Rollin Simeon Belknap), soon became popular for their medicinal qualities, being especially efficacious for rheumatism, kidney and stomach troubles. These with the excellent fishing afforded by this stream continue to make this section a great resort."

PROMINENT CITIZENS

Gale Burwell of Leaburg, formerly Willamette National Forest public affairs specialist and forest history coordinator, reported all members of the McClung party became prominent citizens of Eugene.

McClung, born in Ohio, came to Oregon in 1856 via the Isthmus of Panama. He purchased 160 acres of land west of Eugene and farmed until 1859, when he and an uncle established the first drug store in Eugene. He later sold the store and became a surveyor. In 1863, he bought the old Grange Store, known from then as McClung and Johnson. He served as county surveyor, councilman and Lane County representative to the state legislature for two terms. He was one of the founders of the Oregon Central Military Wagon Road Co.

Joel Ware, born in Columbia County, Ohio, Feb. 14, 1832, where he was educated, crossed the plains in 1852, driving an ox team to California. He settled in Sacramento, where he learned the printing trade. He came to Portland, Ore., in 1857 and to Eugene City in 1858. He worked on the first newspaper, started by B. J. Pengra. With Harrison R. Kincaid and William Thompson, he founded the *Oregon State Journal* in March 1864. He sold to Kincaid, when he was employed as chief clerk in the surveyor general's office in Eugene. He was elected Lane County clerk in 1870. He married Elizabeth Cochran. They had six children.

Dr. Renfrew, Eugene hotel owner, said to be an uncle of Melvina "Auntie" Frissell, of McKenzie Bridge, explored extensively for gold on Gold Hill. He died there in 1876. A marker at Renfrew Springs and Renfrew Grave commemorate his name. (See Lucky Boy chapter).

Patterson, born in Indiana in 1824, came overland to Oregon in 1853, settling in Eugene. He was elected to the state assembly in 1858, was engaged in mercantile pursuits 10 years, then was appointed Eugene City postmaster July 1, 1869, serving many years. He was one of the founders of the University of Oregon and the Oregon Central Military Road Co.

A. G. Welch, Lane County treasurer 1856 and 1862, died in La Grande in 1864. Moses and Stevenson were not well known.

McKENZIE RIVER swift flowing westward from Belknap Springs.

CHAPTER 14

The Scott Trail

Felix Scott Jr. made the first epic crossing of the Cascades with cattle and wagons in 1862. The hard winter of 1861-1862 killed all the cattle in the upper country (eastern Oregon). There was a great demand for beef. He decided to make the venture and take freight with him.

Born in St. Charles County, Mo., July 2, 1829, Felix Jr. emigrated to California with his family in 1845. Wintering there, he came to Yamhill County in 1846. In 1849 he moved to Lane County and located on a claim along the McKenzie on which his brother, Rodney, lived many years later. Felix ran stock between Oregon and California, frequently going to the aid of pioneers. He had an early interest in the possibility of an easy wagon route over the Cascade Mountains from the Eugene area.

"In 1851, *The Oregon Statesman* reported introduction into the Oregon Territorial Legislature of House Bill 16 (ultimately passed). It provided that the legislature authorize as commissioners 'Felix Scott Jr., Jonathan Keeny and Soloman Tethero. . .to view the practicality of a road from the Willamette Valley, at some point between the South Fork of the Santiam River and McKinzy (sic) fork of the Willamette River across the Cascade Range. . .' No evidence was found they ever viewed the road." (Menefee and Tiller, 1972: 319-21).

Early in the 1860's, gold was discovered in Idaho's Florence area. Felix Jr. conceived the idea of supplying miners there as he had California miners earlier. His plan involved crossing the Cascades by following the McKenzie River into the mountains, then striking boldly over the range.

Starts From Crescent City

It was from Crescent City where he had a large herd of stock that he started with his cattle and wagons to go to Idaho. One wagon was very large and heavy, carrying 10,000 to 15,000 pounds of freight. There were eight smaller wagons, sixty yoke of work cattle and 900 "beeves," a news story in the *Oregon State Journal* said.

George Millican in an interview late in life said he had returned to Lane County (route not given) from the Florence mines in 1862 and had gone up to where Scott was camped with his cattle at the John Latta place above Walterville. With Scott was John McNutt of Thurston. John Cogswell also was reported to have been a major participant in this expedition, and so was John Templeton Craig.

"Felix had heard I had been on the upper country and came to talk to me about it," said Millican.

At this time the eastern terminus of the McKenzie road was some

30 miles east of Springfield at the "Rock House," a natural formation making a sort of crude shelter, four miles east of Vida.

Millican said: "Scott had so much team power he could pull over almost anything. He went through without making a road, taking to the river frequently. As soon as the party got across the summit, the laborers were dismissed and they returned to Lane County."

Robert Sawyer in *Oregon Motorist* wrote: "Scott's party of 50 to 60 men hacked their way east through thick forests, up the steep slopes and passed the jagged and difficult lava beds near the summit.

"It was not until fall that the 900 head of cattle and nine wagons of supplies were over the summit to open pines of the eastern slopes. The party wintered at Trout Creek in what is now Jefferson County and in 1863 went to Boise, where the Boise mining district had been discovered, instead of going to Florence."

What was historically called the Scott Wagon Road followed the ancient Indian trail up the McKenzie River and left Highway 126 about 58 miles east of Eugene, beyond Belknap Springs, originally Salt Springs, to the mouth of Scott Creek. It followed Scott Creek east about two miles, leaving the creek to proceed up a very steep ridge, known as Big Hill, north of Deer Butte. It passed through Finger Board Prairie, past Irish Camp Lake, Melakwa Lake, Scott Lake, south skirting the lava beds, then turning east, reaching the Cascade summit in the vicinity of Yapoah Crater.

Scott Pass is about 3 1/2 miles south of the present McKenzie Pass. At Yapoah Crater the trail ran north along the crest to North Matheu Lake, then east past Yapoah Lake to Trout Creek.

The Scott Trail was a difficult route. Tremendous obstacles had to be overcome. Scott at times was forced to use as many as 26 yoke of oxen to one wagon to surmount the grade. Men suffered from the rough, dangerous lava. Shoes and gloves were torn to shreds.

However, having proved the feasibility of the route, Scott attempted to develop the road and form a company. Articles of incorporation were filed Dec. 20, 1862, for The McKenzie Fork Wagon Road Co. ". . .to construct the road from the eastern terminus of the county road near the John Latta place, 16 miles east of Eugene. . ." But there is no record of any tolls collected. Another group was formed, but it too became defunct.

Felix Scott Jr. lived on his Lane County ranch until 1869, moving then to Crescent City where he had spent much of his time. In 1872, he emigrated to Arizona, where he was engaged extensively in freighting and the stock business up until his death in 1879.

Route Retraced

James Drury, a life-long McKenzie resident, said the old Scott Wagon Road crossed the McKenzie River about a mile east of Blue River to the south side, went east through the South Fork bottoms, then crossed to the north just above old Crib Point. He wasn't sure where it crossed to the south side again. John Craig built the first crude bridge, across the river at McKenzie Bridge in 1869.

Drury had worked on the U. S. Forest Service McKenzie District, beginning with the Civilian Conservation Corps in 1934. He did trail maintenance and retired as fire control officer in 1970.

On July 22, 1982, he led a party over the section of this route historically called the Scott Wagon Road, where it leaves the McKenzie River Highway 126, near Belknap Springs, about 58 miles east of Eugene at the mouth of Scott Creek. It continues over the Cascade summit.

In the party were Jerry Williams, Umpqua National Forest sociologist and historian, chairman of Region-6 History Committee; the late Dave Burwell, consulting forester, and his wife, Gale Burwell, Willamette Public Affairs Specialist and Forest History coordinator, who wrote an account of the trip.

Mrs. Burwell wrote: "On this reconnaissance trip Drury was able to locate many remaining sections of the Scott Trail and Scott Wagon Road, including the spot where it left Scott Creek and began the steep ascent described in many accounts. He stated that in other areas he had found ruts over a swampy area and could possibly relocate the spot, though there was not time on this trip."

Dave Burwell, a resident of the McKenzie for 30 years, was familiar with forest trails. He passed away in June of 1993.

CASTLE ROCK at 3808 feet elevation dominates the landscape as viewed looking south from vicinity of Rainbow.

CHAPTER 15

Craig's Obsession

John Templeton Craig, known as John Tom, was a member of Felix Scott Jr.'s cattle drive party. Development of a road over the Cascade Mountains then became an obsession with him. Later, he became an organizer of the McKenzie Toll Road. He died while carrying mail over the Cascade Summit in December 1877.

Of Scotch-Irish parents, Craig was born on a farm near Wooster, Ohio, in March 1821/22. His grandfather, as a mere lad with a dream of America, had run away from his home in Glasgow and boarded a vessel for the new world. John Templeton Craig, the eldest of ten children, was born of the first American generation. During his youth he worked on his father's farm, earning and learning what he could.

In the summer of 1853, he joined the great trek westward. Thinly-clad in homespun, he walked barefoot and drove an ox team for his brother-in-law, M. D. "Dill" Ritchey. They came to Oregon via the Barlow Pass and Oregon City, thence to the Camp Creek Valley.

"John Tom, always ready to stretch out his sinewy arm to a friend or neighbor in need was soon to become known far and wide for his kindliness and gentleness," wrote Agnes Millican McLean in the *Lane County Historian,* Vol. 1, March 1963,

"Upon his arrival at the little settlement, he found that a number of the newly-come families were without shelter, and his heart was moved by the thought of the suffering that must follow with the storms of winter. Immediately he set to work to build a sawmill of the whipsaw type on Camp Creek near the old ford across the McKenzie. In this enterprise he was assisted by Ritchey, but when shortly thereafter a disagreement arose, Craig left to work on the Rodney Scott farm in the lower McKenzie Valley." Some reports say Craig helped build the sawmill for Charles Patterson.

Craig early became interested in surveys for new roads. During the greater part of his life he made his home among the great forests and hills of the West he loved. Up and down through the deep forests of the McKenzie he plodded, learning the lay of the land. Under the great trees he baked his sourdough biscuits upon hot rocks beside his campfire, killed and fried the flesh of deer and bear for his meat. When his supplies ran low he turned to the tender growth of the forest such as fern sprouts or miner's lettuce.

Deeply religious, ". . .his philosophy of brotherly love was firmly founded on the tenets of the old Scotch Presbyterian school," wrote Mrs.

McLean. "The Rev. Jeremiah Dick, who preached those days in the log cabin school house at Camp Creek, was his pastor. He always carried his Bible in his knapsack, along with his coffee pot and frying pan, and he read it daily for guidance and inspiration. The gospels and the prophets were his literature, and the psalms of David, set to the melody of the wild birds of the forest were his songs."

During the Rogue Indian War of 1856, Craig joined Company B as a private. In a skirmish the Indians cut him and nine other men off from their company and stole their horses. They escaped and, after much hardship and wanderings in the southern Lane County mountains, made their way to Cottage Grove, half famished having subsisted on wild berries for 14 days. Craig contacted George Millican, who, with John Latta and Walker Young, went to their aid, wrote Mrs. McLean, Millican's niece, daughter of Robert Millican.

In 1859, Craig was one of the four McBride Party members, including George Millican, James Storment and Joseph Carter, credited with the discovery of Belknap Springs.

John Tom joined Felix Scott Jr.'s party in crossing the Cascades with 900 head of cattle. Early the next summer with his Bible in his knapsack, he plodded up and down the valley searching for an easier route. He knew the Scott Trail was too steep and rugged for the building of a passable road.

With his friend, John Latta, Walterville, pioneer of 1852, he made another trip up the McKenzie in 1863. They left the river near the hot springs (Belknap), explored the Lost Creek canyon and, arriving at Alder Springs, the two men came to the conclusion this was the answer to an easier route.

"The road carried through the deep gorge, between high wooded hills to the north and south. Deer Butte to the northeast extends in a long precipitous ridge toward the west. Eagle Rock juts out from the center of the south range and the three sisters rise majestically eastward. White Branch flows between salmon berry and willow-bordered banks through the canyon to join Lost Creek as it gushes out from under its hidden lava bed," wrote McLean.

The route led passed Alder Springs, up Dead Horse Hill to the lava fields. A way was picked on which a trail was built. It was rough and tortuous, but crossed the Cascades 1,000 feet lower than the Scott Trail.

Craig consulted with George Millican and received much encouragement toward building a road over the Cascades on this route. Other parties had shown an interest in developing Scott Trail.

John Tom worked incessantly, often single handed, on toward the summit, through the summer season and far into the fall, grubbing brush and roots, smoothing the road. He always carried his frying pan and coffee pot. He never carried bedding but made his bed of moss and ferns. He burned out old fir logs to sleep in.

One such log, called "Craig's Bedroom," was 42 miles from Eugene, near Finn Rock -- about two miles west of Blue River. This natural shelter was the mere shell of a tree, perhaps seven or eight feet in diameter at the swollen base above the sprawling surface root. The hollow center extending upward ten to fifteen feet formed the four walls of the chamber. The out-of-doors was his living room.

Hendricks Ferry

Meanwhile, Hendricks Ferry was established just upstream from the present site of Hendricks Bridge southwest of Walterville. Owned by Caswell Hendricks, it began operating in 1862. The county approved ferriage fees in April 1863.

The Oregon State Journal, Eugene, June 16, 1864, wrote of several trips of families and wagons over the mountains via the Scott Trail. "They are getting along very well. Already travel between here and the mines, in wagons, droves of stock and pack animals, is becoming quite an important feature in the business of the country and will surely increase as the roads are improved, until Eugene will rival The Dalles as a depot of mining supplies."

By October, 1864, the road was graded a distance of 60 miles east of Eugene, with only 20 miles of pack trail remaining over the summit. W. A. Masterson left Boise with 50 wagons of immigrants who intended to come to the Willamette Valley by way of the McKenzie road. In 1865, Marion Scott and Pressly Scott and party, including Charles Hardesty and John Evans, took a herd of cattle over the road wintering at Trout Creek. Travel, such as there was, used Scott Trail for about 10 years.

On Sept. 25, 1865, a third attempt was made to form a corporation to establish a new route over the mountains. George Millican, William Y. Miller, J. M. Dick, and James W. Gray filed articles of incorporation for the McKenzie Valley and Deschutes Wagon Road Co.

The purpose of the corporation was to construct "said road from Robert Millican's place by way of the Valley of the McKenzie and the most feasible pass over the Cascade Mountains north of the Three Sisters to the crossing of the Deschutes above the mouth of Crooked River." This effort also failed to materialize.

Craig, as engineer and builder, established himself at Rock House for the winter. He traveled up and down the valley, telling the farmers of the advantage of this road. He said it could be built with their united efforts from which a substantial toll could be collected.

Agnes McLean wrote: "Thenceforth, Craig's enthusiasm never waned. He worked the remainder of his life constructing this road. Under his pick and shovel hillsides were leveled into road beds, deep gullies filled, streams bridged and timber shaped with his meager tools. Floors of bridges were nailed down with cedar pins whittled from trees of the forest. Trails that wound in and out to avoid the majestic trees standing in the way were straightened. Patches of the winding trail and deep earth scars were years afterwards to remind the tourist of the former road bed."

Some people thought Craig was demented. But if he was his dementia went in the direction of doing good for his fellow men. There was no kinder, gentler person, despite his unkempt appearance. And to quote a curious little daughter of Robert Millican, after Craig had stopped in Walterville to talk about his road:

"How can Mr. Craig work so hard in the cold and rain to make a road for us? I -- I think he is beautiful -- not his clothes, but him."

To which Millican replied: "No other man on earth could withstand the toil and exposure. I don't know, daughter. Perhaps he is -- beautiful -- within."

The first bridge across a major stream in Lane County is believed to be the one Craig constructed across the river at Craig's Pasture, now McKenzie Bridge, in 1869.

Crossing the river at this point had become a vexing problem to Craig. One day, or so the story goes, he began to build a bridge by felling a large tree across the river. Clambering over it to the opposite bank, he felled another tree to serve as a bridge stringer. Unfortunately, it swerved to the side, striking the first tree, breaking it into pieces. The swift water carried both trees down the stream, leaving Craig on the side of the river farthest from his supplies.

Nine days he searched for another tree suitable for a stringer, felled it across and was able to reach the opposite bank. He had survived on miner's lettuce and sour dock and was almost exhausted.

As he started trimming the limbs from a tree he had felled, his ax slipped from his trembling hands into the surging waters. He did not have time to go after another, nor did he have the money to buy one. Setting to work to retrieve it, he planned to fill a sack with rocks and tie it across his back to sink before the swift water could carry him down stream. He intended to grab his ax, slip off the sack and rise to the surface. Other helpers winked at each other. But John Latta protested vigorously and managed to dissuade him in this perilous undertaking.

After the fir stringers were positioned, a cedar puncheon floor was laid and nailed down with cedar pegs fashioned during the long winter evenings around his camp fire. The railing was set up and the bridge was pronounced safe for travel June 16, 1869.

Others seeking to control the road development formed companies, but none materialized. "Instead we find Craig at last at the goal of his ambition and at the head of a wagon road company that was to control this McKenzie road for 25 years," wrote Sawyer in The *Oregon Motorist.*

The company, originated by Craig and George Millican, was reorganized. On Jan. 14, 1871, articles of incorporation of the "McKenzie Salt Springs and Des Chutes Wagon Road Co." were filed by M. H. Harlow, P. (Philander) Renfrew, J. T. Craig and A. (Alexander) Renfrew. Its goal was "to construct a clay wagon road from the terminus of the present county road at Clark's Point on the north side of the McKenzie River in Lane County, thence up the north side of said river to the point known as Craig's Bridge, thence across said river and by way of Lost Creek and through the low pass to the Des Chutes River at a point near the north end of the Paulina Mountains."

Harlow, P. C. Renfrew and J. A. Odell were named as directors and stockholders, Harlow as president, and Odell, secretary. On Jan. 16, 1872,

Craig was elected president and L. F. Scott, secretary. On Dec. 6, 1873, A. G. Hovey, banker and one-time Eugene mayor, was elected president. He held the office many years.

After building the bridge and reorganization of the company, John Tom, as president, filed on a homestead at Craig's Prairie or Strawberry Acres, now McKenzie Bridge. He built a log cabin under the fir trees on the river bank south of the bridge. Cracks between the logs he chinked with sticks and mud. One window without glass could be closed and pegged from within. The fireplace where he cooked his meals was fashioned with boulders to the height of four feet. The chimney was made of sticks and clay. He lay a puncheon floor over the packed earth. This was the only home he ever had.

In addition to giving the company a franchise to improve the road, the Lane County court authorized it to collect tolls. How soon travel was started over the road is not known, but the first disbursement of toll receipts was made for the period Nov. 8, 1872, to Dec. 3, 1873, in the amount of $219.62 receipts and $714.25 disbursements, signed by Craig as president of the company.

Others to whom payments were made were J. H. Belknap, W. W. Craig, P. C. Renfrew, M. Fountain and George Millican.

Just what part J. H. (James) Belknap played in this toll road is not known. But this was pretty much the situation when he came on the McKenzie in 1869 from the Rogue River Valley to take up a homestead, six miles east of Blue River. His father, Rollin Simeon Belknap, established Salt (later Belknap) Springs in 1871. It is not known whether others, aside from the McBride Party, knew the location of the springs. There was no access road. Rollin had to cut his way, a distance of a mile from the old Scott trail. Big and Little Belknap Craters on the Cascade summit were named for James.

Lane County Commissioners records of 1872 indicate the road company, under Craig as president, gave a 13-mile section of the newly-constructed road to the county to keep the road in good condition and open for travel. The gift section lay between the Robert Millican place, a mile east of Walterville, and the Rock House, four miles east of Vida.

Apparently the last week in October, 1874, saw the first emigrant wagon train cross the Cascades on the toll road. The train was from Walla Walla, Wa.

While the McKenzie road development was under way, like interest was being taken in Linn County in a road into Central Oregon by way of the south fork of the Santiam River. By 1859, a route was discovered by Andrew Wiley, and by 1864 there was some form of road on the route proposed. A Linn County company, The Willamette Valley and Cascade Mountain Wagon Road Co., finished its Wiley Pass Road in 1865 and 1866. Thereafter for many years it was an important route of travel from the valley to Central Oregon.

CHAPTER 16

The Millicans

Two highly influential men in McKenzie Valley history were George Millican, pioneer stockman, founder of Walterville, and his brother, Robert, who settled in the community. George was an enthusiastic supporter of the toll road over the McKenzie Pass.

Their parents emigrated from the border of Scotland to the United States. George was born at sea on the trip on Nov. 22, 1834. The family settled in Osteco County, N. Y., south of Utica, where Robert was born June 19, 1837. Their father was killed just prior to Robert's birth. His brother joined the family in 1843. In 1844, they moved to Jefferson County, Ind., locating at Hanover where the boys were educated.

George Millican

George Millican with his faithful shepherd dog, "Nellie," crossed the plains in 1854, assisting with a cattle drive to the Sacramento Valley. After a short stay at Marysville in the Yuba River gold fields of California, he went to Yreka, then to Happy Camp in Northern California and engaged in gold mining operations there.

He was known to have been in Lane County in 1856. Agnes Millican McLean, his niece, wrote that Millican, John Latta and Walker Young went to the aid of a party cut off during a skirmish with the Indians, who stole their horses during the Rogue Indian War of that year. In this party was John T. Craig. In 1859, George was one of the four McBride Party members who discovered Belknap Springs.

In 1861, George prospected for gold in Idaho. On his way via the overland route to California in July, 1862, he stopped in Walterville and purchased some land from Ross Pollock, pioneer of 1852. In California he traded his gold, mined in Idaho, for $15,000. Returning in the fall, he settled on his McKenzie property. He conferred with Felix Scott Jr. prior to Scott's historic trip over the Cascades with 900 head of cattle in 1862.

In 1863, George and Susan Ritchey were married, standing in a wheat field along Camp Creek, according to Carl Stephens, Walterville historian. Susan, born in 1840, was the daughter of M. D "Dill" and Mary Ritchey, Camp Creek settlers of 1853.

George traveled to Central Oregon to look for grazing land. Apparently he stayed there two years raising cattle and horses before returning to the McKenzie. In 1868, he went to Central Oregon with a band of cattle. Two years later he established a cattle ranch in the Ochoco region on McKay Creek, near Prineville, with the intent of selling cattle in the Willamette Valley.

Walling (1884) wrote: "Marketable cattle were driven west over the Willamette Valley, Salt Springs and Cascade Wagon Road" (actually the McKenzie, Salt Springs and Des Chuttes Wagon Road) "to his ranch on the McKenzie and sold." The company operating the toll road originated by Craig and Millican was, "in the first instance started by private subscription, the object to cut a road from the valley across the mountains to pasture lands of Eastern Oregon."

George, an incorporator and stockholder in the toll road, maintained homes in both Walterville and Central Oregon.

"The railroad was completed from Salem to Eugene in 1871. George shipped his cattle from the McKenzie to a butcher shop he operated in Salem. . .traveled the 135 miles to Eugene for his mail and supplies. He took two saddle horses and a half dozen pack horses to make the two-week trip, to visit his family, relatives and friends on the McKenzie and return to Eastern Oregon with some 1,000 pounds of supplies." (Jo Smith Southworth, *Millican Memories,* 1977:2).

George and Susan had three children: Madella (1866-1890), Margaret Elizabeth (Maggie) (1869-1954) and Walter (1872-1964).

Susan died in 1874.

George brought his family back to Walterville. He was appointed postmaster of the first post office established there Feb. 24, 1875. He named the office for his son, Walter, the first white child born in Central Oregon, at Prineville. The post office was located on the Millican Ranch, a mile north of Hendricks Ferry.

He was reported by Walling's *History of Lane County* to have owned 280 acres of valuable land at Walterville, in addition to 220 acres which he pastured near Prineville.

On Sept. 23, 1881, he married Ada C. Bradley, daughter of Kenno Witt and Elizabeth (Pierce) Bradley. Ada, born in 1859 in Marin County, Cal., grew up in Coles Valley, Douglas County. (Charles Carey, *History of Oregon,* 1922). At the time of their marriage, Ada, 23, was teaching school at West Point in Douglas County.

They spent several years living and working in Salem and Eugene. Ada and George had one child, Scott Bradley, born in 1890. He died two years later (1892).

Hard times fell on the Millicans and they lost their Walterville home. Ada began teaching in rural Linn and Lane County schools. George took up a ranch near Pine Mountain, now known as Millican (in Millican Valley), in Central Oregon.

"We had to have money. . ." Ada wrote in 1920. "I secured a

position (in October 1899) as teacher at White Rocks, Utah, in an Indian school. Later, I was transferred to the school at Yuma, Ariz., and still later to the Indian school at Pima, Ariz., where I taught eight years. From there I was transferred to the Indian school at Puyallup, Wa., then to our Pine Mountain Ranch, for we got on our feet again. The last few years we lived at Prineville."

In 1916, after 30 years operating the Pine Mountain place on the High Desert, Millican sold the 1,800 acres of land at Millican and on Bear Creek and the livestock to Frank Sloan of Stanfield. That was the year Deschutes County, including the Millican and Bend country, was formed from Crook County.

Ada, very active in Women's Clubs of America, a teacher in Indian schools, and a collector of Indian artifacts, was author of *Heart of Oregon, Legend of the Wascos*, published in 1914. Her Indian artifacts collection is in the University of Oregon Museum in Eugene.

George Millican died in Prineville Nov. 25, 1919, age 85, after three years retirement from a productive life. Ada died in 1927.

WALTER MILLICAN

Walter Millican was born in 1872 on McKay Creek in Wasco County, a part of which became Crook County and later Deschutes County. He was the first white child born east of the Cascade Mountains in Central Oregon. His mother died in 1874, and his family moved back to Walterville in 1875. Walter returned to the family farm on McKay Creek with his father in 1882.

Dave Fountain, Walter Millican and John Fountain

Father and son moved from their Eastern Oregon ranch to one 40 miles south of the original location in 1886, near the community of Millican. In 1896, Walter married Mable Dodson in Walterville. They moved to the ranch in Central Oregon, then in the fall of 1905 moved back to the McKenzie to their Anderson place ten miles east of Walterville. During the 1920's, Walter operated the community store in Leaburg. He died in 1964.

ROBERT MILLICAN

Robert Millican, writing his life history by family request May 19, 1917, shortly before his death Feb. 28, 1918, said: "In April 1854, I went to Cincinnati to learn the carpenter trade. In the fall of 1856, I went to McDonough County, Ill. . .worked on some frame houses (all brick work in Cincinnati).

"Went back to Illinois in the spring, didn't like the climate. Worked in Indiana until the fall of 1859. Started for Oregon Nov. 2 (at age 22, five years after brother George crossed the plains). Spent a few days in Osteco. Sailed on steamer Atlantic Nov. 21, 1859.

"In about six days we landed at Colon (north side of the Isthmus of Panama). Spent a day getting the passengers and freight (overland) to Panama (on the Pacific side).

Robert Millican
with son Oscar

"I boarded the steamer Golden Age for Frisco. Coaled at Acapulco, Mexico. Spent the day ashore sightseeing. Had to wait in Frisco for the Portland boat. The ice in the Columbia was running so the boat couldn't get to sea. Came to Albany on the river boat. Then walked to Eugene. I stayed most of he winter with John Latta" (mp. 13.5, just east of Walterville).

"On May 1, 1860, I joined a prospecting party" (of 53 men and 107 head of horses and mules, under G. W. Bunch of Linn County. Bunch, a pioneer of 1852, was born in Kentucky in 1816).

The party was "bound for Eastern Oregon (a country of hostile Indians). . .Crossed the mountains near Diamond Peak May 20. On the headwaters of the Malheur River, Indians stampeded our animals. They took 67 head, while 40 were saved as they were hidden by willows across the stream. They burned all they didn't need. We started for home and were ambushed by the Redskins. They put up a good fight, but their aim was not as good as ours. We got an Indian every time," he wrote. One man in the party was shot through the leg. "We were a hard-looking lot when we reached the settlements.

"There was nothing to do here, so I walked to the mines in Southern Oregon, bought a claim in Douglas County near the Jackson

County line. I made some money. . .left there in January 1862 for Idaho. Located in Florence on the Salmon River. The mines were very rich. . .I then left for Auburn, Baker County, Ore. There were four of us. The second night south of Lewiston, an Indian stole my saddle. I tracked him home. Well, I didn't get my saddle but they gave me the worst scare I ever had. I spent all night trying to get even. Went back to Lewiston, bought a new saddle and started for Walla Walla. . .

"I got a fresh horse and crossed the mountains. It was not safe to go farther than Auburn alone. Not catching the party, I got 25 men together bound for Boise. The Indians fled when they saw us. I mined in Boise nearly two years. In 1864, I went to Canyon City, Grant County, Ore. Three of us went over to the middle fork of the John Day to prospect. We began where Susanville afterwards was located. The Indians scared us away. It was dangerous outside Canyon City. Susanville was a very rich camp afterwards.

"In the fall of 1864, I came here to Walterville. I bought the ranch we live on" (from John Latta. Family members said George Millican had written to Robert urging him to come west, and that George had asked Latta to file for homestead rights on the property to make it available for Robert to purchase).

"I worked for George (Millican) three years. On Aug. 13, 1867, I married Mary E. (Abigail) Beals." (Millican 1963:28-30-31).

Mary, born in 1850, came to Oregon with her parents on the Lost Wagon Train of 1853. Robert and Mary had eight children by 1884. Oscar, the eldest, was born July 19, 1868. Maria Belle was born in 1869.

Oscar Millican owned vast acreages of farm land north and west of Walterville, including most of George's original homestead. In later years he acquired property at Hayden Bridge. Oscar ran mostly white-faced Hereford cattle on his land, along with general farming. Oscar and his sister, Belle, lived at the junction of Camp Creek Road and Millican Drive. She and Oscar died the same year, 1950. Neither had married.

The others were Agnes (Aggie) (1871-1958), married George McLean; Fannie (1875-1961), married Harry Laverage; Ada, (1877-1962), married Marion Brubaker; Lawrence (1878-1952), married Verna Sharp (they made their home in Walterville); Inez (1879-1972), married Bruce Garrison, and Lester R., born July 19, 1882, married Ada Belle Collins.

Century Farm

Lester Millican, prior to his marriage, homesteaded land on the west adjacent to his parents. He built a small house on the hillside and lived there with Ray Rennie.

He married Ada Belle Collins Jan. 12, 1910. Ada, the daughter of Mr. and Mrs. Zachary Taylor Collins, was born June 9, 1888. Collins came to Oregon with the Jesse Applegate party and settled at Cottage Grove. He married the former Mary Eldora Damewood, who was born in Oregon.

Ada was working for the Post's Stage Stop at Walterville when she and Lester met. They purchased additional property, lying south of the McKenzie Highway, from the Vern Hucha family and built their large house and farm buildings. After Robert Millican Sr.'s death, Lester and

Ada rented the property from the heirs, then bought the place in 1935. Lester farmed the land and raised livestock. He also was involved in sawmill operations earlier in life.

Lester and Ada had three children, all born at Walterville. They were Robert II, born Aug. 9, 1912; Lucile, Aug. 12, 1915, and Dorothy E., Feb. 5, 1919.

Lester died in 1946. Ada died May 13, 1989, a month short of age 102 years.

Their home is occupied today by their daughter, Lucile, and her husband, Gordon Hale. They have three children, ages as of 1996, Lester, 52, Robert, 50, and Mary Johanna, 49.

Dorothy married Henry Lindsay Calhoun April 6, 1947. They have two sons, Harry Robert and William Gordon, both married, and five grandchildren. All live in Bremerton, Wa.

Robert Millican II married Neva Mae Currant. They moved into the senior Robert Millican house in 1933. Their children are Kathleen, Karen, Sandra and Sharen. Robert died in 1977.

A Century Farm designation was conferred by the state of Oregon on the Robert Millican Ranch -- originally a 160-acre donation land claim, grown to 320 acres by acquisition -- being continuously farmed for more than 100 years. The designation was made Aug. 31, 1965, during the Oregon State Fair. It was one of eleven so designated in Lane County.

Mr. and Mrs. Robert Millican II and his mother, Ada, were the occupants and owners at the time of the Century Farm designation. The 88-year-old (at that time) house on the place was a sturdy and architecturally balanced structure, with a porch on three sides.

MILLICAN MEMORIAL HALL

Robert Millican Sr. is credited with building the first Walterville schoolhouse, a log cabin, about 1864. It was built with upright planks and plank floor. First teachers were Inez Henderson and Martha Reasoner. Church was also held in the cabin. Before that, area residents had to go to lower Camp Creek to attend church and school. Twelve boys and 12 girls attended.

The original school house was replaced in 1889 with a one-room frame building erected on land donated by George Millican. Robert built the desks and seats.

In the early 1900's, the building was enlarged to include a second room. In 1951, the Walterville school was consolidated with another.

The George Millican Memorial Hall in Walterville was named for George. After the school's closure Millican family members, Walter and Maggie, agreed to donate the land to the Walterville Grange and the Welcome Rebekah Lodge on the condition it be maintained as a community center. The empty frame building was turned 90 degrees and enlarged. Over the years it was added to and enlarged again.

CHAPTER 17

The Storments and Reasoners

James Wilson Storment, born in November, 1811, brought his family to Oregon from Illinois in 1852.

A. G. Walling's *History of Lane County* gives the year of their arrival and place of settlement as Walterville. An early-day map shows a large holding, 1200 acres, in the name of Jas. W. Storment, extending from the heart of what is now Walterville two miles east toward Deerhorn on either side of today's McKenzie River Highway and the Eugene Water and Electric Board's power canal.

Family descendants were under the impression the Storments had settled in Camp Creek and the Walterville property was acquired later by their son, Alexander Franklin (Frank). The confusion may arise from the fact early-day Walterville and points east were included in the Camp Creek precinct for voting and census records. The name Walterville didn't exist until 1875, when the first post office was established. The homestead of Alexander Franklin connected on the east side and extends north into the hills and south to the river.

Very little information is available on James Storment's early life. What is known, Storment, a farmer, was very active in McKenzie River Valley explorations. He was a member of the McBride Party, with George Millican, John Craig and Joseph Carter, credited with the discovery of Belknap Springs in 1859.

He also is reported to have named Gate Creek, which flows into the McKenzie River at Vida (river mile 41.4). The *Eugene Daily Guard*, July 12, 1893, said: "The name was given to the creek by Mr. Storment, now dead. A few hundred yards below where the road now crosses are two immense rocks between which the creek flows and over which was a foot log. Storment remarked the rocks had the appearance of gate posts. He also gave names to other points and creeks along the river." James Storment died Jan. 5, 1875, at age 63.

Storment's wife, Harriet, was born in South Carolina March 3, 1816. The 1880 census for Camp Creek Precinct, including Walterville, lists Harriet, the mother, age 65; Harriet E., daughter, 33; James, 29, a farmer, both born in Illinois, and Amanda, 22, born in Oregon. James died Sept. 19, 1888. Another daughter, Margaret, died in 1862. Harriet died May 29, 1892.

Alexander Franklin Storment, oldest son of James and Harriet, was born in Jefferson County, Ill., July 14, 1842. He was 10 years old when he crossed the plains to Oregon with his parents in 1852.

Frank (as he was known) and Martha Tryphena Reasoner were

married Oct. 31, 1866, at Brownsville. Martha, at age 16, was the first school teacher at Walterville in 1865. She boarded with friends. While there she became acquainted with her future husband.

Born May 6, 1849, in Terre Haute, Ind., on the banks of the Wabash River, Martha was the daughter of John Stout and Sara Tryphena (Northway) Reasoner. Martha was two years old when her family moved to Oregon from Illinois in 1852. They settled first in Sellwood, 20 miles west of Portland, then lived near Scappoose on the Willamette Slough and later near Brownsville.

Settle on Homestead

Frank and Martha in 1868 settled on their homestead east of Walterville. They filed for their donation land claim at the nearest Federal Land Office in Roseburg. The deed was signed in 1872 by President Ulysses S. Grant. It became a Century Farm in 1968. Frank took over the James Storment homestead after his parent's deaths. Much of the western portion was sold off in later years.

Frank and Martha grew hops, as the main crop, and vegetables on the river bottom land south of the present highway, and pastured livestock on the hillside. They had three separate houses. First, they lived in a hop-drying house built on the bottom land.

The hop house was replaced with another built on the hillside. This house burned. The present large, two-story house, which sets back from the highway, was built in 1908. The home served as an eating place for workers during digging of the Walterville power canal about 1910. It was rented out during the depression 1930's.

A great-granddaughter, Virginia Gamache, her husband, Allen, and children now occupy the home.

Martha Storment, as mid-wife, assisted with the births of several children in the community, including all but one of the Johnny and Lynn Fountain children, who lived nearby.

Alexander Franklyn Storment died April 11, 1909. Martha died March 2, 1940. They are buried in the Camp Creek Cemetery.

Frank and Martha's four children, all born at Walterville, were: Henrietta, known as "Hat", b. Aug. 25, 1867; John Wilson Storment, b. Dec. 6, 1869, d. June 23, 1937; Marrietta, b. April 10, 1872, d. at age 26, March 27, 1898, from scarlet fever, and True Frances Lynn Storment, b. March 29, 1889, d. in 1974.

Henrietta married T. J. Henkle Feb. 21, 1888. Children were: Hazel M., b. 3-4-1889, in Oregon; Venita Maple, b. 4-22-1894; Mark Forest, b. 1-14-1898, and Clark W., b. 8-8-1909, the latter three born in Washington. Venita married Del E. Benson 11-25, 1915, in Moro, Ore. Mark married Florence Scott in Portland June 29, 1929.

John W. married Estelle McNutt July 3, 1896. They had eight children: Vera LaVelle (Ogden), b. 11-19-1897; Franklin Bush, b. 8-18-1899; Marrietta Aletha (Buckner), b. 11-15-1900; Ura Grace (Moore), b. 3-15-1902; John Alexander Wilson, b. 4-15-1907; Elton McNutt, b. 6-8-1909, and Estelle June (Harkema), b. 6-6-1910, all born in Oregon, and Ivan Truman, b. 12-25-1917, in Washington.

John was killed at age 67 June 23, 1937, in the Mohawk Valley near Mabel, when he was trampled by a team of run-away horses and run over by a sled. He was raised in Walterville but spent several years in Washington before settling at Mabel.

True Storment was quoted as saying she rode her horse and sometimes walked to school at Walterville. The land was open hillside and grassy. There was constant danger from wild animals, primarily cougars and bears. She was joined by Fountain and Millican children. They were usually accompanied by Frank Storment's dog "Old Shep."

True married Marion Bigelow Aug. 21, 1912, in the Storment home. Marion's father owned People's Meat Market, the first in Springfield, on Main Street. Marion drove his team into Eugene for ice at the old ice house, then hauled meat to Walterville and other McKenzie communities. He sold it to the residents along the way.

"This was a love affair that lasted 59 years of marriage," said Virginia Gamache, a granddaughter. She told the following account:

"True Storment (who grandpa teasingly referred to as 'Torment'), met my grandpa when he was delivering meat. Her first encounter with Marion Bigelow was to run out of the house and tell him to be careful because their dog, named Bounce, would bite. She said he chuckled it off. Little did she know he had a way with animals and probably dealt with mean dogs with scraps of meat.

"Grandma said he was 'quite a catch.' All the eligible young ladies swooned over him and acted like 'silly geese,' waiting for him at the fence posts. So she always made herself scarce when he came around. At one time Marion listened in on a party-line telephone as the young ladies discussed him."

Marion and True had sons, Francis Marion, born Sept. 26, 1918, and died in 1992, and Donald Reasoner Bigelow, born June 27, 1925.

Donald Bigelow married LaVane Marylin Johnson Feb. 10, 1945, in Blaine, Wash. She was born Oct. 5, 1927, the daughter of Arthur and Marie Weppner Johnson. They had five children: Donald Jr., Gary of Walterville, Glenn of Monroe, Virginia (Mrs. Allen) Gamache of Walterville and Kenneth of Springfield.

LaVane, who had lived in a home on 200 acres of the original homestead next door to her daughter, Virginia, died of cancer Aug. 28, 1995, at age 67. She was preceded in death by a son, Donald, and two grandchildren. Her other children, Gary, Glen, Virginia and Kenneth, also a sister, Delores Johnson, 18 grandchildren and three great-grandchildren survive.

Mary Fountain Gillispie, 95 at this writing, who grew up next door to the Storments, wrote, "Early-day memories of our friends Martha, Frank and True Storment."

"They lived down near the McKenzie River on what Martha referred to as the bottom land, in an old hop yard. In my memory Frank made a nice home of the old hop house. I remember the large rooms and high ceilings. The pump in the kitchen for the water was a miracle to me, as our water up on the hill first ran in a wooden trough, then later in a pipe. The big white geese my mother helped Martha pick, and we had a pair of (down) pillows. Onions, grain, apples, grapes and black walnuts were grown on that wonderful river bottom land. We four Fountain children went down with Martha to thin and weed onions.

"Maybe they built on the hill to homestead the hill place. They were our nearest neighbors. Martha took us in the buggy with the old white horse to help her on the bottom place and to Sunday school each Sunday at the Deerhorn school-house.

"When Frank built the home down the hill, True was a young lady and was married there. How I admired her beautiful clothes. Our childhood was filled with memories of these dear friends. Martha came as mid-wife when we last six children were born."

The Reasoner Family

Martha's parents, John Stout and Tryphena (Northway) Reasoner, were missionaries with the Presbyterian Church. Rev. Reasoner, born April 25, 1799, in Maysville, Ky., was the son of Nicholas II, who was the son of Peter. Peter's father was Nicholas I. Peter emigrated from France to escape religious persecution during the French Revolution of the 1700's. He settled in Pennsylvania.

Nicholas II moved to Kentucky from Pennsylvania prior to 1790. He married Polly Stout March 2, 1797. Polly died in December 1807, leaving Nicholas with four children. He returned to his old home in Pennsylvania, where his father Peter and several brothers and sisters remained.

In 1809, Nicholas II accompanied his father and brothers, Solomon, Benjamin and Jacob to Ohio to join brothers, John and Henry who were already there. They went down the Ohio River and up the Muskingum to Zanesville, where John met them and took them to New Concord. Nicholas II taught school in winter and farmed in summer. While teaching he had two of his sons, John Stout and Aron, with him. He lived in the homes of patrons according to customs.

There is a gap in the life of John Stout Reasoner until after his marriage to Tryphena Northway of Steuben County, N. Y., Dec. 29, 1833, at Painted Post, near Corning, N. Y.

Tryphena was born in Vermont in October 1814. Her father was a colonel in the army. She received her education in Corning, and taught school for many years before and after her marriage.

In 1833, John Stout went to Danville College and Auburn Seminary in New York. He worked for a time in Pittsburgh, where he learned the blacksmith trade and became an expert ax maker. A fluent reader in Greek and Latin, he often read from the Greek Bible.

The Rev. John Stout and Tryphena Reasoner, devout Presbyterians, had a strong calling to be missionaries. Her teaching and his blacksmithing supplemented their meager missionary pay. In 1837, when they took their first assignment they had two children, Francis Northway and Lucy Case Reasoner.

John applied for missionary assignment in the Presbyterian Church and was assigned to Kaskaskia in Randolph County, an early capital of Illinois, on the Mississippi, 75 miles below St. Louis. He probably had less than $25. With friends, Mr. and Mrs. Blakeslee, who wished to go to Cincinnati, he built a boat at Olean, N. Y., to carry them to Pittsburgh. Fortunately, they were on the headwaters of the Allegheny River which goes to form the Ohio River.

Tryphena Reasoner sent back a description of this trip, which has been preserved (Vol. I, Chapter 17, No. 601-a. Letter dated A. D. 1837, Mary's River Township, Randolph Co., from Tryphena Northway Reasoner to her parents at Painted Post, Steuben Co., N. Y.)

They left Olean, N. Y., in early October, 1837, in this boat and with a few provisions and their scanty belongings and a few dollars started on their voyage. The boat, 25 feet long and eight feet wide with 16 feet boarded up to form a cabin, housed the four adults and three children. They had straw for mattresses, a little Franklin stove for cooking and heating, a glass window and six lights. But the floor was so low they could not keep the boat properly bailed out. Water slopped through cracks in the floor. When they put their bunks down at night there was room for only a couple of chairs and firewood.

Several dams on the river, used to run flour mills and sawmills, proved a problem to negotiate. They stopped from time to time for provisions and once Rev. Reasoner held religious services. The river became wider and deeper and they encountered fall storms. Finally arriving at Pittsburgh, they sold the boat for $5.00, and arranged for accommodations on the river boat "The Detroit," which eventually took them to Kaskaskia.

Tryphena wrote: "Thursday we landed at Kaskaskia landing, about three miles from the village. Francis is quite ill with a high fever. All of us are sick. There were three hundred passengers and poor accommodations."

A descendant, Col. M. A. Reasoner, in the 1930's compiled an account of this missionary experience from letters and other material. He commented: "It was a mean trick of the Board of Missions to send them out to such a place as this. It was almost exclusively a Catholic settlement with no church or house available. It was in the river bottoms where malaria and dysentery were plentiful and the conditions in general were such that they never had a chance. The man who drove them to their destination asked $3.00. They gave him $2.50 and had $4.00 left. They moved to the Widow Pettitt's where they all lived in one room. Within a few weeks they were, with the exception of Mrs. Reasoner, feeling better."

Rev. Reasoner had only 16 members in his church. Tryphena taught school. Other letters, one written Dec. 5, 1841, from Newton, Ill., tell of hardships and illnesses and birth of another child, which died "while her husband was unconscious with the fever." At that time, John's father Nicholas II came to live with them.

A letter tells of their moving to Indiana. "Always there is a recital of sickness and hardship but never a complaint," wrote Col. Reasoner. In 1847 they were living in Terre Haute, Ind., when Nicholas II died.

Martha was born there.

Finally in 1852, a letter of Tryphena tells of their waiting to start on their trip across the plains to Oregon. They left Sullivan, Ind., May 9, 1851, and traveled by wagon to Silver Creek in southwest Iowa, just 15 miles from the starting point at Kainsville, Ia.

During the summer they laid in a supply of hay and forage for their cattle and horses. There was a colony of Mormons waiting until spring to continue their trip. During the winter John worked "ironing" their wagons and otherwise preparing them for their journey, while Tryphena "taught school for young and old."

Tryphena's letter, written to her parents, Mr. and Mrs. Francis Northway, at Dundee, Harnes Co., Ill., just before their departure for Oregon, shows her concern for the long trip and the unknown perils that lay ahead. She expressed concern that she probably would never see her parents and brothers and sisters again. At the time of departure in 1852 they had ten children.

They crossed the plains in two wagons, one drawn by three yoke of oxen loaded with supplies, driven by son Frank; a light wagon drawn by a team of horses carrying camp supplies, driven by Rev. John Reasoner. Son Martin brought up the rear driving loose cattle whose milk provided partial subsistence. Cholera broke out, but the Reasoners escaped. On the trip two young men quarreled over a girl. One shot the other. Frontier justice was meted out.

Incredible difficulties were described after crossing the Snake River as they approached the Blue Mountains. They had to abandon most of their belongings which had been brought along at the expense of so much toil and labor.

They experienced many hardships along the way. The wagon train picked up an Indian boy who was sick and had been cast out by his tribe for fear of spreading the disease. The boy recovered but one day he disappeared. Days or weeks later he reappeared and warned the wagon train of possible trouble ahead. He advised against continuing this route because of imminent danger.

Here the train divided. Some members followed the Indian boy's advice and turned off to follow the Oregon trail. The others, fearing a trap, continued along their selected route. They were set upon by Indians and some of them massacred.

When they came in site of the Columbia River, Rev. John Stout officiated at a marriage. Tryphena walked the last 110 miles to The Dalles to save throwing away some of their goods.

Arriving at The Dalles too late in the season to take the Barlow trail, they left their remaining six head of cattle and a mare with some men who offered to care for them until the following spring. Needless to say they never saw the stock again. They floated down the Columbia and landed at Portland at night Nov. 6, 1852. In less than 24 hours the remainder of their property was stolen. Their daughter, Abigail, had picked up a little lamb along the way. This lamb and their dog were the only animals they got through with.

They first located where Sellwood now stands near Cornelius, about 20 miles west of Portland. However, when the fall rains came, they had to leave in a boat. They next located at Scappoose on the Willamette Slough. The winter of 1852 was a hard one and the emigrants had a difficult time getting along. However, their health improved in the mild Oregon climate.

Reasoner told of the election, a result of which, by a small margin, the Oregon Territory decided to go with the United States rather than with Canada. In 1845, the U. S. Marshall took a census and found 2,100 inhabitants of whom 1,000 were women, and probably half of those were half-caste.

In 1853 and 1854, Rev. Reasoner and son, Frank, built a sawmill and a turning lathe and built furniture for themselves and others. It was his mechanical ability which came to his rescue so many times and made it possible to carry on through the obstacles which confronted him and his family. Then there was the Indian uprising and the alarm in the night and their hurried departure.

In 1860, the Reasoner family was in Aumsville, 10 miles southeast of Salem. That same fall the family moved to Brownsville. In 1870, they were in Benton County, south of Corvallis.

The Reasoners had 13 children. Born in New York were Francis Northway, b. 10-12-1834, d. 8-21-1920; Lucy Case, b. 6-13-1836, d. 8-24-1920. Born in Illinois, Martin Luther, b. 3-21-1838, d. 1-22-1862; Mary Abigail, b. 8-24-1839, d. 12-14-1925; John Calvin, b. 1-29-1841, d. 8-18-1841; Ellen Amelia, b. 9-1-1843, d. 7-1918.

Born in Indiana were John Calvin (same name as child who died), b. 11-8-1845, d. 1918; Matthew, b. 3-5-1847, d. 9-11-1849; Martha Tryphena, b. 5-6-1849, d. 3-2-1940; Henry Arba, b. 2-25-1851, d. 11-16-1927. Born in Oregon near Forest Grove was Emma Tryphosa, b. 9-24-1853, d. 1-24-1884. Born on the donation land claim in Columbia County were Melissa Jane, b. 8-8-1856, d. 9-12-1895; and Royal Froman, b. 12-17-1857, d. 7-29-1930.

The Rev. John Stout Reasoner died in Oregon June 12, 1892. Tryphena, died May 4, 1905 in Seattle. Both were buried at Seattle.

CHAPTER 18

The Fountains

Sensing the winds of Civil War between the states, James Davis Fountain and his wife, the former Matilda H. Sims, sold their plantation, freed their slaves and with five children and Matilda pregnant left their Missouri home in the spring of 1857 and headed west.

James Davis, born in 1820 in Missouri, and Matilda were married Dec. 18/28, 1846, in Boone County, Mo.

Boone County census records show Matilda was born Sept. 12, 1828, in Kentucky. She was the daughter of Thomas Anderson Sims, a farmer, born about 1802, and Elizabeth (Morris) Sims, born in 1809. Sims families and relatives migrated from Virginia to Kentucky to Missouri.

Matilda probably was a sister of John Whitlock Sims, who at age 34 married Dora Belknap, age 15, and homesteaded west of McKenzie Bridge in the mid-1870's. John, born in Sedalia, Mo., was working at Belknap Springs for Rollin S. Belknap when he met and married Dora.

The Fountains traveled the Santa Fe Trail in their covered wagon to the crowded mining areas of California, but soon moved to Oregon.

They traveled by boat to Portland and arrived at Harrisburg -- known as "Old Muddy" -- by stern wheeler in 1858. They did not move into the McKenzie Valley until almost ten years later, about 1867.

Carrol Fountain the youngest of the John Fountain family, with his wife, Thelma, lives on the old home place on Buck Point Way, two miles east of Walterville. Carrol listed from family records the children of James Davis and Matilda Fountain.

The first five born in Missouri were: (1) Amanda, born Sept. 23, 1847, married first, Spores; second, John Sumpter, moved to Washington, died in 1903. (2) Matthew, b. Feb. 20, 1849, moved to Palouse Country, near Spokane. (3) Thomas Anderson, b. Dec. 18, 1851, m. Melissa Hendricks, settled near Elmira, west of Eugene. (4) Elizabeth Josephine, b. Feb. 18, 1853, married William (Bill) Neely, lived in the McKenzie Valley. (5) Jeannette, b. Feb. 5, 1855, married Olias Johnson.

(6) Martha Jane, born June 26, 1857, apparently after the family arrived in California; married Jake Nicholson. They lived in Marcola and were parents of Ernie Nicholson, who married Sara Ann (Sadie) Sims, daughter of John and Dora Sims..

Born at Harrisburg, Ore., were: (7) Laura Ellen, April 24, 1859; married Al Lane. They lived on the McKenzie. A son, Guy, married Mamie, daughter of Mr. and Mrs. Matt Emmerick of Walterville.

(8) Sarah Emmaline, b. April 9, 1861; married Jim Kennerly. A son, Ervin, born May 22, 1882, died Sept. 7, 1902. The Kennerlys kept the

store at Leaburg, then known as "Jim Town," named for Jim.

(9) Icyphena, b. Oct. 3, 1863, married Albert Moore Feb. 25, 1881. They lived in Eastern Oregon. (10) John William "Johnny", born Nov. 6, 1865, married Salinda Paxton in Eugene May 11, 1893.

Sometime after John's birth, James Davis and Matilda moved to Walterville, where two more sons were born. They were: (11) Henderson Davis (Dave) Fountain, b. Feb. 24, 1868. He married Georgia Barnes. They lived in Walterville. Their children were Marvin, who married Rosella Smith of Walterville; Nettie LaVerne and Merle. Merle was killed during World War I. Dave Fountain was killed in a logging accident Nov. 13, 1923. After his death Mrs. Fountain and Nettie moved to Riverside, Cal.

(12) Hudson (Hud) Fountain, b. April 17, 1870, married Minnie Price. They had daughters, Elma and Neata, born at Walterville. After Minnie's death, Hudson married Louise Hickson, widow of Andy Hickson. He lived all his life on the McKenzie, mostly in the Leaburg area, working as a logger and in later life for the Eugene Power and Electric Board. Elma Fountain married Beryl Slavens.

James Davis Fountain died Oct. 1, 1894, at Walterville. Matilda moved to the home of her daughter, Martha Jane Nicholson, at Marcola and lived there until her death March 2, 1898.

"Johnny" Fountain married Salinda Paxton in Eugene May 11, 1893. Born in Sandusky, Ohio, March 3, 1873, Salinda (known as Lynn) came to Oregon with her parents. The Paxtons settled at Cedar Flat.

Salinda taught before her marriage at a school where the Greenwood Cemetery is now located. That school, built in 1884, was used until 1893, when a new building was erected at the present Leaburg site (now the Leaburg Community Center) on land donated by Jim and Emma Kennerly. Salinda lived with the Kennerlys while teaching.

Johnny and Salinda first lived on Johnson Creek, Leaburg, then moved east of Walterville, up on Buck Point, north of the McKenzie Highway, now accessed by Buck Point Way. John was a farmer.

They had three daughters and four sons, all born in a small clap board house on Buck Point. They were:

(1) Edna, born March 11, 1894, married Earl Ray Johnson. He was killed in a logging accident. She later married Dan Miles. (2) Bessie Jane (Beth), born May 3, 1896, married Harold Robinson. They had a son, Bill.

(3) James Lee, born July 26, 1898, married Rose Anna Minney of Vida. They had daughters, Rosalee (Lloyd) and Roberta (Bradford).

(4) Mary Matilda, born Dec. 4, 1900, married Vincent Gillispie of Deerhorn. He died in 1945. They had children Brian and Marjorie.

(5) John William (Jack), named for his father, was born Jan. 6, 1903. He married Ovetta Mae Uber, daughter of William and Lyda Uber, Brownsville. They had two sons, Loris William, born in 1925, and Raymond Harold "Bud" in 1927. Jack, a logger, died in 1991.

(6) Ervin Thomas, born July 6, 1909, married Margaret Perry. Their children were Gary and Karen.

(7) Carrol, born Jan. 19, 1913, married Ethel Currant (deceased). They had four children, Dick, Mike, Pam and Tom. A logger, Carrol has

lived all his life on the Fountain homestead on Buck Point, which he acquired from the other heirs. Part of the property is occupied by Carrol's married children. He is now married to Thelma (Minney) Baker, whose first husband died of multiple sclerosis.

John Fountain died Feb. 6, 1937. Salinda died Oct. 6, 1936.

Mary Gillispie, at age 95, and Carrol are the only living members of the John and Salinda Fountain family at this writing.

James Lee Fountain, born in Walterville July 26, 1898, attended Walterville schools. A World War I veteran, he served in France and was wounded. After the war he attended Oregon State University. He became active in the Disabled Veterans of Foreign Wars.

He and Rose Anna Minney, daughter of James Kapp and Nettie Alice Minney of Vida, were married Dec. 26, 1919, in Eugene. Rose was born Feb. 13, 1899, in Newport, Ohio. They met while working for Booth-Kelly Lumber Co., he as a logger and she as a camp cook at Wendling.

They lived at Leaburg, where their daughter, Rosalee -- a combination of their names -- was born Dec. 3, 1920. They moved to Wendling. In 1926, they built a home just west of Leaburg. Daughter Roberta (Bobbie) was born there June 30, 1931.

Lee later worked for the U. S. Forest Service and the Civilian Conservation Corps, supervising construction of roads, including the Box Canyon and Clear Lake roads. He then became a building contractor.

He and Rose were active in the Leaburg community. He served on the school board. Rose was chief observer of the Aircraft Warning System during World War II. She became a nurse with a degree in licensed practical nursing. Lee died in Crescent City, Cal., July 23, 1975, and is buried at Brookings, where he lived many years. Rose died Aug. 1, 1984, and is buried in Greenwood Cemetery.

Rosalee, now Mrs. Edward Lloyd, said: "I attended the first grade at Booth-Kelly Camp. Then my sister, Roberta, and I attended school at Leaburg until my senior year, when the high school was consolidated with Springfield. I graduated from Springfield High in 1938. My children, Steve Clark and Judi Lloyd, attended Leaburg Elementary.

Rosalee Fountain Clark and Edward "Bill" Lloyd were married Jan. 1, 1945. Lloyd, born July 26, 1909, in Elk City, Okla., to Wyatt and Martha Lloyd, was graduated from Elmira High School and attended the Eugene Vocational School. During World War II he was a naval ship inspector in Tacoma. He worked in logging and construction.

Lloyd died of respiratory failure June 3, 1996, at age 86.

Mrs. Lloyd said: "I have lived in Leaburg all my life, except for about five years when my husband had a portable sawmill and we lived in Lorane, Coos Bay and Bandon. I worked for the Springfield School District 22 years, 21 of them at the Walterville Elementary School." Roberta lives in Springfield and works for the school District.

Life on the River

Reminiscences of life on the McKenzie are contained in an article in *Historic Leaburg* by Ray Nash from an interview with the late Jack Fountain in the mid-1980's. Nash wrote:

"Jack Fountain is a product of Oregon pioneer heritage, one of that scarce breed which has known the McKenzie Valley intimately since the days of river ferries and horse-drawn travel. . .

"Jack has memories of those days. His father, John, played the violin, as had his father, James, and there was an old organ in the home. There would be occasional song-fests in the evening. Other people would come and join in the singing and party games as well. Jack recalls a game called 'Skip to m' Lou' in which everyone entered the dancing. His oldest sister, Edna, played the organ, entirely self-taught. 'Dad played the fiddle, playing Turkey in the Straw and other old favorites.'

"Social life often included exchange visits between families. The Matt and Kate Emmerick family (who lived south across the river, accessed by a ferry) with five girls and two boys, including Frank, Matt, Clara, Mamie, Matilda, Hilda and Bertha, exchanged visits with the Fountains several times a year. They would hitch up the wagon, and the whole family would pile in to spend the day with their friends.

"'Dad was a good provider, and Mom was a good cook.' Jack remembered her 'delicious sourdough biscuits, of which she always made 39, because of the exact capacity of the two pans she used.'"

Jack recalled as a boy "being offered money for his string of 12 to 18-inch redsides by some sportsman headed for Thomson's Lodge.

"He knew the location of all the old ferries on the lower river. He used them and remembered the problems they presented when the ferry was on the other side of the river where the last user left it. Once as a teenager he solved the problem at the Deerhorn ferry by climbing onto the cable and hitching his way across the river. He also remembered his dad yelling from the bank at Hendricks Ferry to rouse Grant Hendricks to get the ferry to their side of the river.

"Jack graduated in 1921 from McKenzie Union High School (composed of Walterville, Deerhorn, Cedar Flat and Camp Creek districts; each had its own grade school). His diploma was signed by V. V. Willis, teaching principal; E. R. Schwering, chairman of the board, and M. J. Wearin, clerk. The class included Lilly Minney of Vida and Roy Ranald Chase of Camp Creek.

"The high school had a baseball team, even if a grade school player had to be recruited to round out nine players. Jack was a pitcher. Thurston was a favorite opponent. Jack remembered teammates George Momb, Ranald Chase, Don, Vincent and Darrol Gillispie, Ad Chaffee, Ted Gebauer, Adrian Thomas, Kenneth Tobias and Roy Mead."

Jack, a logger, began as a "whistle punk" (signal caller) at age 16 for Booth-Kelly Co. "It was while he was eating in the Booth Kelly Camp 34 cook house in 1923 that he met and later married (1924) Ovetta Mae Uber of Brownsville, a 'hash slinger' at the camp," Nash's article said. Their two children attended the camp elementary school, but Jack moved his family to Walterville in time to enter high school.

CHAPTER 19

Upper River Settlements

With wagon road improvements, such as they were, up the McKenzie, families began moving into the Deerhorn, Leaburg and Vida areas, and the upper McKenzie, including such well-known names as the Martins, Pepiots, Thomsons, Belknaps, Finns, Sims and Wycoffs.

Gate Creek, named by James Storment, flows into the McKenzie River at the community of Vida (river mile 41.4). First area settlers aren't known, but the account of Felix Scott Jr. driving cattle over the McKenzie Pass in 1862 refers to the eastern terminus of the road 30 miles east of Springfield at "Rock House," a natural formation making a crude shelter, four miles east of Vida.

Thomas M. Martin (1840 - ?) for whom famous Martin (sometimes spelled Marten) Rapids was named, and his wife, Caroline, in 1864, purchased property four miles east of Vida from William Allen, who settled there in 1863 (Walling's History of Lane County). The property, river mile 45, was on the south side of the river where the famed Thomson Sportsman's Lodge was later located.

Martin accompanied Rollin S. Belknap on the first recorded trip to Clear Lake, headwaters of the McKenzie River, in the early 1870's.

"The Gate Creek Post Office (elevation 783 feet) was established Dec. 30, 1874, with Martin as postmaster. It was discontinued Sept. 30, 1880, and re-established May 29, 1891, with Benjamin F. Finn as postmaster. The office, discontinued July 22, 1895, was again re-established Jan. 22, 1897. On Dec. 3, the name was changed to Ellston. The Ellston Post Office was later discontinued." (McArthur, 1982).

Martins Move to Eugene

The Martins moved into Eugene in 1888 so their sons, Carie and Willie, could attend school. Both became lawyers. Martin taught in Eugene schools. He also served in the state legislature. A Civil War veteran, he took part in all local parades, playing the flute.

The Regis Augustus Pepiot family, in 1868, settled at Gate Creek, on land first occupied by Nicholas Oliver in 1863. The Pepiots were followed in 1870 by the Fayette Thomson family, a mile down river on what is now the Goodpasture Ranch.

There were no settlements beyond the Martins until James Belknap, at age 21, moved up from the Rogue River in 1869 and settled 25 miles east of Vida across from what is now Rainbow.

These were the only families in the area when Benj. Franklin "Huckleberry" Finn brought his family to the McKenzie from Missouri in 1871, according to Finn's son Peter. Pete in interviews late in life referred to a man named King, who was surveying in the area. There were scattered settlers down river.

The Finns "squatted" on land on the south side of the river. The children had to cross the McKenzie in a boat with Thomson children, joining the Pepiots, to attend the first school established in the area, taught by Mrs. Thomson.

THE PEPIOT FAMILY

Regis Augustus Pepiot (also spelled Pepioz or Pepio) was born Jan. 10, 1823, in Verdun, France, the fourth son of Peter Joseph Emme and Mary Josephine (Milliard) Pepiot.

Peter, a Catholic and a shoemaker, was born in France in 1785. He was married first to Mary Josephine Milliard (no further information), and second to Mary Celestine Pequinot from Switzerland, according to Marianne Doyle of Beavercreek, Ohio.

Peter, to escape persecution, brought his family to America from Le Havre, France. They sailed across the ocean on a tall ship, the New Orleans "Fortune." They had to spend the time below deck with other emigrants, and arrived in New Orleans Jan. 22, 1837. They then made their way to Ohio on the Mississippi River flatboats, arriving in winter with several feet of snow on the ground. Peter died in May 1839 in Shelby County, Ohio.

Peter's six children, all born in France, were:

(1) Frederick George, a carpenter, b. 1812, married Angelique Pour Jan. 5, 1859, in Piqua, Ohio; d. April 1, 1893, in Russia, Ohio. (2) Francis Emme, a gardener, b. 1815; d. before March 17, 1845, in Shelby, Ohio. (3) Mary Virginia, b. July 2, 1820; d. Sept. 5, 1856, in Russia, Ohio. (4) Regis Augustus, b. 1823 (see below). (5) Barbara Peliza, b. in 1826 and d. before March 18, 1848. (6) Mary Cecilia, b. in 1830, married Joseph Laurent in Miami County, Ohio, in 1847.

Since Regis was the fourth son of Peter and Mary Josephine, Mary was also the mother of at least the three older children.

Regis was 30 when he traveled with his family to America. On Jan. 7, 1843, in Russia, Shelby County, Ohio, he married Mary Marie Octavia Pierron. Born Jan. 29, 1824, in Hennemont, Meuse, France, she was the daughter of Joseph and Marie Francois (Thiebaux) Pierron.

Fifteen years after marrying and starting a family, Regis and Marie came across on the Oregon Trail by wagons, pulled by ox teams, arriving in Eugene in 1852. They settled in Lane County and were living in the Coburg area when their ninth child, Frederick, was born in 1864.

The Pepiot family moved to Gate Creek in 1868. Benjamin F. "Huck" Finn, pioneer of 1871, was quoted as saying Regis first came up the river on an old mule.

The Pepiots established the community of Gate Creek Ranch, a famous stopping place for stage coaches that traveled along the McKenzie prior to the coming of the automobile.

Regis, a highly respected brick layer and stone mason, died Dec. 15, 1894. The *Daily Eugene Guard* Dec. 17, 1894, said: "He kept the half-way hotel between Eugene and the McKenzie springs for many years and is well known all over the state. . .The many tourists who annually go to the springs will greatly miss the old gentleman, for by his good nature and cordial hospitality the time spent at his place was one of pleasant remembrances of their trip."

Marie died Sept. 10, 1906, at Coburg. Both were buried in the Greenwood Cemetery, Leaburg.

Regis and Marie had 10 children. The first five were born in Ohio, and the others after they came to Oregon. They were:

(1) Octavia, b. Feb. 2, 1843, in St. Valberts, Ohio.

(2) Mary Catherine, b. Dec. 20, 1845, in Dayton, Ohio, married Williamson Gatewood Allen Jan. 26, 1861, in Lane County; d. June 4, 1935, in Monument, Grant County, Ore. Part of the Pepiot genealogy was supplied by Mary Catherine's granddaughter, Maxine M. Schafer of Scholls Ferry Road, Portland.

(3) Joseph Amie, b. May 26, 1848, married Adelle Burnham May 26, 1872, in Harrisburg, Linn County, Ore. They moved to Freewater, Ore., then to Walla Walla, Wa., where at some point in time he started using the name James Aimie, perhaps so as not to be confused with his younger brother, John Joseph, according to his great-grandson, Robert Bostrom, of Lacey, Wa. James was a prison guard for many years. He died in February, 1922, in Freewater, Ore.

His son, Clifford, lived in Walla Walla, then Seattle, moving back to Walla Walla the last half of his life. Bostrom's mother, Carmen Pepiot, and his father, George Bostrom, were married in Seattle and stayed in Western Washington. Bostrom said he was unaware of his Oregon relatives until he and his wife, Marlene, began researching his family.

(4) Mary Adeline, b. in 1850, married Robert Baker; d. in 1878 in Harney County, Ore.

(5) John Joseph, b. Aug. 15, 1852, in Shelby County, Ohio, married, first, Etta Simmons Sept. 21, 1881; second, Mary Matilda (Mollie) Goddard Jan. 2, 1889, in Lane County. Mary was born Jan. 2, 1864, in Tennessee, the daughter of Andrew Jackson and Martha Ann (Simson) Goddard. John died March 8, 1938.

John and Mary had four children: (a) Joseph Elmer, b. 6-2-1891, m. Lena Grupp 9-18-1923, d. 4-10-1970. (b) Martha Eleanor, b. 3-16-1893, m. Walter Wilbur Carter. (c) Elden Harris, b. 1-17-1902, m. Ruth Bivens.

(d) Bertha Viola, b. 10-28-1904, m. Charles E. Brown. She died in Redmond April 10, 1996, at age 91. Her husband died April 22, 1959. She lived most of her life in Springfield. Surviving are sons Harry of Crescent Lake and Harold of Redmond; nine grandchildren, 16 great-grandchildren and four great-great-grandchildren.

Born in Lane County

Other children, born in Lane County, were: (6) Mary Frances, b. Apr. 23, 1855, married Henry Thomson; d. July 23, 1937. (7) Anne Victoria, b. March 10, 1858; married, first, James O'Brien Oct. 8, 1874, second, James Mundell Dec. 21, 1921; she d. Sept. 17, 1942. (8) Cecilia Josephine, b. April 27, 1861; married Charles Powers; she d. Sept. 6, 1952.

(9) Frederick R., born March 8, 1864, in Coburg; married Bertha Belknap July 12, 1888; d. June 6, 1942, in Vida.

(10) Francis Augustus, born Feb. 19, 1867, in Vida, married Florence Ann Goddard Dec. 18, 1889, in Eugene. Florence also was a daughter of Andrew Jackson and Martha Goddard. Francis was postmaster at Gate Creek/Vida around 1900. Reports show the post office after being closed was re-established April 12, 1898, under the name Vida, because the Gate Creek name was too similar to Gales Creek in Washington County. Pepiot selected the name Vida because that was the name of his oldest daughter.

In later years, Francis and his wife moved to Douglas County. He died in Sutherlin July 15, 1953. Florence died in Elkton Jan. 30, 1958. They are buried in Fair Oaks Cemetery, Sutherlin. Their children, all born at Vida, were: (1) Vida Marie, b. 12-21-1892, m. John Willard McCollum, 3-26-1916 in Eugene. Vida died 12-31-1975 at Roseburg. (2) Eva Martha, b. 9-12-1896, m. John James Richard 12-27-1918 at Roseburg, d. 8-6-1977. (3) Regis Andrew, b. 10-18-1899, m. Liola Vista Rowe 7-6-1931 at Silverton, d. 12-11-1978 at Roseburg. (4) Amie Francis, b. 12-9-1903, m. Winnie Thornton Kelly 3-17-1924 at Roseburg, d. 7-18-1981 at Veneta. (5) Pearl Ann, b. 10-12-1906, m. Carl Clyde Thornton 9-17-1924 at Roseburg. (6) Margaret Mellisa, b. 6-17-09, m. Lynn Thornton Moore 5-14-1932.

Fredrick R. Pepiot

Fredrick R. Pepiot, born March 8, 1864, at Coburg. was one of the first settlers, 1888, on Greenleaf Creek, which flows into Lake Creek west of Triangle Lake. He came by the Nelson Mountain route. The combined mail, stage and freight wagon came only to the junction of Nelson and Lake creeks, then went west. There was no road, only a trail in the easterly direction. From there Fred carried all his belongings, including a cook stove and a heavy tool box, on his back to his homestead. He settled on his claim and built a house.

Fred and Bertha Belknap, daughter of Rollin and Mary Belknap, founders of Belknap Springs, were married July 12, 1888, at the home of her brother, James, six miles east of Blue River, by Justice of the Peace C. E. Powers. O. H. Renfrew and F. A. Pepiot were witnesses.

Fred and Bertha, both 24, moved to Greenleaf Creek. He filed for homestead rights July 25, 1889. They farmed the land and raised goats They had no children, but they raised two nieces, Mable Pepiot and Dessie Bressler. (See Rollin Belknap chapter).

A slide nearly buried their house. A *Eugene Register* news item Jan. 14, 1891, said: "Fred Pepiot has succeeded in clearing away the monstrous avalanche that came out of the canyon and lodged near his home in time of the flood." That canyon is now called Slide Canyon. Part of the orchard can be seen on the Bureau of Land Management road off Highway 36.

CHAPTER 20

THE THOMSONS

The name Thomson has long been associated with the McKenzie River Valley. Fayette (Faye) Thomson settled his family in 1870 on the south side of the river on what later became the Goodpasture ranch, one mile west of Vida.

The Thomson name is spelled without a "p". The story goes that when the family emigrated from Scotland, they were too "Scotch" (stingy) to use the extra ink to include a "p" in their name.

Fayette (1823-1913) crossed the plains from Wisconsin in 1852, and took up a donation land claim near Philomath. His wife, the former Marie Tewksbury (1827-1912), with daughter, Lena, sailed around The Horn of South America to Portland three years later. Fayette was soon attracted to the California gold fields, where he spent nine years. Returning to Oregon, he moved his family to the McKenzie in 1870.

John West, long-time McKenzie River guide, in 1980 said Fayette picked the location because it was across the river from Indian Creek, where he had been on a highly successful deer-hunting trip. Everett Thomson, a grandson, in 1980, remembered spending several years at this location at a young age.

Fayette Thomson homesteaded on the south bank of the river below Gate Creek and "wrested a part of the rain forest from the wilds," wrote Nick Bella in the *Springfield News* Dec. 18, 1977.

"When they came on the river in 1870, the road up the McKenzie was little more than a muddy trail from the Willamette Valley to the Cascades. Private contractors operated the highway as a toll road. The Thomsons built several swinging bridges from their cabin to the road across the river, and prayed floods wouldn't leave them completely stranded.

"Life was not easy. Cougars slipped stealthily into their barnyard at night and feasted on unwary livestock. The women washed the family laundry in the river after boiling the clothes in heavy iron pots. Midwifery was an accepted art."

The Thomson's children were: Lena Lacota (1851-1931), Carey Sr. (1856-1940), (see Carey Thomson chapter); Henry (Frank), born in 1859; Winthrop (Winnie), born in 1864; Theron, born in 1866, and Clarence, born in 1869. Birth dates are based on census records. Fayette died in 1913. Marie died six months later.

Lena, born March 31, 1851, near Fox Lake, Dodge, Wisc., married Orren Elisha Brownson Sept. 26, 1869. Brownson, born March 7, 1847, in Franklin, Del., was the son of Julius and Mary (Ogden) Brownson. His occupation was listed in the 1880 census as "mineral baths."

According to information furnished this compiler by Mrs. H. L. (Martha J.) Brownson of Myrtle Creek, two of Lena and Orren's children, Bertha Estelle and Wallace Clifford, are believed to have been born at Leaburg. They had moved to Pendleton by 1889, where their third child, Fogatle (Fayette) Orren, known as Faye, was born. Two other children were Irene Caroline and Florence Goldie. Unverified information is Orren Elisha died a month after arriving in Pendleton. Lena died in 1939. H. L. Brownson is a grandson of Lena.

Henry Thomson married Mary Frances Pepiot. Clarence Thomson died from injuries suffered from hazing while a student at the University of Oregon. Hazing often went to extremes in those days. It was not uncommon for a freshman pledge to be tossed into the icy waters of the nearby millrace for some infraction even in the 1930's.

Theron Thomson, a farmer, homesteaded on property adjoining that of his parents. He lived with them and took care of them in their declining years. Needing help, he hired Miss Frances Morris of Walterville to assist in their care. He ended up marrying her.

Frances Morris was born in England. Her mother, the former Leticia Easton, was married to a man named Morris. They had another child, Ned Morris. Frances and Ned were brought to America at a very young age by their grandparents, Tom and Jane Easton, who settled in Walterville about 1882.

Jane was the sister of Stephen Smeed, who with his wife, Eliza, had emigrated from England earlier and settled in Walterville about 1877. Ned never married. He lived on Millican Lane.

Theron and Frances Thomson had eight children, born in the old Fayette Thomson home. The oldest was Everett.

Blanch, born in 1908, attended Walterville High School. She married Paul Ray. They had eleven children, nine living at this writing. They lived in Cedar Flat. Blanche now lives in Springfield.

Other children of Theron and Frances are: Eileen, married Leo Martin; Fayette; Clarence, who was killed in an auto accident; Homer; Geneva, married Joe Long, and Lena, died young.

It was Blanche Ray who corrected this compiler on the spelling of the Thomson name in an earlier writing in which the conventional spelling of Thompson, with a "p," was used. So I had to go through about a hundred books and knock the "p" out of Thompson with a whiteout. The error was corrected in later printings.

Winthrop Thomson took possession of the Fayette Thomson homestead after his parent's deaths. There were 386 acres with two acres on the north side of the river on Indian Creek at mp. 26. He constructed a shingle mill and a feed grinder operated by an overshot water wheel. A ferry and footbridge spanned the river at Indian Creek.

Goodpasture Ranch

The Thomson property was sold first to Dr. Gullion, a Eugene eye, ear, nose and throat specialist. It then was acquired in 1923 by Benjamin Franklin "Frank" Goodpasture, a Eugene car dealer, and his wife, Mazie.

Benjamin was born in 1877. He was the son of Thurston and Susan Goodpasture.

Thurston, born in 1856, was one of six children of Alexander and Elizabeth Goodpasture, both of whom were born in Tennessee. They came west in the early 1850's and settled north of Eugene near today's Valley River Center. Alexander was listed as 36 in the 1860 Lane County census, and Elizabeth, 35. The children, ages as of 1860, were: Martha, 15; Salinda, 12; Nancy, 9; Thurston, 5; William, 2, and May, three months. Tnurston's wife, Susan, was born in 1852.

Indian Creek Ferry operated across the McKenzie, at mp. 41.0, just above the present covered Goodpasture Bridge, which now serves the area. Just before the B. F. Goodpastures could take possession of the Vida property, the footbridge and ferry were swept away by a flood and had to be replaced. Carey Thomson rebuilt the footbridge and Henry Daughenbaugh, the ferry.

Thurston and Susan Goodpasture, who had just retired from their 500-acre farm near Spencer's Butte, moved to the Vida property in 1925.

Benjamin sold his car dealership and set out a filbert orchard. Filbert stock was acquired from the Dorris Ranch at Springfield.

The water wheel was converted to a five-kilowatt light plant during the late 1920's, providing the only electric lights on the river. Lights were installed on the footbridge and operated night and day.

Benjamin donated land for construction of the Goodpasture Bridge, serving the south bank of the river. The bridge, built by Lane County in 1938-39, also was referred to as the Thomson Bridge, as it traversed from the McKenzie Highway to the old Thomson place. Benjamin died in 1958.

Robert F. "Bob" Goodpasture, son of B. F. and Mazie Goodpasture, was born in Eugene Oct. 4, 1915. He attended Vida Grade School, University High School in Eugene and the University of Oregon. He served in the Oregon National Guard.

On April 13, 1940, he married Marjorie Osborn. They had two sons, James of Vida and Joseph of Everett, Wa., and two grandchildren.

Robert was a filbert farmer and river guide until the mid-1940's He then turned to cabinet making. He built cabinets for Sears Roebuck and the R. S. Chamber's home in Eugene. Recently he built cabinets for the Tourist Information Center at Leaburg Lake.

He died at his home Nov. 15, 1996, at age 81.

Rollin Simeon Belknap   Mary Ann Belknap

CHAPTER 21

The Belknaps

The names Belknap, Finn, Wycoff and Sims, interrelated through marriages, were almost synonymous with early days on the upper McKenzie River.

James Henry Belknap (my grandfather), for whom Big and Little Belknap Craters on the Cascade Summit and other McKenzie landmarks were named, was the first settler of duration on the upper river. In the summer of 1869, at age 21, he established a claim six miles east of Blue River across from what became Rainbow, now Holiday Farm.

Two years later, 1871, his parents, Rollin Simeon and Mary Ann (Smith) Belknap, with three of their four daughters -- Dora A., Cora Alzina and Bertha A. -- literally hacked out a road into what became Belknap Springs, and developed the resort.

The Belknap ancestry can be traced to the year 1450 in Sawbridgeworth, Hertz Co., England, where a Richard Beltoft had large farm holdings. Historians say the name appears originally to have been Bealknap -- Beale or Beal, a passage between hills; a narrow pass. Knap is a low hill or knoll, which gave rise to this surname.

The lineage follows through a son, Henry; his son, Richard (1520-1599), then Bennet Beltoft (1560-1624) to Abraham (1589/90-1643/4), the immigrant, who settled in Lynn, Mass., in 1635, and adopted the name Belknap. The line continues from Abraham's son Samuel I (1627-17 - ?), a joiner or cabinet maker-farmer, through Ebenezer (1667-1762), a joiner-farmer, whose family was the longest-lived on record, several reaching or exceeding one hundred years of age.

Next came Samuel III (1703-1757), then Simeon I (1726-1804), a prosperous New England farmer; Simeon II (1758-1841), Revolutionary War captive involved in a most bizarre escapes from a St. Lawrence River island prison, and one of the first to settle in Randolph, Vt.

His son, Simeon Belknap III, born in Randolph, Vt., Aug. 13, 1795, married Sophia Pierce June 6, 1826. They had two children, Alzina, born Feb. 2, 1822, and Rollin Simeon, Nov. 30, 1823. Simeon III died when Rollin was three, and his mother died when he was 11. Rollin and Alzina grew up in the home of an uncle, Levi Belknap.

BELKNAP SETTLEMENT

Jessie Belknap from another branch of the Belknap family, traceable back to the same Samuel III, located in what became known as Belknap Settlement in the Belfountain area, three miles northwest of Monroe in Linn County, Ore., in 1848.

Samuel III had a son, Samuel Jr. or Samuel IV. He died of heat prostration during the Battle of Bunker Hill in the Revolutionary War. His son, Jonas Newton Belknap (1758 - 1824), was Jessie's father.

Jessie, born Jan. 26, 1792, in Cherry Valley, Ostego County, N. Y., married Jane Garlinghouse Feb. 20, 1812. She was born March 26, 1792, in Pennsylvania. They had seven children: Kezia or Kesiah, Hannah, George, Ransom A., Talitha Cuma, Harley A. and Corrington.

Ransom (1820-1896) founded Belknap Settlement Oct. 15, 1847. Coming west with Ransom were his wife, Mahala, and two children; L. D. and Hannah Belknap Gilbert and their six children; Oren and Nancy Belknap Starr and their four children; Samuel Fletcher and Talitha Cumi Belknap Starr and their two children. They came overland by ox team on the old Scott-Applegate trail with the migration of 1847, and traveled for a time with the Oskaloosa Company, headed by David D. Davis.

Jessie, Jane and other Belknap family members came in 1848. Jessie died in November 1881. Jane died in December 1876.

ROLLIN SIMEON BELKNAP

Rollin Belknap married Mary Ann Smith in Boston Oct. 8, 1844. Mary Ann was born in Raymond, N. H., Jan. 5, 1822. Two children born in Boston were Clara Sophia, Nov. 17, 1846, and James Henry, March 25, 1848. In 1849, Rollin left Boston by boat, via the Isthmus of Panama, for San Francisco and the California gold fields. Two years later he had drifted to newly discovered gold fields in the Rogue River Valley.

In 1853, he joined 40 men, recruited by Perry B. Marple and outfitted with horses, guns and supplies, who left Jacksonville to explore Coos Bay. Rollin, 30 years old, strong and robust, was described in his Rogue Indian War pension papers as 5 feet, 10 inches; weight, 176 pounds, blue eyes, light hair and fair complexion.

Twenty-one men, disillusioned because they found no gold, only some coal deposits, turned back in the vicinity of what is now Myrtle Point. The remaining 19 men, including Rollin, continued on to establish the first Coos settlement at what became Empire.

During that period, Rollin sent for his wife and children, who sailed around The Horn of South America. They landed at Port Orford, which was settled in 1851 and the only port open between San Francisco and the Columbia River. Rollin then located his family on a homestead -- Riverbanks Farm -- on the Rogue River at Wilderville.

He fought in the Rogue Indian War of 1855-56, part of the time as a spy. Mary and their two children, left alone, were threatened by Indians. She cowed them with a dog and a gun left by a friendly Indian chief who had warned her of impending danger. The Indians murdered a nearby family. Mary went to Fort Vanoy and served as a nurse.

Rollin participated in the formative years of fledgling Josephine County, serving as the first chairman of the board of commissioners, 1856-57, according to official Josephine County records. The first county seat was at Waldo, known as Sailors Diggings, a mining hamlet in the southwestern part of the county where seafaring men dug for gold. The county seat was moved to Kerbyville a year later, then to Grants Pass in the early 1880's. Rollin served in other official capacities, was councilor to the Oregon Territorial Council, equivalent to senator, from Josephine and Jackson counties, 1857-58, and again as commissioner, 1860-61.

Three more children were born in Josephine County -- Dora A., Dec. 30, 1859; Cora Alzina, 1861, and Bertha A., July 12, 1863.

Clara Sophia, their oldest daughter, married Robert Edwin Lockwood Sr. Feb. 19, 1863. They lived in Kerbyville but moved to Canyon City in Grant County, Ore., prior to 1870.

Rollin farmed his homestead at Wilderville, worked a gold mine near Kerbyville and worked for the county. About 1869, he moved his family to Albany. That same year, James, at age 21, located on property across the river from the future Rainbow. In 1873, he married Ella Jane Finn, 19, daughter of Benj. F. and Mary Finn, pioneers of 1871. James and Ella had fifteen children, only seven of whom lived to adulthood.

In 1871, Rollin and Mary moved to the McKenzie, where they founded Belknap Springs, discovered in 1859 by the McBride Party. He is believed to have relocated the springs while exploring in 1869, and conceived the idea to develop them as a health resort.

Mary Ann Belknap was quoted in a newspaper interview as saying about 1871 they bought "what is known as Belknap Springs on the McKenzie. They traveled in a wagon and camped along the route for several weeks, cutting the road." The McKenzie road, such as it was, extended to Central Oregon, but bypassed the springs by a mile. They "opened the bathing resort and kept the place four years," Mary said.

Maple Stobie (1969: 48) wrote: "Rollin built a hotel on the south side of the river on a beautiful level, tree-shaded bench and piped hot water from the springs across the river in a cedar flume."

Belknap and Thomas M. Martin of Vida were the first white men of record to visit Clear Lake, generally considered to be the headwaters of the McKenzie River. The lake, 20 miles beyond the Springs, "is fed by numerous underground springs, Great Springs, Fish Lake Creek and Ikenick Creek. The water is exceptionally clear and one can see nearly 100 feet to the bottom. The southeast corner or arm was once known as Bock Bay. There is a unique, preserved evergreen forest-underwater in the lake." (Williams, 1991).

Whether the McBride Party actually found the lake is not certain. One of the first descriptions of the underwater forest was contained in an article in the *Oregon State Journal*, Eugene, Sept. 1, 1894, recounting a trip into the lake by Belknap and Martin some 20 years before. The article, telling of a much later visit by some Albany residents, began:

"Some gentlemen from Albany have returned from a trip to the headwaters of the McKenzie river and are enthusiastic over the beautiful scenery and especially the great falls of that river. Very few people have ever seen those falls although they were known to the early settlers of the McKenzie fully 25 years ago. People generally suppose the McKenzie river has its source in the snow mountains called the Three Sisters. This is a mistake.

"The McKenzie heads in Clear Lake 25 or maybe 35 miles north of the most northern peak of the Three Sisters. The river is nothing but a small stream here and after leaving the lake rushes down a canyon and leaps over a great precipice, making one of the grandest falls in the world. After leaving the great pool below the falls, we are told the river entirely disappears under the lava beds and for many miles is only seen now and then through crevices in the lava.

"Talk about scenery, why there is yet some of the grandest in the world on the upper McKenzie and it has never been fully explored. It is very difficult to reach this country. Tourists usually go to the snow mountains, leaving the beautiful Clear Lake and the magnificent water falls many miles to their left.

"About twenty years ago (1874) Mr. Belknap and T. M. Martin went to the scenic country at the head of the McKenzie. They packed food and blankets on their backs and explored a considerable amount of mountain country, which few if any white men had ever seen. They followed up the river from Belknap Springs to its head.

"At the great falls the river was crossed. Just on the brink of the precipice above the falls the river is very narrow. They cut long fir poles and laid them clear across. On these wiggly poles, Belknap stood upright and walked across the river, when one misstep would have carried him to eternity over the falls. Mr. Martin, being a minister at that time, got down on his hands and knees and 'cooned' it across. They camped there overnight and caught some mountain trout. Just below the falls, Mr. Martin got into a monster 'yellow-jacket' nest, a fact he remembers vividly to this day.

"They built a raft and reconnoitered on Clear Lake for several days. They told about how their raft would occasionally strike the tops of huge fir trees, many of which were standing upright in the deep clear lake. The country offers more inducement to the genuine tourist and explorer who is willing to rough it a little than any section of country in the Cascade Mountains."

Rollin and Mary had daughters, Dora, Alzina and Bertha with them. Dora, on Jan. 1, 1874, the day after her fifteenth birthday, was married to John Whitlock Sims, 34, employed by Rollin as proprietor.

John and Dora homesteaded two miles west of McKenzie Bridge.

A post office under the name Salt Springs was established Oct. 26, 1874, with Rollin S. Belknap first postmaster. In 1875, he and Mary sold the Springs to Peter Settle and John Miller, who changed the name to Belknap's Spring. (See Belknap Springs chapter).

Listed variously as a farmer, wool grower and stock trader in census records, Rollin didn't stay on the McKenzie. The 1880 census for Brewster Precinct in Coos County listed Rollin, Mary and Bertha, also a year-old granddaughter, Hadassah (Dessie) as residents. He also worked as a ship's carpenter at Scottsburg.

CLARA SOPHIA LOCKWOOD

Clara Sophia, oldest daughter of Rollin and Mary Belknap, was born Nov. 17, 1846, in Boston, Mass. On Feb. 19, 1863, she was married to Robert Edwin Lockwood Sr. The wedding took place at her parents' home, Rev. P. M. Starr officiating, the *Jacksonville Sentinel* reported.

Lockwood was born in 1843 in Van Diemans Land, Tasmania, Australia. They lived in Kerbyville but moved to Canyon City in Grant County, Ore., prior to 1870.

Robert and Clara had ten children. The first three, born in Kerbyville, were Alonzo, Laura Bell and Robert Edwin Jr. (Laura Bell died young). The other children, born in Canyon City, were Willie Clyde, Nellie P., Reuben Dale, Lennie A., Leon Oliver and Bertha M. and twin.

Lockwood Sr. was shot to death July 5, 1888, by two escaping prisoner in Canyon City, where he had served as a deputy sheriff and jailer for eight years. He was killed his last day as a deputy. The sheriff had held him on the job one more day. He went to the jail for a final check on the prisoners, when he was overcome and shot with his own gun. The culprits were caught and summarily hanged.

Robert Lockwood

Clara Sophia Lockwood

Clara and Robert were divorced at the time and he had remarried. He was buried in the Canyon City cemetery, under direction of Homer Lodge No. 78, Ancient Order of United Workmen.

Clippings from the Canyon City newspaper referred to frequent and lengthy visits by Clara to the McKenzie River Valley. The last visit of record was for three months, prior to the births of the twins at McKenzie Bridge. It is known Rollin Belknap spent some time in Canyon City in the mid-1880s. Clara was residing in Boise, Ida., at the time of her death Oct. 13, 1921. Two of her children, daughter Lennie Fife and son Leon, also were living in Boise, Ida., when they died.

CORA ALZINA BRESSLER

Cora Alzina Belknap married John Henry Bressler Feb. 16, 1878. Jackson County records show the marriage took place at the house of R. S. Belknap, conducted by Abraham Miller Jr., minister. Witnesses were Belknap and G. W. Bressler. We have no knowledge Rollin and Mary were living in Jackson County at that time.

A daughter, Dessie K. Bressler, was born to John and Cora Alzina Nov. 27, 1878. The 1880 census for Brewster Precinct, Coos County, listed a year-old granddaughter, Hadassah (Dessie), living there with Rollin, Mary and Bertha. Alzina died in 1893, at age 32, at the home of her sister, Bertha, on Greenleaf Creek in Lane County.

Bertha Belknap and Fredrick R. Pepiot were married July 12, 1888, at the home of her brother, James at Blue River, by Justice of the Peace C. E. Powers. O. H. Renfrew and F. A. Pepiot were witnesses.

Fred, born March 8, 1864, at Coburg, was one of the first settlers on Greenleaf Creek, west of Triangle Lake. He and Bertha, both 24, moved there the year of their marriage. Bertha described many lonely nights when Fred was gone for supplies, with just her horse, dog and her gun for protection. A slide nearly buried their house in the 1890's.

Fred and Bertha had no children, but raised two nieces. An August 1897 news item said, "Two nieces are living with the Pepiots -- Miss D. (Dessie) Bressler and Mable Pepiot." Dessie is shown in a picture of school children in the little log schoolhouse on the Sims' place in 1890 or 1891. She also attended school at Walterville. She was listed as living with James and Ella Belknaps in the 1900 census.

Dessie married Frederick Easton, of Walterville, Aug. 18, 1900. A daughter, Cora, was born Oct. 10, 1901. Dessie died in 1910. Easton, on Jan. 15, 1912, married Katie Hartwig. Their children were Ivan, Marvin, Veola (Rasmussen), Erma (Brooks) and Nellie (Holcomb).

Cora married John Sherman Sheasley Oct. 29, 1919. Their children were Wade, Springfield lumber broker, Irene (Curts) of Hillsboro and Shirley (Fisher) of Waldport.

Rollin spent some time in Canyon City with his daughter, Clara. He went to Seattle in 1885, then to Alaska for two years around 1890, and to California until 1895. He returned to live for 10 years with his son, James, at Rainbow. Mary during that period lived part of the time with James and also with daughter, Dora Sims. She moved to Bertha Pepiot's home at Greenleaf about 1900.

Cora Alzina Bressler   Bertha Belknap Pepiot

Although separated many years, both Rollin and Mary were at Bertha's home at the times of their deaths. A news item in October 1900 said, "Mrs. Mary Belknap comes to live with her daughter, Bertha Pepiot." An item in April 1903 said, "R. S. Belknap arrives at the Pepiot home. He returned to the McKenzie after a week."

He returned again in September. Mary died March 16, 1904, following a lingering illness. Rollin died at age 84, Oct. 23, 1907.

Mrs. Elma Rust of Triangle Lake Road commented: "Fred and Bertha Pepiot were kind and helpful people and were always taking someone into their home. When Bertha's mother became paralyzed, she stayed her remaining years there, and Bertha also cared for her ailing sister (Alzina) and her father, who both died at her home."

Fred, a road supervisor, was a delegate to the Republican convention in April 1904. He and Bertha moved to Junction City. Bertha died there of cancer at age 66, Feb. 6, 1930. Fred died at Vida June 18, 1942. Both were buried in the Greenwood Cemetery near Leaburg.

Mrs. Rust received a letter from Cora Sheasley (date not given), from Lowell, asking: "Do you have any record of Fred Pepiot who lived up Deadwood Creek about the turn of the century? A landslide nearly buried their home. She (Bertha) was a Belknap. Her parents were Rollen (Rollin) and Mary Belknap. They were separated in their last years. Both died at Bertha Pepiot's home.

"My grandmother, Cora (Alzina) Bressler, also passed away at the Pepiot home and is buried beside her parents in the little cemetery on the hill."

Benjamin "Huck" Finn   Mary Ann Finn

CHAPTER 22

Benjamin F. "Huckleberry" Finn

Although Benjamin Franklin Finn (1832-1919), didn't come on the upper McKenzie until 1871, long after Oregon became a state, he made his name as a teller of tall tales. He claimed to be the original "Huckleberry" Finn immortalized by Mark Twain (Samuel Clemens).

Of Irish and German ancestry, B. F. "Huck" Finn brought his family west by wagon train from Ohio, via Michigan, stopping off for a time in Missouri, where a daughter, Ida, was born in 1869. They joined other western-bound pioneers before proceeding on their four-month trip to Oregon to settle along the McKenzie near Vida.

Six feet tall, Civil War navy veteran, wounded when shot in the leg by a poison arrow, Finn was 39 when he went up the McKenzie. One of his greatest feats -- by his own admission -- was rolling a huge monolith out of the way with his span of mules. Fact or fiction, the rock, 35 miles east of Eugene, still bears his name -- Finn Rock.

Born in Elyria, Lorain County, Ohio, March 4, 1832, as near as we can establish, Finn was 87 years old when he died Feb. 11, 1919. However, a birth year of 1823 and ages of 93 and 95 keep popping up in certain newspaper articles, a Bible record and a legal document which mention an age of 93.

Finn's claim to being the immortal Huckleberry Finn is best told in his own words quoted in a news story in 1915, at age 83 years.

Contrary to historical records, Finn claimed to have been raised on a farm in Missouri near the home of Samuel Clemens. Finn said he was first mate on the Mississippi River boat Shotwell, and Clemens was one of the pilots. Later, Finn, Clemens and Tom Sawyer bought the riverboat Gray Eagle, he said.

"'I was 26 years old at that time' (making the year 1858). 'I got the name Huckleberry Finn on the Gray Eagle in a little racket that happened. . .You see, I was first mate, and if anything didn't go right I was the "huckleberry." That was what we called the man who gets in between a fight. . .We stayed on the river until 1860. . ."Charley" Clemens went to Denver and stopped there to write books, and he didn't do much of anything else, I guess. Tom went to St. Paul and lived there until he died. He has been dead about 12 years.'

"Finn claimed to be Clemens' traveling companion around 1860 from Missouri to Denver, that they lived for a time together in Denver, when Twain wrote his stories about 'Huckleberry Finn.' He claimed Clemens was actually writing about the life of B. F. Finn."

In a Seattle *Times* interview June 24, 1917, with his picture, Finn's age was given as 93 years. Excerpts follow:

"SEATTLE TIMES, June 24, 1917 -- Ask Dad! He knows. He'll tell you this photograph of B. F. Finn is 'just exactly' like the picture of Huckleberry Finn's father as conceived by the illustrator of Mark Twain's masterpiece printed when Dad was a boy. But 'Ben' Finn doesn't claim to be Huck's renegade father. He says he is Huckleberry himself, the one original, dyed in the wool, Injun-hunting partner of Tom Sawyer.

"'Huck' spent last week with his younger brother, E. A. (Erastus) Finn at 313 Thirty-second Avenue. Mark Twain's famous character is no longer the knobby-fisted, indomitable 'Huck' of the days of long ago, when he and Tom and 'the rest of the boys' sought adventure and found it. He is now 93 years old, with the same long willowy white whiskers draping his chin and neck as did the father in Mark Twain's description. He is bent and withered with age.

"When 'Huck' left Seattle yesterday for his home 30 miles out of Eugene, in a farm hewn out of the woods, he announced time had forced him to draw the curtain upon the one thing he liked best -- roaming.

"'I was on my way to Bellingham, but when I reached Seattle I was just tired out,' said 'Huck'. 'I am going back to my farm in the woods now and stay there my remaining days. Ever since I was twelve years old when my father died and I started down the Mississippi, I have loved to travel -- rather to roam. But I guess I must settle down now.'

"As he sat in a reminiscent mood at his brother's home yesterday morning, just before his departure, 'Huckleberry' recalled a trip across the plains from Missouri to Denver, Colo., with Mark Twain when he was 25 years old (year 1857).

"'I had just about mastered my trade as a bricklayer,' said Huck. 'Twain, of course, was writing some. When we got in Denver we were both broke and we rented a house on the outskirts of town. The money wasn't coming in very fast, and in order that we might make it appear we were not so bad off financially, Clemens and I would go about the neighborhood at night and collect a lot of tin cans with the labels on. We would scatter those cans about our back door so the people would think we were eating oysters, peas and other things that our palates had lost acquaintance with.'" (A typical Finn story?)

"'Finally Clemens got work on a Denver newspaper, but he did not make much money,' continued Huck. 'I was doing some brick laying.'

"Finn declares it was during the time he and Twain lived together in Denver that the famous author started to write the 'Huckleberry Finn' stories. 'Of course, he added some fiction for his stories,' reflected 'Huck.' 'He exaggerated things somewhat, but he pictured the lives of Tom and myself pretty well.'

"If there is one thing Finn is proud of it is his cognomen 'Huckleberry.' It is really a cognomen, he says.

"From the time he was 12 years of age until he bought a tract of land in Eugene (should be Vida), Finn says he had 'no place where he could call home. In fact, I really didn't want a home,' he said, 'I wanted to roam.'

"'They called me Huckleberry because I was always on top,' he said. 'I only fought when I felt I was in the right, and I always won. I was ready with two fists when the challenge came.' 'Huck' admits he was a prety (sic) mischievous fellow in his younger days but he doesn't think he was 'such a bad kid.'

"There is no glitter of mischief in 'Huck's' features now. Back of the white whiskers the wrinkles of age are marked. His step is uncertain and his hands quiver.

"'I've about spent the time I've been allotted,' said Finn. 'I suppose I should be satisfied, but I long for return of the day when I was 'Huckleberry Finn' of the Mississippi Valley.'"

If such were true, I cannot but marvel at the versatility of Benj. F. "Huck" Finn to be in so many places at the same time. It is our humble opinion he'd told the story so many times he had grown to believe it. At least, he was not about to change his story in old age.

Finn mentioned his destination was Bellingham. His son, Pete, was logging in the area (1917). His brother, Erastus, who lived in Seattle, came across the plains in the 1880's, after his wife died.

A Convincing Story

A most convincing story of Huck Finn's life on the Mississippi is told in a newspaper interview, found in a scrapbook at the Oregon

Historical Library in Portland, date line Eugene, Ore., March 27, 1915. A headline read, "Huckleberry Finn, 90, Recalls Life on the McKenzie."

He "crossed the Plains and Rockies to the McKenzie, arrived broke and looked for a place to winter." He "lived by the rifle and sold hides in Eugene and came out money ahead." He "erected the largest turpentine factory in the state," sold rosin and turpentine of his own preparation. He conducted a hotel and catered to fishermen.

The news story repeats Finn's claim he grew up on a Missouri farm, which he apparently told to many friends, and about his life on the Mississippi. It repeated his claim to being the "Huckleberry who got between two fighters," and lost a couple of fingers in a fight.

He said, "I was first mate under Capt. Hull -- whose death was noted a few days ago -- on the Steamer Shotwell, the fastest boat on the Mississippi. Its fastest time was four days, seven hours from New Orleans to St. Louis." He said he and Clemens found the boat, The Gray Eagle, downstream in pretty bad condition, but they "fitted her out" and two years later challenged Capt. Hull to a race, which, of course, they won, including a bet for $5,000.

He said he was 26 at the time, making the year 1858. He said they stayed on the River until 1860, but hostilities between the states were brewing, so they headed north. They got as far as Cairo, in southern Illinois, when their ship was seized. He said the boat cost them $9,000, but the government paid them $12,000. Clemens went to Denver and Tom (Sawyer) went to St. Paul.

"I don't know where he got those stories about Tom and I," he commented. "In the War (date not listed) I served on the Mississippi, first on the gunboat Carondalette." The Carondalette "was the second monitor ever built and sure was a dandy."

Webster's Dictionary defines a monitor as an ironclad warship with flat deck and low freeboard fitted with one or more revolving turrets carrying heavy guns -- like The Monitor which fought the Merrimack in the Civil War.

The Carondalette was disabled at the Battle of Memphis, Huck said. "They punched her there, at Memphis, and it took the whole crew to keep her afloat. We got her plugged and rammed her up to Mound City (Ill.), three miles above the junction of the Ohio and Mississippi rivers. There were no docks and we hauled her up on ways." He was transferred to the Great Western. "I stayed on that boat as signal quartermaster. After the War I went home to my family in Kalamazoo, (Mich.)"

He stayed there four years, then traded for a plantation in Missouri. "I buried one child there, then sold out for what I could get." He said they crossed the Plains and the Rockies. They "came up the Platte (River) to Salt Lake, then to Boise City and over the Barlow Trail to Brownsville (Ore.) We came here in 1870 and reached Eugene with six children, a wife, two mules, two horses and $14.10."

Huck said they arrived broke and came up on the McKenzie looking for a place to winter. "I had my old needle gun -- the same gun with which the Germans licked the French. I was first on the McKenzie.

Old Regis Pepiot came the next spring with pack horses."

(It is generally conceded the Pepiots and Thomsons already were there, when the Finns arrived).

Finn continued: "I hunted all winter and killed deer and hauled the hides to the Valley. I gave all my money to my wife, and at the end of winter she had $350, so we could live on the McKenzie. That was 45 years ago. My wife died there and I'll be there when I die." He ran a turpentine business and worked in Eugene in summer. "I built a third of the houses in Eugene.

"It's a pretty life to look back on," he reminisced, recalling his days on the Mississippi. "In the spring we started for Lake Pippin, but many times we had to lay over in Capital Prairie, until the ice would melt so we could get to St. Paul. But I'd rather whip fish out of the McKenzie anytime," he concluded.

Much of this news account is true, but portions are open to question. This writer remembers my Great-grandpa Finn at age 85 as a tottering old man, with a long white beard and white hair, who had to have his "Jamaica Ginger" (whiskey) brought up the McKenzie on the stage. He was living at the home of his daughter, Ella Belknap, his last few years. He was always there when my family visited.

Benjamin Franklin Finn's Civil War pension application papers clearly state he was born March 4, 1832, in Elyria, Lorain County, Ohio. That is the birth date written on his death certificate, signed by his daughter, Ella Jane Belknap, and on his tombstone in Greenwood Cemetery at Leaburg. This date also corresponds with census records.

Irish Ancestry

Finn's death certificate shows his father was born in Ireland, and his mother, last name Snider, born in Germany. However, the 1880 census shows both Benjamin and his wife's parents being born in Pennsylvania. The 1910 census is quite clear Finn's mother was born in Germany. His father's birth place appears to be Pennsylvania but was written over and is almost illegible.

Our unconfirmed information is Benjamin's father's name was James. The 1790 census lists a "James Finn" and a "Solomon Finn" living in Lucerne County, Pa. The 1840 census lists a James Finn living in Elyria, Ohio. It may have been Benj. Finn's grandfather who was born in Ireland, and either his mother or his grandmother born in Germany.

Thomas "Tom" Trotter, a great-great-grandson of Finn, has a copy of Erastus Finn's death certificate. The certificate, identifies Erastus' father as 'Erastus' Finn and his mother as Rebecca Snyder (note spellings of Snider-Snyder). It also indicates both the father and mother were born in Pennsylvania. The informant was J. M. Arnold, Erastus A. Finn's son-in-law who died many years ago.

The only information we have on the Finns' immediate family is contained in a quotation from Erastus Alvenza Finn. He, too, was interviewed by the *Seattle Times*. Erastus, born in 1835, confirmed his brother's claim to being the prototype of "Huckleberry" Finn. He told *The Times'* reporter, "Mother called him Benjamin Franklin Finn. There were six children, two girls and four boys, all born in Lorain County, Ohio. When Dad died the boys were all bound over but Huck ran away. He hired out on the boats running up and down the Mississippi River and the Ohio and the Missouri."

Marriage License

Finn married Mary Ann Halter, also born in Elyria, in 1833. Their marriage certificate, somewhat blurred by water damage after being rescued with other family papers from a flood, lists their marriage date as Nov. 30, 1861, but the ink-written date was later changed in pencil to Nov. 30, 1851, believed to be accurate. By 1861 Benj. and Mary already had two children, the first born in 1853/54.

The certificate says they were married in Schoolcraft, Kalamazoo County, Mich. Schoolcraft is given as Finn's residence and his age 27, and Elyria, Ohio, as Mary's residence, age 24. Finn's pension papers list their marriage date as 1850. We cannot reconcile these variations.

Benjamin and Mary had seven children, according to census and family Bible records obtained by Finn's great-great-grandson, Gary Kernutt and his wife, Donna, of Eugene, Ore.

The oldest, Charles Eugene, was born Feb. 12, 1853/54. Next was Ella Jane, Aug. 31, 1855, both born in Elyria. The others were Mary Ada, March 3, 1861; Lewis (Louis) Napoleon, Oct. 12, 1862; Emma B., April 18, 1864; Arthur Peter, March 13, 1867, all born in Schoolcraft, Mich., and Ida Druscilla, July 29, 1869, in Montevallo, Mo. Mary Ada died in 1869.

If Huck Finn cavorted with Sam Clemens in the early days it would have had to be some time after Ella's birth in 1855 in Ohio and before Mary Ada was born in 1861 in Michigan.

Encyclopedia Americana says:

"In April 1857, while en route from Cincinnati to New Orleans, Clemens apprenticed himself to Horace Bixby as a river pilot. He was licensed two years later, and continued in that lucrative profession until the Civil War closed the river. . .In July 1861, after serving briefly in a volunteer company, which disbanded before being sworn into the Confederate army, Clemens went west with his brother, Orion, who had been appointed Territorial Secretary of Nevada." In August, 1862, Clemens joined the staff of the Virginia City, Nev., Enterprise.

"Huckleberry" Finn

The true "Huckleberry" Finn was the son of the town drunk in Hannibal, Mo. James Playsted Wood's *Spunkwater, Spunkwater* "A Life of Mark Twain," Copyright 1968, says:

"Huckleberry Finn was no composite but one. He appears in both *Tom Sawyer* and in *The Adventures of Huckleberry Finn* just as he was when Mark Twain knew him when they were boys. His real name was Tom Blankenship. Son of the town drunkard, clad in rags, living as he could, 'Tom' or 'Huck' was the envy of Mark Twain and all the rest of his gang. Huck came and went as he pleased with none to answer to, none to forbid him to smoke or indulge in any of the other delights they all found precious. It was Tom Blankenship who had the raccoon skin which the boys sold over and over to a storekeeper, who was slow to suspect their trickery."

It is not our purpose to debunk a wonderful yarn that provided so much amusement in days gone by, but to set the records a bit straighter for historical documentation. While it was not uncommon for husbands and fathers in those days to leave their families for long periods sometimes to fend for themselves, we have no information that was the case. As for "Huck" growing up in Missouri, that is open to question.

But here the mystery thickens!

Benjamin F. "Huck" Finn is not listed in the July 15, 1860, census for Elyria Township, Lorain County, Ohio. That census shows his wife Mary Ann, age 27, and children, Charles Eugene, 6, and Ella Jane, 4, living in the household of Mary's mother, Rosanna Halter, age 64, and her sons, Abraham Halter, 31, and Peter Halter, 22.

Where was Benjamin Franklin "Huck" Finn? It was during these years he claimed he was on the Mississippi with Samuel Clemens.

John Craig (*Springfield News*, 1970) wrote: "Although known as 'the biggest liar on the McKenzie River,' 'Huck' presented a good case for having been the prototype of author Mark Twain's masterpiece, 'Huckleberry Finn.' Only the very self-confident or a history expert could dismiss Finn's claim without further investigation."

The Seattle *Times* quoted Erastus Finn as saying, "After a while the war broke out and Huck joined the army. That's where he and Hank (the author's nickname, he said) Clemens got acquainted. Hank was in the quartermaster's department and Huck helped him. I suppose they were two of a kind and got together on the story part."

From this account, it appears Erastus may have been as much a liar -- pardon, a teller of tall tales -- as his more famous brother. Clemens did serve in the Civil War -- for about two weeks in 1862 with a volunteer group which disbanded.

Huck Finn also served in the Civil War, after he had three more children. Veterans still place a United States flag over his grave. His pension application papers state he enlisted Aug. 26, 1864, and was discharged by Fleet Paymaster Davis June 13, 1865. He served in the U. S. Navy as acting quartermaster on the USS Great Western. Chances he and Clemens met during the Civil War are remote.

Nevertheless, Erastus declared his brother's claim was true. "I was in many of those pranks myself," he said "You see, I traveled with Huck part of the time after I ran away from my foster father."

Erastus' pension papers state he was born Feb. 18, 1835, in Elyria, Ohio. If Huck was born in 1823, he would have been 12 years old when Erastus was born. That was the age Huck said he was when he ran away from his foster home. But he would have been only three years older than Erastus if he (Huck) was born in 1832.

Finn's granddaughter, the late Mrs. Clayton (Mabel Ward) Nestle, said one of her uncle's cousins, Ed Rice of Hanna, Ind., and his family visited the Leaburg area many years ago. Rice said he had documentary evidence proving Benjamin to have been Clemens' friend and the model for his novel. She had no idea what that "proof" might have been.

Benjamin Finn's son, Peter, didn't believe his father's story. "Perhaps casting the longest shadow across Finn's story is the fact he was notorious for his tall yarns," the Springfield News item said.

Remote Possibility

Benj. Finn in his Times' interview said he ran away from home at age 12 after his father died. That would have been in 1844. Erastus said Huck worked on river boats.

The part about "Huck" living as a child in Missouri seems far fetched, unless it was after he ran away from home at age 12. There is the remote possibility Finn was with Twain on the Mississippi riverboat. And there is the possibility Clemens did name his all-important character after Benjamin Franklin "Huck" Finn. There is even the possibility he went to Denver with Twain, but if he did it was only briefly. Clemens didn't write his books in Denver, according to authorities. His books came much later, after he went to Nevada.

Finn truly was an actor. Everything he did was an act, as evidenced by his ability to entertain guests or strangers at his hotel, keeping them spellbound, while, with a perfectly straight face, spinning yarn after yarn which had little, if any, basis in fact.

"Huck" Finn definitely did serve in the Civil War. Tom Trotter obtained copies of pension application papers for both Ben and Erastus from the U. S. Department of the Interior, Bureau of Pensions. Both Ben and Erastus suffered wounds in that War. Ben had an arrow wound, one inch above the ankle in his right leg, which in later life caused erysipelas. Erastus lost a leg in the fighting.

Finn's declaration for pension, filed May 27, 1912, stated he was 80 years of age, that he served as an able seaman on the USS Great Western in the Civil War, was quartermaster at time of discharge at Mound City Navy Yard, Ill., June 13, 1865. The late Mrs. Nestle said Finn regularly drew a $50 a month pension, and that she cashed it for him.

His personal description on enlistment was height, six feet, fair complexion, blue eyes, dark hair; occupation, mason. He was born March 7, 1832, at Elyria, Lorain County, Ohio. Since the war he had lived in Michigan, Missouri, and the last 40 years on the McKenzie, 30 miles east of Eugene. He said he was married to Mary A. Halter in 1850 in Elyria, Ohio. His living children at time of his application were Eugene, Ella, Lewis (Louis), Emma, Peter and Ida.

ERASTUS A. FINN

Erastus Alvenza Finn claimed acquaintanceship with both Mark Twain and Col. William "Buffalo Bill" Cody. He was thrice wounded while fighting in the Civil War, resulting in the loss of a leg. He was interviewed in the *Seattle Times* Feb. 18, 1917. The following is taken from Washington Biography (479.719) records:

"With reminiscences of slave markets in Southern cities, of life as a pilot on the Mississippi and as a wagon master in pioneer days in the West, Erastus A. Finn celebrated his eighty-third birthday anniversary at his home, 313 Thirty-Second Avenue (Seattle).

"Mr. Finn was born in Lorain County, Ohio, Feb. 18, 1835. In 1852, (at age 17 years) he was wagon master of a horse train hauling supplies from Fort Leavenworth, Kan., to the government posts in Kansas, Nebraska, Colorado and New Mexico. In 1856 (at age 21) he was pilot on a Mississippi River steamboat from St. Louis to New Orleans. He frequently attended the slave markets and saw slaves sold in New Orleans and Memphis. He was half owner in the steamboat and was at Memphis when the Civil War broke out. His partner also was a northern man. They both fled north and their boat was confiscated.

"Mr. Finn went to Michigan and enlisted in the 13th Michigan Infantry Volunteers. He served until 1864, when he was shot in the right ankle and had his leg amputated below the knee. After his recovery he returned to Michigan."

We do not question Erastus' work as wagon master at age 17, nor that he was a pilot on the Mississippi River steamboat nor that he knew Mark Twain and Buffalo Bill. As with Ben Finn, it is more a matter of where truth left off and fiction began. Both apparently were great storytellers, as were many western plainsmen, and if they and their listeners found pleasure in their stories, so do we.

He said there were six children in the family -- two girls and four boys. After their father died, they were "bound over." He said he ran away from his foster home, but didn't say at what age.

Erastus' pension application papers say he enlisted in Company G, 13th Regiment, Michigan Volunteer Infantry, U. S. Army, at Schoolcraft, Kalamazoo County, Mich., Jan. 8, 1862. He was 26, five feet, nine, light complexion, blue eyes, brown hair, occupation, teamster.

Thrice wounded, he suffered a wound in his left arm between Corinth, Miss., and Pittsburgh Landing on the Tennessee River May 15, 1862, by a rifle ball from "Bushwhackers." He was treated in the field. He suffered a second wound in his left leg at Stone River, on or about Dec. 31, 1862, when struck by a piece of shell below the left knee and was treated by the same surgeons. Wounded a third time, his "right ankle was shot and mangled at (the battle of) Chickamauga, Tenn., Sept. 19, 1863. Gangrene set in. His right foot was amputated above the ankle at the military hospital, Stevenson, Ala. Gangrene was not eradicated, and his right leg was re-amputated about 2.5 inches below the knee at Schoolcraft, Mich., in 1866."

Erastus' Army certificate of disability for discharge, Dec. 6, 1864, lists his birth place as Ashland, Ohio, (south of Elyria). The certificate, signed by his commanding officer, Capt. Balch, mentions loss of his right leg, amputated as a consequence of a gunshot wound in the Battle of Chickamauga. He was discharged Dec. 14, 1864, at St. Louis, Mo.

In papers filed Dec. 12, 1921, Erastus said he married Marion A. Shoecraft in 1868 in Flowerfield, St. Joseph County, Mich. She was born in Marcelus, Cass County, Mich., May 1850.

Marion had been married to a man named Hubbard, by whom she had a son, Willard. Erastus said Hubbard was "a bigamist. At the time he

(Hubbard) married her he had a wife by a prior valid marriage who was living and undivorced. Later and before my marriage, his first wife came after him and he went back and lived with her in another state and abandoned the woman I subsequently married and her baby. I was advised before my marriage that my wife's previous marriage to a married man as above stated was void and then she did not need a divorce. Her son, Willard Hubbard, died about the year 1890."

Erastus and Marion had five children, Ella Marie, born Aug. 18, 1868; Wilbur, Mar. 14, 1869; Marion, Jan. 25, 1870; Erastus, Nov. 19, 1873, and Rebecka (note spelling), Nov. 29, 1877. Wilbur died at age two. Erastus' wife died at Huntsville, Mo., in August, 1879, at age 29.

Finn brought daughters, Ella Marie and Rebacca, to the Territory of Washington in 1882, settling in Marysville. In 1889 they moved to Seattle where he was engaged in the transfer business for 18 years. Ella Marie married John M. Arnold. They lived in Seattle. Rebacca (sic), married J. Nelson They lived in Vancouver, B. C.

A pension paper filed in 1923, listed places Erastus had lived since leaving the service as Detroit, Mich., Chicago, Ill., Huntsville, Mo., Scranton, Kan., and Seattle, Wash. Occupations included shoemaker, engineer, fireman, coal miner and expressman. After retiring Finn lived in Seattle with the Arnolds until his death March 17, 1930.

CHAPTER 23

Wycoff Family

The story of the Wycoffs involves three pioneering families --
the Wycoffs, Redmans and Millers -- and the tragic events that brought
them together. A fourth family figured into the friendships and
cooperation typical of the people who settled the West.

The book, *The Wycoff Family in America,* traces descendants of
Nicholas Wyckoff (cq). A Peter Wicoff (spelled with an "i"; names are
spelled variously as Wichoff, Wychoff, Wicoff and Wycoff) was born
Feb. 26, 1775, in Somerset County, N. Jer. They lived in western Virginia,
moved to Erie County, Pa., then to Ohio. He married Elizabeth Jane Bruce,
daughter of James Bruce. She was born in 1777. Peter died Sept. 26, 1841,
in Wayne County, Ohio. Elizabeth died Aug. 8, 1849.

They had ten children, the oldest being James Finley Wycoff.
James, born July 28, 1798, married Rachel Cisel (or Cisal), born Oct. 20,
1799, in Maryland. He died Sept. 12, 1855, in Marion County, Iowa. Rachel
died July 27, 1846, in Jefferson County, Ohio.

Peter Jackson Wycoff, the seventh of James and Rachel's ten
children, was born March 15, 1831, in Wayne County, Ohio. About 1850
in Iowa, Peter married Elsie Jane Stillwell. She was born in 1830.

A son, James William, was born in Iowa Oct. 19, 1852. The
following spring, when Peter was 22 and Elsie 23, they headed west over
the Old Oregon Trail, settling near Brownsville in Linn County.

Four more children were born there: George Washington, June 4,
1856; Harriet, 1857; Rachel, 1858, and Joseph Wesley, 1860.

About the same time, Benjamin Washington Redman, born Nov.
10, 1816, in Clarke County, Ind., brought his family west from Iowa with
two heavily-laden wagons to The Dalles. They arrived via the Columbia
River route at Howell Prairie near present-day St. Helens, in Columbia
County Oct. 20, 1852. The family in 1853 moved to a homestead at the
North and South Santiam rivers forks, but a flood in the spring of
1854/55 wiped them out. They moved to a farm northeast of Brownsville.

Benjamin's wife Amanda E. Craven, was born June 3, 1822, in
Fleming County, Ky. They were married in 1838 in Van Burren County,
Iowa. A daughter, Amanda Evelina, was born there April 14, 1844. A son,
John T., was the subject of a write-up included in *History of the
Northwest, Oregon and Washington*, vol. II, 1889, Page 533, published by
the North Pacific History of Oregon.

The Miller Family

John Miller, born Feb. 7, 1830, in Indiana, was the son of George
and Mary Ann Stockton Miller. George was the father of 24 children.
Mary Ann was his third wife. They were married in Indiana.

John married, first, Hannah Miller (same last name but not cousins). Hannah, born in 1842, was the daughter of Isaac and Elizabeth (Coddington) Miller. Isaac was born Feb. 8, 1806, and Elizabeth born Dec. 20, 1827, in Tennessee. Isaac sold his farm in Miami County, Ind., and returned to Montgomery County, Ind., where he lived with his elderly mother until she died two years later in 1847. He and his brother, Christian, went to Missouri where they spent the winter preparing for their trip west.

John and Hannah apparently came with them. One report says they came about 1848. Another report says the Miller family came west in the late fall of 1853, settling in what is now known as Millersburg in Linn County. There were other family members.

A daughter, Mary Elizabeth, was born Dec. 6, 1857. Hannah died June 30, 1859. On July 18, 1863, John Miller married Amanda Redman in Linn County. They had four children, Rebecca (known in later years as Aunt Lettie) born in 1866; Perry, born at Scio, Ore., May 21, 1868; Norton born May 18, 1870, and Curtis, born June 3, 1872, at Scio.

Tragedy Strikes

Peter Wycoff in the early 1860's was serving with the military at Fort Lapwai, east of Lewiston, Ida., where soldiers protected wagon trains from the Indians. While he was there, his wife, Elsie Jane, and daughters, Harriet and Rachel, were killed in a runaway horse and buggy accident in August, 1862, probably in Linn County.

Family members have been unable to locate their graves, but they most likely are on a 320-acre homestead (Claim No. 145) eight or nine miles southeast of Brownsville, as told to Wilbur S. (Bill) Johnson by James Frederick Wycoff, son of George Wycoff. Johnson's wife, Ardyce, is a great-granddaughter of Peter from a second marriage. About 1980 they moved to a parcel of the old Wycoff homestead on the McKenzie. In January 1996, they moved to Springfield.

Elsie Jane had left her young son, Joseph "Baby Joe," in the care of a neighbor woman, Mrs. Thomas (Nancy) Barrett, near Brownsville. The 1870 Linn County census shows Joseph Wycoff, age 9, residing with Nancy Barrett, 70, and Thomas Barrett, 38, probably her son, on a 281-acre farm, four or five miles west of Peter Wycoff's original homestead.

Peter Wycoff, left a widower with sons, James, George and Joe, moved to the McKenzie, 12 miles east of Vida, in the mid-1870's. From 1874 to about 1877, he was back in Fort Lapwai.

John and Amanda Miller at some time in the 1870s also moved to the McKenzie. John is reported to have carried mail in the area.

Miller and a partner, Peter Settle, in 1875 purchased Belknap Springs from Rollin S. Belknap. Settle emigrated to Oregon and filed for homestead rights in 1862, just where is not known.

The year 1875-76 was a sad one for the Millers. John became ill that winter and had a huge abscess on his shoulder that may have been cancer. Amanda also was in ill health, having given birth to a nine pound daughter, Leona. A letter John wrote to a brother and sister tell of problems at the springs resulting from his illness. He died Oct. 5, 1876.

Belknap Springs was closed for a year then reopened by Settle. Probate records show Miller had a half interest, valued at $1,000.

The Wycoffs and Redmans had been close friends at Brownsville. In 1878, Peter Wycoff and Amanda Redman-Miller were married. On May 4, 1879, a son, Archie, was born at Walterville. The 1880 census lists Peter Wycoff, 47; Amanda E., 36; their son, Archie, age 1 year, and Amanda's children, Rebecca, 13, Perry E., 12, Norton, 10, and Curtis J., 8. The baby, Leona, died young.

Peter Wycoff and Benj. "Huck" Finn found the body of John Templeton Craig, who perished in heavy snows on the McKenzie Pass in December 1877, while carrying the mail to central Oregon. After this tragedy Peter took over the job of carrying the mail over the Cascades summit for two years, followed by Carey Thomson.

The Wycoff homestead, known as the Wycoff Ranch, was the location of a toll gate on the old McKenzie Toll Road. Peter built a toll gate and two lean-to sheds for overnight camping. He constructed the road along his property, hence a toll was charged.

In 1882, Peter turned his McKenzie property over to his eldest son, James, who on April 19, 1879, married Emma Bertha Finn, age 15, daughter of Benj. and Mary Finn. (See James and Emma chapter).

Peter with wife Amanda, son Archie, age 3 years, and daughter Daisy Dell, born Feb. 4, 1881, at Millers Station, with the Miller children, Rebecca, Perry, Norton and Curtis, moved all their possessions and a herd of cows to a 160-acre homestead, nine miles north of Sprague, Washington Territory, southwest of Spokane. They sold milk, butter, cream and cheese and other farm produce to employees of the Northern Pacific Railroad being built across Washington. Another child, Anna Elsie, was born June 13, 1884, at Sprague.

George Washington Wycoff, Peter's second son by Elsie Jane Stillwell, moved to Freeman, Wa., before 1880. He was married Oct. 5, 1891, in Spokane, Wa., to Eliza Caroline (Parker) Bare, according to notes of Orville Wycoff, a great grandson of Peter.

The daughter of Sarah Parker, Eliza was born May 1, 1858, in Benton, Marshall County, Ky. She was the widow of Owen Rinehart Bare, who died Dec. 16, 1889, at Mt. Hope, Wa., after being kicked in the head by a horse. She and Bare had five children -- Rosie, May, Alice, Celia (died young) and Ernest Earl.

After their marriage, George asked his father, Peter, to move up from Sprague to Freeman to take over his homestead so he could move onto Mrs. Bare's existing farm. Archie, 13 in 1892, drove his father's cattle from Sprague to Freeman.

Peter developed leg ulcers. His stepson took him to Nez Perce, Ida. He died Jan. 5, 1906. Amanda died in Spokane Mar. 5, 1934. Daisy, born in 1881, married Dave C. Shore. She died in 1944 and was buried in Freeman Cemetery near Spokane. Anna Elsie married Floyd Huffman March 9, 1908, in Freeman, Wa. Children were Evelyn, Glenda and Murray Jack.

George and Eliza had five children: (1) Georgia Beaulah, born Aug. 6, 1892, in Rockford, Spokane County, Wa. (2) Sarah Eliza Myrtle, born Sept. 10, 1894, in Mt. Hope, Spokane County, Wa.; married July 3, 1928, in Seattle, Wa., to Murrel Winfield Sprague. (3) Barnett Lester, born Oct. 29, 1895, at Mt. Hope, Spokane County, Wa.; married Leah Gertrude Fiedler July 6, 1918. (4) James Fredrick, born Aug. 4, 1899, in Waterville, Douglas County, Wa.; married Lela Marie Johnson. (5) Hester Edith, born March 29, 1902, in Douglas County, Wa., married Charles Merle Deane Aug. 29, 1921.

When James Wycoff was killed at age 53, Nov. 25, 1905, in an accident with a team of horses, brother George came from Washington to help care for his sister-in-law, Emma Finn Wycoff, and her children. He then sent for his wife and family. They lived for a time on the Wycoff Ranch. Etha Wycoff, a daughter of James and Emma, married Ernest (Curley) Bare. Chester Wycoff, a son of James and Emma, married Ona Pearl Bare, a half sister of Ernest.

George died Sept. 10, 1930, at Redmond, King County, Wa. Eliza died Jan. 27, 1944, in Kirkland, Wa. Both were buried in Kirkland.

Joe Wycoff, son of Peter and Elsie Jane, never married. In 1906, at age 45, he was killed in a sawmill accident, when the crank of a windlass flying through the air struck him on the head.

Archie Merton Wycoff, son of Peter and Amanda Redman-Miller, married Rosa Montgomery. They had three children, Cecil Vernon, born Dec. 28, 1902 (dec.); Vera Crystal, born July 21, 1905, and Wayne LaVerne, born July 4, 1907 (dec.)

After Rosa's death Archie married Grace Snodgrass. She was born May 24, 1890, in Mt. Hope, Wa. Children were Ardyce Grace, born July 16, 1913; Norma Clarice, Sept. 6, 1915; Archie Lloyd, Aug. 24, 1917; Orville Merton, Oct. 19, 1919; Leona Dell, Jan. 16, 1921; Betty Gene, Jan. 6, 1923, and Joan Carmen, Apr. 12, 1930. Ardis married Wilbur (Bill) Johnson.

Mary Elizabeth Miller on March 12, 1875, married Henry Frank Newman Jr. His parents were Henry and Elizabeth Wamsley Newman. The senior Newmans bought Isaac Miller's 640-acre land claim. Henry Sr. became postmaster and named the post office Millersburg, which name has remained. Isaac Miller moved to Ashland, Ore.

Henry Jr. and Mary Elizabeth were parents of John Henry Newman, who married Cynthia Adeline Harpol. They were the parents of the late Ralph E. Newman, who established the retail-wholesale Newman's Fish Market in Eugene in 1927.

Another son, Ethan Newman, was Eugene city postmaster for many years. Mary Elizabeth died Aug. 20, 1933. Information on the Millers and Newmans was supplied by Zelma Newman, Ralph's widow. She has been researching family history since 1960.

Perry Eli Miller on Dec. 23, 1889, married Anna E. Simpson in Adams, Ore. She died in 1901. He moved to Tacoma, Wa. On Dec. 31, 1911, he married Daisy Hoffman. After his death she moved to Nez Perce, Ida.

Curtis John Miller married Pauline McGlade in Sprague, Wa. They had three children. Pauline died in 1912. He married Eva B. Henderson in 1913. Curtis died at age 82.

John Whitlock Sims and Dora Belknap Sims

CHAPTER 24

Sims Family

John Whitlock Sims, tired of family bickering at his home in Boone County, Mo., got on his horse and rode west. Aside from the place and date of his birth, we have no record on Sims' movements as to when he left Missouri and arrived on the McKenzie. In the early 1870's he was working for Rollin Simeon Belknap as "proprietor" at Belknap Springs.

Born April 12, 1840, in Sedalia, Mo., John probably was the son of Thomas Anderson and Elizabeth (Morris) Sims. Thomas was born about 1802 and Elizabeth about 1809, in Virginia. The 1850 Boone County census listed Thomas, a farmer, age 48, and Elizabeth, 41. They migrated from Virginia to Kentucky, then to Missouri.

And John probably was a brother of Matilda Sims, daughter of Thomas and Elizabeth. She was born in Kentucky Sept. 12, 1828. On Dec. 28, 1846, Matilda married John Davis Fountain, born in 1820. The Fountains migrated to Oregon in 1858, settling at Harrisburg, then moving to Walterville on the McKenzie ten years later.

John Whitlock's identity is unclear due to the fact three John Sims lived in Boone County. The 1850 census lists a John Sims as one of Thomas and Elizabeth twelve children. Two other John Sims were found in the records: John W., born in 1833, and a John S., in 1839. We are unable to fully establish which was Matilda's brother.

John is said to have had sisters Virginia Turman and a Mrs. Hicks, also a brother, James. But these names do not come up in the 1850 census for Boone County. Likewise, a John Sims, at age 15, is reported to have married Elizabeth Wade Feb. 25, 1855.

John Whitlock Sims was an experienced hunter and trapper, an old "coon skinner," said his grandson, Kermit Sims of Elmira, Ore. He may have been with Rollin Belknap when he relocated Belknap Springs about 1869. Jack Sims of Eugene, another grandson, told the unverified story that Rollin and John, hunting in the vicinity, shot a bear, which stumbled into the bubbling hot springs.

Dora A., daughter of Rollin and Mary Belknap, was born Dec. 30, 1859, on Riverbanks Farm, the Belknap homestead near Wilderville, Josephine County, Ore. She had just turned 15 when she married John, who, at age 34, was more than twice her age. Both were living at Belknap Springs. The wedding took place Jan. 1, 1874, at the home of V. S. McClure, address not listed.

The late Maple Stobie wrote (1964: 64): "Mrs. Sims, the former Dora Belknap. . .told of planting the maple trees at Belknap Springs." Dora was 11 years old when the family moved there in 1871.

Dora and Melvina "Auntie" Frissell (1838-1926) were said to be the first white women to view Clear Lake, headwaters of the McKenzie River. Mrs. Frissell's uncle, Philander Renfrew, was surveying in the area and they accompanied him to the lake.

After Rollin sold the resort in 1875, John and Dora homesteaded half a mile north of the McKenzie River, one and a half miles east of the James Belknap Ranch. The homestead was just west of the present Tokatee Golf Course along Mill Creek Road. The late Rolland Sims was quoted in 1979 as saying his parents, John and Dora, "bought 64.8 hectares (160 acres) for $1.00 per hectare ($2.50 per acre), the going price for land in the late 1800's."

Established First School

The Sims established the first upper McKenzie school, a small room built of hewn logs on a nearby land claim. Jane Bigelow, quoting Smith Taylor in *Historic Leaburg*, said the school was establish in 1885. The pupils were mostly from the Sims, Belknap, Isham and Thomson families. The school operated only three months a year, because of lack of money to hire a teacher. By 1902, the Sims children were the only ones attending. Classes were moved into the Sims household, with Dora Sims as teacher. Soon the O'Leary family moved into the district with 11 children. The school was moved into an unoccupied store building at McKenzie Bridge.

John and Dora Sims were responsible for naming Goose Creek, which joins the McKenzie River from the north at McKenzie Bridge.

McArthur's *Oregon Geographic Names* (1969: 64) related: "Scott (probably Smith) Taylor (district forest ranger) of McKenzie Bridge (said that) about 1870, Mr. and Mrs. John Sims were traveling eastward along the road on their way to have Thanksgiving dinner with Uncle

George Frissell (their closest neighbor). Mrs. Sims had her baby in one arm and a dressed goose in the other. When her horse reached the creek, he jumped suddenly, and the goose fell into the water. Ever since, the brook has been known as Goose Creek."

The date probably was closer to 1880. The Sims weren't married until 1874. Their first living child, James Edwin, was born in 1876. Frissell didn't come on the McKenzie until 1879.

Census Report

Mrs. William G. (Gloria Caroline) Jenkins of Salinas, Calif., a granddaughter, supplied records from the family Bible, which is very fragile and the script very light. Other information was obtained from Kermit Sims, a grandson of John and Dora; from Kermit's mother, Mrs. Rolland (Adelene) Sims; Mr. and Mrs. Jack Sims, Eugene; Emily Woolsey, Wilderville, and Mary Ragsdill, Medford.

Ten Sims children are listed, all born at Blue River (mailing address at the time), probably on the Sims Ranch:

(1) Unnamed child, born Nov. 13, 1874, died same day.

(2) James Edwin (Eddie) Sims, Dec. 7, 1876, died at age 13. (Gloria Jenkins lists his death date as Jan. 23, 1887). He was buried in a small cemetery at McKenzie Bridge.

(3) Sarah Ann (Sadie) Sims, born Sept. 3, 1878, married Ernest Nicholson, Oct. 11, 1899. They had two children, Donna and Ethelyn. Sadie and Ernest are buried in the Marcola Cemetery.

Donna married, first, Bonnie G. Fletcher. A son, Fredrick Ernest (Rick) Fletcher, was born Sept. 15, 1941, in Eugene, Ore. Donna's second married name was Roberts. She died in July, 1965, and is buried in Lane Memorial Cemetery. Ethelyn (Wheeler) is buried in West Lawn, Eugene.

Fredrick Fletcher married Bessie Mae Alldridge Sept. 24, 1962, in Seattle, Wa. They have lived in the greater Seattle area since January, 1966. Both work for The Boeing Company, he as an analyst for the logistical branch of the quality assurance department, and Bessie as a technical instructor.

They have daughters, Delaina Rae, born Nov. 25, 1965, in Eugene, and Michelle Lynn, born June 17, 1968, in Seattle. Delaina married William J. Bochsler July 20, 1985. An adopted son, Shawn, was born April 7, 1991, in Seattle. Michelle married Timothy J. Terrill Oct. 19, 1991, in Auburn, Wa. They have no children of their own, but Timothy has two daughters by a prior marriage.

(4) John Ervin Sims (known as Ervin or Ervie), born March 12, 1880, married Leota V. Close June 17, 1917. Leota was born Aug. 27, 1886. A son, Norman, was killed at age 12 riding his bicycle in Eugene. Leota died Nov. 30, 1920, Ervie in 1927. They are buried in the Pioneer Cemetery, Eugene.

(5) Robert (Robbie) Henderson Sims, born April 10, 1884, married Pearl York. They had four sons: Harold, Loris, Jack and Cleo. Robert and Pearl were divorced Jan. 27, 1923, and Robert married Janie Martin in September 1924. Both are buried in Antioc Cemetery in Sams Valley, Jackson County, Ore. Pearl then married a man named Barker. She is

buried in Sand Ridge Cemetery near Lebanon.

(a) Harold Homer Sims, born Jan. 30, 1909, and his wife, Ruth, live in Wilderville. They have four children: Roger, Viola (Sims) Means, John and Jeanette (Sims) Smith.

(b) Loris Garland Sims, born Sept. 10, 1910, and wife Elizabeth E. (Murphy) had three children: Virginia Wassom of Salem, David of Roseburg, and Dorothy Whitten. Loris died Feb. 9, 1975, at age 64.

(c) Jack Robert Sims, born June 23, 1912, married Margarette (Andrews) of Eugene at Sweet Home Sept. 18, 1936. Children are: Roberta Fay, born Oct. 1, 1937, and Jack Russell (Bud), March 12, 1939. Both live in Medford. Jack Sims first married Mary Lee Dulder. They had a son, Mark, born in Tacoma, Wa., Sept. 11, 1962. Jack then married Annette Camerado. She had a son, Christopher Lee, born May 26, 1956. Mark and his wife have a daughter, Silvia Rae Sims, born July 15, 1989, in Tacoma.

(d) Cleo James Sims, born July 8, 1914, lives in Myrtle Creek.

(6) Leo Edwin Sims, born Dec. 4, 1888, married Helen Caroline McCormick Nov. 24, 1920, in Eugene, Lane County. They had two daughters, Gloria Caroline, born in Roseburg, Ore., Feb. 11, 1924, and Helen Patricia, born Sept. 19, 1926, in Eugene. Leo died in Paso Robles, San Luis Obispo County, Cal., Dec. 27, 1960. Helen, born Oct. 12, 1899, in Salem, Marion County, Ore., was the daughter of James Jay and Jessie May (Smith) McCormick. Helen died Nov. 13, 1970, in Mt. Shasta, Siskiyou County, Cal. She and Leo were buried in Pacific Grove, Cal.

Gloria married William G. Jenkins Dec. 28, 1944. They live in Salinas, Cal. Their son, William Avery, born Nov. 21, 1948, has three sons: Nathan, who lives with his mother; William Joseph, born July 25, 1979, and Matthew Christopher, March 8, 1981.

Patricia married Alan Stewart Jan. 24, 1947. They lived in Mt. Shasta, Cal., where they were in business, until they retired and moved to Port Orford on the southern Oregon coast.

(7) James Vincent (Vinty) Sims, born Oct. 3, 1890, married Ica White. Both are deceased.

(8) May Melvilla Sims, born Dec. 6, 1892, married William H. (Bill) Nutter Sept. 29, 1911. Nutter, a civil engineer, came from Wisconsin to the McKenzie on a surveying job in 1909. He homesteaded near Vida. Later he and May moved to the Sims Ranch. Nutter was interested in mining. May had dairy cows and sold milk. Their first child, Charles, was born on the ranch. Their second child, John, was born at Lebanon.

They moved to a farm on Bear Creek near Medford, where Loris, James and Emily were born. Then they moved to Merlin where Mary was born. May died Jan. 10, 1972, and William, May 21, 1961.

(a) Charles William Nutter in 1934 married Charlene R. Neal, born on the McKenzie in 1915 to Charles and Cora Neal. They had sons, Kenneth Leroy and Norman Jay. Charles and Charlene are deceased.

(b) John Edwin Nutter married Irene Rachor (dec.) They had a son, John Edwin Jr. John Sr. lives at Grants Pass.

(c) Loris Raymond Nutter married Juanita Alreid. A daughter, DaLoris Raylene, was born soon after Loris' death.

(d) James Franklin Nutter married Viola McCormick (both deceased). Children are: James (deceased), Jerry and Darlene (Nutter) Shepherd, of Stherlin.

(e) Emily Mae Nutter married Darrell Woolsey. They live in Grants Pass. They have daughters, Myrna Cournoyer of Carlsbad, N. Mex., and Marla Watson of Grants Pass.

(f) Mary Ellen Nutter married Merlin D. Ragsdill. They live in Medford. They have daughters Dianna Graham of Portland; Christie Classen of Medford, and Brenda Perry of Ashland.

(9 and 10) Twins, Raymond Garland and Louris Rolland Sims, were born Aug. 3, 1895. They enlisted in the U. S. Army during World War I. Raymond died Feb. 24, 1918, during the flu epidemic while he and Rolland were at Ft. Stephens in Oregon waiting to be sent over seas.

John Sims Death

John Whitlock Sims died Jan. 25, 1902, at age 61 years He was buried in an unmarked grave in a small cemetery at McKenzie Bridge. He is one of seven persons buried there, along with John Edwin Sims, possibly the Sims' first born child, and some Belknap children.

Dora lived on the homestead until her death in Eugene May 15, 1931, at age 71. She was buried in the Pioneer Cemetery, Eugene, beside her son, Raymond.

Rolland Sims served as a private in France during World War I. On his return he lived all of his life on the McKenzie. On Aug. 18, 1927, in Eugene, he married Mary Adelene (Addie) Williams. The daughter of Burley and Daisy (Walker) Williams, she was born July 28, 1910, at Vida. Children were: Kermit, born in 1929, and Betty (Sims) Dierker, Portland.

Rolland and Addie built a home on the timbered portion of the homestead. After Dora's death the ranch was sold to Glen (Pat) Bandy, who ran a milk route. Bandy and his wife had a son, Greg. They sold the ranch to Clarence Belknap and moved to Idaho. Clarence ran stock. Art Belknap earlier leased the big open field and grew hay for his horses.

Rolland died May 7, 1985, and was buried in Greenwood Cemetery at Leaburg. After his death, Addie sold her McKenzie property and moved to Elmira, next door to her son, Kermit. She died March 27, 1997.

Kermit, a logger, had lived at McKenzie Bridge until 1975, then moved to an eight-acre tract near Elmira, west of Eugene. He and his first wife, Anita, have three daughters Cermalean, born in 1960; Brenda, 1962; Tamara, 1967, and a son, Kermit, 1966. Betty and her husband have four children, Becky, KayC, Kelly and Julie.

Sims Butte, elevation 5,648 feet, lies east of McKenzie Highway Route 242, south of Frog Camp in the Three Sisters Wilderness. It may have been named for John Sims, according to the late Manena Schwering (1979). However, Forest Service District Ranger Ray Engles, (1978) said Sims Butte probably was named for Ray Sims (1901-1980), who was actively involved with The Obsidians, organized in 1927 as a mountain rescue group after an unsuccessful attempt to rescue two University of Oregon men lost in the area. Their bodies were found two years later (at Chambers Lake).

Sims Burn was located on the south side of Lookout Ridge above McKenzie Bridge. "The Sims family had a hunting cabin on the ridge, to which they directed hunters (for a fee). Said hunters stayed in the cabin and watched deer stands until the one they wanted came along, then 'Bang.' To give their patrons more open (rifle) shots at game, (the Sims) kept the area burned off. Hence the named 'Sims Burn'." (Lawrence E. Baxter, 1974). Kermit Sims, who grew up on the homestead, said this wasn't a cabin, but more of a blind on poles up in some trees.

Mysterious Death

Mystery shrouds the gunshot death near Canyonville in 1877 of James B. Sims, reputedly a brother of John Whitlock Sims of McKenzie Bridge and Virginia Turman of Princeton, Cal.

Authorities ruled it a suicide, but there was little in the man's make-up to indicate he was suicidal. He appeared in good spirits and left considerable personal possessions. Possibility of murder or accidental shooting were not discounted. James Sims, staying at a farm at Canyonville, left in search of cattle. A shot was heard by the farmer, who found the body, according to a news story in The *Roseburg Plaindealer* Jan. 25, 1877.

We are unable to connect James B. Sims with either John Whitlock Sims or Virginia (Sims) Turman, remembered by family members as "Aunt Vir." Harold Sims of Wilderville, Ore., said Virginia married Joseph (Joe) Turman. A Caroline V. Sims, born in 1846 in Boone County, Mo., was listed as a daughter of Thomas and Elizabeth Sims. The "V" could stand for Virginia. She reportedly married William Lampton Feb. 13, 1866. So we can't verify these as facts.

John also is said to have had a sister, Mrs. Hicks, but these names and James do not come up in the 1850 census for Boone County. Thomas Guthrie Sims, son of Thomas and Elizabeth, married Margaret Ann Hicks. So there may be a connection. Likewise, a John Sims, at age 15, reportedly married Elizabeth Wade Feb. 25, 1855.

Martha Belknap said W. R. Turman in 1881 homesteaded Lost Creek Ranch, in Lost Creek Canyon on scenic McKenzie Pass Highway, three miles east of the Clear Lake Junction. An 1882 journal/diary of W. R. Turman showed he was building a barn at the ranch. His journal noted that every week or so he would take several dozen eggs and other farm products for trading to McKenzie Bridge. (Williams, 1991).

Forest Service records, dating from 1907, show Joseph Turman, who may have been related to W. R. Turman, squatted on this famous ranch. Apparently, Joseph Turman bought the land with a quit claim deed for $1,065, ". . .from someone who bought the land from others. . ." The property consisted of a five-room house, barn, fencing, and some cleared land. Turman cut hay from the cleared acres and sold it for the animals on the old hot, dusty, steep toll road over the Cascade summit. The ranch served as a road house or hotel for weary travelers. He later filed a homestead claim on 102.5 acres.

CHAPTER 25

Craig Disaster

The death of John Templeton Craig in the snow on the Cascade Mountains was a significant event in McKenzie Valley history. This is not just another chapter in the saga of "John Tom" Craig, the rough, unshaven pioneer, who never had his picture taken, but reveals early development on the upper river.

Craig, a mail carrier, made regular trips over the McKenzie summit between the Willamette Valley and Central Oregon. The *Oregon State Journal,* Jan. 8, 1878, contained this brief item:

"We are informed by B. F. Finn, Esq., that John T. Craig, mail carrier on the McKenzie and Ochoco route, has been out fourteen days without being heard from. It is feared he has perished in the snow; yet there is some hope he may have reached Camp Polk in safety. Parties have gone in search for him. Mr. Craig is an old mountaineer and we have some hope he may have come out safe."

Ruth Ellsworth Richardson's article, "John Craig, a Pioneer Mail Carrier," in the *Lane County Historical Quarterly,* recounts Craig's early life, the part he played in developing the road over the McKenzie Pass and early-day problems leading up to his disappearance.

Treaty With Indians

"Indians of eastern Oregon had been causing trouble for some time. In 1864, a treaty had been made with the Klamaths, Modocs and the Yahooskin band of the Snakes, but other Snakes had been troublesome. In 1866 the roads were unsafe because of Indian raids.

"George B. Curry, assigned the command of the Department of the Pacific Aug. 6, 1865, selected nine sites for winter camps. One was on the Santiam not far from the present junction with the McKenzie Highway, three miles northwest of the town of Sisters.

"In the late summer of 1865 a detachment of Company A, United States Army Volunteers, came to this site under Capt. Charles La Follette. The post, located on Squaw Creek, was given the name of Camp Polk for the county from which La Follette came. The detachment spent the winter at Camp Polk, but when spring came the volunteers were mustered out and returned to their homes.

"Samuel M. W. Hindman in 1870 settled across the road from the cabins left by the military and was appointed postmaster of Camp Polk in 1872. With the establishment of the post office and the opening of the McKenzie Pass road, the contract was let to carry the mails from Eugene

City to Prineville by way of Camp Polk. A. S. Powers, one of the early mail contractors, an officer of the road company and a toll collector, gave the contract to Craig, 56. Craig's contract was to carry the mail weekly over the route between McKenzie Bridge and Camp Polk."

The article recounts how Craig started out on snow shoes one December morning in 1877 from Belknap Springs with the mail on his back. He felt sick, but told the men not to worry. He planned to stop at his cabin, which was about half way. It was snowing when he left.

Searchers Turned Back

When Craig failed to return after a week had gone by three men -- John Sims, Philander C. Renfrew and Ben Finn -- started out to look for him. Sims became blinded by the glare of the snow and all three turned back before reaching the cabin near the summit.

"Powers wrote to Hindman at Camp Polk, but the letter had to go through Portland and by way of The Dalles and Prineville, much of the way by stage coach, which meant another week's delay. Finally word was received from Camp Polk that Craig had not reached there. Powers then knew Craig probably had perished in the mountains."

Peter Wycoff and Ben Finn, both able mountaineers, started out in search on snow shoes, as the snow was eight to ten feet in the pass. They reached Craig's cabin with little difficulty.

"The cabin, about seven feet high at the eaves, contained one room, a fireplace and a lean-to used as a woodshed. It was almost buried in snow. The customary way to enter a snowed-in cabin was through the spacious fireplace chimney. Craig's body was found lying wrapped in his blanket among the fireplace ashes. The two men removed and buried the body as best they could a few feet from the cabin. They built a cairn of stones over the grave to keep the wild animals away.

"Rufus Robertson, an old-time Eugene resident, crossed the McKenzie Pass in the spring of 1878, the same year Craig, the pioneer carrier lost his life. With Robertson were two other Eugene men who had driven a large herd of cattle to Prineville over the Santiam. They were returning by way of the McKenzie. It was spring and most of the snow had melted. They stopped at Craig's cabin. Mr. Robertson said there was plenty of wood which John Craig apparently had been too exhausted to use. In the ashes was a partially burned spool of thread and scores of burnt matches, with which he had futily tried to start a fire.

"It is possible Craig didn't reach his cabin the first night out from Belknap as we knew he was sick and it was storming. The trail to the cabin was very steep. He may have become exhausted and very ill from the exposure. He may have made a fire on reaching the cabin and laid down to sleep. He may have rolled out the back log and crawled exhausted into the warm ashes. And so, days later his body was found. High in the mountains, beside the road he helped build, lies the grave of John Templeton Craig, unseen and unknown by thousands passing upon the scenic highway," Mrs. Richardson concluded.

Today near the McKenzie pass, a marker bears this inscription:

"In honor of John Templeton Craig, March 1821 -- December

1877, Pioneer Mail-Carrier over the wagon road he himself located and built, where this present highway runs. He perished in a little log cabin near this point from exposure in a terrific storm while attempting to carry the mail over this route. The adjacent tomb is the final resting place of his immortal remains. Erected by the Rural Letter Mail Carriers Association, 1930."

Peter Wycoff took up carrying the mail over the mountains. Two years later Carey Thomson carried one relay of the mail, making a 15-mile trip daily from Alder Creek to two miles east of Windy Point, often using Craig's cabin for shelter. The Camp Polk post office was abandoned in 1888, the business transferred to Sisters.

Craig had lived the life of a hermit at Craig's Pasture, which became McKenzie Bridge. A large pond at the side of the highway near the McKenzie Pass is named Craig Lake for the man who did so much to provide the link between the west and central Oregon.

Mrs. Lester (Ada) Millican, in 1978, recalled that, after a fire in 1909 destroyed Craig's cabin on the McKenzie Pass, she and other Millican family members placed rocks around the burial site, before the memorial plaque was placed. Craig's sister was the wife of Dil Ritchey of Camp Creek. The Ritcheys' daughter, Susan, married George Millican.

Bridge Construction

Meanwhile, considerable agitation developed in Lane County during the 1870's to replace toll ferries with bridges. Eugenians, as early as 1857, the *Oregon State Journal* said, complained they were losing too much Mohawk Valley farm produce trade to Harrisburg because of costly and unreliable ferry service into Eugene.

The county court in 1874 employed A. S. Miller and son, H. B. Miller, to build bridges to cross the Willamette at Springfield and the McKenzie at Hayden Ferry, the county to pay half the cost and the remainder to be collected from the people by the contractor.

"Bridge fever" ensued. Eugene residents, not to be outdone by the Springfield bridge, in 1877 prevailed upon the debt-ridden county to build Ferry Street Bridge across the Willamette at Eugene City. New-design Smith Trusses went into these bridge constructions.

Jacob Spores' Ferry at Coburg was replaced by a bridge in 1878. A toll bridge, built in 1878 by Carey Thomson, replaced John Craig's original crude bridge at McKenzie Bridge.

Perilous Journey

Illustrative of the treacherous and difficult journey over the McKenzie Pass is the story told by Martha (Gay) Masterson in her diary, as recorded in "One Woman's West," edited by Lois Barton.

In the spring of 1878 she rode by stage to McKenzie Bridge to meet her husband to travel by horses and wagon to Eastern Oregon. About nine miles out, a wagon wheel broke.

"We were in a deep forest, going up hill," Martha wrote. Her husband had to return to McKenzie Bridge to get the wheel repaired. This left her and their children alone in the forest "miles from anyone with wild animals prowling around."

While they were eating their evening meal, a man on horseback came in sight. It turned out to be her husband's nephew, traveling to the valley from the Cascades. She told him of their plight and invited him to eat with them. But after eating, much to her chagrin, he got on his horse and rode off. They rebuilt the fires, but a storm put them out. There was further danger from falling trees. They spent a fretful night, but her husband rejoined them next day, and they moved on.

One night they camped near the summit and saw the snow-capped Three Sisters. The next day they crossed the lava beds "during a frightful storm," she wrote.

"The black lava on every side extended far to the south. To see immense trees growing here was a mystery, as there was no soil visible. I looked down into the deep channel where the molten lava had flowed and thought of the intense heat, and of the long years it would take these miles and miles of burning mountains to cool off. Then for the seeds of trees to be carried there in some way and grow to such wonderful size in that dry lava bed. All marvelous to behold!

"The graded road which leads around on the very brink of the precipice was a frightening place to pass during a storm. Our wagon nearly capsized several times in the wind. Rain, hail and snow beset us while crossing the lava. The grade was narrow, only room for one wagon. To our right was a steep mountain, while on the left was the chasm, deep, dark and dismal. I hoped we would not meet anyone, for one would be almost compelled to turn back or be pushed from the precipice into the yawning abyss below. We saw dead horses and cattle down there. Where we crossed, the lava beds were several miles wide."

After leaving "this dreary looking place," they continued along a fairly good road to a wayside cabin, where they stopped for the night. After retiring Martha was disturbed by a noise on the roof.

"My bed was near the door on the floor and the door was ajar. I got Dot (baby daughter) in my arms as I lay there. We could not close the door at all. Just then a heavy thud on the ground caused me to almost scream." Her husband aroused. He thought the noise was from one of the horses. "Next morning we found the tracks of a mountain lion in the mud in the yard. Fortunately I heard it on the roof, for it could easily have clawed baby from my arms if I had been asleep."

They rounded up the horses which had strayed during the night. "The road lay down the eastern slope. We made a quick run for Squaw Creek Station (near Sisters)," she wrote.

Great Floods Take Toll

The great flood of 1881 took its toll on the Willamette Valley and McKenzie River bridges. Several collapsed or were washed away and had to be replaced. The Springfield bridge on more than one occasion washed down river toward Eugene.

Toll gate tender A. S. Powers at McKenzie Bridge was on the bridge (built in 1878 by Carey Thomson to replace Craig's bridge) when it was washed downstream in the destructive 1881 flood. The *Oregon State Journal*, Jan. 22, 1881, reported the bridge "was carried down river about half a mile, when he (Powers) succeeded in making his escape on a drift. By alternate swimming, wading and walking drift logs, he made his way to shore and reached home safely, but it was a narrow escape."

The first McKenzie Bridge toll gate tender, an elderly man named Hill, died in a fire in 1883. Neighbors found him in bed. A lighted candle apparently had fallen off a post. The bedding had only burned a ring about a foot wide around his head when the fire mysteriously went out.

Although several ferries continued to operate along the McKenzie, Lane County became a pioneer in constructing bridges, many of which collected tolls. Carey Thomson's bridge at McKenzie Bridge which washed away in 1881 was replaced the same year by one built by Lord Nelson (Nels) Roney (1853-1944), a famous bridge builder.

This covered bridge lasted 25 years. Roney replaced it in 1907 downstream from the present McKenzie Bridge Market, according to Carl Stephens. In 1929, a steel and concrete bridge replaced the covered structure. The new design bridge remained in service until 1968, when replaced by the present bridge at mp. 50.4.

James Belknap's ferry, at present-day Rainbow, was replaced by Carey Thomson in 1889 with a covered bridge. He collected tolls.

The road was reported to have been graded 64 miles east of Eugene, but this was a very crude wagon road. Stage routes were established in the late 1870's, as noted in Martha Masterson's diary. But, in spite of later heavy use occasioned by mining developments on Gold Hill above Blue River starting in 1885, travel up the river was an ordeal. The road consisted mainly of two wagon tracks, dusty in summer and muddy, almost impassable, in winter.

Records show, except for two years, toll road accounts were filed annually until 1894. Craig's name is not found after the first account. Names of A. S. Powers, George Millican, A. G. Hovey, W. R. Walker, A. V. Peters and George A. Dorris appear as officers and directors. Toll collectors were A. V. Peters, M. G. McCarty, J. (James) W. Wycoff, G. O. Powers, J. R. Atkinson and a Mr. Hill. Until 1891 tolls were collected at McKenzie Bridge. In 1891, '92 and '93, the collection was at Blue River, and in 1894, the last year of tolls, to quote from the report, "at the gate."

There was increasing agitation from residents in the upper McKenzie to abolish the toll road and make it a public roadway, even though the residents could travel the road for six months of the year without charge. Indians reportedly were unwilling to submit to tolls and whenever possible made their crossings at other locations.

Lane County Commissioners resolved the matter May 9, 1895, when they denied the petition of A. G. Hovey and G. A. Dorris for a renewal of tolls, after declaring "the bridges unsafe and the road in poor condition." In 1896 the road from Rock House to Belknap Springs was declared a county road. Two years later the entire road was taken over and renamed the McKenzie and Eastern Road (*Eugene Register-Guard*, Feb. 22, 1959). Upkeep was by private subscription, until state and county financing was authorized after 1900.

Hotel at Belknap Springs on the McKenzie under new owners.

CHAPTER 26

Belknap Springs

Hot mineral springs played a significant part in the early development of the upper McKenzie River Valley, long noted for its recreational values and its attraction for such personalities as ex-President Hoover, movie stars and European royalty.

Belknap on the McKenzie and Foley on Horse Creek, a tributary, were developed in the 1870's. A third springs, Terwilliger, on the South Fork of the McKenzie was never developed as a resort, but in recent years has been used for bathing by counter culturists. Foley has been closed since 1940.

Belknap Lodge and Hot Springs was acquired in July 1995 by McDougal Brothers Inc., a Eugene/Springfield company with diverse business interests. Principals in the company are Norman and Mel McDougal. Jeanne Blillie has been hired as manager.

Planned improvements include a new swimming pool, extensive remodeling of the main lodge and hotel, installing steam baths, building new cabins and increasing the amount of RV sites and camping on the upper level. Improvements are geared to increasing the clientele. The ultimate plan is to build it into a destination resort.

Plans also include constructing a new foot bridge across the McKenzie River to the hot springs. The new owners purchased about eighty acres of land on the north side of the river, including thirty-five acres which had been held by the Bigelow family heirs.

Sale of the resort follows a transaction in 1991, in which Jim Nation, owner since 1975, sold the Belknap Springs operation to a San Francisco, Cal., investment company, the RYT Corporation, headed by R. M. Bowman, chairman of the board. The property was involved in foreclosure litigation, prior to the McDougals' acquisition.

Discovery of Belknap Springs is generally credited to pioneers, George Millican, John T. Craig, James Storment and Joseph Carter, who, about 1859, were "first to seek for the headwaters of the McKenzie." (Walling's *History of Lane County* 1884).

Long before white settlers entered the Pacific Northwest, Native Americans frequented hot springs throughout North America. At Belknap, exact archeological dating has not been done. However, due to the types of the many artifacts found on both sides of the river, it is possible native inhabitants used the hot springs at least seasonally for more than 8,000 years for medicinal and ceremonial purposes. Many established trails existed leading to hot springs of the Northwest.

The Springs, 63 miles east of Eugene, was named for developer Rollin Simeon Belknap, who came west to San Francisco from Boston, Mass., in 1849. After a 20-year sojourn on the Rogue River in Southern Oregon, he moved with his wife Mary and daughters, Dora, Alzina and Bertha, to the McKenzie and opened the springs. He built a hotel on the south side of the river on a level, tree-shaded bench. The resort at first consisted simply of cabins used as steam baths for hunting parties Rollin Belknap guided.

First known as Salt Springs, they are composed of six, hot, mineral spring sources at the base of Coronet Point across the river. They also were called the Pool of Salome and Siloam Springs.

The *Oregon State Journal*, Eugene, March 8, 1873, mentioned various improvements under way: "Mr. Belknap at the Springs on the McKenzie by a fair patronage last season will also be found to have enlarged the grounds and made other improvements. Having engaged a mechanic (carpenter) he will, March 15th, begin a building 16 x 32 feet (4.9 x 9.8 meters) with additions to contain bathrooms and spacious porches. The main building is to be used as sitting rooms for ladies and gentlemen and near it will be the feature of the establishment an ample swimming bath."

An *Oregon State Journal* advertisement, June 20, 1874, said:

"To Those in Search of
HEALTH AND PLEASURE
The Undersigned, Proprietors of the
SILOAM SPRINGS
"The undersigned proprietors of the Siloam Springs would call attention of those in search of health or pleasure to the properties and excellent situation of the above springs. They are situated on the McKenzie River 60 miles east of Eugene

surrounded by scenery beautiful and grand. The neighborhood abounds in game of every kind and the streams with fine trout. The medicinal properties of the water have been tested by the cure of those who have visited them who have been afflicted with various diseases, particularly Female Weaknesses, Scrofula, Rheumatism, Inflammations both internal and external and general debility. Experienced males and females always in attendance. Charges moderate. Good pasture near by."
Signed "R. S. Belknap, MD,"
"John W. Sims, proprietor."

Rollin Belknap was not a medical doctor. His prescribing no doubt was limited to claims for the magical healing powers of the mineral water. Sims, 34, on Jan. 1, 1874, married Dora Belknap, who turned 15 years of age the day before. The Sims later homesteaded on the north side of the McKenzie along Mill Creek Road.

First Post Office

A post office under the name of Salt Springs was established Oct. 26, 1874, with Rollin S. Belknap as first postmaster. (McArthur's *Oregon Geographic Names*). The name of Salt Springs was changed to Belknap's Spring after it was sold June 5, 1875, to Peter Settle and John Miller. Miller died a year later.

Whether Rollin thought he owned the springs is not clear. Records show he established a preemption land claim near the location. Surveys were informal. He isn't on record as owning the property.

Northwest Ruralite (1967) reported: "Mrs. (R. E.) Newman (of Eugene) located an 1873 survey by Lorenzo Gesner, marking an 'X' to locate the 'Belknap cabin' across the river from the 'hot Siloam or Siloam Mud.' She also found the first owner of record to be Peter B. Settle, who received a patent on his homestead signed by President Arthur May 7, 1886. Linn County probate of the estate of John Miller in 1876 mentions a half interest in a quarter section owned by Miller in partnership with Settle, known as Belknap Mineral Springs. Mr. Miller is thought to have at one time carried mail in the area."

Walling (1884) wrote: "The springs are enclosed on three sides by high hills. . .The property. . .was taken up in the first instance by Mr. Belknap in the year 1870, his claim extending to both sides of the river. He commenced improvements, with the object of making it a resort, and a few years later erected the building now used as a hotel." (Belknap) "Having conducted the establishment until 1875, Peter Settle and John Miller purchased it, when the latter dying at the end of twelve months, it was closed for two years. In 1882, J. W. Hickson took charge and now conducts the spa."

Miller's story is told in the Wycoff Chapter. The 1880 census listed Peter Settle, 50, as being born in Iowa, his father in Indiana, and his mother in Georgia. Children were listed as Lorina P., 20; Mary C., 16; John C., 14; Minnie M., 10; Stephen, 8, and Percilla R., 7.

Walling (1884) said: "The hotel is placed in a short bend, or elbow, of the river, on a level plot of two acres in extent, where are built the bath houses to which the water is conveyed from the north bank, where the springs are located, through pipes, the springs themselves being reached by means of a substantial bridge.

"Besides the hotel accommodations there are six cottages for the use of families. The temperature of the water is 185 degrees and that of the river, flowing only six to ten feet away, 44 degrees in the hottest weather. The environment may be termed the hunter's paradise. Elk, deer, and other game abound in the woods and mountains, while the stream teems with trout that offer tempting sport for devotees of the gentle art. Improvements are being made daily while it is contemplated to construct six additional cottages for the accommodation of the increased patronage that had arisen."

The post office was closed between 1877 and 1891, when it was reopened and the name changed to Belknap Springs. The office was closed again 1895-96 and 1902-16. It finally closed April 22, 1953.

The resort's popularity continued to grow. By 1890, some 700 guests were visiting the springs during the summer months. Hotel rooms were $15.00 per week and camping sites, $1.50 per week.

The springs and resort were sold in 1893 to A. P. Ostrander and George Hill. Apparently unable to keep the springs profitable, the following year they sold their rights back to Hickson.

An advertisement in the *Eugene Guard* May 20, 1897, shows George Hill as proprietor and C. M. Hill, manager. The stage left the hotel in Eugene Mondays, Wednesdays and Fridays, returning on alternate days, a distance of 60 miles each way. It advertised "fine hunting and fishing, a fine swimming rink, cures of rheumatism, skin diseases, liver complaints, catarrh, ague and private diseases."

Over the years a bathhouse, with tubs hollowed from a single, mammoth cedar tree, provided privacy for guests and offered both vapor and plunge baths. The springs, natural mineral water gushing from the ground, was a so-called magical cure from rheumatism to female problems. By the early 1900's, a daily stage coach was taking tourists to the site, a trip that took 16 hours from Eugene. Later, a swimming pool and other services were added.

The late Coy Lansbery said, when he arrived on the McKenzie from Pennsylvania in 1907, George and Alice Croner, who owned the Log Cabin Hotel at McKenzie Bridge, "had the Belknap Springs leased. They drove a two-seated, one-horse hack from the Bridge to the Springs each day to take care of the tourists which were quite brisk in the summer." The Croners were reconstructing the Log Cabin Hotel, which was destroyed by fire in 1906. Lansbery and his cousin, Freeman, helped rebuild the hotel which stands today.

Haak Acquires Ownership

John Howard Haak, Michigan timber baron who got his financial start in Pennsylvania oil, acquired Belknap Springs in the early 1900's, according to his grandson, John Bigelow. John's family owned and operated the resort for more than half a century.

Haak moved his family to Portland in the early 1900's and invested heavily in Oregon timber. Bigelow said everything his grandfather did was on a grand scale. Haak made and lost fortunes. Timber he purchased for fifty cents per thousand board feet couldn't be sold for half that much in the 1930's. The Springs constantly was under a mortgage from money borrowed to finance improvements.

During our visit with John Bigelow in the summer of 1991, he said he didn't have details or the date of his grandfather's takeover. His sister, Betty Jean Smith, quoted in *Ruralite* (1967), gave Haak's acquisition date as 1908. A manager, Sloan, was responsible for many early improvements, he said. (This was Bert or Buck Sloan, who later joined Al Kuhn in construction and operation of Cascade Resort, one and a half miles west of McKenzie Bridge, in the late 1920's).

The first "highway" reached the springs in 1913, about a mile distance across Lost Creek from Yales' Ranch, at the old Belknap Junction. This highway was really a dusty, dirt road in summer and an impassable muddy, heavily rutted road in winter.

Belknap Springs remained pretty much as described for many years. This writer's first visit was about the end of World War I. The "substantial" swinging bridge spanned the swift flowing McKenzie River from the resort to the springs. We used to put salt in the mineral water and said it tasted like chicken soup. Beyond the springs, a trail continued upriver another 20 miles over rugged terrain to Clear Lake, headwaters of the McKenzie.

Bigelow commented the Springs was in its heyday in the Roaring Twenties. Haak sent in his son-in-law and daughter, Frank and Helen Bigelow, to take over the management. At least four bridges washed out by high water were replaced. The last bridge, destroyed by the 1964 flood, was not replaced.

John, born in 1910, was the oldest of the Bigelows' five children. The others were Betty (Smith), Tom, George and Frank Jr. (all deceased). His family divided their time between Portland and Belknap Springs. He attended schools both places. He was a student of Martha Andrews, who became the wife of Clarence Belknap, grandson of Rollin.

In the summer of 1925, extensive improvements were begun. By the late 1920's the Springs boasted a large new lodge, post office, two restaurants, a swimming pool, dance hall, several cabins, grounds improvements and a suspension bridge that allowed access across the river and served to support the pipe for the hot mineral water.

Clarence Belknap, in the 1920's, constructed a flume from cedar sawn in his sawmill at Rainbow to carry hot water from the springs across to the resort. The flume consisted of numerous lengths of split and hollowed cedar clamped with wire and suspended over the river. Today the hot water flows across the river by means of a metal pipe, suspended by steel cables to the opposite river bank.

Early-day Crowds

Bigelow recalled those early days, when one Fourth of July more than 2,500 visitor crammed into the lodge, cabins and campsites. Live bands and minstrel shows were regular features of the dance hall. Belknap probably was the most popular resort in the Northwest.

Other resorts, such as the "more elegant" Foley Springs, which catered to the aristocratic; Cascade Resort, Yales Ranch, Lost Creek Ranch and Sparks Ranch on the upper river thrived prior to and in the early part of the Hoover administration.

Many famous people visited, including President Herbert Hoover, who held a fondness for the valley's recreational opportunities; movie stars, such as Clark Gable, and Gen. George C. Marshall, World War II commander of the American armies.

Activity at the springs flourished until the great 1930's depression, which cut heavily into patronage. Frank Bigelow was replaced as manager by John Haak, son of the senior Haak and brother of Mrs. Bigelow. Frank and son, John, returned to the management in 1933. They enlarged the lodge and made extensive other improvements. John, meanwhile, operated the Blue Lake Resort and Lodge, which he established near Suttle Lake, west of Sisters.

Business never fully recovered from the depression. With modern transportation and other recreational opportunities, including free government-owned campgrounds built by the CCC, interest in hot springs, at one time so extensive around the state, slowly waned. The so-called "magic" cure of mineral springs water ceased to hold the lure it once had, even if the rest and recreational value still remain.

After Frank Bigelow Sr.'s death in 1952, the resort ownership passed to his daughter, Betty Jean Smith, who worked in a California brokerage office in winter and at the lodge May to September.

In the late 1960's, the resort fell victim to public health regulations, which forced its closure. With Mrs. Smith's failing health, no effort was made to reactivate the Springs. After her death ownership passed to her son Randy and daughter Shelley.

The Haak and Bigelow families -- Frank Sr., and sons, John, Tom, George, Frank Jr., and Betty Smith and Betty's children, Randy and Shelley -- owned the property for more than 60 years.

Jim Nation, a U. S. Army Corps of Engineers retiree, purchased the property in 1975. With the sale, the Bigelow ownership came to an end. The Bigelows and Smiths, however, retained ownership of the three hot springs. The flow of one is piped across the river to the resort. The others were retained for family use.

Nation remodeled and reopened the resort in 1979. Extensive reconstruction was necessary. Floods had washed out the swinging bridge, which spanned the river to the springs and caused other damage. Improvements had to be made to meet health requirements.

Springs Property Sold

In the summer of 1991, the 70-year-old Nation sold the Belknap Springs Lodge/Belknap Woods Resort to the San Francisco-based investment firm RYT Corp. for a reported $900,000. The sale included the 12-room lodge, mineral water swimming pool, 21 recreational vehicle sites, five cabins and quarter mile of river frontage. The property was tied up in foreclosure litigation prior to the McDougal Bros. acquisition.

The Bigelows and Smiths no longer own any part of the Belknap resort. John, the last surviving child of Frank and Helen Bigelow, has long-lasting memories of what served as his home for so many years. He owns 160 acres a mile down river. He constructed a metal vehicle bridge across to his property and built a house.

Property in the vicinity held by surviving Bigelows has been sold to the McDougals. This included land east across the river owned by the late Frank Bigelow Jr.'s estate. His son, Brad, had property northwest of the springs, accessed by a cable car suspended from a cable strung across the river. Randy Smith also had property nearby.

John Bigelow, an engineer in his own right and a firm believer in the future of geothermal energy, has made unusual developments on his property. By diverting a small flow of water from the river, he has created an 18-acre lake with a small island. He has his own hydroelectric plant, sufficient to supply his needs, and has his swimming pool heated with hot mineral water.

He has used the springs for geothermal energy experiments and drilled his own geothermal well reaching hot water at about 680 feet. He said this is the only hot-water well in the state drilled for personal use. It is used to heat his swim pool and for other purposes.

John speaks with nostalgia of his youth, schooling, life at the Springs, of good times and bad. But he waxes with enthusiasm on the subject of geothermal energy. With his electrical background he has focused on energy development and geothermal consultation. He has new and bigger tests in mind hoping to prove the molten spine of the Cascade Mountains can make the area a hotbed of geothermal activity. In 1986, he proposed to the Committee for the Development of the McKenzie River Valley that a series of pilot projects explore the feasibility of geothermal-pressurized food processing, greenhouse and aqua-culture projects, even full-scale electric-generation facilities.

He sees unlimited possibilities by tapping the energy from the molten mass beneath the Cascade Mountains, extending from Belknap Springs east into the Metolius region. He believes firmly there is enough energy to supply the state of Oregon with enough hot water left over to heat all of Eugene and Springfield. As for tourism, he also sees great potential for further recreational development, especially if winter sports can be expanded to the fullest extent.

John still has unwavering faith in the health benefits from drinking the mineral water. He said he drinks a liter of the water a day or uses it in his cooking. Then, he added, "all my family died of cancer," and he wondered philosophically if there was a connection.

CHAPTER 27

Foley Springs

Credit for the actual discovery and early development of Foley Hot Springs, on Horse Creek four miles southeast of McKenzie Bridge, is still a bit in controversy. But any way you want to cut it, Foley Springs was Ella Haflinger, personified.

The grand old lady, upper McKenzie River pioneer and as controversial as the history about the origin of the development, ruled her domain with a "strong arm and voice." She often was affectionately referred to as "Mrs. Hell-flinger" who made sure young couples were married before she'd admit them to her hotel.

The resort, long since defunct, closed in 1940 with Mrs. Haflinger's death. Because of costly health and environmental requirements, it was not reopened. The grand old hotel burned down March 4, 1981, but the hot mineral springs remain, pouring out 1,000 gallons of water an hour at 180 degree temperature. And Foley Hot Springs, once known as Bethesda and as Siloam Hot Springs, lives on in the memories of the many people who visited in years gone by.

Mrs. Haflinger's grandson, William "Bill" Runey, who took over after his grandmother's death, sold the property in 1993. He also sold his home at McKenzie Bridge and moved to the Eugene area. There are no plans to revive the resort.

Gerald Williams, quoting from Howard Horowitz unpublished thesis, 1973-8, reported: "The water for these springs derives from an area near Avenue Creek. Paul Bristow related 'sometime in the middle 1860's Doctor (Abram) Foley was acquainted with the Indians who lived up near the head of the McKenzie River. They told him about a spring of water that smoked. He went with them and discovered the Foley Springs.'

"The Indians continued to use the hot mineral springs for many years after the building of the private resort. William Runey recalls Indians were frequent visitors to the waters, and they came in groups for occasional visits as recently as 1920, when the resort was in full swing."

Walling's *History of Lane County* (1884: 466) had this account:
"Foley Hot Springs are located on Horse Creek, about sixty miles due east from Eugene City, amid the fastness of the Cascade Mountains, and were first discovered by Wm. Hanley and Wm. Vick (in the early 1860's). In 1865, Mr. (J. B.) Alexander settled on the premises and, in 1870, Dr. Foley purchased the interest of the last known gentleman; and in that year opened the springs to the

public under the name of Bethesda Hot Springs."

Lewis McArthur (1982: 282) related: "Lane County records seem to show what Dr. Foley bought from Alexander was little more than squatter's rights. Abram A. Foley received a government patent dated March 30, 1882, filed and recorded Nov. 30, 1889."

Apparently the first improvements to Foley began in 1873, the same time improvements were also beginning at Belknap Springs.

The Oregon State Journal March 8, 1873, reported: "By way of the new road which Dr. Foley proposes to have finished early in May you may visit him at the Siloam Springs where he is erecting a hotel and bath house this winter. His main building 18 x 36, two stories, is already roofed and the floors laid. His faith in the value of the springs is unbounded, and, as it is based on actual experiments, is akin to positive knowledge."

Bill Runey said this building was little more than a one-room, cedar cabin. His grandfather, Peter Runey, constructed a lodge, with guest rooms, around it. The cabin was used as a kitchen.

The Springfield News (1981) reported: "Following the winter of 1949-50, when heavy snows crumpled the lodge, Bill Runey dismantled the wrecked building and found the cabin still intact. Before taking the building apart -- in the never-realized hope that someone would reassemble it elsewhere -- Runey snapped a few pictures, which are now the only record of its existence."

The first wagon road into the springs followed up stream bottoms. Foley made only minor improvements, Runey said.

An advertisement for Bethesda Springs in the Oregon State Journal (June 20, 1874) stated:

"Ho! Ye Weak and Weary
BETHESDA SPRINGS

"These springs are located about 55 miles east of Eugene City and within 4 miles of the celebrated Big Prairie of the McKenzie. They are within a few hundred yards of Horse Creek, one of the most famous trouting streams in Oregon. Deer and Elk are very plentiful near these springs, having been the resort for ages of these animals. The grandest and most picturesque scenery of the North Pacific. We have the best buildings and the best accommodations of any springs in this part of the state. Our bathhouse is constructed with reference to the wants of those visiting us from the valley. We also have an excellent vapor bath room constructed near the head of the spring, and we propose to keep up with the demands for an institution of this kind.

"An experienced physician in attendance at all times. Board and lodging in good style for those who prefer it. Animals can be pastured for small cost with us, and be perfectly safe."

A. N. Foley |
J. B. Alexander | Proprietors

Dr. Foley owned the hot springs for about nine years. Upon his death in 1880, the springs ". . .passed into the hands of Henry Hill, who in March 1882 sold to Peter Runey, the present proprietor, the property comprising 160 acres. Runey, henceforth, commenced its improvement, removing the log cabins that were originally built and substituting a large and comfortable hotel in their stead, with cottages, bath house, etc." (Walling, 1884.)

Runey, an Irish immigrant, fought for the Union during the Civil War, then served as Astoria's mayor before entering the construction business in Portland. He bought the springs for $1,200 in 1882. An Astoria newspaper recounted the event. He built the first road into the resort and the lodge around Foley's one-room cabin. He established a post office, called Foleysprings in compliment to Dr. Foley. Postal authorities spelled the name as one word, but "ordinary mortals use the style Foley Springs." (McArthur).

(Walling 1884): "The water is obtained from two springs in close proximity to each other and, as it leaves the rock, has a uniform temperature of 180 degrees. It is a specific against all diseases save consumption, while in the surrounding country we have the hunter's elysiun. The stream abounds with the finny tribe, and the scenery is unsurpassed. Three miles from the springs is a view the like of which is nowhere else to be found. No fewer than fifteen snow-capped peaks are in sight at one time, while all around the grandeur of mountain ranges is intense."

McArthur (1982) said: "The water is hot, about 188 degrees, rendering the baths very agreeable when adequately tempered."

Bill Runey said today the temperature of the springs water is about 176 degrees. He doesn't know whether the water has cooled or if the early temperature readings were inaccurate.

On March 10, 1886, Peter Runey married Ella Kenyon. Ella, born in Nebraska in 1860, had moved with her family to Junction City, Ore. Peter and Ella had two children, Arthur (father of Bill), born May 13, 1887, and Nellie, born in 1890.

Peter Runey sold the springs Oct. 14, 1891, to Dr. Barr and Mr. Mulford for $18,000. (*Oregon State Journal*, Oct. 17, 1891). "They returned the springs to Mr. Runey in 1893 as the financial burden of the loan was too heavy."

Tragedy Strikes

Tragedy struck the family in 1895. Peter Runey and daughter, Nellie, at age 6, both died from diphtheria on Christmas day.

Defying Runey's dying request that she close the springs and move to Eugene, Ella took over operation of the resort. On April 20, 1897, she married Albert Haflinger. The 1905 Blue River Precinct census shows Haflinger was born in Switzerland. That census listed him and his wife as age 45, making their birth years 1860.

Haflinger owned a restaurant in Portland. He apparently met Ella Runey on a visit to the springs. They continued the Portland business several years, since Foley was a summer-only operation. The family moved to Portland in the fall, then returned in the spring.

The Haflingers began extensive improvements in the early

1900's. The stately white old hotel was built in 1916. James "Jimmy" Yale, life-long McKenzie resident who lives at Yales' Ranch, six miles east of McKenzie Bridge, recalls his father, William "Bill" Yale, operated a small steam-powered sawmill at McKenzie Bridge. Employed to cut lumber for the Foley Springs construction, he moved his mill to the site and cut lumber from timber on the property.

An old advertisement about the highly mineralized water from Foley Springs stated with authority that "these waters are most valuable in cases of Liver and Kidney Complaints, Rheumatism, Gout, Dropsy, Skin Afflictions, Dyspepsia, Catarrh, Female Diseases, Private Diseases and Brights Disease."

The advertisement listed: Board, lodging and bath $2.50 per day, $14.50 per week and camp grounds and bath, $1.50 per week. It offered horse and automobile stages, and stated: "U. S. Mail will leave the hotels (in) Eugene, Oregon, on Mondays, Wednesdays and Fridays at 6 a. m. from April 1 to June 15, and from June 15 to Sept. 15 daily except Sunday, arriving at the Springs the same day."

During summer months, before advent of the automobile, the open stage "run" to Foley from Eugene took 12 hours. But "the long trip was worth it as passengers were greeted with beautiful mountain scenery, spacious grounds, fine food and good accommodations, making this one of the most popular places for the well-to-do to come and stay for the summer. (Horowitz, 1973: 67).

"In Oregon there was an unwritten but very clear distinction between the springs for the wealthy and the springs for the 'common man.' Foley Springs for the most part catered to a more affluent and pretentious class of people than nearby Belknap Springs. This is not apparent from any differences in advertising or literature, but is the opinion of many personal informants based on their recollections."

The *Springfield News*, April. 28, 1981, quoted Smith Taylor, Forest Service district ranger at McKenzie Bridge, recalling what the resort was like before the advent of the motor car:

"In those days people came from all over the United States to stay, not overnight, but for the summer. Many a time I walked to Foley Springs Resort, Log Cabin Inn and Belknap Springs, which were miles from nowhere, to find their dining halls crowded with people. Whole families came to take trips into the wilds."

Bill Runey, describing the resort as it was in the 1920's, said: "I've never seen a place which had such an atmosphere of tranquillity. People traveled by horse and wagon from as far as Pendleton to spend a month or two there." Arrival of the stage was a gala occasion. Hotel guests and employees would come out to meet the stage. As it came up over the hill approaching the springs, the driver would whip the horses to a fast speed before coming to a quick stop.

Mrs. Haflinger built the stately old white hotel in 1916 and added a wing in 1927. She ran the resort, reportedly, with a "strong arm and voice." She served as postmaster until the post office was closed Jan. 22, 1940. She died in 1950.

The great depression and changing vacation habits of Americans -- automobiles and better roads made other areas more accessible -- "conspired to squelch the resort's economic vitality by 1930," said the *Springfield News*. "Mrs. Haflinger, who 35 years before defied her husband's dying instructions to close the resort and move to Eugene, refused to face the new reality." Peter Runey had owned a home in Eugene at 13th and Willamette streets. This home was occupied for a number of years by Bill Runey's mother.

Bill Runey said, "By 1930 she was 70 years old and a very strong-willed, domineering person. She refused to let anybody do anything with it, and it just deteriorated. She charged fees for people to camp there and use the hot springs, but the hotel didn't operate."

Years of vandalism and petty thefts during Mrs. Haflinger's aging and failing health added to the problem. Ella Haflinger lost many valuable antiques kept in the hotel to souvenir hunters. The usual method of operation was someone would engage the elderly woman in conversation while another would steal anything they wanted, according to Runey. Vandalism, thievery and trespassing at Foley plagued the Haflinger and Runey families for years.

Health restrictions in the 1960's brought a permanent downfall of the resort, which had long since become defunct. The beautiful old lodge burned in March 4, 1981. The blaze destroyed a 3,000 to 4,000-volume book collection, the guest records dating back to 1882, a small gun and tool collection and Peter Runey's desk, which he used as mayor of Astoria, and the only remaining photograph of him.

Even after the hotel burned, curiosity seekers snooped around following a false rumor "the walls were stuffed with coins," said Runey. The fire melted no coins, but it came close to snuffing out the life of his son. Young Peter Runey was sleeping in the hotel when a wood-burning furnace ignited a wall. He escaped after a vain attempt to put the fire out with a fire extinguisher.

Runey, brought up at the springs, remembers its early splendor. He tried to revive the resort before World War II, but the expenses to satisfy new building codes persuaded him to enter the logging business. He continued using the springs for bathing, but his dreams of restoring the resort remained just dreams.

Arthur Runey, son of Peter and Ella, married Alma Dickert, who was born in Arkansas in 1895. They had two sons, William "Bill," born in 1920, and Jerry, of Leaburg, 1924.

Bill and his wife have four children, Peter, born in 1958; Brian, 1961; Steve, 1963, and Heather, 1972. Bill Runey's grandmother on his mother's side divorced Dickert, then married Albert Walksmith. The Walksmiths in 1925 purchased Log Cabin Hotel at McKenzie Bridge and operated it until 1944.

Martha Belknap, commenting on Belknap and Foley Hot Springs, said in a taped interview in 1976, "Yes, they were very beautiful places. People would come and spend the summer, camped and take their water and do their fishing. And Foley especially was a beautiful place. Mrs.

Haflinger had so many flowers and nice buildings. She dearly loved beautiful things. She had cut glasses and beautiful tablecloths. But, she was an old-timer. She wouldn't do anything she couldn't pay for and she got sick and didn't have the money to run the place. She left it to her grandson, Bill Runey."

Over the years, Mrs. Haflinger provided summer employment for many people. My mother, Cora Belknap Inman, and her older sister, Alice Odell, both worked there in the early 1900's prior to their marriages. Alice's daughter, Metta, who worked at the resort in the summer of 1937 after graduating from Springfield High School, was married there to Ernest Watson with Mrs. Haflinger's blessing.

Ella Haflinger, Ella Belknap, Dora Sims and Melvina "Auntie" Frissell were the original pioneer women of the upper McKenzie.

Bill Runey said the bodies of Peter and Ella are buried on Foley Springs property. A tombstone bearing their names has been erected in the Pioneer Cemetery in Eugene. The bodies haven't been moved.

Names that will live in history, besides Foley Springs, include: Haflinger Creek, which empties into Horse Creek four miles above Foley Springs. Foley Lake -- a small lake in the Three Sisters Wilderness area, listed in an Oregon Game Commission report by Frank Young, 1962, is located just south of the Foley Ridge trail, southwest of Proxy Falls and northwest of Proxy Point in the headwaters of Rainbow Creek. Foley Ridge follows a generally east-west direction, separating the Horse Creek (south) and McKenzie River-Lost Creek-White Branch (north) drainages. Foley Ridge Road, beginning above the McKenzie Ranger Station on the McKenzie Highway, skirts near the crest of Foley Ridge. (Williams, 1991).

LOG CABIN INN is located on property at McKenzie Bridge homesteaded by Philander Renfrew in 1874. The inn was built originally by "Uncle" George Frissell in 1885. The property was purchased in 1991 by Dave and Diane Rae.

CHAPTER 28

Log Cabin Inn

Log Cabin Inn at McKenzie Bridge is famous as an old stage stop and hotel. Open-top stages once traveled from Eugene, bringing mail and passengers to the upper McKenzie. Many people were traveling to the Blue River mining district and either to Belknap or Foley Hot Springs, popular during the summer months.

The Inn, built originally in 1885, was rebuilt in 1906 following a disastrous fire. But we have to go back a few years to establish the history of this landmark, which was taken over in the summer of 1991 by new owners, Dave and Diane Rae, of Southern California.

The hotel stands on an original 160-acre tract, settled in 1872 by Philander Renfrew. He filed a homestead claim in 1874.

Renfrew was born in Ohio in 1817. His father was born in Ireland and his mother in New York. Just when he came to Oregon is not established. He was around Eugene and the McKenzie prior to the 1870's. His name kept popping up in records and news accounts of early-day events. Philander, with Dr. Alexander Renfrew, John T. Craig, and M. H. Harlow, joined in 1871 to incorporate the McKenzie Salt Springs and Des Chutes Wagon Road Co.

Philander may have been a brother of Dr. Alexander Renfrew, Eugene hotel owner, whose name was almost synonymous with gold discovery on Gold Hill. Alexander, also born in Ohio in 1816, brought his wife to the Oregon Territory in 1852.

The McKenzie Bridge Post Office, established Dec. 30, 1874, with Philander C. Renfrew as postmaster, was named for the bridge, built by John Craig in 1869, that crosses the river at this point. The name first came out as McKinzie Bridge. After years of protest by local residents, the name was changed to McKenzie in 1918. The post office was closed July 10, 1974, and taken over as a rural route.

Philander died in 1880 from a self-inflicted gunshot wound, the first reported case of suicide on the McKenzie. His heirs secured title to the Log Cabin Inn property from the U. S. Government in August 1882. O. H. Renfrew, Philander's nephew, born in 1847 in Ohio, was administrator of the estate.

On March 7, 1884, George Colby Frissell (1848-1921) and Melvina Frissell (1838-1926) paid $480 for about 120 acres of mostly timbered McKenzie River frontage (an old Log Cabin Inn menu said he paid $350 for 160 acres). The land extended about a mile upstream from the bridge, one fourth mile wide. Improvements built by Renfrew included an hotel, house, camp house, barn, woodshed, smokehouse, hen house and outhouse. O. H. Renfrew was living in the hotel at the time.

Philander was Melvina "Auntie" Frissell's uncle. An unverified report said Dr. Alexander Renfrew also was an uncle. An Oscar (probably O. H.) Renfrew is believed to have been her brother or half brother. Her death notice in 1926 listed a W. W. Renfrew of Farmington, Wa., as a surviving half brother.

"Uncle" George Frissell was quoted in an *Oregon State Journal* interview, in 1915, as saying: "I was born in Vermont Nov. 5, 1848. From Vermont I moved to Michigan then to Wisconsin. When I came to McKenzie Bridge in 1879, my nearest neighbors were Jim (should be John) Sims and Jim Belknap."

First Married at Age 14

"Auntie" Frissell, born in Ohio in 1838, was first married at age 14 years. She was playing outside her home, when her parents called her in and told her she was to marry a certain man, apparently without prior courtship. That would have been in 1852. We do not know where her family was living at the time. A son was a product of that marriage a year later. But the marriage was a failure.

My sister, Gladys Myers, lived with "Auntie" one year while she taught school at McKenzie Bridge, 1923-24. She recalled meeting the son, who was visiting from California. He was 71 and Auntie 86.

Dates and sequences are a bit confusing. George said he arrived at McKenzie Bridge in 1879. It is not known when he and Auntie were married. Maple Stobie, late of the McKenzie, wrote (1969: 26): "Captain George Frissell and his wife, Melvina, arrived at McKenzie Bridge in 1879 in a wagon drawn by a mule and a bull."

Auntie's death report, Nov. 22, 1926, said: "Coming to Oregon from

California in 1873 on a visit, Mrs. Frissell and her husband, known as 'Uncle George', returned to Oregon in 1878 and took up residence at McKenzie Bridge. They lived there until they died."

"Uncle" George in the Journal interview said, "In 1874 my wife's uncle, Philander Renfrew, a surveyor, was cutting a trail into the Clear Lake country. My wife and Mrs. (John) Sims went with him to see Clear Lake. They were the first white women to visit the lake."

Melvina would have been 34 years of age, and Mrs. Sims, the former Dora Belknap, 15, her age when she married Sims. Auntie's death notice observed she "was the first white woman to visit McKenzie Falls." Her trip to the lake must have occurred during her visit to the McKenzie in 1873-74.

Frissell in his 1915 interview said: "When I came here I could have bought thousands of acres of fire timber (burned over timber land) at two dollars an acre. Now it sells for $40 or $50 an acre. I paid three dollars an acre for my quarter section, but it was a particularly desirable place. I am a fisherman and no hunter. I never carry a gun. When I came here 35 years ago, this road was operated as a toll road. The toll was $2 at the bridge. Not many people came here. We often got plenty short of money and necessities, particularly tobacco. We used to smoke manzanita bark. After a year or two I raised my own tobacco. I had enough for the whole neighborhood."

Inn Built in 1885

Construction of the Log Cabin Inn was begun in 1885. It was opened for business in 1886. "Travelers from as far as Los Angeles came to visit the new resort on the McKenzie," the old menu stated. The hotel was operated by "Uncle" George and "Auntie" Frissell. The building, constructed of rough peeled logs, contained 19 rooms, 32 windows and 22 doors, with covered porches around the building.

A *Daily Eugene Guard* advertisement July 6, 1898, said:

"Frissell's 'Log House' Hotel. Neatly built. Splendid accommodations. Table supplied with fresh trout and venison in season. Splendid hunting and fishing in season. Stages and mails three times a week. Very reasonable terms for guests. Only about one-half the usual charge of summer resort places. For terms and further particulars, address Geo. Frissell, McKenzie Bridge, Ore."

In 1906, the inn was destroyed by fire. Frances O'Brien of Blue River (1979) said hotel guests were up the river at Belknap Springs when the fire occurred. All their food and belongings, except the swimming suits they were wearing, were lost in the fire. The guests were put up by local residents until a rescue wagon loaded with supplies arrived from Eugene three days later.

Reconstruction of the inn was begun soon after the fire. Coy and Freeman Lansbery finished the new hotel in the fall of 1907. Uncle George then turned the property over to his foster daughter, Alice Tuttle Croner, wife of George Croner, a deputy sheriff stationed at McKenzie Bridge. They were married March 3, 1895. The Frissells also reared George Moody, a packer and guide.

Auntie Frissell operated the McKenzie Bridge Post Office for 34 years. Uncle George was justice of the peace. He served in other capacities during his life time and conducted a stage barn for horses.

Annie Laura Miller, writing in *The Oregonian* Sept. 27, 1908, quoted Frissell as saying about early settlers: "There was 'Ole Man' Pepiot, a Frenchman who kept the eating house at Gate Creek. He is dead (1896) and so are 'Ole Man' Belknap (1908), and 'Ole Man' Sims (1903), who lived far up in the big timber. 'Andy' Hickson, tall and gaunt, a great hunter in days gone by, has retired from life on the trail and works in the salmon hatchery, while 'Pood' his dog and 'Mouser', the little gray pony, grow fat and lazy with inaction. 'Ole Man' Finn, the greatest liar on the McKenzie, still lives in a lonely big white house with 'Finn Hotel' painted in long letters on the side.

"Uncle George rises early in true mountain fashion. When we came down to breakfast he was driving the cows out of the barn to pasture. He is some 60 years old. . .but covers the ground like a boy. Behind his round spectacles his keen eyes can see a fish far down in the water where untrained eyes see only the rocky river bottom. He wears sad-colored clothes in deference to the fishes' feelings, an old gray hat, brown suit coat, gray trousers and blue shirt.

"After breakfast I saw an-eight pound Dolly Varden on the back porch. Uncle George was in the garden. I asked him where and why of the fish. He said he caught it in the garden walking among the cabbages.

"There is a beautiful big pool just beyond. The garden is the pride of his life. . .But the love of his life is 'Auntie', his sweet old wife, a plump little old lady who walks with a cane. She was the postmistress at McKenzie Bridge. . .Next to Auntie in his affections comes Brutus, the old asthma-smitten white terrier. . .We carried lettuce to the chickens.

"'I've got 160 chickens,' he said, 'not big enough to fry yet. An' tell you I don't like to kill 'em. . .They know me and come runnin'.'

"'See where the limbs are broken on the trees,' he said as we went through the orchard. 'Where the high water came, some of those big redsides roosted on the limbs. That's what broke 'em off.'

"Then we went fishing. . ."

"After supper, all the people thereabouts began to gather for the mail: the trapper who lived across Horse Creek; three of the cattleman's children; the old mountaineer who was a living botany book; the homesteader's wife, very picturesque in a short skirt, blue flannel shirt and a felt hat, with the revolver by her side; the summer boarders and a wiry dark man who is the most fearless hunter in the forest reserve. I asked Uncle George about the hunter.

"'Afraid? He ain't afraid of nothin'. He'll climb right up in a tree and shake out a wildcat or cougar. . .' The four-horse stage came jingling in from Eugene. Uncle George took the mail sack into Auntie. Just now as I sat on the upper porch watching the stars come out above the rugged mountain tops, I saw him starting out patiently with a lantern to find the straying cows."

Property Subdivided

The new hotel built in 1907 is the same building that occupies the site today. The Log Cabin has been described as a "... Rustic inn -- a close replica of the original (1885) stage station and resort hotel developed by George Frissell, which burned in 1906. Only native materials were used in its hand-crafted construction. Walls were built of logs with saddle-notch comers and clinked with moss while poles were used for short joists. Small poles were used decoratively as railings and as siding on the gable ends where they were split and set vertically. Cottages behind the main building were also built in the rustic style." (Williams, quoting Dale and McCulloch, 1983: 124).

In 1909 the property was subdivided into 29 lots, following the river upstream a mile. Most of the lots were sold.

George Frissell died at Mercy Hospital in Eugene Oct. 9, 1921, age 73. His obituary said Frissell "pioneer at McKenzie Bridge, coming from California in 1879 and for several years owning and operating the Log Cabin Inn. . ."

Melvina "Auntie" Frissell died Nov. 12, 1926. (Death records and the 1905 census spell her first name Melvilla). The death notice said, "After a life that has been particularly blessed by a sunny disposition and a personality that attracted all who came within her sphere, Mrs. Melvina Frissell. . .of McKenzie Bridge died at her home this morning.

"For nearly a half century, Mrs. Frissell mothered the children and grown-ups of that country. A short illness resulted in her passing and with her a custom that prevailed for many years. The first wild flowers of spring have annually been gathered by the children and presented to her."

"Uncle" George, "Auntie" Frissell

The Log Cabin Inn has had a number of owners. In September 1925, Mr. and Mrs. Albert Walksmith purchased the hotel and adjoining properties from Alice and George Croner. Mrs. Walksmith was Bill Runey's grandmother on his mother's side. Bill's other grandmother, Ella (Runey) Haflinger, operated Foley Springs.

A Log Cabin Inn menu reprinted in the *Lane County Historian* 1969, says the Walksmiths operated the resort until 1944, when they sold to the Taylor family. They in turn sold to the Robert Tuttle family in April, 1946. The Tuttles had the property for 21 years. The inn gained a certain amount of fame as the place where such notables as President Herbert Hoover, Clark Gable and the Duke of Windsor stayed. Stories are they closed the highway while Hoover went drift-boat fishing, and Gable used to rent the entire place.

The Tuttles sold the present eight-acre property with approximately 900 feet of McKenzie River frontage in September 1967 to Paul A. Krumm and Arthur J. Lucey, ex-Californians who held executive positions with a national food chain and with Knott's Berry Farm. For seven years prior to the purchase by Krumm and Lucey, the inn lay vacant. The new owners leased the inn almost immediately to Mr. and Mrs. A. J. Marastoni (Peggy and Tony), who "maintained the character of the log structure with furnishings in keeping with its age. The only departure was a spotless stainless steel kitchen with ultra modern cooking and serving facilities."

Dave and Diane Rae, the most recent owners of the Log Cabin Inn and Guest Cottages, purchased the property and business in the summer of 1991. The Raes originally hail from Montreal, Canada. Dave, in the banking business, moved his family to the Los Angles area in 1980 to open a foreign office in Mission Viejo. When that office closed, the Raes saw the Log Cabin Inn advertised in the Orange County, Cal., Register. They had been considering a change of lifestyle and were impressed with Oregon on a trip north to explore business opportunities. Diane was a housewife. They have three children -- ages 13, 12 and 10 (as of 1991).

The Raes extensively renovated the kitchen and enlarged the banquet room, while maintaining the atmosphere and rustic features of the historic establishment. The inn offers eight cabins, a gift shop, a lounge, outdoor dining, concerts and dinner theater. They keep the hotel open year-around, catering in winter months to special groups.

FRISSELL LANDMARKS

The name Frissell appears often on the upper McKenzie. Frissell Point, at 5,144 feet elevation, is about two miles north of Paradise Campground along the ridge separating the McKenzie River and the Blue River drainages. The point served as a fire lookout for many years. It is within easy walking distance of Frissell-Carpenter Road (FR. 1506), which begins on the Clear Lake cutoff portion of the McKenzie Highway (mp. 17.2), climbs westward toward Frissell Point, then turns northward toward Carpenter Mountain, to Blue River Road. Frissell Crossing was a shallow ford on the South Fork of the McKenzie along what is now Aufderheide Forest Drive at (mp. 21.8). A bridge now spans the river.

CHAPTER 29

Goddards-Stephens

The Goddard and Stephens families, related through marriages, were among early settlers in the Camp Creek and Walterville areas. Samuel Munchy Goddard Sr. came to Camp Creek in 1876. The Stephens' families did not come until 1886.

Born Sept. 18, 1810, in Knoxville, Tenn, Samuel Munchy was the son of Joseph and Elizabeth (Betsy) Jordan Goddard. On Aug. 20, 1835, Samuel married Harriet Jones in Knoxville, Knox County, Tenn. Harriet was born May 10, 1819, in Knox County.

Carl Stephens, Walterville historian, is a great-great grandson of Samuel Munchy. His parents, Charles O. and Arvilla (Knowles) Stephens, were married July 1, 1922, in Eugene. Charles, born in Walterville, Sept. 29, 1890, was a son of David and Rose Ann (Dennison) Stephens, pioneers of 1886. Charles died Feb. 22, 1977. Arvilla died April 5, 1993.

Carl was born Sept. 5, 1925, in Springfield. He married Judith Ann Swanger June 20, 1955, in Thurston. She was born in Eugene July 19, 1936. Carl lives in Walterville on property occupied for many years by the late Lawrence and Verna Millican. The old Millican home was destroyed by fire in August 1943. It was replaced.

Samuel Munchy Goddard

Grace Mae (Stephens) Lindsay, of Springfield, died there Jan. 28, 1996, age 95. She was born in Camp Creek Oct. 4, 1900, daughter of David and Rose Ann Stephens. Prior to her death, she was the oldest alumnus of the old Walterville school, having attended 1906 to 1912. She finished the seventh and eighth grades at Camp Creek, returning to Walterville for a year of high school. She married Richard Lindsay in Eugene April 1, 1924. The Lindsays lived in Walnut Creek, Cal., from 1953 until 1975 before moving back to the McKenzie. Richard died in 1979. Survivors include a daughter, Velma Hammer of Walnut Creek, three grandchildren, six great-grandchildren and two great-great-grandchildren. A grandson, Richard Hammer, died previously.

An aunt of Carl Stephens, the last of a family of nine, she was affectionately known as "Aunt Grace." As one of the longest-lived native-born McKenzie River residents, she was chosen a grand marshal for the Walterville Fair parade of 1991, along with classmate the late Wanda (Schultie) Myers, 97, and former teacher, Veda Gray, 95.

Ancestry Traced

"The war between the States destroyed many of our east Tennessee county records, making the search for our ancestor, Joseph Goddard, most difficult," wrote Jane Crouch Bell in 1965. Jane was a great-great-granddaughter of Joseph. "We are reasonably certain Joseph Goddard was born in the United States, rather America, since there was no United States at that time. From the birth date of his wife, Elizabeth (Betsy) Jordan, in 1782 in Guilford County, N. Car., we can guess Joseph's birth date around 1780.

"My oldest relatives tell me our line of Goddards are German -- perhaps Von Goddard or Gotthardt. There is extensive history on the Goddard family from England but to date none of it fits our family. Therefore I must agree our Goddard family is German. This seems plausible since Joseph married Elizabeth, daughter of John Jordan (born in Germany) and Catherine Scherrer, daughter of Jacob Daniel Scherrer, who emigrated from Germany.

"In 'The Goddard Family' by Jubert Lacy, it is stated the Scherrer family served in the Revolutionary War; that John Jordan did and Goddard relatives are 'said to have served.' I am certain Scherrer and John Jordan served, but whether Joseph Goddard's father served, I am unable to ascertain. (Joseph was not old enough).

"In letters from the 'Scherrer Family History' we are reasonably certain Joseph Goddard lived in Sullivan County, Tenn., probably around 1800. His father-in-law, John Jordan, is known to have lived there or in Virginia in 1800. It seems likely Joseph and Betsy Jordan were married in Sullivan County. Their eldest son, John, was born in 1805 in Tennessee.

"Some sources believe the marriage took place in Guilford County, N. Car., Elizabeth's birthplace. This is hardly logical since the marriage most probably took place after 1800, placing the Jordan family in Sullivan County, Tenn. Elizabeth's brother, John Jr., was born in 1790 in Virginia, according to the 1850 census. We are prone to believe this could have been Bristol, Va., or even Washington County, Va. At any rate, it proves to me John Jordan Sr. and family had moved from Guilford County, N. Car., to somewhere in Virginia, possibly Sullivan County (now Tennessee) before 1790."

Joseph Goddard died in 1825. Elizabeth died in 1863 in Knox County, Tenn. They had eleven children:

(1) John, b. 5-6-1805, m. Martha Johnson, d. 10-24-1860. (2) Joseph, b. 9-11-1806. (3) Catherine (Katie), b. 10-11-1808, m. George Maines. (4) Samuel Munchy Sr., b. 9-19-1810, in Knoxville, Tenn., m. Harriet Jones 8-20-1835, d. 9-16-1897, in Springfield, Ore. (5) William Russell, b. 8-13-1812, m. Margarete Kerrick, d. 5-21-1889. (6) Elizabeth Ann (Betsy), b. 8-14-1814, m. Richard S. Stephens. (7) David Thomas, b. 8-24-1816, m. Matilda Keith. (8) Sally (Sarah F), b, 1818, m. Joseph L.

Hackney. (9) Nancy, b. 1820, m. Hardin Hope. (10) Polly (Eleanor), b. 1-16-1823, m. Joseph Harris. (11) Andrew, b. 1-16-1825, m. Mary F. Boyd.

Samuel Munchy Goddard Sr.

Samuel Munchy Goddard Sr. and Harriet Jones were married Aug. 20, 1835, in Knoxville, Tenn. She was born May 10, 1819. They had twelve children, the first four born in Knox County, Tenn. They were:

(1) Lousinda, b. 2-21-1837, m. (first) Wallis, (second) Samuel Thomas Couey. (2) Harriet, b. 6-9-1838. (3) Andrew Jackson, b. 9-12-1840. (See below). (4) Nancy, b. 4-1-1843. (5) Manervy, b. 3-18-1844. (6) Rutha, b. 11-1-1845, m., (first) John Alexander Dennison, (second) William West, (third) John Kemery; died in Eugene. (7) Marinda, b. 5-1-1848, m. Jacob Hileman, settled near Mabel, Ore. (8) Henry, b. 10-1-1850, m. Mary Jenkins; d. in Lane County. (9) Malissa, b. 1-13-1853, m. James Allen, 7-10-1882. (10) Samuel Munchy Jr., b. 2-2-1855. (See below). (11) Tennysee, b. 4-3-1857 in Mt. Vernon, Ill. (12) Barbary, b. 9-20-1858.

Harriet died March 13, 1861, in Mt. Vernon, Ill. Samuel then married Nancy Jane Boyles (or Bayless) May 20, 1868. Born in Kentucky in 1826, she had two daughters by prior marriage. A daughter, Burga, was born 4-19-1869. Samuel Munchy and Nancy, with Burga, came to Oregon in 1876 and settled in Camp Creek on a donation land claim. They also purchased a part of an original claim of Jeremiah M. Dick.

Apparently Lousinda, her daughter and son-in-law came to Oregon at the same time. About 1885, Burga married William McBee. She died in Camp Creek.

Rutha, daughter of Samuel Munchy Sr. from his first marriage, came to Oregon in 1886. Her son, Alexander, daughter Rose Ann and son-in-law, David Stephens, and children, Cora, Walter and Leonard, were in the party. Alexander married Laura Couey, adopted daughter of Thomas and Lousinda (Goddard) Couey.

Samuel Munchy Goddard Jr., born in Mt. Vernon, Ill., Feb. 2, 1855, and known as Uncle Bud, m. (first) Delzeva Martin, 7-4-1875, (second) Isabelle Tefeteller, 8-30, 1878. Both were born in Blount County, Tenn. He came to Oregon in 1889. He died in Springfield.

Henry and Marinda came to Oregon in 1891. Henry was married twice. Both of his wives were named Mary.

Samuel Sr. died Sept. 16, 1897, in Springfield and was buried in the Camp Creek Cemetery. At his death his Camp Creek property went to his daughter, Rutha Dennison, who later sold it to her son-in-law, David Stephens, husband of Rose Ann Dennison.

ANDREW JACKSON GODDARD

Andrew Jackson Goddard, son of Samuel Munchy Sr., was born July 12, 1841, in Knox County, Tenn. He served in the Civil War as a private with K. Company, 49th Infantry. He enlisted in January 1862 and was discharged Sept. 9, 1865, serving three years, eight months. He suffered chest wounds and was pensioned. He married Martha Simpson July 3, 1864, in Mt. Vernon, Ill. She was born Feb. 19, 1836. They came to Oregon about 1875. Andrew established a farm in Deerhorn. He died there March 19, 1906. Martha died July 29, 1907. They were buried in the

Camp Creek Cemetery. They had six children as follows:

(1) Harriet Lucinda (Hattie), b. 3-28-1865, m. Richard Raymond Deadmond. They had a son, Dolph. (2) Martha Melissa, b. 1-10-1867, m. (first) Allen, (second) Parish. (3) Mary Matilda (Mollie), b. 1-2-1869, m. John Joseph Pepiot 1-2-1889, in Lane County, Ore., d. 12-7-1942. (4) Florence Anne, b. 12-14-1870, m. Francis Augustus Pepiot, d. 1-30-1958. (5) Samuel Jackson, b. 11-9-1874. All the above were born in Illinois except Mary, born in Tennessee. A sixth child, a boy, was born and died March 15, 1876, after Andrew and Martha came to Oregon. He was buried in the Camp Creek Cemetery.

John Joseph and Francis Augustus Pepiot were sons of Regis and Marie Pepiot of Vida.

Samuel Jackson Goddard acquired his father's Deerhorn farm. On May 16, 1896, he married Emma J. Eulrey in Vancouver, Wa. He died in 1958 in Creswell, Ore. He and Emma had ten children:

(1) Hazel, married Robert Vaughn. (2) Fanella, b. 3-5-1899, m. Dewey W. Bennett, d. 5-27-1982. (3) Denzel, m. (first) Ethel Ward, (second) (?). (4) Fannie, m. Clyde Dulley, d. 1979. (5) Erma, m. Harry Cunningham. (6) Eula Mary, m. Lane Smith. (7) Gladys, m. Ivan Bryant. (8) Emma, m. George Kochis. (9) Hugh, m. Sharon Baxter. (10) Mae, m. Willard Cyrus. Mae and Willard died in late December 1995 as the result of an auto accident on Highway 20 at Santiam Pass. Hugh is the sole survivor at this writing (March 1996).

Eula Mary (Goddard) Smith, lifelong area resident, died at age 84, Oct. 12, 1992. Born Jan. 12, 1908, at Walterville, she attended Deerhorn grade and Walterville high schools and was a University of Oregon graduate. She taught science and art at Creswell Middle School and Creslane Elementary for 30 years. She also taught at Lower Camp Creek, Walterville and other schools. She had several grandchildren. Interment was in Greenwood Cemetery.

Stephens Family

The Stephens family goes back to Richard S. Stephens, a farmer-freighter, born in the early 1800's. He resided in Maryville, Blount County, Tenn. He married Elizabeth Ann Goddard, daughter of Joseph and Elizabeth Jordan Goddard, June 5, 1840, in Maryville. She was born Aug. 14. 1814. Richard died about 1858 or 1860 as a result of injuries suffered when run over by his freight wagon.

They had 12 children: (1) Henrietta, b. 4-20-1841, m. Riley Long. (2) Calvin, b. 3-24-1842, m. (first) Jane Hedrick, (second) Martha Matilda Davis, d. 11-18-1897. (3) Polly (Mary, M. E., Molly), b. 4-1-1843, m. William H. Keller, d. 6-1-1880. (4) Frances S., b. 6-30-1844, married James Clemins. (5) Richard Jr., b. 12-4-1845, m. Sernia Ann Long, b. 2-15-1842. She died 3-22-1933. Richard died 5-6-1899. (6) Margaret (Mag), b. 8-8-1847, married William Murr. (7) William Russell, b. 9-17-1848. (8) Samuel Phillip, b. 12-17-1849, m. (first) Elizabeth A. Clemmon, (second) Mary A. Long in 1892, d. 3-29-1924. (9) DAVID, b. 12-5-1851. (See below). (10) Matilda (Tildy) b. 3-19-1853, married Martin F. Murr. (11) Febe (Phoebe) Jennie, b. 3-16-1856, m. William H. Keller, d. 8-31-1930. (12) Reuben

Andrew, b. 9-13-1859, m. Sarah Emmaline Thompson, d. 6-5-1928.

David Stephens, born in Blount County, Tenn., married Rose Ann Dennison, known by all as "Aunt Ann", Oct. 21, 1880. The daughter of John Alexander and Rutha Goddard Dennison, she was born, April 10, 1865, in Illinois. David and Rose moved to Oregon from Tennessee in 1886. He filed for homestead rights on property in east Camp Creek.

After Samuel Munchy Goddard Sr.'s death, his daughter, Rutha sold his property to David Stephens. David died Sept. 5, 1937, in Springfield. Rose Ann died Feb. 9, 1964. Both were buried in Laurel Grove Cemetery (formerly commonly called Laurel Hill).

David and Rose had nine children: (1) Cora Ethel, b. 9-5-1881, m. Victor Stroud in Oct. 1902, d. 5-30-1951 in Walnut Creek, Cal. (2) Fredy Walter, b. 8-18-1883, m. (first) Minnie Myrtle Long in 1912 in Eugene, (second) Ora Irene Logsdon, d. 1-1-1964 in Seattle, Wa. (3) Roy Leonard, b. 2-5-1886, m. (first) Erie Jane Kennedy 9-15-1913 in Eugene, (second) Katie Grace Workman Trotter, widow of Walter Trotter, d. 2-11-1962 in Springfield. Cora, Fredy and Roy were born in Maryville, Tenn.

Children born in Springfield, Ore., were: (4) Garther Guy, b. 6-14-1888, m. Harriet Adeelia Gossler 6-30-1927 in Eugene, d. 6-30-1975. (5) Charles Orville, b. 9-29-1890, m. Arvilla Rebecca Knowles 7-1-1922 in Eugene, d. 2-22-1977. (6) Roe Chester, b. 6-30-1892, m. Beverly June Jefferson 6-27-1943, in Eugene, d. 3-10-1975 in Eugene. (7) Elvin Otto, b. 5-9-1895, m. (first) Myrtle Lindley 6-7-1929, (second) Virginia (Bonney) Jefferson, d. 10-7-1970 in Springfield. (8) Toby Eldon, b. 3-20-97, m. Marguerite (Moore) Stafford, widow of Glen Stafford, Mohawk Valley pioneer family, Nov. 1956 in Eugene, d. 7-18-1977 at Springfield. (9) Grace Mae, b. 10-4-1900, m. Richard Lindsay 4-1-24, d. Jan. 28, 1996.

At his death David owned three farms, from which all of his nine children inherited a portion. Stephens Road begins on Camp Creek Road at mp. 5.5. It apparently was named for Toby Stephens.

Reuben Andrew Stephens

Reuben Andrew Stephens, known as "Andy", youngest brother of David, was born Sept. 13, 1858, in Blount County, Tenn. He married Sarah Emmaline Thompson, Nov. 30, 1881. She was born April 15, 1863. They came to Camp Creek in 1888 and settled in between property of Goddard and David Stephens. Reuben, a farmer, died June 5, 1926. Sarah died Jan. 17, 1901, in Walterville.

They had eight children: Born in Maryville, Tenn., were Nolia, b. 6-4-1883, died in Tennessee. (2) Callie Adria, b. 4-21-1884, m. James Madison Tipton, d. 2-15-1941. (3) Grover Paris (Jack), b. 5-15-1886, m. Lilly Craft 6-29-11, d. 11-17-53, in Springfield. (4) Robert Franklin, b 3-29-1888, m. Clara Anna Goracke in 1923, d. 5-6-1942 in Springfield.

Born in Springfield were: (5) Phoebe Jennie, b. 12-7-1889, m. Roy Granville Coe 10-20-1912, d. 5-2-1938 in Eugene. (6) Bessie Valietha, b. 3-9-1892, m. Thomas Ray, 2-14-1917, d. 9-12-1958 in Springfield. (7) Lee Roy, b. 7-4-1894, m. Bella (Mahoney) Smith, d. 10-24-1951 in Springfield. (8) Ray McColey, b. 1-11-1901, d. 1-31-1901.

CHAPTER 30

Lucky Boy

Those fever germs need but a start
To exercise uncanny art
    And breed ten billion more;
Those germs that urge to venture bold
And launch men out in search of gold,
    Dame Nature's ancient lore.
He braves the desert's fiery breath,
On mountains shakes the dice with death,
Success, in dreams, accomplisheth,
    The rainbow just before.

Perhaps the most significant chapter in the upper McKenzie's early development came with gold discovery on Gold Hill in 1863 and further developments in the 1890's and 1900's.

Additionally significant was the part my own family played, small though it may have been, in this important phase of Lane County history. My father, Clifton L. Inman, was working at Lucky Boy, operating a stamp mill, when he met and married my mother, Cora Edith Belknap. His association with Lucky Boy shaped his life for many years. The above poem is the opening stanza of an epic story in poetry, titled *Whisperings from Ancient Oregana,* he wrote late in life personifying life and thinking of the seeker of gold.

"Broken dreams of centuries past can be found 45 miles east of Eugene up an abandoned road on Blue River. Mines with names as romantic as the frontier spirit itself -- Lucky Boy, Treasure, Durango, Blue Bird, Cinderella, Red Star -- are now little more than rusted ruins, curious settings for a hiker's lunch. Once, however, the men who dug for gold in this district dreamed of more treasures than could be found in California and the Yukon combined." So wrote Bob Keefer, Eugene, in *Historic Leaburg* (1986).

The story of the Lucky Boy and adjacent mines cannot be fully told without a glimpse into the life of Dr. Alexander Renfrew, who found the first evidence of gold in the region.

Born in Richland County, Ohio, in October 1816, Renfrew brought his wife, Catherine, whom he married May 6, 1836, to the Oregon Territory in August 1852. They settled on a donation land claim in Linn County near Brownsville. Soon they moved to Eugene, where Renfrew bought property at present-day Broadway and Willamette. In 1856, he built the 50-room, brick St. Charles Hotel and saloon, often referred to as Renfrew's.

Dr. Renfrew accompanied the John H. McClung party up the McKenzie River in 1860. Others in the party were A. S. Patterson, A. J. Welch, Joel Ware, C. H. Moses and Joseph Stevenson, all of whom became prominent in Eugene business circles in later years.

McClung, writing years later, described how undeveloped the McKenzie was. There was no road beyond Walterville. On the fourth day out Renfrew, a big man with top hat and wig, and Moses began prospecting at Elk Creek, a mile below Blue River.

"On the first day," wrote McClung, "they reported small particles of gold along the McKenzie at the mouth of Blue River, but above Blue River, no indications." They continued exploring up Blue River, where prospects improved. They thought gold in paying quantities would be found later.

Began Prospecting

Enthusiastic, Renfrew made frequent prospecting trips to Gold Hill, which lies northeast of the Blue River community. His discovery started a gold fever. The *Portland Oregonian* Dec. 8, 1863, reported: "About 1,000 pounds of specimen rock were taken from lodes on Blue River at a site just discovered."

The name Blue River, selected the year gold was discovered there, was used in a descriptive sense, as the clear water of the stream appears blue-green due to the color of the rock formation of the river channel.

Eugene F. Skinner, co-founder of Eugene, filed two claims in 1864 on Summit Lode and Wilbur Lead. He died that same year. The claims, on file at the Lane County Museum, cannot be examined.

Apparently Renfrew, though called "Doctor," never practiced medicine. He was one of a party which formed the McKenzie Salt Springs and Des Chutes Wagon Road Company, with M. H. Harlow, John T. Craig and P. H. (Philander) Renfrew, which was instrumental in establishing a toll road over the Cascade summit at McKenzie Pass.

The relationship of Alexander and Philander has not been determined. Philander homesteaded at McKenzie Bridge in the mid-1870's. Both are reported to have been uncles of Melvina "Auntie" Frissell, long-time McKenzie Bridge resident at Log Cabin Inn.

Alexander later became quite unbalanced. His wife and adopted daughter had him committed to the East Portland Sanitarium in 1872. He was released and made a will, signing over his estate to his wife in 1876. He continued prospecting on Gold Hill. However, he never benefited from his discoveries. He died there 16 years after his first discovery.

In August 1876, Renfrew set off alone from Blue River to visit some gold diggings on United States Creek, north of Gold Hill. He was found dead two days later by prospectors, who buried him near a spring on the south slope of the mountain and sent word of his death to Eugene. The spring was named Renfrew Spring. "Renfrew Grave" is marked on U. S. Geological maps.

His wife ran the Renfrew Hotel (St. Charles) at the northeast corner of Ninth and Willamette until 1877 or 1878. Their adopted daughter, Thursa Ann (listed as Annie, age 9, in the 1870 census for Eugene), was married to Hobart A. Dyer in the St. Charles in May 1878.

In that year Mrs. Renfrew sold the hotel to Henry and Jim Hoffman, who renamed it the Hoffman House. It stood as a Eugene landmark until destroyed by fire March 2, 1960. In 1962 the Equitable building was erected on the site.

Mostly Placer Gold

Bob Keefer in *Historic Leaburg* explained, "What early prospectors found was mostly placer gold, nuggets or flakes mixed in with gravel in stream beds. Placer gold comes from gold buried in the ground in the form of lodes, or veins through the rock, and it was the discovery of large quantities of lode gold in the Blue River area that turned the trickle of prospectors into a rush."

The Blue River mining district, comprising two townships, was established during this early period of activity. It lies about four miles north of the town of Blue River, within Townships 15 and 16, Range 4 west, and along the divide separating the Calapooya and Blue River drainages. The area is steep, rugged, heavily timbered terrain, with elevations ranging for the most part from 3,500 feet to 4,744 feet, peak elevation of Gold Hill. Most of the mines and prospects lay within 1,500 feet of the summit of the divide.

Chinese immigrants also prospected on Gold Hill, but "were crowded out by the whites," wrote one prospector in 1890. A black man, John Downs or Downing, worked a claim for 20 years, later selling out. The claim became the Treasure mine, one of the largest.

George A. Dyson, Nate B. Standish and John W. Moore discovered what became known as the Lucky Boy ledges, 1,400 feet from the summit of Gold Hill June 24, 1887. The three prospectors filed claims, built cabins and trails and dug about 200 feet of tunnel. Insufficient money kept them from mining as much of the gold as they would have liked.

Blue River Growth Noted

"While growth of the Blue River area was considerably influenced by the discovery of gold in 1863, it was later in the century that any significant development took place," wrote the late Manena (Sparks) Schwering of Blue River.

Samuel Sparks, with sons, Dexter and Felix, moved into the area in 1883. Mrs. Schwering, born Jan. 24, 1905, was the daughter of Dexter and Rosa (Lane) Sparks who operated Sparks Ranch west of Blue River for many years. After earning a bachelor of arts degree in journalism, she worked as a journalist for the Lane County Historical Society, also the U. S. Forest Service and the U. S. Department of Agriculture as a personnel officer. On Dec. 26, 1926, she married Walker Edwin Schwering of Walterville. He died Sept. 16, 1974.

Manena died at age 90 Jan. 13, 1996, in Bend, Ore. Survivors were a daughter, Gloria Donoho of Yuma, Ariz., a son, Ray Baker of Eugene, two grandchildren and two great-grandchildren.

"Interest continued to grow in the McKenzie country," Mrs. Schwering wrote. "In addition to those looking for free land, there was activity and speculation in the mines northeast of Blue River. Almost every able-bodied man in the community staked a claim hoping for a bonanza. Without exception, these expectations provided little more than hard work and disappointment."

The first Blue River post office was established Jan. 18, 1886. Jim Davis was postmaster. The office was located one-half mile west of the community on his property acquired later by the Sparks.

Glen O. Powers, born in Springfield, came to Blue River in 1890 and commenced business in general merchandise. In August 1892, he was appointed postmaster. His business was chiefly with the mines and miners of the district. With increased business he built a large new store and was agent for sale of lots in the town's Watts addition.

The area now needed a stage and freight route. This service was coordinated and developed with the delivery of mail. The horse stages delivered mail, carried passengers and small parcels of freight. Later, a separate freight service was operated by Frank Moore, a cousin of Rosa Sparks.

Probably the first contract for delivery of mail was awarded to Eli Bangs, who owned a livery stable at Eighth and Pearl in Eugene. Early drivers included Earl McNutt, Orel and Percy O'Brien, Ed Walker, Joe Jones, Arch Shough and others.

"It was necessary to establish stables for fresh horses and eating places for people. The trip from Eugene was usually made using four horses for each rig -- occasionally two. Fresh horses were required at Walterville, Vida and Blue River. The noon meal was eaten at Leaburg (at the Kennerlys)," Mrs. Schwering wrote.

"Vida also provided a small hotel and livery stable, owned by Ben Minney. The Sparks' Hotel at Blue River was the next stopping place. During the early years, limited accommodations for meals and overnight stops were provided in the old log homestead house owned by Samuel and Robena Sparks." The Log Cabin Inn at McKenzie Bridge and hotels at Foley and Belknap springs offered additional lodging.

"At one time more than 250 men were moving in and out of the area. Except for scattered homesteads with their families, Blue River was almost exclusively a male community. Robena Sparks stated at one time she did not see another woman for a period of three months."

The Sparks were part owners in several mining claims, including the Bronco and Burro and the Lexington and Cracker Jack claims.

In 1897, Dyson said there were about 150 claims in the district, some having been worked for 20 years. J. S. Silver, a U. S. Geological engineer, wrote in 1898 there were no producing mines in the district. The *Portland Oregonian* quoted Dyson that the Lucky Boy produced more free gold than all the other mines combined, then offered to sell his interest for a sum represented by six figures. His offer drew results.

In October 1898, Portland meat packer Louis Zimmerman and two other men incorporated the Lucky Boy Mining Co. of Portland and bought the Lucky Boy claim. This and other Blue River mines enjoyed their heyday at the turn of the century.

The company installed a 10-stamp mill to crush ore Jan. 1, 1900, and was producing $250 in gold a day. Two years later the company increased capacity to 15 stamps and started planning a 40-stamp mill to handle a greater output. Ore was carried from mine to mill by a 1,400-foot aerial tram. Electricity was generated at a plant on the McKenzie. The owners planned to boost their gross to more than $1,500, with a profit of $1,300.

"Just east of Blue River was a stamp mill run by electricity for pulverizing ore," Martha Belknap was quoted as saying. "An electric plant was put in and wires run over to Lucky Boy. These stamps were great big brass cylinders that would crumple the ore. Then they washed it and got the gold out. I was up there when the old buildings were there. The Lucky Boy was seven-stories high."

At the turn of the century Samuel Sparks and sons, Felix and Dexter, laid out the town on property they owned as part of the 360 acres Samuel acquired from the Jim Davis and Smith homestead in 1893. They built a first class hotel for tourists, a store, livery stable and sawmill at the site of the present community of Blue River.

A considerable number of transients were moving in and out of the area due to the development of mining projects. Felix Sparks' lumber mill cut 500,000 board feet of lumber just for the flume, and had nine men working full time just to keep up with the mine's demands.

A second hotel in town catered to miners who didn't have lodging at the mines. Other new facilities were built at the present site of Blue River. Some additional services were provided, including several saloons, a blacksmith shop and Chinese laundry.

The Lucky Boy Post Office was established Feb. 16, 1901, with George A. Dyspan (this could be Dyson) postmaster, to serve the mine, some four or five miles northeast of Blue River. The mine reportedly was named "in the spirit of optimism." (McArthur, 1982).

In 1904, the *Eugene Morning Register* reported the Lucky Boy held 186 acres of claims. Other mines prospered, especially the Treasure Consolidated Co. The company erected its own stamp mill, bunk houses and livery stable and operated day and night shifts.

High Hopes Dashed

Despite high hopes, the gold of Gold Hill largely ran out in the first decade. Zimmerman and his partners found there wasn't enough gold ore for their 40-stamp mill. The mine owners lost a small fortune through the grandiose expansion, *The Oregonian* reported.

The post office was closed Nov. 26, 1906, when mining ceased, with papers sent to Blue River. The Lucky Boy closed in 1907, when all that remained in the mine was low-grade ore that would require extensive costs and pollution in order to extract the gold and silver.

Other important mining developments included Great Northern (six claims), two miles north of Lucky Boy in Linn County. This mine had a four-stamp mill and operated until 1917, said Mrs. Schwering. It reportedly had the longest single tunnel development in the district. Production was second only to the Lucky Boy group.

Higgins mine lay northwest of Great Northern. Rialto (formerly Blue Bird), located at the head of the North Fork of Quartz Creek, included 12 claims in Linn and Lane counties. Rowena group was located on the North Fork of Quartz Creek. This property was closely associated with the Rialto group in development and family ownership. Work continued on these properties for many years. Reports vary.

Treasure mine, located on the east slope of the eastern part of Gold Hill, one-half mile northeast of Lucky Boy properties, had a small production. It was one of the most extensively developed properties in the district. A 15-stamp mill was built in 1902, also a small sawmill, which provided lumber for a large complex of offices, kitchens, living quarters and storage sheds. The mine had a 4,000-foot tunnel. Work was discontinued in 1916. A caretaker was employed. Eventually the premise was abandoned and the huge, rambling two-level structure of 50 to 60 rooms was taken over by hordes of rats, mice, squirrels and bats.

"After 1912, there was no significant activity in mining," wrote Mrs. Schwering. "The supply of free milling ore processed in the stamp mills was largely exhausted. Material would require shipment to smelters in Denver or Tacoma to extract the minerals from this low grade ore. Transportation problems made this impractical."

By 1910, the Blue Bird Mining Co., which operated the Blue Bird, Red Star and Red Cloud mines, was the only company still producing, Diller wrote in 1914. In 1923, the Lane County Court ordered the wagon road closed, as unused and unsafe for travel because of decaying bridges and washed-out roads.

A changing economy and way of life was developing. In 1911, the Sparks completed a subdivision, which included Cascade Park and Sparks Addition to Blue River City. The area came to attract notice from a recreation standpoint about 1914, with fishing, hunting and use of the two hot springs near by.

Cottages were available for renting during the summer months and swimming pools were used most of the year. Roads were improved and use of the automobile became common place. By the end of W. W. II, the pioneer character of the valley largely disappeared. A few sawmills were in production. Clarence Belknap's sawmill on the Belknap homestead six miles east of Blue River, begun in 1920, was the largest.

Clayton and Mabel Nestle in 1920 made a purchase-option on the Lucky Boy mine from Mr. Lyman and Mr. Scott. The Nestles paid off the contract in 1952. They worked the mine for a number of years, cleaning out the tunnels and selling timber from their claims. During W. W. II they operated the No. 5 tunnel at a cost of $32/foot without labor. They cleared the No. 6 tunnel by the end of W. W. II, mining mostly lead, zinc and copper. (Williams, 1991).

Mrs. Schwering recalled walking through the place when many furnishings were still in place, including a fully-equipped kitchen.

In 1930, the buildings were set afire by vandals and destroyed.

Only a few remains of the former large-scale operation exists today, as fire and the intervening years have taken their toll at the mine. The most visible sign of the former activity are piles of ashes and scattered rusted metal machinery that serve to mark the spot.

The late Martha Belknap of Rainbow, interviewed about 1975, was asked how mining affected the area. "Well it made Blue River. At one time it had ten saloons. It was quite a place," she said.

"Were women allowed in saloons?"

"I don't know. There were many with doubtful reputations. The miners came in. . .The Blue River mines, especially Lucky Boy, turned out a lot of gold. But at the turn of the century, when the Forest Service came, about 1904, the mines ran out of base ore, which means the gold and everything is mixed with other minerals. You know that in Anaconda, for example, there are no trees at all -- where they smelted. That put an end to the smelting, although people occasionally think they are going to start up again."

Family Involvement

I mentioned family involvement in Lucky boy operation and its influence on the life of my father, Clifton L. Inman. Born in New Brighton, Pa., he came to Oregon with his family in 1890. He was employed in the stamp mill when he and my mother, Cora Edith Belknap, were married in 1903, they lived at Lucky Boy in a cabin provided for workers before and after the birth of their first child.

After Lucky Boy closed for all practical purposes, Inman and Nate Standish developed a mine at Great Northern, working a gold ore vein that appeared promising. They were offered $25,000 for their claim, but Standish held out for $100,000. They sank their earnings into equipment to further develop the mine, but the vein played out.

Inman moved back to Walterville about 1906 and went into the sawmill business. But gold fever still burned in his mind. About 1914, he prospected unsuccessfully in the Trinity River country in northern California. War in Europe was on. He went into San Francisco to work in a machine shop, returning in 1918. His years of prospecting were reflected in his writing of a mythological story in poetry, about early-day northern California Indians. The book was published under the title "*Whisperings from Ancient Oregana.*"

CHAPTER 31

Murder at Isham Corral

The air is fresh and bracing, Mother;
The sun shines bright and high.
It's a pleasant one to live --
A gloomy one to die.

"Three can keep a secret only when two are dead."

Three men, tired from a hard day of driving a herd of horses westward over treacherous McKenzie Pass, relaxed around their campfire at Isham Corral. The horses secured for the night, the men had eaten a hastily prepared meal of bacon, biscuits and coffee.

There was little talk, as they rested prior to bedding down for a presumed night of sleeping under the stars that clear, cool night June 15, 1898, before heading down the valley toward Eugene next day.

The older man arose, stoked the fire, then got his blanket. The two younger men exchanged glances, nodded slightly. One of them stood up, stretched and yawned. He was a big man, young, handsome, robust. He took a few steps, then quick as a flash, he whipped out his revolver. A shot rang out. The older man, struck in the chest by the bullet, gasped, then slumped over dead.

Thus was spawned one of the most sensational murder cases in Oregon's history, culminating in Lane County's first public and legal hanging.

It was 2 o'clock in the morning July 4, 1898. Lane County Deputy Sheriff H. J. Day, in answer to a knock at his door, stood sleepily in the doorway of his Eugene home holding in his hand a coal oil lamp, which revealed the figure of a young man.

"I've got -- I've got -- I've got to tell you something, Mr. Day."

"Who are you?" demanded the deputy.

"Why, don't you recognize me? Court Green from Thurston."

"What, are you Court Green? What's happened to you?"

"It's this -- this what I've got to tell you. It's on my mind all the time -- I can't eat -- I can't sleep. . ." He burst into strangling sobs and hid his face in his hands.

"Come in," said the deputy.

At 4 o'clock Deputy Day and Courtland Green came out of the house and walked to the nearby home of Deputy District Attorney Lawrence T. Harris, where a partial account of the grisly murder at Isham Corral was retold.

That day crowds had gathered around the Eugene City Hall, where Harris was scheduled to deliver a patriotic Fourth of July speech. But the people were more interested in news accounts of Admiral Dewey crushing the Spanish fleet at Manila Bay.

Following a brief speech and not waiting for applause, Harris hastened away to join Deputy Sheriff George Croner, Green and Coroner V. L. Cheshire to travel in a "hack" Sheriff William W. Withers had rented at Bang's Livery Stable. They went as fast as a team of horses could take them up the McKenzie River. The very rough road became a mere rutted trail on the upper river and climbed into the darkened forested steps of the Cascades.

At White Branch Creek they waded out and searched unsuccessfully for a man's watch. They camped nearby. The next morning they turned off at a landmark boulder into an enclosure known as Isham Corral, a favorite stopping place for travelers over the McKenzie Pass.

The corral, about 15 miles east of McKenzie Bridge and some 70 feet south of the old McKenzie toll road, was built in 1895 by upper McKenzie resident John A. Isham and his son, Ira. They had cut long, slender fir poles and fenced in this two-acre tract of land to rent overnight to ranchers making the tortuous trip across the mountain with herds of sheep, cattle and horses being driven up the Lost Creek Canyon to the high mountain meadows of Central and Eastern Oregon. No water nor feed was available for the animals.

"After seven hours at the corral the men from Eugene, very grimy and weary, started down, taking with them, among other things, a small box. They stopped for the night at McKenzie Bridge, where Dr. Cheshire impaneled a coroner's jury of six men, including John Isham," wrote Mary Baen Thompson, in a 1948 *Eugene Register-Guard* news story. A sequence of events follows.

The evidence laid before them included a blood-spattered ax. "That's my ax," exclaimed Isham. "I'd know it anywhere. My boy, Ira, lost it when we were fencing in the corral in 1895. But it's not the same handle."

The coroner's jury signed as their verdict that one "John Linn, a rancher late of Condon, in Eastern Oregon had on the night of June 15, 1898, come to his death at the hands of Claude Branton, 21, of Walterville, Oregon."

Reports on the murder of John Linn by Claude Branton and Courtland Green on that lonely mountain side, about one and one-half miles below present-day Alder Springs, thereafter filled the columns of local and statewide newspapers for months. While early days on the McKenzie were not without criminal activity, this one crime stood out in the minds of local residents for many years.

Horses Driven Madly

The Ishams told the officers that on June 16 they had seen a herd of about 60 horses galloping madly down the McKenzie road led by a splendid black stallion, lashed on unmercifully by a young horseman they recognized as Claude Branton, of Walterville. A mare and gelding dropped out, exhausted. The Ishams gave them refuge.

On the night of June 23, there was a knock on the door of the Isham home. There stood a broad-shouldered young man, about five feet, eight inches tall with black hair and eyes and a small mustache worn by young men of the day. It was Branton! He was on his way back to Eastern Oregon, he said, and wanted to stay the night.

Claude Branton

Usually good natured, he was always smiling, as if to display his perfect white teeth, but this night he was silent and preoccupied. Before turning in with Ira, he laid under his pillow a loaded pistol. He left early, riding a horse and leading a stallion.

June 23, continued Isham, he and Ira had gone up the trail to work. On reaching the corral they found the remains of a large camp fire.

The lowest branches of a fir alongside, though 40 feet from the ground, were seared and charred, and a large section of their fence had been torn down, presumably to feed the flames.

Meanwhile Sheriff William V. Withers, who took office July 1, and his deputy searched for Branton along the lower McKenzie. Branton's description and $250 reward for information leading to his arrest was published. He was last reported seen June 26 in the desert town of Prineville, where he sold the black stallion for $400.

Actions Arouse Suspicions

Branton's actions aroused suspicion prior to his disappearing from the valley with the stallion, which he tried to sell for a fraction of the value. Seven men told officers they had been approached by Branton with the story these horses were due him as wages from his employer, John Linn of Condon, that he had some trouble with Linn and was willing to give a team -- "your pick" -- to anyone willing to declare he'd seen Linn in the McKenzie Valley with the horses.

"If anyone asks you who turned these horses in here," he said to Walden and Walter Trotter, 16-year-old twins, "tell them it was John Linn of Condon. I'll make it worth your while. If you don't -- "

"We never saw any John Linn and we're not going to say we did," retorted the twins, who lived on Camp Creek.

Deputy District Attorney L. T. Harris, 25 at the time, became speaker of the Oregon House in 1903 and served as a justice of the Oregon Supreme Court from 1914 to 1924. In a talk before the Lane County Bar Association about 1953, Judge Harris recalled many of the details of the investigation. He said Branton, after the slaying, mounted his horse, and, donning a set of chin whiskers made from a horse's tail, went down the river and tried to pose as his victim.

Sheriff Withers made arrangement with the postmaster to intercept any mail Branton might send to his girlfriend up the river. This maneuver, "not kosher these days," Judge Harris said, paid off. A letter from Kansas City to the girl, which described life in the midwestern town, was steamed open. Withers decided Claude was coming back to Eugene soon.

Meanwhile, the sting of conscience and prodding of officers completed the capitulation of the unhappy Green. On July 10, he surrendered to the sheriff, saying, "I haven't told you everything. I helped. I'm guilty, too." He was placed under $7,500 bond.

On July 20, Branton, with a two-week's growth of beard, was spotted on a Eugene street by tobacco-shop owner A. C. Austin, who notified Deputy Day. A defiant Branton was placed under arrest and taken to jail. He had no gun, but a new watch, a poke containing $40.30, and a pocket knife were found on his person. The wallet was traced to the Condon leather worker who sold it to Linn.

Branton refused to talk. Green, on seeing him, turned ghastly pale. Before long they were quarreling, each accusing the other as being the instigator, with himself the unwilling witness. Both were indicted for first degree murder.

Armed with additional information, Harris and Withers left for the mountains to see if they could "smoke" something out of Claude's brother, Clarence. A sheepherder took the officers to him. They obtained a statement that he "suspicioned something was wrong when I talked to Claude at Cobb's Place before the murder."

"Well, we got Claude in jail," Harris answered Clarence.

Clarence's reaction was immediate.

"I could see right then he wanted to get that written deposition back," Harris recalled. "'Say,' he said, 'I'll bet I can beat you shooting at a mark.' I knew he was looking at Bill Wither's gun, which he kept under his arm. We just backed off and spread out, so he couldn't get both of us in a hurry," said Harris. But Clarence didn't act.

On trial, Branton arrogantly maintained his innocence. Green, however, admitted participation and pleaded guilty to second degree murder. He turned state's evidence and testified against Branton.

Among witnesses at the trial was Stephen Smeed, Walterville hop grower. He testified Green had worked for him and had shown himself trustworthy. When Green returned from Eastern Oregon, his apparent mental distress aroused his employer's suspicion. He finally succeeded in getting from Green a partial confession of his "dreadful secret" and persuaded him to go immediately to Eugene and turn himself in.

State's exhibits brought from the crime scene included a slender 12-foot pole, probably torn from the corral fence and charred at one end; fire-blackened buttons and suspender buckles; the long-lost, blood-spattered ax, and a crumpled receipt for dues paid by Linn to the Condon Woodmen of the World. In a small box handed over to the jury were Linn's mortal remains: charred and splintered bones, toe and finger bones, scattered teeth and a three-inch skull fragment.

Branton was convicted of first degree murder and sentenced to "hang by the neck until dead." The Oregon Supreme Court upheld his conviction. May 12, 1899, was set for the hanging. Green pleaded guilty to second degree murder and was sentenced to life in prison.

Gruesome Murder

Much has been written over the years about the gruesome murder at Isham Corral. Although facts of the crime are essentially the same, newspaper accounts differ on what actually took place. Many of the details came out during the trial of Branton after his partner in crime, Courtland Green, turned state's evidence.

Judge Harris, in his talk to the Bar Association, said Branton and Green, engaged to "McKenzie River girls," needed money to get married. Together with Claude's younger brother, Clarence, they hatched a plan to rob Linn, a wealthy cattleman.

Mary Thompson wrote: "In the spring of 1898, the two young men, far from home in the McKenzie Valley, were working on neighboring ranches near Condon, a small desert town in north central Oregon. John Linn, a thrifty, industrious rancher, had employed Branton as a cowboy. Five or six times that spring, Claude, meeting with Green, had outlined a plan to decoy Linn away, rob and kill him. Revolted at first, Green agreed to help.

"Branton knew a man to whom Linn had lent $1,000 had repaid the debt June 1. They knew he had cash. Branton persuaded Linn to drive his horses over the mountain into the McKenzie Valley, either to sell or exchange them for an imaginary ranch Branton said he owned."

A news story on the day of Branton's hanging said evidence showed that on or about June 10, 1898, a party left Gilliam County in northwestern Oregon with 60 head of range horses bound for the Willamette Valley. The party included John A. Linn, owner of the horses; Mrs. S. C. Branton; her two sons, Claude and Clarence; some younger children, and Courtland Green. (Linn's brother C. E. Lind, spelled the name differently). The Brantons lived west of Walterville near the McKenzie River, due south of the present-day Eugene Water and Electric Board power plant. Green lived in Thurston.

Mary Thompson gave the date of June 5 when the party set out, saying, "First came Linn with the horses, some of them wiry Cayuses of the plains, led by the splendid black stallion for which he had paid $1,500; then the three horsemen -- the two cowboys, handsome, mustached, both 21 -- flanking the toil-stooped rancher."

The third man, although not identified, could have been Clarence Branton, arrested as a co-conspirator, though never indicted.

Their route took them through Prineville, Ore. At the Cobb place on Squaw Creek, near Sisters, Mrs. Branton and Clarence took the smaller children and went on ahead of the slow-moving herd. If Clarence knew of the plot, he had no direct part in the actual killing. Later newspaper stories made no mention of Mrs. Branton and her children, nor what she might have been doing in Gilliam County.

Claude Branton and Green stayed behind to help Linn with the horses. "As it turned out 'helping' was euphemistic, to say the least," to quote Lewis McArthur in *Oregon Geographical Names.*

They crossed the desert lands and finally were "confronted by the Cascades, which divide the desert on the east from the vast, evergreen forests on the west. Travel over the McKenzie pass at that time was a terrible ordeal for man and beast," wrote Thompson.

Although the route was firmly established, little had been done to improve the road from that John T. Craig built in the late 1860's.

"Steep, rutted, boulder-strewn, the trail looped and twisted like a tortured snake. Vast floods of lava, poured out ages ago in some tremendous upheaval, had cooled off into fantastic chunks of porous rock that rolled and clinked and shredded the stoutest boots from the feet of those who crossed them," wrote Thompson.

"Up through the sparse pines of the eastern slopes toiled the cavalcade. It was John Linn's funeral procession, and like that of a king it included his steed and his dog. He was riding his favorite dappled gray, behind him limped his collie, loyal until death.

"One of the homesick cowboys rode in silence; the other sang, played his harmonica and pointed out the landmarks: raw, triple snow peaks called the Three Sisters, Belknap Crater, and 25-foot-high stumps, the slender trees, twisted like corkscrews by the snows, the nameless cairns, now marked in bronze, where mailman Craig perished in a blizzard in 1877. A horse broke its leg -- they shot it. Like a string of ants they crawled along toward the sunset."

After the arduous trip driving the herd over the McKenzie Pass, the three men arrived at Isham's Corral in the afternoon of June 15. They secured the horses and made their camp for the night, reported *The Eugene Daily Guard* July 6 and Aug. 11, 1898.

Branton, searching through the dense underbrush for firewood, found a rusty ax, its handle rotted away. The callused hands of Linn soon were busy whittling a new handle from a piece of vine maple.

"See? Ay make him goot as new," he said.

"They built a fire and fried bacon. Then, Linn wrapped himself in his blanket and lay down with his dog beside him. Two hours later, Branton finally arose, stood over the sleeping man and fired three revolver shots into him," wrote Thompson.

Judge Harris said Branton "put a single shot into Linn's heart."

Green, sickened by the spurting blood, hugged the frightened dog and tried to quiet its howls. From the victim's pocket Branton pulled the long buckskin poke that Linn carried for a dozen years and had marked three notches "to make it mine." To Branton's chagrin, it yielded only $61.40. Branton took Linn's pocket knife and watch, which he later threw into White Branch. He did not know that the day Linn had been paid the $1,000 he had lent it again.

Forcing Green to help him, Branton dumped the body face down into the fire. He knocked poles from the fence with the ax, built a roaring blaze. Then he sat down on a log and played his harmonica, while the dog howled throughout the night. With the dawn, the two men raked the bones from the embers, carried them in a pan to a distant slab of lava, smashed them into bits with the ax and hid the fragments under the slab.

Smith Taylor, for many years district forest ranger at McKenzie Bridge, wrote in 1937 that the two men intended to bury the body but found it impossible to dig a grave in the lava, so they built a big fire against a log and burned (the body) piece by piece.

The "murderers" continued down the McKenzie River to Eugene, selling horses as they could, but leaving about 40 horses with William Seavey at Hayden Bridge.

Taylor continued: "Claude Branton went to Omaha, Neb. (Some doubt exists he ever left the Eugene area). Courtney Green went to work at the Smeed ranch near Hendricks Bridge. He confessed (the night of July 3) to his employer, Mr. (Stephen) Smeed, that he was guilty of a terrible crime." Some reports say Green first told his story to a girl friend before going to Smeed.

One of the McKenzie River girls Judge Harris alluded to in his talk was Stephen Smeed's 17-year-old daughter, Carie. It appeared Courtney Green earlier had sought permission to marry her. Smeed asked Green if he thought he could support a wife, and said he would need at least $500 on which to get married.

Green, deeply disappointed, told the story to Branton, who also had a girlfriend. On learning of Smeed's edict, Branton asked Green to go along with him on a plan, which he assured would bring him at least the $500 he needed, as well as to sweeten his own coffers. Green was reluctant but finally agreed in principle.

Green acted very suspicious that something was wrong, when he approached Smeed after the slaying, and finally broke down.

They went immediately to Eugene, where Green in the early hours of July 4 made a partial confession. A great manhunt was started for Branton, who was arrested July 20 in downtown Eugene.

Branton, described as a very handsome man, strong and robust, was brought to trial in the Lane County Courthouse in Eugene before Circuit Court Judge J. W. Hamilton, in a crowded courtroom.

Following a sensational trial and much publicity, on Nov. 4, 1898, he was convicted by a jury of ". . .murder in the first degree in that on the 15th of June, 1898, in Lane County, State of Oregon, he. . .did purposely and of deliberate and premeditated malice kill John L. Linn."

Judgment was passed by the court Nov. 8, 1898, that Branton be "hanged by the neck until dead." Branton appealed to the Oregon Supreme Court, which affirmed the conviction April 3, 1899. Friday, May 12, 1899, was set for the hanging.

Changing Moods

Although calm and apparently remorseful in the final days, Branton had shown "moods ranging from docility to absolute treachery," the *Eugene Daily Guard* said. On being taken back to the jail after hearing the jury's verdict, he "made a murderous assault upon Deputy Sheriff Day in an attempt to secure his revolver. Sheriff (W. W.)

Withers soon brought him to time, however.

"Another time Branton made an ingenious fake pistol, from two potatoes, bones, a suspender clip and tinfoil, and attempted to force Sheriff Withers to throw up his hands. Later he confessed religion and studied the Bible, sang and read a little and wrote a great deal."

It was reported that after a religious conversion he was baptized in a borrowed bathtub.

Since this was to be Lane County's first hanging, there was great excitement and opinions were expressed on both sides.

George Croner, a Lane County deputy sheriff, later stationed at McKenzie Bridge, had a personal invitation to attend the hanging. Martha Belknap, in 1978, said the invitation card was quite distinctive, printed with gilt letters on white with large black border.

The *Junction City Times, reported,* "The invitation reads as follows: 'This permit will entitle you to witness the execution of Claude Branton in the City of Eugene, Friday, May 12, 1899. Not transferable.' The card, surrounded by a large border, contains the sheriff's official signature. This will be the first legal execution in Lane County and, while Branton deserves death, we have no desire whatever to witness the revolting spectacle and will not therefore be present (*Daily Eugene Guard,* May 6, 1899)."

Big Crowd Gathers

On the day set for the hanging, the courthouse square attracted many people. The death warrant said the execution should occur between the hours of 10 a. m. and 2 p. m., but by 8 o'clock a large crowd began to assemble and increased until after the execution.

The *Eugene Daily Guard* devoted most of Page 1 to the hanging.

"The death of John A. Linn Is Avenged," read a headline. Subheads stated, "LIFE OF CLAUDE BRANON (sic.) THE PENALTY." "His Accomplice, Courtland Green, Is in the Oregon Penitentiary for Life." "The Prisoner Was Game to the Last." "Out of Seventeen Murders Committed in Lane County, This is the First Execution Made."

The news story, dated May 12, began with a brief poem:
"The air is fresh and bracing, Mother;
The sun shines bright and high.
It's a pleasant one to live --
A gloomy one to die."

"The first legal execution of a criminal ever held in Lane County occurred today," the story said. "Claude Branton, the condemned man, displayed the greatest fortitude, and during the past few days, has been busily engaged in making preparations for his death. He has been calm, eating and sleeping well, wrote messages to friends, studied his Bible, and showed by acts and speech his appreciation of the kindness of the officers. Around the jail every preparation was made for the event. The stockade which had been built was guarded from inside and out by special deputy sheriffs, some of whom were stationed at various places to keep all persons out of the jail yard.

"Branton's parents, Mr. and Mrs. S. C. Branton, his sister, Mrs.

Bailey, brother Clarence and other relatives made their last visit to the condemned man's cell at 9:35 this morning, remaining about 20 minutes and were greatly affected. Rev. E. M. Patterson, who baptized Branton, and Rev. Joe Handsaker, students of the Eugene Divinity School, were with the man until the last, mounting the scaffolding with him. After his relatives retired they held a short prayer and song service, and comforted him with assurance based on his belief in divine forgiveness.

"At 10:05 Sheriff Withers read the death warrant to Branton who remained composed through the trying proceedings.

"Only once did Branton become tearful. Before leaving the jail and as the straps binding his arms to his sides were being placed in position by Sheriff Withers and Deputy Day, Branton took his final farewell. With tears in his eyes, Branton thanked Sheriff Withers, Deputy Day, Guard Andrews and the two ministers for their consideration. He said no one could have been more kind to him than the officers had been. He forgave everyone, holding nothing against them, believed the officers had forgiven him and that God would do so. Branton shook hands with all, giving a firm handshake. It was an ordeal men pass through but seldom, and it is greatly to their credit as officers and men alike that their humility was tenderly shown.

"Branton was attired in a neat fitting black suit, low collar and black tie, with a bouquet of pansies on the coat lapel. After his hands were strapped to his sides, the march to the scaffold began. Messrs. Patterson and Handsaker were first to go, then came Branton, with Sheriff Withers and Deputy Day on either side and Guard Andrews at the rear. In this order they mounted the scaffold. Branton was placed on the trap, a strap placed around his arms and waist, one around his legs above the knee and one around his ankles."

Those holding invitations filed into the enclosure about 10 o'clock. The execution was witnessed by about 50 persons. Among those present were members of the jury convicting Branton, seven newspapermen, 12 physicians, the undertakers, officials, the 12 citizens selected by the sheriff to officially certify the execution, etc.

"An unidentified woman, standing on a box, witnessed the execution from a window in the courthouse, and from this point of vantage saw the gruesome spectacle," the news story said.

After the hanging the body was turned over to the Branton family and, the news story said, taken to the Pleasant Hill Cemetery.

Actually, Branton was buried in the Camp Creek Cemetery. A tombstone bearing his name and date of burial, May 12, 1899, stands in that cemetery. The name of Claude's sister, Amanda, and date of 1934, also is on the tombstone. Whether Claude was first buried at Pleasant Hill then the body moved is not known.

Green had turned state's evidence and pleaded guilty to second degree murder. Sentenced to life imprisonment, he was sent to the Oregon State Penitentiary. He was pardoned after a time. Smith Taylor (1937: 52) wrote that Green "served about 20 years. He was given his freedom and told to leave the state, when it was discovered he had consumption (tuberculosis). He lived only a short time."

Branton's diary, found after the hanging, spoke his concluding sentiments: "Three can keep a secret only when two are dead."

County's Last Hanging

Judge Harris characterized Sheriff Withers as "The most super-human bloodhound of any man I ever saw." Renowned as a lawman, he was considered a Wyatt Earp and Sherlock Holmes rolled into one.

Lane County had a second and last hanging four years later, when the popular sheriff was himself a victim of a slaying.

In February 1903, Sheriff Withers and his constable went to Walton, 29 miles west of Eugene, to arrest Elliott Ellis Lyons for horse theft. The constable guarded the door. The sheriff went into the living room where he found Lyons with his pregnant wife and his parents. A scuffle ensued. Lyons shot Withers in the throat and escaped through the mud and snow. Withers died 36 hours later.

Sheriff Withers

Lyons was caught in Creswell Feb. 9, four days later. Deputies successfully guarded him from a bloodthirsty mob outside the county jail. Convicted in a one-day trial March 4, he was sentenced March 6 and hanged in the county courtyard April 7, 1903.

The scaffold stood higher than the fence. A huge crowd outside had an unobstructed view. After that all capital punishment was moved to the state capital in Salem.

CHAPTER 32

Carey Thomson

Carey Thomson, McKenzie River Iron Man, was born near Philomath-Corvallis, Ore., in 1856. He would have been 14 years old when he moved with his parents, the Fayette Thomsons, to the McKenzie Valley and settled south across the river at Vida in 1870.

He would have been only 22 when he built a new bridge across the river at McKenzie Bridge, replacing John Templeton Craig's crude bridge, in 1878. His father, Fayette, no doubt assisted.

After Craig's death in heavy snows on the high Cascades in December 1877, Peter Wycoff carried the mail over the McKenzie Pass to Camp Polk for two years. Carey took over the job for two more years.

Ray Engles, who succeeded Smith Taylor as district forest ranger at McKenzie Bridge, was quoted in 1937 as saying: "The heaviest article Mr. Thomson ever carried as part of the mail going to Eastern Oregon was a pair of cowboy boots. For the most part the mail carrying consisted of very few letters. Mr. Thomson continued carrying the mail on this route until 1881, when it was abandoned."

Carey was married twice. His first wife's name was Wagner. Their only child, Jennie, married "Doc" Paulette. His second marriage in 1884 was to Mary Isham (1869-1953). She was the daughter of John and Catherine Isham.

The late John West, long-time McKenzie River guide, said the Ishams settled at Vida. A 1930 Metzger map, however, shows an area in Section 17 lying north of the Belknap Bridge at present-day Rainbow on the upper McKenzie as the homestead of John A. Isham. Isham children attended the log school on the nearby Sims' property. John and his son, Ira, built and maintained Isham Corral, where John Linn was murdered in 1898. They moved to the Vida area at a later date.

Carey and Mary homesteaded on the upper McKenzie after their marriage. His movements prior to that period are not clear. He filed for homestead rights about 1885 on property on the north side of the river across the McKenzie Highway from the Belknap Bridge, "but the highway and bridge were not there when the Thomsons settled." (Lewis McArthur, 1982).

That would be near the Isham property, which lay farther north. Bureau of Land Management records show a patent was granted May 11, 1896, for tract No. 3704. The C. W. Thomson property was located in Section 17, Township 16 south, Range 3, west of Willamette Meridian.

Carey built the first bridge across the McKenzie at the Belknap Bridge location in 1889 by felling several large trees across the river to use as stringers. This bridge replaced James Belknap's ferry. It was first known as Thomson's Bridge, and he collected tolls. It later became Campbell's Bridge, named for residents of the area, then Belknap Bridge, which name has remained.

The Thomson Land Co. established a post office April 15, 1891, between Blue River and McKenzie Bridge with Mary C. (Isham) Thomson as postmaster. It was believed to have been located near the present bridge site at Rainbow.

McArthur reported: "Thomson was an early-day post office on the McKenzie River, but should not be claimed as a pioneer establishment. Mary C. Thomson (probably Carey's wife) was appointed postmaster April 15, 1891. She ran the office until June 24, 1893, when it was closed to McKenzie Bridge. An effort was made to revive the office in May, 1895, when Cynthia J. Isham (probably Mary's sister) was appointed postmaster, but the order was rescinded in July, 1895."

Carey and Mary had four children: Milo, Dayton, York and Carey Jr. An Effa Thomson, presumably a daughter, is shown in an old picture of children who attended the little log school on the Sims place.

The late Clayton and Mabel Nestle reported Carey Thomson in 1896 built and occupied the present Nestle home on the north side of McKenzie River Highway 126 just west of the Ben and Kay Dorris State Park, four miles east of Vida. The fine old home served for many years as a stage stop between Eugene and Belknap and Foley springs, before the stages began stopping at Gate Creek Ranch.

The lumber for construction came from the Ben Finn sawmill. The land, originally homesteaded by a man named Bone, later was occupied by the Al Montgomery family. The house, remodeled by the Nestles, is currently the home of their son, Ervin.

The Thomsons also are reported to have built a home at Blue River around 1900, but we have no further information.

Carey Thomson, a noted woodsman, was a skilled trapper, hunter and marksman who earned his living by providing restaurants in Eugene and Springfield with fresh game.

Thomson's Lodge

In 1902, Carey moved to property on the south side of the McKenzie River, below Ben and Kay Dorris State Park. He built a home and, in 1912, established the well-known Thomson's Sportsman Lodge.

The land, accessible only by ferry and a swinging bridge, was first homesteaded by William Allen in 1863. Thomas M. Martin, Vida's first postmaster, purchased the property from Allen in 1864.

Carey acquired the name McKenzie River Iron Man, because, wrote Nick Bella in the *Springfield News* Dec. 18, 1977, he "stands among the handful in history who helped carve the narrow, winding McKenzie River from the wilderness. He earned a reputation as a true renaissance man who built homes and bridges, carried the mail, served as a deputy sheriff, invented the prototype of the modern McKenzie River boat, hunted for the market, guided fishermen, established an inn and played the fiddle for dances."

He was the first man to take fishermen down the river in a boat for a fee. The Thomsons spent much of their time from 1900 on as river boat and hunting guides. Thomson's lodge was well known for many years among hunting and fishing circles. Milo, Dayton and York owned and operated the lodge after 1923.

They built an addition so the lodge could hold 14 overnight guests. The Thomsons developed lighter and better boats -- a light dory, easily maneuverable through white water -- for running the river. They were founders of the McKenzie River Guides Association in 1932, along with other original members, John and Roy West, Rube and Howard Montgomery and Prince Helfrich.

When Carey died in 1940 at age 84, reportedly "an entire valley mourned, and condolence cards poured in from all over the country. Thomson was a personal friend of President Herbert Hoover, the Weyerhaeusers, the Huntingtons of Pasadena, the Franks and Terwilligers of Portland and several crowned heads of Europe who vacationed on the McKenzie and visited the lodge."

Thomson could "capture the curiosity of dinner guests and weave yarns which held their rapt attention until the wee hours."

"Grandma" Mary died in December 1953. A *Eugene Register-Guard* news story said:

"Many of the women were taken care of by Mrs. Thomson, who could be counted on to come to their assistance at any time, riding horseback to even the most remote homestead. . .Mrs. Thomson became famous with sportsmen for her cooking, and especially for her way of frying trout."

The lodge was sold in 1948 to Mr. and Mrs. A. P. Gannon. It burned down in 1954. The famous fishing lodge was not replaced.

Milo Thomson, after 50 years of boating on the river and the first guide to run treacherous Martin Rapids, died in 1955 in a boating accident at the McKenzie River confluence with Blue River. He and two passengers were drowned.

Carey Thomson Jr. (1909-1974), who guided for many years, died of a heart attack while visiting Yellowstone Park. Dayton (1897-1974) started rowing at age 11 and later managed Thomsons Lodge for many years. In 1926, he married Elvira May Dyer, who died two days after Dayton's death in 1974. York Thomson (1902-1979) told the compiler he stopped guiding in 1940. (Williams, 1991).

Martin Rapids

Martin Rapids, known for their ability "to sink the unwary boat or leave it in small pieces," are located within Ben and Kay Dorris State Park above Vida at river mile 45. The rapids were named for Thomas M. Martin, well-known state legislator and first Gate Creek postmaster.

The first person to successfully negotiate Martin Rapids was Carl B. Dehne (1889-1936). Wilber Dehne said his father had a homestead on the south bank of the river just above Martin Rapids and used a boat to get to the road. When crossing one day, the swift current swept him downstream through the rapids, which he successfully maneuvered, though he was "scared half to death."

He told the Thomsons, who either didn't believe him or thought he was just "lucky." On a $2.00 bet, they lined up along the bank. Dehne went through the treacherous rapids just to prove it could be done. Afterwards, the Thomsons negotiated the rapids successfully.

Prince Helfrich Landing, commonly known as Thomson Landing at the end of Thomson Lane, was named to honor the late Prince Helfrich (1908-1971), well-known hunting and fishing guide. His family moved to the McKenzie early in this century. Prince worked for the U. S. Forest Service, was a logger and ran a trap line. He acquired Thomson Landing after the property was sold. The Helfrich family donated the landing to Lane County in 1972 after his death.

John West (1901-1986), who worked 58 years as a guide on the McKenzie and other rivers, recalled Prince was one of the oldest river guides in Oregon. He pioneered many streams no man had floated, and he coordinated the White Water Parade.

Elvon and Lydya Skeen, 46585 Goodpasture Road, both retired school teachers, bought the Carey Thomson property shortly after the lodge burned in 1954. They built their own house overlooking the river and have renovated the old foot-swinging bridge several times, replacing the old wooden supports, planks and suspension towers.

The bridge, built around 1900 and known as the Thomson Bridge and McKenzie River Suspension Bridge, has been added to the Oregon Inventory of Historic Properties. It connected what was then the Thomson Sportsman Lodge on the south side of the river to what is now the Helfrich Boat Landing. Except by ferry, it was the only access to the north bank

The covered Goodpasture Bridge, sometimes referred to as the Thomson Bridge, four miles down river, with a connecting road, now serves the area. It was built by Lane County in 1938-39 just above the old Fayette Thomson ferry site at mp. 41.0.

James Henry Belknap and Ella Jane Finn Belknap

CHAPTER 33

James and Ella Belknap

James Henry Belknap, the first settler of duration on the upper McKenzie, was born March 25, 1848, in Boston, Mass. With his mother, Mary Ann, and sister, Clara, he may have lived for a time in Vermont, after his father, Rollin Simeon Belknap, went west to San Francisco via the Isthmus of Panama, during the gold rush era in 1849.

Franklin Belknap, Rollin's cousin, writing from Chicago in 1905, mentioned occasions when "your mother, yourself and sister, were at Father's (Levi Belknap) when you were very small." Franklin referred to an incident when James cut his foot with a little "cunning ax."

He was about six years old, when he came with his mother and Clara to Oregon, sailing around The Horn of South America to join his father in Southern Oregon about 1855. He grew up on the farm at Wilderville. The family moved to Albany in 1869.

The same year, at age 21, James moved to the McKenzie and took up homestead rights on 165.2 acres, six miles east of Blue River across the river from present-day Rainbow. Others had explored, hunted and fished in the area. But there were only scattered settlements beyond Walterville and none on the upper river.

James built a log cabin, cleared and farmed the land, but relied upon hunting, trapping and fishing for much of his livelihood. Living 50 miles from Eugene-Springfield, he had to make periodic trips into town to sell or trade his pelts and acquire staples. After his parents and three of their daughters moved to the area to found Belknap Springs in 1871, they were about 12 miles away -- an easy day's hike for a hardy, young woodsman. He no doubt had explored the area with his father when he relocated the springs, and probably helped cut the road.

Four years after he had settled, James, 25, married Ella Jane Finn Oct. 1, 1873. She was the daughter of Benjamin Franklin "Huckleberry" Finn and Mary Ann (Halter) Finn, pioneers of 1871.

Ella was born in Elyria, Ohio, Aug. 31, 1855. Her family migrated from Ohio to Michigan, then to Missouri. At age 16, she drove a mule team all the way when the Finns came to Oregon. James and Ella were married at the Gate Greek (now Vida) home of the bride's parents.

Just when and how he met and wooed Ella Jane Finn, age 18, can only be conjectured. The Finn family settled 25 miles down river on the south side, accessible only by boat. Somehow they met and somehow they were married Oct. 1, 1873, to begin a life together and raise a large family in relative isolation.

James filed for homestead rights in 1875. Ben Finn, his father-in-law, filed for his Gate Creek property at the same time at the nearest land office in Roseburg. The patent was granted Dec. 15, 1882, for 165.2 acres, Bureau of Land Management records show.

His homestead, lying south across the McKenzie River from what became Rainbow, now Holiday Farm, was one of the most fertile and picturesque on the upper river.

Access was by boat only. There were two places to ford the upper river: the old Indian ford east of Blue River, where Joseph Carter operated a ferry briefly, and below the Belknap homestead. Both sites were treacherous. Reports say the river had to be forded six times between Belknap Ranch and Walterville in those days.

James installed a ferry 0.5 of a mile west of the present Belknap Bridge. He operated it until about 1890, "when wear on the ferry ropes required its replacement. Instead of spending $80 of scarce money, he decided to construct a bridge which would be more permanent," to quote Martha Belknap. The ferry access points are still visible.

The first bridge was named Thomson Bridge, for Carey Thomson, who in 1889 felled several large trees across the river and covered them with an open, wooden deck. He charged tolls. The bridge later became known as Campbell Bridge, named for a resident in the area, then Belknap Bridge in the mid-1890's.

James, a farmer, grew food stuffs, along with dairy products, chickens, beef, and he had an orchard. Berries and nuts grew wild. Game in the woods was plentiful and the streams abounded with fish. He made trips in the spring and fall by horses and wagon into Eugene and Springfield to buy flour, sugar, salt, spices, clothing, other household necessities and ammunition. The trip took several days.

He had an interest in the McKenzie toll road, which operated from about 1871 until 1894, when the county took over. Records show he and John A. Isham, an area homesteader, served as road viewers to survey or lay out future roads.

BELKNAP CHILDREN

James and Ella had fifteen children, seven of whom lived to adulthood. They were: James Byrd (Nov. 27, 1877), Alice Jennie (Nov. 22, 1878), Arthur I. (Feb. 14, 1881), Cora Edith (March 31, 1884), Clara B. (April 30, 1885), Elva Ann (Sept. 26, 1887) and Clarence Roland (Oct. 21, 1892). Two little girls, Ruby and Pearl, died in childhood. The others were stillborn or died shortly after birth.

Pearl, or Pearlie as her family called her, was born April 7, 1897, and died Aug. 29, 1901. The brief notice states she died at the residence of John Brent, corner of Thirteenth and Willamette streets in Eugene. She "had been suffering from a complication of diseases since June. The grief-stricken parents, one brother and a sister, accompanied by friends, left yesterday for Leaburg for interment of remains" in the Greenwood Cemetery. There is no grave marker.

We don't have Ruby's birth date. It was around 1893. She was four or five years old when she died May 26, 1897, reportedly from sucking honey from flowering rhododendrons. An undated newspaper death notice in my mother's collection states:

"Died From Poisoning. -- Little Ruby Belknap, daughter of Mr. and Mrs. James Belknap of McKenzie Precinct, died last Friday morning, after suffering thirty hours, from the effects of sucking honey out of flowering rhododendrons, so numerous in that locality." When Ruby became ill, an attempt was made to rush her down the McKenzie River in a boat. The family felt that was the fastest and easiest way to travel, rather than by wagon or buggy over the rugged roads of that era. She died before reaching a doctor.

A landmark on the McKenzie, known locally as Belknap Rock, attests to this tragic occurrence. The rock, about 18 feet in diameter and four feet high, is located along the east side of the McKenzie River, one-half mile below Leaburg Dam and Fish Hatchery. . .where the boat was landed and the stricken girl taken out. (Williams, 1991).

Some Belknap children are buried in a small cemetery at McKenzie Bridge. The eight or nine known graves include that of John Whitlock Sims (1840-1902), pioneer settler and husband of Dora (Belknap) Sims, and their son, James Edwin, who died in 1887 at age 12. An Indian also is said to have been buried there.

Stones imbedded in the ground mark these graves. The names have long since weathered away. The cemetery, on land owned by Giustina Lumber Co., some 200 yards south of the highway, is largely over grown. From time to time it has been cared for, otherwise goes unnoticed, yet concealing a small part of the upper McKenzie history.

Early Schooling

How much schooling James and Ella had we have no knowledge. But they provided what education was available for their children. They attended the little log school, built in 1885 adjoining the John and Dora Sims homestead. Smith Taylor, district U. S. Forest Service ranger at McKenzie Bridge, recalled that Art Belknap was one of the first thirteen pupils, starting when he was only four years old.

It is probable Byrd, 8, and Alice, 6, also were pupils. Alice told of walking a mile and a half to school, often in the snow. School was held three months in the fall and sometimes in the spring. The district was too poor to provide year-around schooling. In later years when the other children (Cora, Clara, Elva and Clarence) were of school age, family members moved to Walterville in the fall and stayed until spring so the children could attend the eight-month school.

James' log cabin was about 12 by 16 feet in dimension with a dirt floor, a front door and a window on either side. A barn and other outbuildings were constructed. How long James and Ella lived in the cabin, with their rapidly growing family, we aren't sure. What was referred to as the "big house" was not built until around 1900.

A letter dated April 1, 1899, from Carlyle, Ill., written by M. E. Yerrington, apparently a former school teacher, sheds some light on the early days. Addressed to Mrs. (Ella) Belknap, it asks:

"How are they getting along with your house? You will be proud, won't you, when you get into a new house. . . It seems odd to think your girls are all large now. They must be a good deal of help to you. I suppose they are doing well in school. . . Your neighborhood must be thinned out with so many moved away. Alice said you were to have some new ones in Carey Thomson's house. Does anyone live in Oscar Renfrew's house now?. . . I would like some of the fish Alice told about catching. We don't get any good fish here. . . not like the McKenzie fish or Michigan either. . ."

Letters to Franklin Belknap

Quotations from James Belknap are contained in Franklin Belknap's notes printed in the Vermont *Vital Records* (1017.2, 612, 289, 129.2, 52, 15, 4, 1). They probably are from letters dated Oct. 16 and Dec. 1, 1905, he wrote to Rollin's cousin, Franklin, in Vermont.

James said they had "seven children living and eight dead.

"When we came here the Indians were very bad and the mail was very few and far between. We lost all track of kinfolks. Mother never heard from any of her folks after (age) 55 or 56, and Father did not seem inclined to write.

"I settled here in 1869 and have let the second son (Arthur) have the place, 170 acres. I will try to go down to the Belknap Settlement in the spring. It is 120 miles and a bad road now."

The Indians referred to probably were from the Warm Springs tribe who made summertime visits to the McKenzie Valley to pick huckleberries and catch salmon, which they smoked or dried. The Warm Spring Indians were for the most part peaceful but could have proved a problem by interference and thieving.

The Belknap Settlement was established by Jessie Belknap and family, who came to Oregon in 1847 and 1848, settling in Benton County, west of Monroe. Jessie was a descendant of Samuel Belknap III, a brother of Rollin's great-grandfather, Simeon Belknap I.

James corresponded between 1902 and 1906 with a business acquaintance, W. T. Campbell, a Eugene architect engaged in "plans and specifications made for houses and bridges of every description." This could have been Walter Campbell, who resided near Belknap Bridge in 1880 (Oregon Genealogical Society, 1978), or William T. Campbell, who owned land on the south side of the bridge, as shown in a 1910 Forest Service map of the area. The map also shows a Viola M. Campbell owning land adjacent to the other Campbell property. Campbell mentioned several parties interested in buying the ranch. In another letter Campbell discussed timber sales:

> "Lots of timber is being sold on the Siuslaw but I have not heard of any responsible offers for McKenzie timber. They are only paying $12.00 to $15.00 per acre for most of it, a few pieces going for $20.00 per acre on the Siuslaw. George Croner's wife is trying to get options, at $25.00 to $30.00 per acre but she doesn't pay any down. I don't think there is anything behind it. It's dead easy to take an option as long as there is nothing to pay. I wrote to YALE and tried to brace him up to hold for $35.00 per acre."

(George and Alice Croner were long-time McKenzie Bridge residents. Bill Yale operated a sawmill near Belknap Springs).

Death of James

James Belknap died May 5, 1908, age 60 years, one month, 10 days. His obituary in a Eugene newspaper said he died at a Eugene Hospital from "a complication of diseases." Excerpts follow:

> "Mr. Belknap was one of the Lane County pioneers and was the last of the old settlers of the upper McKenzie River, his home being for many years at Belknap's Bridge, a few miles this side of McKenzie Bridge. His father (Rollin) was the discoverer (should be developer) of Belknap Springs. . .situated ten or twelve miles above the old Belknap homestead.

> "He was married to Miss Ella Jane Finn at Gate Creek (now Vida) Oct. 1, 1873, who has been a faithful helpmate and companion. Besides his wife, he leaves the following children, all of whom live in Lane County (as of 1908): James Byrd, Mrs. Alice Odell and Mrs. Cora Inman of Walterville; Arthur, who lives on the home place; Miss Clara (Mrs. Clyde Lockwood); Mrs. Elva Trotter of Marcola, and Clarence (at home). He also leaves the following sisters: Mrs. Dora Sims of the upper McKenzie; Mrs. Fred Pepiot, of the lower Siuslaw country, and Mrs. (Robert-Clara) Lockwood of Canyon City. He was a member of the Order of Washington, carrying an insurance policy in the order for $1,000." He was buried in Greenwood Cemetery.

Ella Jane's Final Years

After James death, Ella Jane continued living at the Belknap Ranch, with her second son, Arthur. Byrd was working at Walterville, where he had acquired property.

Cora, in 1903, was married to Clifton L. Inman, who was working at the Lucky Boy mine. Alice in 1904 married Joseph Odell. Elva, the same year, married Walden Trotter, of Camp Creek, and Clara married Willie Clyde Lockwood of Canyon City. Clarence married Martha Andrews of Eugene in 1921.

The "big house," occupied about 1900, burned down in 1910. A storage house was converted to a "temporary" home.

This brings us to the period of my first memories of Grandma's place around 1914/15. My family visited each summer and enjoyed the freedom the ranch seemed to offer.

Ella's father Benj. F. Finn, in his declining years from about 1915, and her brother, Louis, "Uncle Lew," who was in poor health, lived in the Belknap home. Louis died in 1916 and his father in 1919.

Grandma's "temporary" house served until the early 1920's, when Clarence and Art built a sawmill on the bench land. They cut lumber from the hillside to build a large new house, and later a house for Clarence and Martha.

Grandma Belknap bore the ordeal of child-bearing well, despite adverse conditions in the small log cabin. She seemed to be in good health, until the summer of 1924, when she failed to survive surgery for gallstones. She died Sept. 2, 1924, in a Eugene hospital at age 69.

Her obituary said:

". . .a pioneer of Lane County. . .she had been a resident of the Belknap Bridge section on the upper McKenzie since 1873, and was the mother of the Belknap brothers, well-known hunters and guides. She was one of four early pioneer women of the upper river, the others being Mrs. Ella K. Haflinger of Foley Springs (about 1884), Mrs. George Frissell of McKenzie Bridge (about 1880), and Mrs. (Dora) Sims (sister of James) of Rainbow (about 1871 at Belknap Springs, later at nearby Sims' ranch)."

Survivors (as of 1924) were sons: Byrd of Bellingham, Wa.; Arthur and Clarence of Blue River; four daughters, Mrs. Alice Odell of Deerhorn, Mrs. Cora Inman of Springfield; Mrs. Clara Siemsen of Amity, Ore., and Mrs. Elva Trotter of Watsonville, Cal.; two brothers, Eugene Finn, Long Beach, Calif., and Pete Finn, Glazier, Wa., and two sisters, Mrs. L. P. Snapp (Emma Finn Wycoff, a second marriage) of Eugene and Mrs. Albert Ward. Ella was buried in the Greenwood Cemetery at Leaburg beside her pioneering husband of 35 years.

Landmarks Named

James explored all through the upper McKenzie and South Fork areas. Belknap Crater, elevation 6,877 feet, located along the crest of the Cascade Range in the Mt. Washington Wilderness on the Deschutes and Linn County boundary, and Little Belknap Crater were named for him. (McArthur's *Oregon Geographic Names*, p. 44).

Other landmarks named for this pioneer settler included Belknap Bridge; Belknap Meadow, on West King Road near Clarence Belknap's old sawmill (part of the Belknap homestead, the Big Field); Belknap Slide, a rock slide area six miles up the South Fork River; now covered by

Cougar Reservoir; Belknap Bar, a gravel bar on the South Fork, also covered by the reservoir; Belknap Camp, the Civilian Conservation Corp. encampment, which operated through the 1930's.

Other sites bearing the Belknap name are derived from Rollin Belknap, who developed Belknap Springs. Included are Belknap Junction, one-time junction on the old McKenzie Pass Highway leading into Belknap Springs, since bypassed by the present Clear Lake Highway; Belknap Dam, a proposed site on the McKenzie above McKenzie Bridge, considered but not developed; Belknap Ranger Station, a U. S. Forest Service administrative site near Belknap Springs, not developed, and Belknap Springs Known Geothermal Resource area, where several test wells have been drilled. The cabin James built in the early 1870's stood until the 1930's, when it fell under heavy snows. My family camped there the summer of 1925.

James Byrd Belknap

James Byrd Belknap was born Nov. 27, 1877, at Walterville. His younger years were spent on the ranch at Rainbow. He attended school at both the log school on the Sims place and at Walterville.

Byrd lived for a time as an adult at Walterville but had lived away from Lane County for about 25 years, most of that time near Bellingham, Wa., where he was engaged in logging.

He died in 1939 at age 62 in Port Angeles, Wa. A news item said he was a saw filer, that he had come to Port Angeles four years before his death and was employed by the Crescent Logging Company. He never married.

The item said Byrd's brothers, Arthur and Clarence of Rainbow, and sisters, Mrs. Elva Trotter, of Eugene, Mrs. Clara Siemsen and Mrs. Cora Inman of Springfield were called to Port Angeles at the time of his three-week illness and resulting death. His body was shipped to Springfield for services. Burial was in the Greenwood Cemetery.

James Byrd Belknap

BELKNAP FAMILY--(Front row, l. to r.) (Back Row) Clara, James Byrd, Alice, James Henry, Pearl, Ella Jane, Clarence; Arthur, Cora and Elva (Picture circa 1900).

CHAPTER 34

Arthur I. Belknap

Arthur I. Belknap, packer, guide, farmer, football player, born on Valentine's day, Feb. 14, 1881, might have been a school teacher. Only things didn't work out that way.

Artie, as he was known, started school at age four years, in 1885, attending the little hewn-log school house on the Sims' place and later at Walterville. He enrolled at Oregon Agricultural College, now Oregon State University, at Corvallis about 1900.

He wanted to become a teacher. But his father, James, still in his fifties but not in good health (he died at age 60 in 1908), wanted him to take over the farm. Byrd was working at Walterville. Art's football career was equally short-lived. About five feet-nine, he weighed around 150 pounds.

Arthur Belknap

Sometime after 1900, Art became a packer and guide. Over the years, he hobnobbed with millionaires. He met all kinds of people, seeking life in the wilds. One party, headed by a San Franciscan named Mills, came every year and one year stayed out all summer. Their destination was the Erma Bell Lakes, high in the Cascades.

These three small mountain lakes, just west of the summit of the Cascade Range, about five miles north of Waldo Lake, were a favorite of fishermen because of their pristine beauty. Rainbow trout grew to 36 inches in length. They were named for Miss Erma Bell, employed in the U. S. Forest Service Portland office. She was killed in an auto accident April 27, 1918. (McArthur).

Other guides on the McKenzie included Sandy Leach, Arthur Moody and Harry Hays. Some packers used mules. Art preferred horses. Some of these knew the trails so well they needed little guidance. Among fishing and boating guides on the McKenzie were the Thomsons, Prince Helfrich and John Shelley West, the last charter member of the McKenzie River Guides Association. West died in 1986.

Art lived on the home place all his life. He farmed, ran a herd of cattle, drilled wells and mowed grass along road shoulders for the state Highway Department.

Using pioneering techniques, probably learned from his father, my "Uncle Artie" made the best jerky I ever tasted. He smoked sugar-cured strips of beef, venison, bacon, hams and fish in his smokehouse.

Always congenial, Art was well liked, not only by his many friends on the McKenzie, but by visitors and people he took into the mountains, who returned year after year. His rosy cheeks, twinkling blue eyes and built-in smile often belied his rugged features.

He was a great tease. He lived with my family in Walterville one winter while working in my father's sawmill. I was three years old. He teased me unmercifully, calling me an "ittie, bittie, ole white-headed kid." I hated him with a passion. But he was only kidding. He had a heart of gold, and I grew to be very fond of him.

Hidden Lake

An excellent fisherman, he often gave me pointers. I'll never forget the time he took me (about 1920 -- I was 9 or 10 years old) into the upper reaches of the South Fork River to "salt the cattle." In the spring when the snow was gone, he pastured his cattle at Frissell Crossing, 26 miles up the South Fork. Unless there was a natural salt lick in the area, he had to put out salt for the animals.

It was a four-day trip with a saddle horse and pack horse. On our return we made a surprise side trip to Hidden Lake, where fish abounded. The trail to the lake left the South Fork about 12 miles out, near Hardy's Cabin, and proceeded up the mountain on the west. We rafted across the lake to the inlet and caught our limit

Ten years later Art said he went into Hidden Lake and found three parties quarreling over the raft. As logging roads were built, this fishing paradise lost much of its charm.

Art loved ice cream. He sometimes "pigged out." One time in the mid-1920's Henry Westbrook, who had a summer home on property purchased from the Belknaps, and Lew Quimby, who owned the Rainbow store, made a bet on how much ice cream Art could eat, the loser to pay for the ice cream. I'm not sure who won or lost the bet, but Art stopped after eating 27 scoops of ice cream.

The Westbrook's granddaughter, Dorothy Dicken of Portland, commented, "When I was a child, Art loved to tell stories, and how his blue eyes twinkled, because I fell for them, if you will excuse the pun, hook, line and sinker. He liked to stump me with riddles."

Upon Art's retirement Jean Webber wrote in the *Eugene Register-Guard*, headed, "Dean of River Guides Pasturing His Horses":

"McKENZIE RIVER -- For the first time in more than half a century, Art Belknap this season won't be heading for the high country with his string of horses. The 'dean' of the McKenzie River guides, Belknap is putting his four remaining pack horses out to pasture -- and is planning to retire himself.

"Belknap, who is 78, explained: Guides once were required to lead fishing and hunting parties into the Cascade wilderness. Now logging access roads have been built and rugged vehicles developed for travel where the going is rough. Sportsmen 'get there on their own.' Besides, a fire at his ranch on the upper McKenzie, (about 1959) destroyed his cabin and much of his camp gear. 'I decided it was a good time to quit.' Belknap now lives in a cabin in the Rainbow community.

"A member of the McKenzie River Guides Assn., Belknap has made pack trips into the Cascades for the past 59 years.

"'I've hunted and trapped every kind of critter that makes a track in this part of the country,' he said.

"'Fish and game were more plentiful in days gone by. In the early 1900s, the fish were so thick in Hidden Lake their backs stuck out of the water. There wasn't any limit in those days. I caught 97 trout the first morning out.'

"One of the highlights of his career, the guide recalls, came in 1906, when he led a party of 10 into Rider Creek on the South Fork of the McKenzie. The party was out 21 days and bagged 21 deer. With this party was James J. Jeffries. Belknap still chuckles at the memory of the world heavyweight champion (boxer) being downed by slippery rocks along the McKenzie. 'Darn near every day he would slip and fall in,' Belknap said.

"Just to keep busy during his retirement, Belknap said he plans to follow his hobby -- well digging. 'To date, I brought in 80 wells along the upper McKenzie'."

Jeffries Point on the South Fork, partly submerged in Cougar Reservoir, was named for Jim Jeffries, who came out of retirement for his title fight which he lost to Jack Johnson in Reno in 1910.

Art came from a hardy, pioneering stock. He loved the McKenzie and he loved to hunt and fish and to explore. Sturdy, strong and robust, he was a pioneer in his own rights.

Old Oregon Magazine, the University of Oregon Alumni Association publication, in its January-February 1965 edition, featured Art's picture as its cover page, at age 83, with long white hair and beard. An article by J. Barre Toelken, a graduate student and instructor in English at the University, was titled "*Adventures in Folklore.*" A portion pertained to Art and "Huck" Finn. It began:

Magazine Feature
(Used by Permission)

"In the main, Americans have not liked to think of themselves as easily fooled. Hardheaded and practical, they have either wanted to believe a story is the truth or admit with a grin it's an outright lie.

"Witness Arthur Belknap, grandson of Benjamin Franklin Finn, who claimed to be the real Huckleberry Finn of Mark Twain and also prided himself on being the biggest liar on the McKenzie River. Arthur, a fine story-teller in his own rights, spins a whole collection of tales he learned from his grandfather, none of which he actually believes."

The article relating some of Finn's best stories concludes:

"It is needless to point out the stories are not at all spoiled by our knowledge that they are also told of Jigger Jones, an old Maine logger, and they crop up here and there in oral tradition wherever there's a memorable character to celebrate."

Great-granddad Finn had many stories, which he always told with a straight face. My mother used to crack up when she related some of his best. A couple of them are recalled here:

One time Finn out hunting saw a deer run around the side of the hill. Quickly he struck his rifle against a tree, bending it so he could shoot around the hill. He killed the deer.

Another time while hunting he became tired and crawled inside a hollow log. While he slept a storm blew a tree across the open end. Only a tiny hole emitted enough light to be seen. Now, Grandpa was a very strong Republican (or was it a Democrat?) As he lay there wondering what to do, his mind wandered to the time he had once voted for the opposite party. He felt so small he crawled right out of that little hole.

Art lived on the farm and took care of his mother. He inherited what was left of the original homestead, except for forested lands acquired by Clarence and tracts which were sold over the years.

After Grandma Belknap died, the Forest Drury family, long-time residents of the King Road, moved in with Art. Drury worked for the Forest Service. During the 1950s, Art sold the farm to Clarence. The house was torn down. Art moved to a small house on the King Road. This house burned in 1959. Not only were his packing gear and personal possessions lost, but such treasures as the family Bible, other historical records, and an 1860 Winchester rifle were destroyed. Art moved into a shack at Clarence's former sawmill.

When his health began to deteriorate in the late-1960's, he moved down river to the unoccupied home of his sister, Alice, who died in 1965. The house was next door to his niece, Mrs. Ernest (Metta Odell) Watson, at Deerhorn. He lived there, under Metta's care, until his death Jan. 20, 1968.

In a taped interview about 1976 by Pat Allensworth and Vicki Koepsel, Martha Belknap, commented: "The first time he'd ever been in a hospital, and the next morning he died -- because he was 88. He'd never been sick, spent all his time outdoors. Ate beans and coffee and survived."

Art displays rack of elk horns bagged on South Fork

BELKNAP GIRLS---Top row, Cora Edith and Clara B.; bottom row, Elva Ann and Alice Jenny. Picture taken about 1900.

CHAPTER 35

Odell Family

Alice Jenny, the second Belknap child, was born Nov. 22, 1878, in Walterville. A life-long McKenzie resident, she grew up at the Belknap Ranch, did housework in Eugene for a family named Kress, who owned a drug store, and worked summers for Ella Haflinger at Foley Springs.

On Sept. 17, 1904, she married Joseph Henry (Joe) Odell at the Belknap Ranch. Joe, born June 12, 1873, in Winonah, Minn., was a son of Henry (Hank) Odell, born Dec. 13, 1852, and Margaret "Maggie" Brown, born in 1855. They were married in Minnesota and had four children -- Joseph Henry, Daisy Dean, Robert (Bunt) and Emma (died in her teens).

In 1887, Joe at age 14 came by train to Oregon from Minnesota with his father. His mother, sister Daisy and brother Robert came at a later date. Hank lived at Walterville. He died Dec. 13, 1939, and was buried in Greenwood Cemetery, Leaburg. Margaret died Feb. 14, 1919. She was buried in Mt. Vernon Cemetery, east of Springfield.

Daisy married Simon (Sime) Putnam. They lived at Deerhorn. Children were Joe, Esther, Glen, Paul, Wilma and Vail. Robert (Bunt) Odell (1875-1927) married Lottie Hilderbrand. Born Aug. 11, 1884, she died Nov. 24, 1926. Their children were Datus, Danny, Violet, and Florence, of Lane County, and Margaret, of Pennsylvania. Another son, Mike, was reared by Daisy and Sime Putnam. Robert and Lottie were buried in Mt. Vernon Cemetery.

As a young man, Joe lived with a half-uncle, Dat Lowell Odell, on a cattle ranch on High Prairie near Oakridge. A cowboy, he drove cattle for Porter Bros. from Eugene to Silver Lake. He later drove stage coach from Eugene to the Lucky Boy mine at Blue River, hauling freight and passengers. He became a hunting and fishing guide, a logger and a farmer. His 1912 hunting and fishing license, at age 37, gave his height 5 feet 5 inches, weight 145 pounds, brown hair, hazel eyes.

Joe and Alice lived at Cedar Flat, Walterville and Deerhorn. Suffering from a terminal illness, Joe died March 29, 1942, age 69. Alice died at Walterville Oct. 13, 1965. Juanita Rebekah Lodge 85 conducted ritualistic rites. Burial was in Greenwood Cemetery. The Odells' first child, Margaret Jenny, born Nov. 14, 1906, at Cedar Flat, died Dec. 19, 1921, age 15, at Walterville. She was buried in Mt. Vernon.

Alice Belknap Odell

Other children were:

Wilbur Henry, born March 18, 1908, in Walterville, served in the U. S. Navy 20 years. After discharge, he homesteaded in Alaska. Returning to the McKenzie, he lived on Goodpasture Road, Vida. He was a member of the Masonic Lodge No. 216, A. F. & A. M., Vida; Fleet Reserve, Veterans of Foreign Wars, American Legion and Springfield Elks Lodge No. 2145. He died Feb. 12, 1983. Burial was in Greenwood Cemetery.

Mildred

Mildred Nettie Odell, born Sept. 10, 1911, at Cedar Flat, attended Cedar Flat, Walterville and Deerhorn schools. She married Joseph Wm. Franklin "Joe" Yoakum June 15, 1929, in Walterville.

Yoakum, son of Mr. and Mrs. Joseph Holt Yoakum, was born in Marshfield (now Coos Bay), March 29, 1903. He began work with the Southern Pacific Railroad in Roseburg in 1923, retiring in 1968 at age 65. He died Oct. 1, 1979, in Springfield. Mildred, a member of Juanita Rebekah Lodge No. 85, Springfield, and the Past Noble Grands Club, died at age 76 July 18, 1988.

The Yoakums had a son, Joseph Holt, born Nov. 15, 1930, and daughter, Marcia, March 18, 1942, both born in Eugene. Twins, born Dec. 3, 1938, died at birth. Joseph Holt married Jeannette Handley April 27, 1951. Children are Joseph Lawnie, born Aug. 22, 1952; Theresa Lynn, born May 27, 1955, and Bobijean, Aug. 17, 1956.

Joseph Lawnie married Laura Lea Dunn Feb. 5, 1985. They adopted a son, Jeffrey Donald, born Oct. 20, 1988. They reside in Roy, Utah.

Theresa married Robert E. Franz Jr., a Springfield attorney. They have a son, Creighton Robert, born Dec. 10, 1987, and daughter, Daschel

Jacquelyn, born May 3, 1995.

Bobijean married Edgar Thomas Watts of Marcola, Ore., Dec. 30, 1976. They have sons, Reuben Lee, born Nov. 24, 1978, and Lucas Gene, Aug. 3, 1981. They live in Thurston. Bobijean has been employed by SAIF Corp. since 1988, and Edgar by Springfield Utility Board since 1979.

Joseph Holt worked 43 years for the Southern Pacific Railroad. He and Jeannette were divorced in 1974. He married Peggy Eden April 14, 1983. He died in Yuma, Ariz., Dec. 26, 1996, at age 66. He was buried next to his parents in Greenwood Cemetery.

Marcia married Rolland Bresee Dec. 10, 1963. Children are Royal Yoakum, born Sept. 3, 1962; Shelli, Aug. 17, 1964, and Shay, March 23, 1968. Royal married Sondra Branch. They have daughters, Stephanie Marie and Makenzie Nicole, born Dec. 5, 1995. They live in Bend, Ore.

Shelli married Rick Schaufler. They have two sons, Brennan Richard, born Oct. 13, 1993, and Blake Augusta, born Aug. 22, 1996. They reside in Springfield. Shay currently resides in Fredricksburg, Va.

Wister James

Wister James Odell, born July 8, 1914, in Eugene, attended Walterville and Deerhorn grade schools and Walterville and Springfield high schools. He served as an armed Navy gunner on merchant ships during World War II with rank of seaman first class. He worked in the lumber industry. He was a member of Springfield V.F.W. Post 3965 and McKenzie Ramblers Good Sam Club.

On Feb. 17, 1946, in Springfield, he married Bessie L. House. She was born April 27, 1925, in Heig, Neb., the daughter of Mr. and Mrs. Arthur House of Springfield. Wister died July 3, 1985, at age 70. He was buried in Greenwood Cemetery. Bessie lives in Springfield.

Their daughter, Betty Marie, married Bill Vaughn July 3, 1966. Children are Ronald Andrew, with the Marines, and Jennifer, married to Gene Sulton. Vaughn died Feb. 14, 1982. Betty later married Don Carlton.

Their son, Andrew Arthur married Londa (Brunum). They have children, Christopher and Tiffany. Andrew served in the Navy.

Myrtle

Myrtle Odell, born May 4, 1916, in Walterville, attended Deerhorn grade and Springfield High School. She married Jack Ryckman in 1940. A son, Matthew (Matt) Lynn, was born Aug. 17, 1941, in Oregon City.

Later, Myrtle was married to Douglas Sproston. Children, all living in the Eugene-Springfield area, are: Noel Delaine, born Dec. 7. 1950; Douglas Arron, Feb. 10, 1953; Mona Darlene, Oct. 4, 1954; Dale, June 11, 1956, and Drew, Sept. 14, 1957.

Noel Delaine (Susan) married David R. Martin Nov. 16, 1969. Their children are: David Douglas, born Aug. 27, 1970, married Kerri Bristow Aug. 22, 1992, and Suzanne Noelle, Dec. 6, 1978.

Douglas Arron married Cindy Rene St. Clair July 15, 1985. A son, Douglas Wesley Sproston, was born Mar. 19, 1988.

Mona Darlene (Donna) married Geneu Dean Winter Apr. 13, 1974. Children are Cheri Ann, born May 22, 1977, and Lacey Nicole, Oct. 6, 1980. She and Winter were divorced June 22, 1985.

Myrtle died June 8, 1988, in Eugene.

Matthew "Matt" Ryckman died May 18, 1996, of complications relating to diabetes at age 54. He married Lola Connant in Muskegon, Mich., Jan. 30, 1989. A disabled resident of the McKenzie for nine years, Matt was a member of the McKenzie Bridge Assembly of God Church. He served in the U. S. Army and was a member of American Legion Post 83. Survivors are his wife; son, Robert Connant; daughters, Beth Delano of Muskegon, and Cheryl Wurthner, Rothbury, Mich.; three brothers, two sisters and several grandchildren. Burial was in Greenwood Cemetery.

Metta Mae

Metta Mae, the last Odell family survivor, was born Feb. 2, 1919, in Walterville and attended Deerhorn and Springfield schools. After graduation from high school in 1937, she was working for Ella Haflinger at Foley Springs when she and Ernest Watson, also a Springfield High grad, were married Oct. 24, that year.

The wedding ceremony was performed by Justice of the Peace Moyer of McKenzie Bridge in the Foley Springs hotel in front of the huge fire place banked with autumn leaves, firethorn and roses.

Watson, born Feb. 20, 1912, in Palisade, Minn., was the son of Mr. and Mrs. Claud Watson who came west from Minnesota and settled in Camp Creek. Ernie and Metta lived in LaPine and Bend, moving then to the Odell farm at Deerhorn. Their children are:

Alice Watson, born Oct. 1, 1939, in Bend, married Richard Laverne (Dick) Wells Aug. 15, 1959, at Leaburg. He was born July 9, 1938. They have four children: (1) Lori Lynne, born May 30, 1960, in Oklahoma. On Aug. 9, 1982, Lori married Lon Steve Dennison who was born Aug. 21, 1945. (2) Randolph Laverne Wells, born Feb. 27, 1964, married Aleta Hadlock. (3) Russell Lee Wells, born May 27, 1967, and (4) Jeffery Lawrence Wells, April 20, 1969.

Lawrence Ernest (Larry), born Dec. 7, 1940, in Bend, on Aug. 3, 1963, married Charoliene Anne Sanne, born Dec. 3, 1942. Children are: (1) Anne Mae, born May 23, 1964; (2) Alicia Lynn, June 12, 1965; (3) Anthony Lawrence, Mar. 16, 1967, and (4) Andrea Kay, April 3, 1971.

Linda Lee Watson, born Dec. 14, 1946, in Eugene, married Larry Edward Hull. The son of Mr. and Mrs. Ed Hull of McKenzie Highway, he was born Feb. 6, 1944. Their children are Amy Lea, born Aug. 17, 1969, married Ramon Rasubala, and Ricky Allen, born Oct. 19, 1973.

Martheda

Martheda Odell, born Sept. 26, 1924, in Walterville, was graduated from Springfield High School in 1941. She served in the U. S. Navy WAVES during World War II as a teletypist.

She married Patrick Gearhart. They had three children, Lynette Ramsey of Harrison, Ark.; Lee Gearhart, U. S. Navy (retired), and Jolane Daniels of Harrison, Ark., and four grandchildren.

After her Navy service Martheda and their children lived in Japan, where her husband was stationed with the Navy. Martheda died Aug. 2, 1981, at age 57 years in Omaha, Ark., where they were living.

Clifton Leverne Inman   Cora Edith Belknap Inman

CHAPTER 36

The Inman family

A shotgun pellet, fired by a man bird hunting in a nearby field, came through the open door of the Walterville school house and struck Cora Edith Belknap on the back. The injury, while not serious, caused considerable alarm.

Born March 31, 1884, on the James and Ella Belknap Ranch, Cora attended school through the eighth grade at the log school on the Sims property and at Walterville. The shooting occurred sometime during the 1890's. She was in the fifth or sixth grade.

As a young lady, Cora worked summers for Ella Haflinger at Foley Springs, and for Rosa Sparks at Sparks Ranch, Blue River. While at Sparks Ranch she met Clifton LeVerne Inman, a stamp mill operator at the Lucky Boy Mining Co. on Gold Hill. They were married Sept. 23, 1903.

Cliff Inman, born Nov. 21, 1873, in New Brighton, Pa., was the son of James, born in December 1844, in Beaver Falls, Pa., and Emily Fidelia (Hyde) Inman, born in Youngstown, Ohio, Oct. 23, 1846. Cliff had a brother, Vernon, and sisters, Stella, Eva Mae and Laurel.

The family came to Oregon, settling in Flournoy Valley, west of Roseburg in 1891. Vernon died there in 1892 from a stomach ailment.

In 1898, Cliff enlisted in the volunteer army at Roseburg and served during the Spanish-American War in the Philippine Islands.

Returning home in 1900, he found employment at Lucky Boy. His mother and father were divorced in 1901. He moved his mother and sisters, Eva and Laurel, to Walterville. Stella was married.

Lived at Lucky Boy

Cliff and Cora lived at Lucky Boy before and after the birth of their first child, Gladys, Aug. 31, 1904.

About 1906, when Lucky Boy operations were being phased down, he and a partner, Nate Standish, developed a gold mine at Great Northern on the Calapooia River in Linn County. The mine showed considerable promise, but the gold vein they were working played out.

Inman returned to Walterville. In 1907, deed records show, he bought a sawmill from Tom Willian for $750. Willian brought his family to Walterville about 1900. He and sons, George, who married Clare Stacey of Walterville, and Robert, who married Madge Hambol, a high school teacher, were in the sawmill business in Walterville and Camp Creek many years. Inman moved the mill to the hillside north of Walterville on the Millican property.

The Inmans had four children: Gladys LaVerne, born Aug. 31, 1904; Arthur Clifton, March 22, 1907; Violet Ruth, July 12, 1909, and Leroy Bertrand, Dec. 23, 1911.

Tragic Events

A string of tragic events occurred, starting with the death May 5, 1908, of Cora's father, James Belknap at age 60. Cliff's sister, Eva Mae, died of tuberculosis July 21, 1908, at age 27.

On Aug. 6, 1909, Arthur Clifton died at age two years from cholera infantum, less than a month after Violet's birth. Arthur Clifton and Eva Mae, were buried in the I.O.O.F. (now Pioneer) Cemetery in Eugene.

Cliff sold the sawmill back to the Willians in September, 1909, and went to work in California mines. Lester Millican, Walterville farmer, bought the mill in 1910

Cliff was again operating the sawmill when this compiler was born Dec. 23, 1911, in a shack beside the mill. Ada Millican, at age 23, was midwife. The doctor failed to arrive. The Inmans moved to the Potter house in Walterville, then to the Sturdevant house, which they rented for $5 a month the next ten years. The house was adjacent to the store.

Mines on Trinity River

The sawmill was closed in 1914. Inman prospected for gold in the Trinity River area of northern California about 1915/16. His prospecting, though unproductive, provided inspiration for a book of poetry, *Whisperings from Ancient Oreganna*, he wrote later in life.

World War I was on. He went into San Francisco to work in a machine shop. He returned home the summer before the war ended. He was not quite 45 and he had received a draft notice.

His mother, Emily, who had lived with Dad and Mother, died Oct. 11, 1918. She was buried in the Pioneer Cemetery in Eugene.

About 1921, Inman and Ray Chase, of Camp Creek, built another sawmill at Walterville, operating as Inman-Chase Lumber Co. After cutting out the timber supply, they moved the mill to the Seavey property, north across the McKenzie River from Springfield. Inman later sold to Chase. A certificate of retirement was filed Feb. 16, 1926.

Inman worked for Booth-Kelly Lumber Co. about 1922, as chief engineer at a logging camp in the Mohawk River drainage out of Wendling. When the Booth-Kelly camp was moved, requiring access by train out of Springfield (rather than a seven-mile hike over the steep hill from Leaburg), the family moved to Springfield in 1923.

The family's long association with the upper McKenzie resumed. Inman quit Booth-Kelly to work as head sawyer at Clarence Belknap's sawmill on the Belknap Ranch in 1924. We spent the summer in a tent-house on the ranch.

Inman negotiated with Grandma Belknap to purchase 18.5 acres of the original homestead which lay across the McKenzie river west of the old meandered channel. In the years after James Belknap homesteaded, a narrow channel had been widened by floods to become the main river, thus dividing the property. Inman subdivided the island into approximate acre-size lots, built a bridge across the meandered stream and an access road. He sold the lots at prices ranging from $150 to $300 each, reserving the choicest lots for family use.

Grandma Belknap died Sept. 2, 1924, at age 69.

The Inman family returned to Springfield, lived briefly on a farm at Pleasant Hill, then moved back to Springfield. While working for the Lane County bridge crew in 1926, Inman suffered injuries when a scaffold collapsed. After that he built houses, hauled wood and worked as caretaker for summer homes at Rainbow and McKenzie Bridge.

In later years, he devoted his time to writing. His love for the McKenzie is spelled out in a lengthy poem, titled "*McKenzie.*"

Gladys Inman, on graduating from Walterville High School in 1921, and Oregon Normal School at Monmouth, taught school several years, the first three at McKenzie Bridge.

She married Horace Henry Myers May 24, 1928, in Springfield. Horace was the son of William and Anna Myers of Hayden Bridge. The Myers came to Oregon in 1901 and purchased farm property a mile up Camp Creek Road from John M. and Louise A. Davis. The original land claim was issued to Octavius A. Spencer Jan. 10, 1865.

The Myers family included Paul Browning, born March 10, 1896; William Russell, Nov. 7, 1900, both born in Oklahoma; Mary Helen, Aug. 19, 1903, and Horace, Sept. 7, 1905, both born in Oregon.

Horace and Gladys lived on the property throughout their married lives. They grew beans as their principal crop, hiring up to 400 pickers each summer. Both were prominent in Grange, Elks and other Lane County activities. Horace died May 26, 1990, at age 84.

Their daughter, Lois, born Nov. 12, 1930, married William Landers. Children are (1) William Jeffery, born Oct. 13, 1952, married Clair Egan June 21, 1980, two children, William Justin, born Sept. 1, 1980, and Alex, Dec. 1, 1983. (2) Douglas Keith, born June 20, 1954, married Carol Ann Zarr Oct. 29, 1994, in Portland, daughter, Madelaine Elizabeth, born Nov. 22, 1995. (3) Lisa Loren, Nov. 26, 1955, son, Michael, born Nov.

14, 1993. (4) Mitchell, born Nov. 8, 1957. Lois is now married to Robert Thomas of Lake Oswego.

Violet Inman, a graduate of Springfield High and Oregon Normal School, also taught prior to her marriage to John Munson (Jack) Larson Nov. 21, 1940, in Springfield. Jack, a World War I veteran, born Nov. 19, 1896, in Pompton Lakes, N. Y., and a graduate of Cornell University at Ithica, N. Y., came to Oregon in the 1920's. He operated a movie theater in Junction City, then moved to Springfield in 1922, where he operated the Bell Theater on Main Street until 1930 and a Richfield Service Station until his retirement.

Jack and Violet were staunch supporters of their community. Larson, active in American Legion affairs, served as state commander. He was a city councilman, helped formulate the Willamalane Park District, servings as council president three years, and headed the McKenzie-Willamette Hospital campaign, serving as president of the founders group. He also worked with Boy Scouts and the American Legion Junior baseball team as manager.

Violet, as an active member of the American Legion Unit 40 Auxiliary and the 8 et 40, Legion subsidiary, served as state president of both groups. She was a member of the Business and Professional Women's Club and Springfield Lions Auxiliary. She served in many local offices and on numerous committees. She was chosen BPW 1956 Woman of the Year. She now lives in Canby near her son and daughter-in-law.

Jack and Violet's son, James Munson (Jim), born Jan. 16, 1942, was a University of Oregon graduate and served in the U. S. Marines. He married Drinda Haagensen of Soledad, Cal., June 3, 1972. Drinda was born Aug. 28, 1948, in Santa Barbara, Cal. An adopted son, Jason Robert, was born Oct. 10, 1979. They live in Canby.

Jack had two other sons by prior marriage, John Richard of Anchorage, Alaska, and Robert F., retired and with his wife, Pat, living near Chico, Cal. Jack had four grandchildren and seven great-grandchildren. He died Oct. 31, 1985, at age 88.

Leroy Inman, a graduate of Springfield High School, attended the University of Oregon and served (1937-1940) in the U. S. Army in Hawaii. He and Iris Barker were married June 20, 1941.

Iris, born Jan. 29, 1916, in Eugene, graduated from Eugene High School. She was a daughter of Wilford Earl, born Jan. 29, 1873, in Red Bud, Ill., and Dora (Rohne) Barker, born March 7, 1876, in St. Louis, Mo. They moved to Eugene in 1902. Other family members were Pearl Elizabeth, Juanita Marie, Russell Edward, Lester Frank, Kenneth Earl and Delbert Elnora.

Leroy and Iris lived in Lebanon, Coos Bay and Springfield, before moving to Roseburg in 1948, where he was employed on the news staff of The News-Review until his retirement Dec. 31, 1976. He is a Life Member of Lions International and a Melvin Jones Fellow.

Their children are: Janet Lee, born March 14, 1942, in Eugene; Lawrence B. (Larry), April 9, 1945, in Lebanon; Kathryn Joan, Jan. 6, 1947, in Eugene, and Laurel LaVerne, Nov. 23, 1950, in Roseburg.

Janet on Dec. 20, 1963, married Ronald J. Crandall, a Methodist minister. He was born June 5, 1937, in Eugene. Both are University of Oregon graduates. They had daughters Elizabeth Laurel, born Aug. 8, 1968, at Tillamook, Ore., and Mary Deborah Kathryn, born Feb. 22, 1971, in The Dalles, Ore. Following a divorce, Janet married Dave Shepherd in 1987. They live in Florence, Ore.

Elizabeth on Dec. 14, 1991, married Scott Ricardo Gaupo. Both are graduates of Willamette University at Salem. They live in Salem. Elizabeth teaches school at Dayton. Deborah is a graduate of Southern Oregon State College at Ashland, Ore. She is employed in Yakima, Wa.

Lawrence, a Roseburg High grad, served in the U. S. Navy during the Vietnam War. He married Maureen Leonard of San Mateo, Calif. Maureen was born in San Mateo, Aug. 3, 1950. Both attended Southern Oregon College at Ashland. Lawrence, a research chemist, received a master's degree. They live in Livermore, Calif.

They have daughters, Jennifer Lynette, born Sept. 23, 1972, and Kelly Therese, born Sept. 30, 1976. Jennifer, a graduate of American University in Washington, D. C., is currently teaching English (1996) in Hungary. Kelly is emploued in Livermore.

Kathryn married Gerald Wayne Cartmell of Springfield, Sept. 10, 1966. Gerald, born in Springfield Sept. 13, 1946, served in the U. S. Navy during the Vietnam War. Both are University of Oregon graduates. Gerald is a computer software engineer. They live in Tualatin, Ore., and have three children, Michael Wayne, born July 27, 1972, in Eugene; Karen Marie, Jan. 21, 1976, and Rian David, June 24, 1980, both born in Portland, Ore. Michael attended the University of Oregon and Portland State University. Karen is a student at Willamette University.

Laurel married Robert J. Everett of New York City, Sept. 7, 1974, in Alexandria, Va. A University of Oregon graduate, she works for the U. S. Government. Robert, after retiring from the Washington, D. C., police department, is a private investigator. Their daughter, Rebecca Miriam, was born Sept. 19, 1986.

Clifton L. Inman died March 17, 1961. He was buried in the Veterans Memorial Cemetery in Portland.

Cora Edith Inman, last surviving child of James and Ella Belknap, died Oct. 7, 1973. She had lived her entire life on the McKenzie -- at the Belknap Ranch, Walterville and briefly at Pleasant Hill. She and Clifton resided in Springfield after 1931. She was a member of the First Christian Church, Juanita Rebekah Lodge No. 85, Springfield, Past Noble Grands Club and the Spanish-American War Veterans Auxiliary. She was buried with Clifton in the Veterans National Cemetery, Portland.

CHAPTER 37

Clara Lockwood Siemsen

Clara B. Belknap was born at Blue River April 30, 1885. She grew up on the home ranch and attended local schools.

She married her cousin, Willie Clyde Lockwood about 1907. The exact date or place of their marriage is not available. Willie Clyde, born at Canyon City, Ore., in 1870, was one of ten children of Robert Edwin and Clara Sophia Belknap. The Lockwoods moved to Canyon City from Kerbyville shortly before his birth.

Willie Clyde and Clara had sons, Robert, born about 1908, and Clyde, born May 22, 1912, in Walterville.

Their marriage ended in divorce. She then married Emil John (Jack) Siemsen, one-time circus performer and electrician by trade. He was born in 1880 in New York State. They lived in Twin Falls, Ida., in Washington state, in the Portland area and at Amity, Ore., before moving to Springfield about 1923.

A daughter, Mable Delorise, was born Oct. 28, 1917, in Raymond, Wa. Other children were Jearld M., born in 1921, and Myrtle D., who was born in 1923 and died in Springfield about 1925, age 2 1/2 years. Jearld died in April, 1977, in Idaho, with burial in Skyline Memorial Gardens, Portland.

After Siemsen's death, in the late 1930's, Clara moved to Portland. She died there Dec. 14, 1961, with burial in Skyline Memorial Gardens.

Clara (Lockwood) Siemsen

Robert Lockwood

Robert Lockwood, around 1923/25, lived at the Belknap ranch on the McKenzie, attending high school in Blue River winters and working in Clarence Belknap's sawmill summers. He joined the Marines about 1926 and spent many years in the service, including time in Nicaragua during an uprising there.

He lived in South America, where he owned a coffee plantation. He also lived in New Jersey. In later life he owned mineral rights and panned gold on Smith River in northern California.

He was married (first) to Florence Martin Brown; (second) to Virginia Adams, born in the East. They had three children -- Ricky, Tommy and Lynn. Robert had another daughter, Carole, by his third wife. He died in 1981 at age 73 in Sacramento, Cal. Ricky Lockwood, a Vietnam War veteran, died about 1985 from effects of Agent Orange. He left a widow and a son.

Clyde "Ikie" Lockwood died in Springfield Aug. 9, 1939, at age 27 years from a heart disorder. He had lived in Twin Falls, Ida., in Washington, Portland and Springfield, Ore. He was a member of the Salvation Army and a charter member of the Springfield Fire Department. Burial was in the Belknap plot in Greenwood Cemetery.

Mable McKinney

Mable Delorise Siemsen, born Oct. 28, 1917, in Raymond, Wa., grew up in Springfield and attended local schools. She and Ivan Quincy McKinney were married Nov. 3, 1935, in Springfield at the home of Mr. and Mrs. C. L. Inman. Cora Inman was her aunt.

Ivan was born at Lake Oswego, Ore., Dec. 1, 1912. He and Mable moved to Portland after their marriage. Ivan served in the U. S. armed forces during World War II. He was a trucker by profession. After retirement they moved to LaPine, in Central Oregon.

Mable died Sept. 12, 1990, at age 72, after a prolonged illness from heart problems. Ivan died Feb. 14, 1991, at age 78. By their request their bodies were cremated, and their ashes scattered on the McKenzie River.

Ivan and Mable's daughter, Dorothy Lee, born in Portland March 26, 1937, was married in Portland to Richard Stuart (Dick) Hall on Sept. 14, 1957. Hall also was born in that city Jan. 25, 1935. They operate Hall Tool Co. in Portland. Their four children are: Denise Rae, David Allen, Michael Scott and Mark Richard.

Portions of the Belknap and Lockwood genealogy was supplied by Mrs. Robert (Georgianna) Bruch of Woodburn, Ore. Mrs. Bruch is a great granddaughter of Robert Sr. and Clara Belknap Lockwood through their son, Robert Edwin Jr. She made extensive genealogical research of the families in Vermont and Massachusetts.

CHAPTER 38

The Trotters

Elva Ann, daughter of James Henry and Ella Jane Belknap, was born Sept. 26, 1887, and grew up on the homestead

She and Walden R. Trotter were married Oct. 26, 1904, at the home of James and Emma Wycoff, 11 miles east of Vida. Emma (Finn) Wycoff was her aunt. Witnesses were W. E. Trotter, and Elva's sister, Clara Belknap.

W. E. Trotter, as shown on the marriage certificate, was Walden's identical twin brother, Walter.

A son, Harold Abel, named for his grandfather, was born Dec. 6, 1905, at Walterville to Walden and Elva.

Abel Trotter, father of Walden and Walter, was born in Guilford County, N. Car., near Greensboro Sept. 30, 1831. Abel's father was Reuben Trotter and his mother was Jane Cranor. Abel had at least five sisters and one brother, Hannah, Elizabeth, Martha, Emily and Emanuel, possibly three more.

Abel married Mary Jane Kirkman, born in North Carolina, Dec. 14, 1854. A daughter, Esther Eugenia, born April 29, 1856, died Aug. 26, 1857. A son, John Ciscero, was born Oct. 26, 1858, in Guilford County.

In 1859 or early 1860, Abel with John moved with his father's family to Hopkins County, Ky., near Charleston.

Elva (Trotter) Cruson

This move may have been because of the threat of civil war. Reuben was said to be against slavery. He had a free black living and working on the farm for more than ten years. He remained loyal to the United States. The Civil War broke out April 12, 1861, at Charleston. In May, 1861, North Carolina left the Union.

Abel enlisted in the Union Army Sept. 3, 1864, at Madisonville, Ky. He was mustered into the 17th Kentucky Cavalry Regiment, Company B, as a private at Russellville. He made the rank of quartermaster sergeant and was honorably discharged at Louisville, Ky., Sept. 20, 1865. He had blue eyes, light hair, light complexion and height five feet, ten inches.

Mary Jane died at Greensboro, N. Car., in 1865. Abel moved back to Guilford County with John. Prior to 1870, he married Julia Ann Cook, born in Guilford County in 1849 to James M. and Martha Cook, both born in North Carolina. Abel and Julia moved to Henry County, near Clinton, Mo., between 1871 and 1874.

Abel and Julia had four children. Louanna was born Sept. 24, 1872, in North Carolina or Missouri. Early in 1874, Abel and Julia, with John and Louanna, moved to St. Charles in Hopkins County, Ky.

Martha Jane was born Sept. 6, 1874, in Scotes Mill, Christian County, Ky. Walden Reuben and Walter E. were born Aug. 26, 1879, in Scotes Mill in a small hand-hewed log house. Their mother, Julia Ann, died at age 30, two weeks later due to birth complications.

John Trotter went to Oregon in 1883 and encouraged his father to come join him. In June, 1884, when the twins were five years old, Abel took his children by train to Oregon. He homesteaded 154 acres on a hillside up Camp Creek in Lane County. It was not the best land for farming, but had a good, year-around spring, and some of the best water in the area. Part of his orchard -- apples, plums, pears, and walnuts -- is there today, but bears are the only ones that harvest the fruit now, said his grandson, Thomas "Tom" Trotter of Maple Valley, Wa.

Roses the children planted now grow wild. Abel had cows, but supplied most of his meat by hunting. Still visible are rocks used to build part of the house, bits and pieces of an iron cook stove. The old wagon road, mostly brush covered, can still be followed, Tom Trotter said.

Abel was living at the Albert Simmons place at Camp Creek when he died at age 77 April 15, 1909. An undated newspaper clipping said Abel died at the home of his daughter, Mrs. Ed (Louanna) Craig at Camp Creek. "The family had been to a revival service at the Camp Creek Church and was accompanied home by the minister of Springfield. They were kneeling at prayer before retiring when he suddenly expired. He was quite an aged man, but always cheerful and hopeful and ready to speak a kind word." He is buried in the Camp Creek Cemetery.

Walden, Walter and sisters, Louanna Craig and Martha Jane Hileman, were listed as survivors. Louanna, known as Aunt Lou, married Ed Craig. Martha Jane, known as Mattie, married Richard Hileman. They lived near Mabel, Ore. Mae and Cora Hileman were their daughters. They had an older brother, Walden. Mae married Earl Charles Daily and Cora married Emery Daily. Earl and Emery, brothers, grew up at Sulphur Springs on Smith River, up river from Reedsport.

Walden attended school through the eighth grade then worked as a logger. He and Elva lived in Walterville, Marcola and Leaburg.

Walden Built House

Forest Service records indicate Walden Trotter in 1908 applied for homestead rights on the property at what became Rainbow, north across the river from the original Belknap homestead.

About 1910, he built the two-story house, since remodeled and now standing as Holiday Farm and Restaurant. He was assisted by his brother-in-law, Richard Hileman of Mabel, Ore., according to Walden's grandson Tom Trotter, and verified by Cora Daily of Cottage Grove, Hileman's daughter. Mrs. Daily, born in 1904, recalls going to the Trotters' place, when she was five or six years of age. Her family returned to Mabel, but her father stayed to help build the house.

Bureau of Land Management records show a homestead patent for this property was granted in 1914. The Trotters operated a stagecoach stop, offering meals, and they had boarders. Elva did the cooking and pretty much ran the place. About 1917, she moved to Eugene. She and Walden were subsequently divorced.

On the death of her mother, Ella Belknap in 1924, Elva was living in Watsonville, Cal., working in a restaurant. Harold was with her.

Elva worked many years at the Osborn Hotel in Eugene. She married Clifford Lee Cruzon. They lived in Oakridge 12 years, prior to her death March 3, 1955. She was a past president of American Legion Auxiliary, Dist. No. 3; a member of the 40 & 8 Auxiliary and Rebekah Lodge 245, Oakridge. She was buried in Rest Haven.

Cruzon, born in Leadville, Colo., retired from the Southern Pacific in 1954. He maintained homes in Eugene and Oakridge for 50 years, was a member of the American Legion and Eugene Elks. He died in Portland from cancer, age 73 years. Burial was in Baker, Ore.

After Walden and Elva's separation, he studied at a barber school in Portland, but later returned to logging.

Walden is on record in the Lane County Courthouse as having sold the McKenzie River property in 1922 to Lewis Quimby of Portland. Quimby established the community of Rainbow and a post office in 1924. The post office was discontinued in 1937 after Quimby sold out. The location today is known as Holiday Farm. The house Walden built has been enlarged and now is a restaurant and bar, as well as the home of owners Pat and Vivienne Wright.

About 1927, Walden married Silvia Van Arden. They were divorced. In the 1930s, he moved to Red Bluff, Cal., felled timber at Mineral Springs, near Mt. Lassen, later working on ranches and at a cemetery. He married a third time and moved to Eureka, Cal. He died there of kidney failure Jan. 21, 1965, and was buried next to his twin brother, Walter, at Merrill, Ore., in the I.O.O.F. Cemetery.

Skiing Enthusiast

Harold Trotter, well-known skiing enthusiast, spent his entire life in Eugene and on the McKenzie. He married Thelma Shubert July 5, 1934, in Klamath Falls. She was born in Great Falls, Mont. A daughter, Le Verda, born Dec. 12, 1934, died two days later.

Following a divorce, Harold married Mary Margaret O'Connor in Reno, Nev., Aug. 19, 1941. Born July 28, 1910, in Stewartville, Minn., she was the daughter of Thomas M. and Margaret (Shannon) O'Connor. She had brothers, Joe, Maurice and Philip. Her father's family homesteaded in Minnesota in the early 1860s. He died in 1917. Her mother died in 1923. Mary came to Portland to live with her mother's sister's family, Frank and Mary (Shannon) Harter.

She graduated with a degree in nursing from Multnomah in 1932 and worked at Sacred Heart Hospital in Eugene as an RN.

Harold and Mary's children, born in Eugene, were: Mary Colleen, March 29, 1947; Sheila Louise, April 13, 1949, and Thomas Walden, April 19, 1952.

Harold, a ski specialist at Hendershott's Sporting Goods in Eugene for 20 years, ran a mountain climbing class at his home. For two years prior to his death, he operated the ski shop at Willamette Pass. He was a member of the Obsidians and the Tri-Pass Ski Club. He died Aug. 26, 1954, in Eugene, from a heart attack at age 49.

Mary Margaret died May 23, 1962, in Portland at age 50 years. She and Harold were buried in Rest Haven Memorial Park in Eugene.

After their mother's death, Sheila and Thomas lived with their father's cousins, Earl and Mae (Hileman) Daily in San Jose, Cal. Mary Colleen lived with Emery and Cora (Hileman) Daily in Cottage Grove.

Mary Colleen lives in Portland. She has a son, Alonzo.

Sheila married Tom Cottingham Aug. 12, 1972, in San Jose, Cal. They live in Klamath Falls. Their children are Matthew Thomas, born June 18, 1978, and Ellen Ann, born Feb. 18, 1981.

Thomas Trotter lived several years in San Jose, Cal. He married Debra "Debbie" Housman March 23, 1985, at Mt. Hermon, Cal. Debbie was born in Santa Cruz, Cal., Jan. 15, 1956. Her father's family came from the same town, Elyria, Ohio, as B. F. and Mary Finn.

Thomas and Debbie, both college graduates, moved about 1985 to Maple Valley, Wa. He manages a biotech company, and she works for a biotech company near Seattle. They have two boys, Miles Thomas, born Nov. 29, 1987, and Nathaniel Abram, Jan. 4, 1991.

Elva, Harold and Walden Trotter

CHAPTER 38

Clarence and Martha Belknap

Clarence Roland Belknap, community leader and lumberman, played an important part in bringing electrical power to the upper McKenzie. Born at Blue River Oct. 21, 1892, the youngest of seven children who attained adulthood, he grew up on the Belknap homestead and attended school at Walterville and at the Sims' place.

Clarence, at age 25, was working as a logger at Maple Falls, Wa., south of the Canadian border, when drafted into the armed service in 1917 during World War I. He served in France with the U. S. Army's famed Rainbow Division. After the war ended in November 1918, he returned to the Belknap Ranch to make his home.

He and his brother Art built a sawmill about 1920. They cut lumber from timber on the property to build a large house to replace Grandma Belknap's "temporary" house, which had served after the "Big House" burned in 1910. He continued in the sawmill business and ranching the remainder of his life.

Martha Andrews Belknap played almost as important a role in life on the McKenzie as her well-known husband. She didn't come onto the McKenzie until 1914 at age 18 as a school teacher at McKenzie Bridge. Except briefly to complete her education she lived the remainder of her life at Rainbow.

Clarence and Martha were married Oct. 1, 1921. The daughter of Cora M. Andrews of Eugene, Martha was a graduate of the University of Oregon.

Clarence R. Belknap

She and her twin sister, Dorothy, were the first women to go into the forest service as lookouts during World War I, Martha on Horsepasture Mountain and Dorothy on Frissell Point

Clarence and Martha's only child, Roy C., born May 17, 1926, was named for her brother, Roy Andrews.

Born in Arkansas

Martha Andrews was born at Tea Ridge Battlefield (Civil War), Benton County, Ark., July 15, 1895, "somewhere in the Ozarks," she commented in a (1976) taped interview with Pat Allensworth and Vicki Koepsel. "And I think that's why I have such hard teeth because of the minerals there."

Martha and Dorothy's brother, Roy, ten years older, was born in 1885 in Waterloo, Ia. In an interview with Gerald and Ellen Williams Jan. 22, 1979, Martha, said: "When we were youngsters living in Arkansas, he (Roy) taught school near Little Rock. He was so incautious as to put up a picture of Abraham Lincoln. He lost his job.

"My father (C. M. Andrews) was a great wanderer," Martha was quoted in *Season of Harvest*, published as a Youth and Senior Exchange Project of the Lane County Social Services Division in 1975.

Interviewed by the Williams Jan. 7, 1979, Martha said: "My mother (Cora) was born in central New York, near Ithica or Rowland in 1860. My father was born in Paris, Maine, five years earlier. Both emigrated to Iowa, where they met, were married and homesteaded out near Cedar Falls. Cora was with the first class that graduated from the Cedar Falls Normal School and taught one year.

"My father, a farmer and carpenter, liked to go around, buy a farm, fix it all up in five years, then sell it. We moved several times when we were growing up. We bought a place on the (Tea Ridge) Battlefield and he raised Poland China pigs. The old house was there during the Civil War. I saw it advertised for the Sinclair Oil people. The historical society was making something of it. I have pictures of it taken when we were babies. We went to Michigan, then to Texas, then we came to Oregon. My mother refused to go any farther."

In Eugene they first lived on Pearl Street. "We came in 1909. It was just a little place, and we knew everybody. In June our neighbor told us about the eighth grade examinations you had to pass to get into high school. We went to the courthouse to take the examinations under Superintendent Dillard. I passed with flying colors. I went four years to high school and never missed a day. We were disgustingly healthy.

"We moved out near the University where Carson Hall is now. One great pleasure was to climb Spencer's Butte. It was only seven miles to the top, a good afternoon's walk. We walked everywhere."

In 1914, upon graduation from high school at age 18, Martha came upriver to McKenzie Bridge to teach school, the first of three terms. She stayed in the home of Smith Taylor, U. S. Forest Service district ranger, across from the present day Paradise Ranger Station. She rode horseback two and a half miles to her school of 10 to 15 children. She saved enough money to attend the University of Oregon three years. Later she stayed with Uncle George and Auntie Frissell.

In 1918, at age 22, Martha became the first woman to fill the position of fire lookout in the McKenzie district.

TWINS---(The late) Martha Andrews Belknap of Rainbow, left, and Dorothy Andrews Brown of Princeton, N. J., pictured during a visit on the McKenzie in the 1960's.

The Forest Service suffered from a manpower shortage. She said, from her prior acquaintance with Smith Taylor, he offered her a job. She served two summers on 5650-foot-high Horsepasture Mountain, named for its excellent pasture. It lies east of O'Leary Ridge in the Olallie Ridge Natural Research area, south of Horse Creek.

One season, her sister, Dorothy, was a lookout on Frissell Point, which lies northeast of McKenzie Bridge. Though this was before the days of two-way radio and telephone, they kept in touch by signaling back and forth with hand mirrors. The Forest Service had phones for periodic reporting.

"They took us up with a tent and alidade (firefinder) and dumped us out," she said. The spring for her water needs was half a mile down the mountain. She said she bathed about once a week at the spring. "I carried water up that hill all summer long. When I went back to the University that fall and enrolled in a physical education class, I had the largest lung capacity of any girl in school."

This compiler's first acquaintance with Martha was about 1920 at age 9, prior to her marriage. Clarence had a nine-passenger Chandler with jumpseats. When he stopped in Walterville to pick up my mother, two sisters and me to visit Grandma Belknap, he had several other people in the car, including Martha. Eleven of us crammed into the Chandler for the 36-mile journey up the McKenzie over the narrow, rutted road with a hundred curves to the mile. We had to get out and walk up steeper grades.

In *Harvest* Martha said, after she and Clarence were married:

"We moved here and put up a tent. . .We slept in the tent and ate with his mother while building our house. I've never moved. Friends would come and help. . .It's amazing what good workmen they were -- for a wooden (building) to last this long.

"We did our wash on the scrub board. You had a big tub to put it in, another tub of rinse water, and another for the last rinse. You always boiled them first. You wrung them out by hand and hung them on a line. . .It wasn't an easy life, but I can't remember when I had such fun. We had a lot of parties and things like that. We just got together and had a good time. Someone would bring something to eat.

"We had an old root cellar for storing vegetables. We pumped our water from the river. A big water wheel pumped the water up into a big barrel on top of the garage, which gave pressure to the house. Pioneers always found a way to do something -- they had to. They wouldn't have survived."

Martha quoted Clarence as saying he didn't know his grandfather, Rollin, very well. "When he was a little boy, and they had a garden, his grandfather thumped him if he didn't hoe fast enough."

In 1923, Clarence and Morton Carlile of Eugene contracted with Ella Belknap to cut timber on the property at $1 per thousand board feet of timber. They operated as McKenzie Lumber Co.

My family lived that summer in a tent house at the Belknaps', while Dad worked as sawyer at the mill. Carlile and his wife, Mary, camped in a tent. Martha's sister, Dorothy, and husband, Douglas Brown, a Princeton University professor, were there for the summer. Dorothy and Douglas had met while she and Martha attended Columbia University in New York City.

Clarence later acquired Carlile's interest. In 1926, he broke his leg in a mill accident. My father again worked for him as sawyer. Our family camped that summer in Grandpa James' old log cabin. My two sisters and I helped Clarence with lumber deliveries, many to Belknap Springs which had a building program under way.

Mill Burned in 1932

The mill burned down in 1932. The crew donated two weeks of labor. Clarence rebuilt the mill, larger and better, Martha said, adding: "It was a pleasant business. The employees were our friends and neighbors. At times Clarence had as many as 75 employees working for him. We milled out the lumber for this house, which we built in 1921. And we traded lumber for a lot of things -- these rugs on the floor, we got them in a trade over at Redmond. . ."

During the depression years, stumpage sold for as little as 75 cents a thousand board feet, Martha commented. Much of this was from timber claims bought up by Boston-Oregon Timber Co.

Ernest Cullen Murphy in *McKenzie Enterprise*, 1974, wrote:

"During those days of rough going because of HIGH PRICES it might be well to reflect on how much tougher it can be in times of real LOW PRICES. This was the situation in 1930-31-32 on the McKenzie following the financial crash of 1929.

"The only business in the upper McKenzie region at that time was the Forest Service, the school, the Brewster's and Penland's stores, and Clarence Belknap's sawmill. . .Wages were 25 cents an hour. No. 1 construction lumber was $9.00 per MBF. And there were few if any buyers. Money was scarce. Eggs were 10 cents a dozen. Milk was 10/15 cents a quart. Hay was $5 a ton. Banks were going broke. The Gross National Product was less than $50 billion. . .Times were tough.

"But Clarence Belknap kept his sawmill running through that Great Depression," Murphy wrote, quoting Martha. "He piled up what lumber he could not peddle. Starting in 1930, he trucked lumber to the Bend-Redmond-Madras area. There he could find some farmer who wanted to build a barn, chicken house or another room on his house, and he'd swap lumber for eating provisions. In one case a furniture dealer wanted to add a funeral parlor. So he traded lumber for furniture.

"Clarence was so successful in his bartering for cloth, eats and all household necessities and in getting lumber into the hands of the denizens of Bend-Redmond that the sawmills and lumber dealers made him a proposition to take his entire output at $9.00 per thousand board feet: CASH. (In those days trees and logs which would not make $1 and better were left in the woods as not worth harvesting).

"Thus all through the Great Depression the workers of Belknap's Mill were well provided for the goods and later with that scarce article viz: MONEY. None of the crew suffered great hardships. Martha said all were hale, hearty and happy. Clarence used to recall the saying, 'Keep your powder dry and wait 'till you see the whites of their eyes.' Then he would add 'My motto is to keep my credit good.'"

Brought Power to Area

Clarence became a pioneer in bringing electrical power to the upper McKenzie in the mid-1930s. Lane County Electric Cooperative originated in that area, according to *Ruralite*, REA house organ. He was one of the incorporators and on the first board of directors.

Martha said Clarence had been trying to get a power line up here. The power companies told him it would cost us $5,000 a mile. "So he was interested in the REA program when it began in 1936. He and others, like Harvey Cooley and Smith Taylor, went to work to get an electric co-op started." Their electricity came into being about 1941 when Roosevelt established the Rural Electrification Administration. It allowed groups of people in a neighborhood with no electricity to borrow money and form a co-op.

"They got easements and ran lines over here. Since it was

wartime, we couldn't get good material. At that time less than nine per cent of the farm people all over the United States had electricity. Now more than ninety-nine per cent have it. It's been extremely successful. Our electricity hasn't been expensive. Sometimes, though, it's hard to keep the lines up," she commented.

Ruralite said: "Along with his concern for Lane County Electric, Mr. Belknap also served as president of the Oregon Rural Electric Cooperative Association and as the state representative to the National REA, headquartered in Washington, D. C."

In the 1930's, Clarence established a lumber and building material sales outlet at McKenzie Bridge. He sold his mill during World War II and operated a truck repair business in Blue River. In the 1950's, he bought Art's property, farmed the land and ran range cattle there and on two homesteads across the river, including the old Sims' Ranch near present-day Tokatee Golf Course.

Clarence and Roy acquired the former Cascade Resort on McKenzie River Drive, west of McKenzie Bridge. They built the Patio Restaurant and Trailer Court. In the early 1960's, the restaurant was destroyed by fire. Bob Rines had operated the restaurant about six years and had just reopened after a brief closure for renovation. Clarence and Roy sold the property to Mr. and Mrs. Hal Boon of Eugene in a three-way transaction in which Roy acquired the Paddock Motel at Yachats.

Cullen Murphy, 1975, wrote: "For many years the Belknaps were community leaders on the upper McKenzie. Martha was 'Dowager Empress,' the social arbiter and Clarence the commercial leader. They split on politics, too, Clarence, a Republican and Martha a Democrat."

Martha was honored during World War II by the Eugene Zonta Club with a citation for meritorious service for her work with disabled veterans by entertaining them in her home.

Brother Taught Science

Roy Andrews, University of Oregon science professor, an ardent mountain climber and camera buff, was a frequent McKenzie visitor.

Martha said: "When we came to Eugene he took his BA and Masters at the University and taught chemistry and botany. He was an old bachelor and loved music. He climbed the South Sister 22 times."

For a time in Lane County he became a sort of rural supervisor, "going around to the schools and seeing how they were getting along. With just a little Brownie camera, he took pictures of every school and the spring, or wherever they got their water. Martin Schmidt (of the University library) said it was the oldest record of schools they had in Lane County." A number of Roy's school pictures were selected for the Ford Foundation of Natural Historic Pictures.

Roy lived with his mother and took care of her until her death in 1953 at age 93 years. He died at age 70 from a brain hemorrhage.

Martha's twin sister, Dorothy, taught in Oregon schools, including Crow and upper Camp Creek, prior to her marriage. She and her husband, Douglas Brown, (both deceased) lived in Princeton, N. J. Douglas was dean of faculty at Princeton University for 25 years, then headed the Industrial Relations section. In the 1930s, as a member of President Franklin D. Roosevelt's "brain trust," he organized and helped start the Social Security Administration.

In an interview, Martha commented on Hugh DeValon, "a man from New York who came every summer from 1904. He had the same room (at the Log Cabin Inn). Quite a wealthy man, he worked for Taylor Instruments, which made doctors' tools. In the depression he lost everything. He came out and spent the rest of his life here."

She shook her head in amusement at one thought: "There was Professor Dunn -- he taught Latin at the University and had a summer home (below Rainbow). When he brought his family up, he also brought along the family cow. It took them four or five days waiting on the cow, but that didn't matter. The Professor stopped and waited. He was a delightful man, wore a top hat and carried a cane."

On places and names, Martha said, "Deathball (Mountain) is my favorite. When they were surveying, it's awfully hard to find new names for everything. The biscuits that morning were infinitely bad. In camp, if the biscuits were not good they'd call them 'deathballs.' So that's how the mountain got its name."

Clarence died Oct. 13, 1968, at age 75, after six years illness. His brother, Arthur, died the same year on Jan. 20.

Roy Belknap died in 1969, at age 43, without providing an heir. He had been married to (Mrs.) Lucia M. Smith, but had no children. Their marriage ended in divorce. So this line of the Belknap family name ended. Roy, a diabetic, was living at Yachats at the time.

The Belknap homestead, so rich in early-day lore, was subdivided into 20-acre tracts and sold. Among purchasers was Wilbur Houmes, founder of the King's Table restaurant chain.

After Clarence's death, Martha sold her home and remaining property to "Mac" McLain of Honolulu with the stipulation she could occupy the house the remainder of her life. McLain spent summers there, but his wife preferred Honolulu.

On Jan. 7, 1979, Martha suffered a hip injury that left her crippled. Gerald and Ellen Williams called that day to conduct an interview. It was very cold, overcast, upper twenties or lower thirties, they wrote. "When we arrived she was lying on the steps -- sitting, really -- and her dog Duke was running around with his leash in the back yard. Mrs. Belknap had slipped on ice, fallen and injured her hip. We helped her inside. . .she called EASE, an emergency number. They summoned a paramedic unit from Eugene."

Martha died at a Springfield nursing home Feb. 4, 1986. McLain died a year later. The Belknap property -- that part of the original homestead not sold in separate tracts -- was bought by Jim and Aurora Hill of Oakland, Cal. The Hills retain their home in Oakland but frequently visit the McKenzie.

CHAPTER 40

Finn Family

So often the unsung heroes of the pioneer families were the wives of adventurous men who sought a new way of life in the great West. Such a woman was Mary Ann Halter, a mere shadow in the life of her more famous husband, Benjamin Franklin "Huckleberry" Finn.

She braved the hardships of a cross-country trip with six children to settle in an isolated area on the south side of the McKenzie River near present-day Vida, Ore.

Mary Ann, born in 1833 in Elyria, Lorain County, Ohio, was the daughter of Peter Halter, a farmer, born in 1793, and his wife, Rosanna, in 1796, both natives of Pennsylvania. The Halters' oldest son, Abraham, was born in New York state in 1828. Peter Jr. was born in 1838 in Elyria.

Elyria Township census of Nov. 7, 1850, lists Peter Halter, 57, Rosanna, 53; Abraham, 22; Mary Ann, 18, and Peter Jr., 13. Mary Ann married Benj. F. Finn Nov. 30, 1851, in Schoolcraft, Mich.

Peter Halter Sr. apparently died during the 1850s. He is not in the July 15, 1860, census, which lists Abraham Halter, 31; Peter Halter, 22; Mary Finn, 27, and her children, Charles (Eugene), 6, and Ella Jane, 4, both born in Ohio, apparently living in the Halter home, and the mother, Rosanna Halter, 64. No mention is made of Benj. "Huck" Finn. Where was he? with Samuel Clemens on the Mississippi?

Family Tree

The Finn family Bible, other records and census show:

(1) Charles Eugene, born Feb. 12, 1853/54, in Elyria, married Martha Hendricks July 3, 1876, in Lane County. He died in 1935.

(2) Ella Jane, born Aug. 31, 1855, in Elyria, married James Henry Belknap Oct. 1, 1873. She died in 1924.

(3) Mary Ada, born March 3, 1861, in Schoolcraft, Mich., died June 9, 1869, in Montevallo, Mo.

(4) Louis Napoleon, born Oct. 12, 1862, in Schoolcraft, never married, died March 30, 1916, in Eugene.

(5) Emma B., born April 18, 1864, in Schoolcraft, married James W. Wycoff April 19, 1879, died Oct. 2, 1938.

(6) Arthur Peter, born March 13, 1867, in Schoolcraft, married, first, Nellie Snow, second, Josephine Houseley, died March 10, 1959.

(7) Ida Druscilla, born July 29, 1869, in Montevallo, Mo., married first, William Ireland, second Albert Ward. She died April 7, 1964.

The July 16, 1870, census for Montevallo Township, Vernon

County, Mo., lists: Benjamin, 37, a stone mason; Mary A., 37; Charles E., 16; Ella J., 15; Lewis (Louis) N., 9; Emma, 6; Peter A., 4, and Ida D., age 1.

With other families the Finns left Missouri in 1871 by covered wagon, headed for Oregon. Ella Jane drove a mule team all the way on the long and toilsome journey across the plains and Rocky Mountains.

The West was wild and the Indians hostile. Several times the party barely escaped Indian attacks. In one instance a band of Indians crept stealthily upon the camp at night, and in the morning were ready to begin a bloody massacre. Fortunately, Finn knew the chief. Years before he had done the Indian a kind deed. When the deed was recalled, the chief without hesitancy, stopped the attack.

Pioneer Life

Life of the early pioneer was far from being a picnic, according to Arthur Peter "Pete" Finn.

Newspaper accounts in the *Eugene Register-Guard*, 1953, and *Springfield News*, July 24, 1970, pretty-well tell the story of the Finn family on the McKenzie. The R-G article by Alma McFadden began:

"LEABURG -- Pete Finn says Friday the 13th isn't a bit unlucky. Fact is, it's a good day. This Friday the 13th was his 86th birthday. He reflected on his life (which), to say the least, has been a full one.

Arthur Peter Finn

"At age four, Pete, one of six children, emigrated from Missouri in a covered wagon train with his father and mother, Mr. and Mrs. Benjamin F. Finn. They arrived on the McKenzie River locating first near where the Alder Grove store stood by Leaburg Lake."

Pete said they left Montevallo, Mo., March 13, 1871, his birthday, and "landed" Sept. 10 at the area known as King's Flat. Although the Finns and others in their party were largely responsible for settling that region, earlier pioneers -- notably a family named King -- had already established themselves, and surveying was under way.

The family had $700 when they left Missouri. That had dwindled to $7 by the time they reached the McKenzie. They had a span of mules (team of two) and span of horses. The horses were sold to raise cash, and proceeds from sale of the wagon was used to buy a cow.

"'Father and Gene (Charles Eugene) felled a cedar tree along the river to make a raft to take the mules and household goods across the river," Pete told his daughter-in-law, Mrs. Earl McClellan, Leaburg, a former Seattle secretary, around 1948.

"'We squatted on unsurveyed land (on the south bank of the McKenzie, below Goodpasture Bridge where the late Dr. Carl Phetteplace years later had a summer home and rhododendron garden). In February Father and Gene worked on the house across the river, made of split cedar. The chimney was made of wood and plastered inside with mud.'

"In 1873, the first Leaburg school, built of logs, was started near Goodpasture Bridge, where a trailer court is now located, just above the present location of the McKenzie River Baptist Church. The Finn children had to cross the river in a boat to get to school, joining the Fayette Thomson and Regis Pepiot children, said Pete."

A bricklayer by trade, Benj. Finn worked during the summer of 1873 on the first building at the University of Oregon, Deady Hall. A later enterprise was distilling pitch to make turpentine.

"'We made a still the same as a whiskey still and distilled it,' Pete said. 'We made resin, too. He'd get the turpentine out of the pitch, then he'd take the resin in and sell that to the soap factories.' When asked if there was any danger of federal revenue officers mistaking the turpentine still for one making whiskey, he replied, 'Yeah, they came up and looked it over. That was about the time moonshining was getting started good up here. I think he'd run off a batch of moonshine before he'd run the turpentine.'

"The Southern Pacific Railroad sold the Finns 69 acres of land, 'This was paid for with proceeds from otter, mink, deer, wildcat and 'any damn thing we could get a hold of,' said Pete. The hides usually were taken into Eugene, The road 'was just a trail swamped out through the timber,' and the trip took four days during winter -- 'two days down and two days back by using part of a day to shop. The journey could be made in three days during the summer, when the road was dry, Travelers could find lodging with almost any rancher along the way.'"

Pete's mother and the children took care of the garden, the cow and chickens. "'My job was to fill up the rain barrel with water.'

"When Pete was 15 years old, he lost his right eye on a deer hunting trip with his brother, Louis. 'I was unable to go to school that year,' he said. 'Next year I started to school and got hit again in the eye with a ball and had to quit again.'"

Hunting was very important to the Finn family as a source of income as well as food. The "men folk" hauled their venison to market in Eugene, then a community of about 300. The hams sold for six cents a pound, and the hides had some value.

"Not too surprisingly, since it was a way of life, Pete became a rather accomplished hunter," wrote John Craig in the *Springfield News*. "There were '10 times as many deer then as there are now.'

"'You had to go a long way,' he remarked in a taped interview by Dr. Phetteplace in 1951, noting that the deer were 'wilder.' Cougars and wolves were considerably more numerous when he was young than they are now, making 'pests' of the creatures, Pete said.

"During his lifetime, he managed to kill quite a number of the 'critters', which threatened the deer population as well as cattle and sheep. He said he killed two cougars one morning before breakfast. 'I was camped in the green timbers. Two came down the ridge.'"

Fishing was a favorite boyhood pastime, Pete told Dr. Phetteplace. Modern tackle was unknown, but apparently not needed. "I started when I was four years old. They wouldn't let me have a hook. I'd use a pin and thread, go down to the creek and catch a bucket of fish."

When he was 18 years old, Pete bought the land on the north side of the river where he built his home. He said he had his eye on the place when he was going to school, because it was "always sunny and sheltered." He bought the land from a railroad company on a ten-year contract, paying $2.50 an acre.

"'Father bought the property next to mine (now Bill Davis' Hidden Valley Ranch) and started a little sawmill. All the lumber in my present house was cut in father's mill. We built my house when I was about 21 years old (1887).

"'I wanted my place for my mother because she was isolated across the river and it was so hard to get to the road,' Pete explained. He wanted the site near the road so the Finn Ranch could double as a stage coach stop. Although mail was delivered only once a week by horseback when he was a boy, stages later made the Springfield-Eugene run to Blue River daily -- 'up one day, returning the next.'"

Mary Finn Died at Age 54

Mary Halter Finn never had an opportunity to enjoy her new home. She died at age 54 years, Oct. 14, 1887, the year father and son built Pete's big house. She reportedly named the Greenwood Cemetery at Leaburg, her final resting place and that of other family members.

Being married to a man like Finn couldn't have been an easy life. Mary had seven children of record, one of whom died at age eight. The family traveled from Ohio to Michigan to Missouri and thence by wagon train to Oregon in the space of about ten years. Life of the pioneer woman was always difficult, and on the McKenzie, to quote her son, Pete, she was isolated across the river.

Pete worked on log drives from Blue River to Coburg. On Aug. 8, 1893, he married Nellie Snow. They moved to Washington, where he lived for 32 years, most of that time logging. They had a son, Jessie Earl. Pete and Nellie were divorced. Nellie married a man named McClellan. Jessie took the McClellan name.

Teller of Tall Tales

Benjamin Franklin "Huckleberry" Finn, Fayette Thomson and Regis Pepiot from the Leaburg-Vida area and James Belknap and John Sims of the upper McKenzie, plus a few homesteaders along the way, were responsible for a large portion of the McKenzie population and much of its history, to paraphrase a quotation from *River Reflections* reprinted in *Historic Leaburg* (1985).

Huck Finn, in addition to being the biggest "liar" on the McKenzie, was a brick layer by trade. He helped build old Deady Hall, the University of Oregon's first building, in the summer of 1873.

"Huck" Finn built the first hotel (Pete's house) along the river in 1886/87. Jerry Williams, 1991, quoted H. J. Cox (1949: 122) as follows: "Huck operated a public inn; that is, he owned the place and the Missus ran it. With a bountiful table and clean, soft feather beds, and a large horse barn. Finn's was a popular overnight stopping place for timbermen, itinerant peddlers, circuit preachers and passengers and drivers of the mail and passenger stage."

Who was the Missus? Mary Finn died in 1887.

Huck Finn occupied Pete's house while Pete logged in Washington. He served as postmaster at Gate Creek (now Vida) from May 29, 1891, until July 22, 1895. He became a fixture on the McKenzie. Newcomers were enthralled by his many yarns.

Cox (1949: pp. 122-123) related one of Finn's most famous stories. "Huck always sat at the head of the dinner table (at his hotel) in the dual role of host and master of ceremonies, regaling the guests with his tales of adventure, hunting prowess and encounters with bear, cougar and other wild beasts of the forest.

"One evening, following a long verbal harangue on his latest expedition, in which he had slain sixteen deer, a stranger spoke up 'Do you know me, Mr. Finn?' 'Can't say I do,' replied Huck. 'I'm the Game Warden,' announced the stranger. 'Well, well, Mister,' said Huck, 'I'm the biggest damn liar in the county'."

Coy Lansbery, who came on the McKenzie in 1907, told this story: "Rennie Koozer, my brother Bruce, Dennis Means and I were going up the river on a hunting trip. The others had never met Mr. Finn, but had heard of his tall tales and said they would like to meet him and have him tell us a story. As luck had it we met him coming down the road just below where he lived. We stopped and I said, 'Mr. Finn, the boys would like to have you tell us a story.'

"He waved his arms and said, 'I haven't got time, boys. My friend, Mr. Pepiot up here died and I have to go down to the mill and cut out a rough box for him.' He kept right on going down the road. We drove on about a mile and met Mr. Pepiot coming down the road in a wagon. The boys didn't know until then that they had their story and Mr. Finn didn't have to stop to tell it."

A 1907 Oregonian news story quoted George Frissell at McKenzie Bridge as saying: "'Ole Man' Finn, the greatest liar on the McKenzie, still lives in a lonely big white house with 'Finn's Hotel' painted in long letters on the side." The writer continues, "As we went up the river, the stage driver pointed out the rock Mr. Finn pulled out of the road with his pair of stout little black mules. To prove the story the rock stands there 'big as a meetin' house' immovable since time began."

Chapter 41

Tragedy on the McKenzie

Benjamin Franklin "Huckleberry" Finn, the elderly gentleman with the long white hair and gray beard, sat leisurely at the oars of his 22-foot logging boat as it drifted slowly down the McKenzie River near the Thurston community.

Finn, age 77, had recently completed building the boat which he was under contract to deliver to the Spalding Bros. sawmill at Salem, on the Willamette River. In spite of declining health and debilitating illnesses, he was able to do some work.

With him were his daughter, Ida Ward; her husband, Albert; their 7-year-old daughter, Mabel, and Mrs. Ward's daughter, Rena Ireland, 19, by a previous marriage; also Norbert Aya of Eugene, who was to accompany them as far as Hayden Bridge and do some fishing.

After delivering the boat, to be used to barge logs, they were to travel by steamboat to Portland, then go on to Seattle to the World's Fair. The party started out joyfully from near Leaburg that Sunday morning, Aug. 15, 1909, with all their effects in the boat. They had run all the rapids safely, until they came to the Craig Rapids above Thurston.

Finn at the oars was rowing head on in smooth water when he stopped and took out his plug of tobacco, preparing to cut off a chew with his knife. His granddaughter, Rena, who sat behind him, told him to take the oars quickly and turn the boat around, as they were approaching rough water.

He did so at once, but not quickly enough, for the boat, caught by the current, was borne rapidly toward a jam of logs. One of the logs hung over the surface, only a few inches above the water, which swept down under it with terrific force. He yelled at Ward and Aya to push the boat off from the log with their fishing poles. They attempted to do so, but their weight on that side of the boat caused it to dip toward the log and in an instant it was overturned.

The old Eugene Register, under the headline "McKenzie Claims Another Victim," recounts the story of Rena Ireland's drowning and the near drowning of Finn and other family members. It said, "Aged Grandfather Acts the Part of Hero in Time of Great Peril."

Finn yelled to Rena to hold on to him, to grab him by the shoulders. She probably did not hear him, as she was partially deaf. She made a dive off the opposite side of the boat into the water and disappeared. The boat turned completely over, but Finn held onto the gunwales, then grabbed the keel of the boat and supported himself on it, as the end of it had been drawn under the log.

Mabel Ward soon appeared on the surface. Finn grabbed her by the hand and dragged her to the boat. He had scarcely got her safe when Mrs. Ward came to the surface, both having been under the boat. Quickly he caught hold of her hair and pulled her onto the boat also, with almost super-human effort. Meanwhile, he looked for Rena, but saw her only once after she jumped overboard.

Ward and Aya escaped and by a miracle, as neither were good swimmers. Had it not been that the latter got hold of an oar he certainly would have drowned. After Ward got out he came up along the bank. Although almost exhausted, he waded out as far as he could. Finn helped Mabel onto Ward's back and he carried her back to shore. He came back for his wife, but as he drew near the boat, he was so exhausted he could not take her back.

Finn helped him onto the bottom of the boat, where all three held on very insecurely. After a time, Aya appeared. Finn sent him for help. Half an hour later Craig came with a long rope. By some most tactful work, he succeeded in getting them all ashore, the boat also.

In the meantime Aya and the Craig family had aroused the neighborhood by phone. Soon a large crowd had gathered and a systematic search was made for Rena. Her body was found about three hours later a quarter mile downstream and was recovered by four men taking hold of each others' hands, the last man diving after the body and bringing it to the surface.

Much of the parties' personal effects were recovered, but a small satchel containing money of Finn, of which some $30 was in silver, is still at the bottom of the river. Finn offered a reward of $20 for its return. He said he thought there was about $100 in the satchel. The gold watch on Miss Rena's person was missing after her body was recovered.

"It was a very sad ending to a trip that promised much pleasure, and Miss Rena, a general favorite in the community in which she lived and the pet of her grandfather, has passed from her beautiful young womanhood to her eternal home. Mr. Finn is almost inconsolable over the affair, although he was the hero of the occasion, for had it not been for his presence of mind, both of the other women would have drowned," the news story concluded.

Rena was buried in Greenwood Cemetery, next to Finn's wife.

Long and Eventful Life

Benjamin Franklin "Huckleberry" Finn lived a long and eventful life. He was 77 by our calculations at the time of the tragedy. His health had begun to deteriorate in the 1890's. His Civil War ankle injury resulting from a poison arrow was giving him problems, according to affidavits accompanying his applications for a pension.

Under the Act of June 27, 1890, Finn at age 57 filed a Declaration for Invalid Pension July 21, 1890, with the Lane County clerk. He stated he was enrolled in the Naval Service as acting quartermaster without rating on the USS Great Western and was discharged at Mound City, Ill.

He declared he was "unable to earn a support by reason of rheumatism and wound in his right leg, one inch above his ankle, and erysipelas from the wound." It was many years later that the pension was granted.

He lived for a time prior to 1915 in the Ward home. In his declining years after 1915 he moved into the home of his daughter, Ella Jane Belknap at Rainbow. In newspaper interviews he held to his claim of being Samuel Clemens' companion on the Mississippi. True to his reputation, he never wavered from stories of his great adventures as he did his part to help conquer the West.

My own recollections, as a child, of Great-grandpa Finn, while he lived with my Grandmother Ella Belknap, were that of an old man with long white hair and long white beard, sitting in a chair by the window and staring into space. He had to have his "Jamaica Ginger," (whiskey), and was very incensed if it didn't arrive on the mail stage.

He died at Ella Jane's home Feb. 11, 1919, age 86 years, 11 months, from "arteriosclerosis and general senility," his death certificate states. However, a family Bible photostat gives his age at death as 95 years, 11 months, six days. The Bible does not list his birth year. His profession was given as brick layer, although this was only one of the many capabilities of this pioneer settler.

A news story of Finn's death in the old Eugene Guard said: "B. F. Finn, who claimed to be the original 'Huckleberry Finn,' around whom Mark Twain built his world famous stories, died at his home at Belknap Bridge, 54 miles east of Eugene, where he had lived for many years, at the age of 90 (age inaccurate), Tuesday.

"Finn had become well known through his ability to tell tales, many of which dealt with the early days on the Mississippi. It was these realistic accounts of his boyhood that led his friends to believe his claim to fame was probably true, despite the fact people in many parts of the United States declared his story false.

"His endless yarns and frequent exploits gained for him wide publicity. His friends tell of many eccentric adventures, one being when he and some relatives started to Seattle to attend the Exposition (Worlds Fair 1909). The plan was to make the trip by water. The party started down the McKenzie River on a raft. The trip ended abruptly, when the raft capsized and one member of the party was drowned."

A final report on Finn's death showed a check for $96 was returned to the U. S. Office of Pensions by the postmaster with the information the pensioner had died Feb. 11, 1919.

Peter Returns to McKenzie

Peter Finn spent some time in Alaska. A letter from his brother, Eugene, to his sister, Ella Belknap, about 1910, mentions, "I haven't heard from Pete since he returned from Alaska."

Gary Kernutt and his wife, Donna, have family heirlooms -- a gold earring and pin -- made from gold Pete mined in Alaska. Pete gave them to his niece, Ellen Fischl, Gary's mother.

Pete and his second wife, Josephine H. Houseley, known as "Josie" and more affectionately by young people as "Ma Finn," were married in

Santa Rosa, Cal., Dec. 20, 1911. She was born in 1883. They were living in Glazier, Wa., at the death of his sister, Ella Belknap, in 1924. He and Josie returned in 1925 to his home east of Leaburg, where he farmed.

Josie served on the school board. At community dances she ruled "with a firm hand." She died May 7, 1940, and "is remembered with affection by all who knew her," a news story said. She was buried in Greenwood Cemetery.

"Finn Ranch, Pete's present home, was built in 1887," said the *Register-Guard.* "The four huge cherry trees planted in front of the home, and a beautiful sight in the springtime, are about 65 years old. A grapevine, planted by Pete, stretches out of all reason and bears heavily. 'In the early days there was no dance hall on the McKenzie, except the upstairs of the Finn House,' he said. 'It took most dancers too long to get home in the early morning darkness, so they'd dance all night and have breakfast, all for one dollar.'"

Pete died March 10, 1956, three days before his 89th birthday. His obituary said he was "well-known for his love of the outdoors and hunting and fishing skills. He was active until a week before his death, resulting from influenza and complications. Before he died he left a number of accounts of his early life on the McKenzie."

Survivors were his son, Jessie Earl McClellan, Leaburg; grandson, Robert McClellan, and sister, Ida D. Ward, Blue Lake, Cal. His obituary mentioned his family connection with other well-known families on the McKenzie -- the Belknaps, Wycoffs, Odells and Nestles. Burial was in Greenwood Cemetery.

Jessie Earl McClellan, born Oct. 11, 1896, in Ocosta, Wa., married Catherine Brown. McClellan, a carpenter and builder, owned his own fuel yard in Seattle. He served in the U. S. Navy during World War I and was a member of American Legion Post 40. After retirement he and his wife moved to Leaburg in 1945. A son, Robert, preceded him in death. His wife died Nov. 2, 1978. McClellan died Sept. 1, 1984.

Finn Hotel, located on the north side of the McKenzie Highway between Finn Creek and Goodpasture Bridge, was sold to the Baptist Church in 1953. When the old house was being torn down about 1970, a sign was found with "Finn Hotel" inscribed on it, recreating the interesting past history of the Pete Finn property.

CHARLES EUGENE FINN

Charles Eugene (Gene) Finn, born Feb. 12, 1853, in Elyria, Ohio, was 18 years old when the family crossed the plains to Oregon in 1871. He married Martha Hendricks, age 17, in Lane County July 3, 1876. Martha, born in 1859, was the daughter of ferry operator Caswell and Hannah Ann Hendricks

Their children, all born in Walterville, were Loren, Herbert, Otis, Elmer and Isa. Otis was born Dec. 18, 1881, and Isa, in March 1894. A minister, Eugene preached in the church at Thurston. The family lived on the McKenzie many years before moving to Idaho.

Eugene and Martha later moved to Lakeland, Fla. Letters to his sister, Ella Jane Belknap, implied they moved to Florida for health reasons. A letter dated Nov. 21, 1910, sends condolences for loss of the Belknap home by fire. A letter, May 4, 1911, mentions Florida's "delightful climate. . .We are in the chicken business."

Another letter said: "Our boys and their families are well. Herbert is still at the Industrial Farm at Weiser, Ida. He is foreman of the farm, and Maud (his wife) is head cook for the hands. They are making about $70 a month. Otis is on his homestead near where we lived in Idaho and doing fine. Elmer is delivering for a bakery in Boise, making about $75 per month."

They were living in Long Beach, Cal., at the death of Eugene's sister, Ella Jane, in 1924. Eugene was living with Otis in Ventura, Cal., when he died March 15, 1935, at age 82.

OTIS C. FINN

Otis C. Finn lived at the family home at Vida until he was 18. He attended Walterville School for nine years. At age 11, he was baptized in the Church of Christ by his father, the minister.

Otis lived briefly in Boise, Ida., moving then to California, where he was foreman for the Haverty Construction Co. He married Florence Suiter at Los Angeles, Jan. 16, 1927. Otis, Florence and son, Stan, born in 1930, moved back to the McKenzie in 1935 (the year Otis' father died). They first lived with Pete Finn. Otis worked on the Harold Mack Ranch, owned by the late Vern Hawn, then became custodian of the Vida School.

When the new McKenzie High School was constructed and the districts consolidated, he moved to Finn Rock and continue his work at the new school. His interest and devotion to his work and to school activities was so intense he was granted a five-year extension beyond retirement age. McKenzie High School's football field was named "Finn Field" in his memory.

A member of the Finn Rock Community Church, Otis was active in church work. He was superintendent and taught Sunday School for years. He sometimes conducted services in the minister's absence. He refinished the church floor each year. Otis Finn died Nov. 21, 1957.

Stan Finn, son of Otis and Florence, attended Vida grade school and McKenzie High, graduating in 1948. He and his wife, Jeanette, now live in Sacramento, Cal. In June 1990, on a visit to the McKenzie they met Ardyce Johnson, a descendant of Peter Wycoff, at the Baptist Church, built on the old Pete Finn property east of Leaburg.

The Finns stayed at the Marjon Bed and Breakfast Inn. They learned from owner Margaret Haas that her house is on the B. F. Finn homestead. She had found some square nails from the old Finn Cabin they tore down. Pete Finn planted the old apple tree in her yard.

LOUIS NAPOLEON FINN

Louis Napoleon Finn, born Oct. 12, 1862, in later years lived in Grandma Belknap's home with my Great-Grandpa Finn and my Uncle "Artie" Belknap. "Uncle Lou" suffered from quinsy, a peritonsilar abscess with recurring episodes. He never married.

He died March 30, 1916, at age 55. (Cemetery records and newspaper obituary spelled his name Louis, although the spelling

"Lewis" appears in some Finn family papers).

The death notice said he died at Mercy Hospital in Eugene "after having made a valiant fight for life. Several days ago Mr. Finn was brought to Eugene, a distance of fifty-four miles, in a wagon. The start was made at Blue River (the Belknap Ranch) at 6 a. m. and the party arrived at Mercy Hospital at 9 p. m. Three different teams were used on the journey to make greater haste." Pneumonia was listed as the cause of death. Burial was in Greenwood Cemetery.

IDA DRUSCILLA WARD

Ida Druscilla Ward, born July 29, 1869, in Montevallo, Mo., the youngest of Benj. and Mary Finn's seven children, was not quite two years old when her family left for Oregon March 13, 1871. Ida loved the McKenzie, but her life did not always run smoothly. A troubled first marriage and a boating tragedy marred her younger years.

At age 17, Ida married William Ireland June 29, 1887. They had two children, Rena, born in Bend, Ore., April 3, 1890, and Ellis, born in Monmouth, Polk County, June 9, 1893. Rena was drowned in a boating accident Aug. 15, 1909.

After divorcing Ireland on grounds of physical cruelty, Ida married Albert J. Ward. He was born Jan. 31, 1860. Their daughter, Mabel, was born Nov. 2, 1902, at Vida. The Wards lived for many years on Greenwood Drive, east of Leaburg.

Ida Druscilla Finn Ward

Ida Ward was interviewed on occasion of her 90th birthday in 1959 by the *Springfield News*. Excerpts follow:

"There's just no place like the McKenzie, and it's well worth the six-hour bus trip from California, just to be back on the river," says Ida Ward, who celebrated her 90th birthday amid old friends and relatives Wednesday in an area where she lived most of her active life.

"Mrs. Ward is the last surviving child of Benjamin Franklin and Mary A. (Halter) Finn, for whom picturesque Finn Rock is named. And the McKenzie River will always be home for the white-haired lady with as many friends as memories.

"A good portion of those friends and relatives stopped at the home of Mrs. Ward's daughter and son-in-law, Mr. and Mrs. C. H. (Clayton) and (Mabel) Nestle, near Vida, Wednesday afternoon to renew friendships and wish her a happy birthday.

"For the past 12 years Mrs. Ward has lived at Blue Lake, near Eureka, Calif. She takes complete charge of her small apartment, although a son, Ellis Ireland, lives at Blue Lake, also. She hopes to be back home for her 91st birthday next summer.

"The McKenzie has changed a lot in the 88 years since she first saw the sparkling waters and timbered mountains, but no amount of change would serve to dim the active, white-haired lady in her opinion that 'there's no place like the McKenzie!'"

Ida Ward died Aug. 7, 1964, in Arcata, Cal., at age 95. She was survived by her son, Ellis Ireland of Blue Lake, Cal.; daughter, Mabel Nestle, of Vida; five grandchildren; six great-grandchildren, and two great-great-grandchildren. Interment was in Greenwood Cemetery at Leaburg, with her husband, Albert J. Ward, who died Feb. 27, 1944.

THE NESTLES

Mabel Ward married Clayton Nestle June 19, 1918, in Eugene, Ore. Nestle, born Sept. 5, 1898, at Alma, Mich., to Henry and Julia Nestle, lived most of his life in the Eugene-Springfield area and on the McKenzie.

A partner in the Elspass and Nestle Concrete Construction Co. in Eugene, he later was a shovel operator in road construction. He then worked in logging and cared for his filbert acreage, 46707 McKenzie Highway, east of Vida, where he and his family occupied the fine old home built in 1896 by Carey Thomson. The house was used as a stage stop, and the upper story served as a community dance hall.

After the Lucky Boy mine was abandoned, Nestle acquired the properties and worked the mine. But the remaining ore was low grade.

Nestle died at a Eugene retirement center June 23, 1981, age 82. He was a member of the Lutheran Church. Following cremation, interment was in Rest Haven Memorial Park. Mabel Nestle died Nov. 1, 1986.

Clayton and Mabel's children were: (1) Elbert E. and wife, Ruth. They live in Kent, Wa. They have a married daughter, Ardy. (2) Ennis H. and wife, Betty, live on the home place at Vida. (3) Ellen L. and her first husband, Kernutt, have two children, Gary and Steve Kernutt. Ellen later married Hal Fischl. They live on the Oregon Coast. (4) Elvin W. lives in the Nestle house on the home place east of Vida.

Elvin's wife, E. Janece, died Oct. 11, 1991, of cancer at age 68. Born Aug. 14, 1923, in Long Beach, Cal., she received a teaching degree in 1945 from the University of Oregon. She taught physical education in Tillamook, Ore. She and Elvin were married April 12, 1947, in Vancouver, Wa. They moved to Covina, Cal., where she worked in the Broadway Store 18 years. On retiring they moved to Vida. Survivors were her husband; daughter, Donna Jean Graham of Irvine, Cal.; sons, Douglas of Denver, Colo., and Michael of Vida; her mother, Katherine Smith of Eugene; an aunt and uncle, Bob and Marge Goodpasture, Leaburg, and eight grandchildren. Interment was in Sunset Memorial Gardens, Eugene.

Elvin and Ennis Nestle operate a filbert orchard on their farm.

Steve Kernutt is unmarried. Gary Kernutt and wife, Donna R., live in Eugene They have three married children: (1) Russ, his wife, Nancy (Adams), and children Bryan and Jeremy; (2) Rick, his wife, Lou (McFaddin), and their son, Chad, and (3) Randy and his wife, Lyndi (Maralynda Robison).

Many Landmarks

The story of Finn Rock -- some 50 feet high -- is legend and told in many ways, how Finn rolled it out of the road with his span of mules when he came to Oregon. Finn Rock Bridge crosses the McKenzie on Quartz Creek Road. The covered bridge collapsed July 12, 1967, and was replaced with a concrete bridge. There are two boat landings nearby.

Finn Creek flows along the west side of the Finn property and empties into Leaburg Reservoir near Angels Flight Road. Finn Grade, a moderate road incline between Finn Creek and Goodpasture Bridge on the north side of the Finn place, extended up the mountain, bypassing the steep area where Goodpasture Bridge is now located.

Finn Rock Ice Cave is suspected to lie in the hills around Finn Rock, Its exact location is unknown. (Williams). "There is a rumor of an ice (cave) above Finn Rock in the McKenzie River. (*The Speleograph*, June 1979)." Could this be another of Finn's tall tales?

Finn Rock Post Office

Just beyond Finn Rock today is Finn Rock Store. The business, first started in the 1930's, was known as The Stockade, owned by the Millirons. A post office was established in 1947. Headed "Recognition Comes from Uncle Sam to Finn Rock," the following item appeared in January 1947 in the *Eugene Register-Guard:*

"VIDA -- We have a new post office on the river, called Finn Rock. The post office and grocery store are being operated by Mr. and Mrs. S. A. Sall. The new post office will give better service to the large number of families who live across the river from Finn Rock who were formerly served by the Vida post office, about 12 miles distant. The store and community, which have been known for many years as Finn Rock, gets its name from a large rock by the side of the road.

"The rock got its name, according to old timers by the following story: 'One day when Huckleberry Finn was driving his mules up the road in the days when he was freighting, he saw this large rock which had rolled down the hill and was blocking the road. This did not bother him, because he just unhitched his mules and hooked them on the rock and pulled it off to one side, where it still sits and you can see the chain marks on the rock.' According to old-timers this story must be true, because, 'Huckleberry Finn' told it."

A tragic event occurred Oct. 6, 1989. Two young men robbed and murdered grocer Howard Emanual Gasper, who with his wife, Eleanor, owned the Finn Rock store for 25 years. The store was reopened in 1991.

CHAPTER 42

James and Emma Wycoff

The further tragic life of the Peter Wycoff family is told in the story of his first son, James, who was born Oct. 19, 1852. He was four months old when his parents, Peter and Elsie Jane (Stillwell), left Iowa and a year old on arrival at Brownsville, Ore.

He and Emma Bertha Finn, age 15, were married April 19, 1879, at Vida. Emma, the daughter of Benj. Franklin and Mary (Halter) Finn, was born in Schoolcraft, Mich., April 18, 1864. At age seven she came to Oregon from Missouri with her family in 1871.

James and Emma had nine children, all born on the Wycoff property near the Wycoff Toll Gate nine miles east of Vida.

James built a large farmhouse used as a school during the week. Saturday nights neighbors were invited to spend the night dancing.

Peter Wycoff apparently did not have adequate claim to the property. Sometimes it took many years to fulfill government requirements. Homestead rights were not granted until April 16, 1892, by the Roseburg Land Office in the name of James Wycoff. Bill and Ardyce Johnson, who built a home on a parcel of the property in 1979, have the homestead patent. They have since moved to Springfield.

James and Emma Finn Wycoff

James was involved with the Blue River mining district and also was a toll collector on the McKenzie Toll Road. Toll collecting was discontinued in 1895, when Lane County took over the road. Koch's map of 1900 showed a J. Wycoff owned 139 acres on the north side of the

McKenzie. Across the river on the south side is Wycoff Creek, named for James and Emma, which flows into Quartz Creek from the east. The creek crosses Quartz Creek Road (FR. 2618) at mp. 4.5. The Wycoff family had a cabin five miles up the creek. Nearby is Wycoff Mountain. Wycoff Road, a private logging road, begins on Quartz Creek Road at mp. 4.6 and follows Wycoff Creek.

James and Emma lived on the Ranch until his untimely death Nov. 25, 1905, at age 53. Bill Johnson related a reminiscence of the late McKinley Yale, James' grandson, concerning a tragic incident which either caused or contributed to James' death. McKinley, son of Bill and Flora Yale, was born in 1896 and died in 1994.

Yale, sitting in the dining room of the Johnson home, was looking out of the window towards the highway and river beyond. "Out there is where it happened," he said.

Yale, age nine, and one of the Wycoff children had accompanied James in his wagon to the Lucky Boy Mine to obtain provisions. On their return, James got off the wagon to open the gate. The horses bolted. James called to the boys to jump, which they did. He ran in front of the team to grab the harness in an effort to stop the horses. Instead, he was dragged as the frightened animals ran in circles, pulling the wagon until they finally stopped. The boys helped the injured man into the house. He died two weeks later. Thus James joined his mother, two sisters and brother Joe in fatal injury accidents. Only his father Peter and brother George died of natural causes.

After James' death, George came down from Freeman, Wa., to help care for the family. Soon after he sent for his wife, the former Eliza Bare, and family to join him. They lived for some time on the ranch. Two Bare children married into the James Wycoff family.

Emma, left with five children under age 21 at home, with little means of support, sold the farm to L. P. Snapp, a music teacher at the Vida school. On Feb. 8, 1907, Emma and Snapp were married. They moved to Grants Pass in 1910. She returned to Eugene in 1919. They were later divorced. She was living in Eugene as Mrs. L. P. Snapp at the death of her sister, Ella Belknap, in September 1924. Emma died Oct. 2, 1938, at age 74, at the home of her daughter, Mrs. Nellie Price, 1351 Olive St., Eugene. She was buried as Emma Wycoff in the Greenwood Cemetery, Leaburg.

The Wycoff Ranch later was purchased by the Al Cook family, who changed the name to Cook's Ranch. The late Etha Bare, daughter of James and Emma Wycoff, was quoted in 1981 as saying Cook's Ranch was a horse changing station for the stage running between Eugene and McKenzie Bridge. It later became Sheppard's Ranch, and still later was known as Heaven's Gate. The homestead was near the present sites of Sheppard's Boat Landing, mp. 35.5, and McMullin Boat Landing, mp. 37. The landings were donated to Lane County by William Sheppard and Prince Helfrich, later owners.

Martha (Mrs. Clarence) Belknap in a taped interview about 1976, while viewing a picture of a group of people sitting on a big Rock, was quoted as saying: "The Wycoffs were a big family. Here they are at Finn

Rock. Mrs. Wycoff was a little woman, and the children were all big people. She was a sister of Clarence's mother."

Wycoff Children

The James and Emma Wycoff family included:

(1) Flora Adeline, born Aug. 23, 1879, married William Yale.

(2) Nellie Jane, born June 26, 1881, married William Price.

(3) Adrian Ernest, born Dec. 25, 1884, married Georgia Beoular Mar. 21, 1908. He died Sept. 26, 1913.

(4) George Lester, born Oct. 23, 1886, married Margaret Olive Barter in 1918. He died in 1969 of diabetes. A son, Francis Wycoff, lives in Livermore, Cal. A daughter, Betty Frazier, lives in Vancouver, Wa. Francis has a son, Francis Jr., who has a son Francis III. A daughter, Michele Marie, is married to Steven Pollard of Burlingame, Cal. They have a daughter, Jenifer, and a son, Jason.

(5) Jessie Peter, born Nov. 22, 1888, married Flossie Violet Doane June 2, 1908. He logged in Washington, where their first child, Ronald, was born July 7, 1910. Jessie also worked in Canada. Twins Hildred and Mildred were born April 14, 1912, at the Wycoff Ranch. Hildred (Mrs. George Logan) recalled as a child going to dances at Vida. The family moved to Springfield, where their fourth child, Geneva (Hemmingsen), was born Dec. 21, 1918. The children attended Springfield schools.

Jessie died Feb. 21, 1933, age 45. Flossie died in 1967, age 79 years.

Mildred died in 1975 and Ronald about 1988. Geneva, married Sidney Hemmingsen June 25, 1938, in Springfield. He died in 1981. Geneva died Sept. 10, 1993. She was survived by a son, Rodney of Carson City, Nev.; daughters Sandra Kirk of Prineville and Teresa Wright of Springfield; sister, Hildred Logan, Springfield; five grandchildren and three great-grandchildren. Hildred married George Logan Aug. 31, 1947, in Springfield. She died March 9, 1994, at age 81. Survivors were her husband; daughter, Nancy Guse, Kelso, Wa., two grandchildren and two great-grandchildren.

(6) Chester, born Aug. 12, 1890, married Ona Pearl Bare June 8, 1908. She was a half sister to the children of Eliza Bare prior to her marriage to George Wycoff. Chester died in 1956. A son, Floyd, and another son, known as "Buddy," live in Sedro Woolley, Wa.

(7) Etha Mae, born May 5, 1892, married Ernest (Curley) Bare March 19, 1908. He was a half brother of Ona Pearl.

(8) James Chauncey, born Nov. 13, 1895, married Nannie Christina Magnuson. He died Aug. 5, 1953.

(9) Archie Percy, born Jan. 10, 1903, married Carrie M. Weisert June 18, 1932. They had an adopted son, Gerald (Jerry). Archie remarried after Carrie's death. He died May 11, 1984, age 81.

WILLIAM AND FLORA YALE

Flora Adeline Wycoff was born Aug. 23, 1879, on the Wycoff ranch. At age 16 years, she married William Joseph (Bill) Yale Jan. 2, 1896. He was born Feb. 1, 1863. They lived first at the Wycoff Ranch. Yale did extensive hunting and trapping.

In the early 1900's, Yale obtained a portable sawmill, which he operated around McKenzie Bridge many years. About 1909, he purchased 120 acres of an original homestead at the old Belknap Springs junction with the McKenzie Highway, since by-passed by the Clear Lake road.

The Yales moved to McKenzie Bridge, then to the large new house he built on the property. During an extensive building program at Foley Springs about 1916, he moved his sawmill, complete with sawing and planing facilities, to that property, and cut lumber for the resort.

William and Flora Yale celebrated their golden wedding anniversary Jan. 2, 1946. Fire in 1949 destroyed their large home at Yale Junction. A news item said:

"'Grandpa Will' Yale, 86, and his wife were homeless Monday, and McKenzie River neighbors talked of a house raising after the pioneer couple narrowly escaped with their lives from the fire which leveled their ranch home Saturday.

"The rambling structure was a landmark of the upper McKenzie country, its porch presiding over the junction of the Belknap Springs-Clear Lake Road and the McKenzie Highway.

"For more than 30 years the Yales had lived in the familiar ranch house. In the late afternoons motorists would see them rocking on their porch.

Bill and Flora Yale

"The rocking chairs were gone Monday, along with their other possessions. All that remains of the landmark is 'the largest fireplace in Lane County.'

"The fire burned a house full of heirlooms and mementos not only of the Yale family but of other pioneer residents who had stored their keepsakes in the big old house, a headquarters for the old-time families of the upper McKenzie. . .Nothing was saved, except a little clothing and bedding and several pieces of furniture near the front door. There was no insurance.

"The Yales were civic leaders for many years on the McKenzie. 'Grandpa Will' is a famed trapper and hunter, making, altering and repairing his own guns and casting all his own bullets. He still runs a trap-line, does a little hunting, and works on his own and neighbors guns. . ." Will Yale died May 18, 1956, at age 93 years. Flora died from diabetes Nov. 3, 1963, at age 84.

The Yales had four children: (1) William McKinley, born in 1896, died at age 97 in February 1994. He and his wife had a son, Melvin, the last of the Yale family name.

(2) Maud married Pete Sheasley. Children were Evelyn and Elvira.

(3) Ruby, born about 1906, had a son, Kyle, and daughter, Helen, with her first husband, Gus Galloway. She married, second, Lorrimy Birch, and, third, Mr. Shochenco.

(4) James (Jimmy) Yale, born April 1, 1909, married Frances Hines of Blue River in 1935. She was born in 1917. Their children were Edith, who lives in Arkansas, and Charlotte, born in 1940 and died Aug. 9, 1971, at age 31. After the death of Jimmy's sister, Maud, he and Frances took care of her children, Evelyn and Elvira.

NIMROD INN

Nellie Jane Wycoff, born June 26, 1881, married William (Billy) Riley Price Sept. 20, 1899. Price, born July 15, 1879, in Gillispie County, Tex., lived in Montesano, Wa., before coming to Lane County in 1894. They had a son, Wayne.

Billy and Nellie owned resorts on the McKenzie, including the famous Nimrod Inn, which was originated by Alfred L. Parkhurst and taken over by Price. It was located on the south bank of the McKenzie River below the Wycoff Ranch. Access was by ferry. Price also was a boatsman and guide for fishing and hunting parties.

Nimrod Inn was described by long-time river boatsman John West, as the "high spot of the county" and "quite a place to go for Sunday dinners." A 1928 pamphlet described Nimrod Inn as ". . .a rustic building with a massive cobblestone fireplace in the lounge, a rustic dining hall, hot and cold running water, baths, and other modern plumbing and electric lights. . .there is dancing on occasions in the evening at the inn. There is a piano and a good phonograph; guests are invited to bring other instruments and their music." The Inn had boats available for anglers. (Williams, 1991)

NIMROD INN, some ten miles east of Vida, across the river, was a favorite spot for fishermen, hunters and Sunday diners for many years. Note the rustic design.

The Prices also owned Anglers Inn. The Anglers was closed when the highway was moved closer to the McKenzie.

Price died March 6, 1937, at age 58, at his home, 1351 Olive St., Eugene. Survivors were his wife and son, Wayne (now deceased), and granddaughters, Marjorie and Dorothy Price, all of Eugene. He was buried in the Masonic Cemetery. After Billy's death, Nellie married Carl Stewart, a world War I Navy pilot. She was listed among survivors as Nellie Stewart, in the death notice of her brother, Chauncey Wycoff, in 1953. She died April 25, 1955, at age 73.

Gunshot Death

James Chauncey Wycoff, born Nov. 23, 1895, was married Feb. 26, 1918, in Butte, Mont., to Nannie Christina Magnuson. She was born in 1892. Chauncey adopted her son, Joseph H., born Oct. 10, 1917. Chauncey operated a garage on the McKenzie, but on the death of his mother, Emma Wycoff, in 1938, he was living in Anchorage, Alaska. He was a member of Eugene Lodge, B.P.O.E. No. 357.

Chauncey died Aug. 5, 1953, at age 57, of a gunshot wound. He was living near the old Wycoff place, known then as Sheppard's Ranch. A news item quoted Coroner Fred Buell as saying Wycoff apparently slipped on the slope between his house and the river. He was carrying a .22 caliber rifle. His adopted son heard the shot. Dr. Paul McGill, a retired Hollywood physician, who operated Hawthorn Cottages, administered first aid, but Chauncey died soon after.

Survivors were his wife, Nannie C., and son, Joe H. of Vida; two grandchildren, Karen Marie and David Arthur; brothers, Lester of Eugene, Chester of Sedro Woolley, Wa., and Archie of Eugene, and sisters, Nellie Stewart, Eugene; Flora Yale, McKenzie Bridge, and Etha Bare, Walterville. Burial was in Greenwood Cemetery.

Joseph and his wife, Jackie, had two children, Karen and David. Joseph died Nov. 7, 1979. Nannie died in 1987. She and Joe also were buried in the Wycoff plot in the Greenwood Cemetery.

JIMMY AND FRANCES YALE

Jimmy Yale, at age 87 (in 1996), one of the few life-long old-timers still living on the McKenzie, is a reliable authority on the early days. When very young and he lived down river, his parents would bundle him up and take him to all-night dances at Vida. They'd start out in the afternoon in a horse-drawn vehicle and return next day.

Yale recalls when he was about nine years old (about 1918), he spent a month with Dorothy (Andrews) Brown on Frissell Point, where she was a Forest Service fire lookout. As a teenager he worked summers at Belknap Springs, helped his father in his sawmill, and later worked for Clarence Belknap in his sawmill at Rainbow.

Jimmy's wife, Frances, revealed when she was still in grade school she made up her mind she was going to marry Jimmy Yale, and she did. They still live on the home place on Yale Lane.

Yale drove a school bus for 20 years. Later, he worked for the Oregon State Highway Department until 1972, when he suffered a serious injury forcing an early retirement.

ETHA WYCOFF BARE

Etha Mae (Wycoff) Bare, who attained the age of 99 years, was the last surviving member of the James and Emma Wycoff family. She was born May 5, 1892, at the family home, 12 miles east of Vida. At not quite 16 years she married Ernest (Curley) Bare, age 19, March 19, 1908. Bare was born in 1889 to Owen and Eliza Bare.

Etha and "Curley" lived many years on the McKenzie, at Walterville and Leaburg. Etha cooked for a number of years in a Marcola cookhouse and in a restaurant. Curley worked in the woods.

Etha's beloved "Curly," the husband she spent fifty-two years with, died in 1960. His passing left a big void in her life, she was quoted as saying in a news account June 9, 1981, shortly after her 89th birthday. "It's awful lonesome now without him. It's no fun being alone. I've enjoyed my life but it isn't the same," she said.

The article by Susan Kennedy in McKenzie River Reflections pretty well summarizes conditions of the times. Excerpts follow:

"Born and raised at Heavens Gate on the old McKenzie Highway, her life has been filled with hard times, good friends and lots of good times." After her marriage, "She left Heavens Gate and her wonderful home behind. She and Curley ventured off into the world together. 'So we were just a couple of kids growing up together. We lived together 52 years.'

"They lived at Leaburg during the 1930's depression and 'we hardly knew it. We never went hungry. We had chickens, cows, pigs. We raised everything and I traded eggs for coffee and stuff like that. I always canned everything.'

"Most of what Etha recalls from her earlier days has to deal with people in her life. 'I've always had lots of company wherever I've lived. . .I was taught to be nice to people.' She does admit that her good cooking helped to bring people around. She recalled, 'Oh, I used to have bunch after bunch up there. The loggers and mechanics and their wives. Whenever they'd have a party they'd wind up at my house.

"'They'd say, "Oh, let's go to Curley's and Goldy's and we'll get a good feed." (They called me Goldy 'cause I had red hair). They'd come up there and order chicken and dumplings at 2:00 in the morning! I'd get up and grumble awhile, but I'd fix it. It was fun. Our house was a place to hang out, I guess.' She said with a keen sense of humor: 'I like company if they'll come after breakfast, bring their lunch and leave before supper'."

Reminiscing Etha said: "'My childhood was nice. There were 10-12 miles between houses, so we made our own fun at home. My Dad played the violin, my brother played the guitar, and I played the piano. We had our concert at home.'

"'The roads were just wagon tracks in the dirt, more like a cow trail through the brush with trees right next to the road. It was pretty. The roads may not have been much but were worth paying a toll for.' In 1900 Etha's father was the road supervisor at

Heavens Gate. That job supported a family of 11. At the toll gate he charged people 25 cents to get through. All the money went to keep the roads a 'goin', for gravel to fill up the chuckholes.'

"The best times Etha remembers was 'Dancing! My Daddy built a dance hall for us nine kids, so we'd give dances there. And boy, did we ever have fun. Tell somebody there's going to be a dance at the Wycoff Ranch and you'd be surprised what a crowd would be there. And mother would cook and cook and cook. She'd make pies and cakes the week before. And the supper she'd serve! Don't blame them for coming.

"'She'd start with oyster soup made in a wash boiler, then roast chicken and everything, because we had everything on the ranch. Everybody came and they said, "Well, if I didn't dance I'd come down for the good ole supper!" The boys and my dad furnished the music and I played the piano.'

"Mrs. Bare had no children of her own. 'I wanted a big family like my mother but it wasn't meant to be.'

"About Oregon, she said, 'Oregonians may drift around, but finally they all end up back in Oregon.'"

Commissioned Painting

An 1895 photograph of the James Wycoff toll gate on the McKenzie shown to Carl Stephens, Walterville historian, by Frances O'Brien, Blue River librarian, led to a meeting of Stephens and Etha Bare, *The Springfield News* reported Aug. 14, 1982.

Stephens in the 1960's became interested in history of the McKenzie and has collected more than 1,000 pictures of early-day events. The great-great-grandson of S. M. Goddard, who settled in the McKenzie Valley in 1875, Stephens recalls his grandfather talking about the old timers. A fire department photo display at the Walterville community fair spurred his interest.

In the background of the Wycoff homestead photo rises the same ridge that over the years has overlooked the Wycoff property. Five Wycoff children -- Etha, Adrian, Lester, Jessie and Chester -- play in the rutted road that eventually became Highway 126. The McKenzie River is visible behind the open sheds where weary travelers rested overnight.

Stephens commissioned Leaburg artist Agnes Baird to paint a picture from the photo and gave it to Etha to hang in her living room.

Chance Meeting

In 1964, Bill and Ardyce Johnson, traveling from California to Spokane, Wa., decided to go up Highway 126 to see if they could find the Wycoff homestead or anyone who remembered the Wycoffs. A stop in Eugene at the Lane County offices showed the land registered in the Walterville precinct. The clerk directed them up Highway 126. At Walterville a woman was working in her flower garden. When asked if she knew anything about the Wycoffs who settled in the area, she said:

"I sure do! I'm a Wycoff!!!"

Ardyce bounced out of the car and a cherished visit was shared with Etha Wycoff Bare -- a cousin!

Bill and Ardyce drove by the old homestead and on to Spokane. They couldn't get the area out of their minds. By 1977 they had decided to migrate north. A trip to Oregon and up Highway 126 was in order. They noticed a "For Sale" sign and called the Realtor.

This was the last acre of Grandpa Peter's homestead. They bought the property and Bill built a home on the 1.19-acre tract at 50069 McKenzie Highway, Vida. On Christmas Eve 1979, Bill and Ardyce moved in. The original homestead had four owners before it was subdivided. The Johnsons were fifth owners.

Ceil Sheppard became a dear friend, they said. Standing on her land at the time was an old Wycoff barn and chicken coop. There also was an old dump site north of the barn.

Etha and Curley Bare

Ardyce found many artifacts, used possibly by Wycoff ancestors.

There isn't much left to identify the old homestead, except the scenic ridge that forms the backdrop, and the McKenzie River that fronts the property.

Etha Bare lived her later years at Walterville. She died Sept. 21, 1991. The *Eugene Register-Guard* listed as survivors: Five nephews, James Yale and his wife Frances of McKenzie Bridge; Francis Wycoff of Livermore, Cal.; Jerry Wycoff and his wife Claudia of San Jose, Cal.; McKinley Yale of Eugene; Floyd Wycoff of Washington; three nieces, Betty Frazier of Vancouver, Wa., Geneva Hemmingsen of Springfield, and Hildred Logan and her husband George of Springfield; many cousins, including Ardyce (Wycoff) and Bill Johnson of McKenzie Highway and many great and great-great nieces and nephews. Burial was in Greenwood Cemetery, Leaburg. McKinley Yale, Geneva Hemmingsen and Hildred Logan are since deceased.

Ardyce, a great-granddaughter of Peter Wycoff, and her husband, Wilbur S. (Bill) Johnson, born in 1912, have two sons, Douglas Lee, born May 24, 1935, and Larry Carl, Aug. 9, 1936.

In August of 1991, Bill and Ardyce hosted a Wycoff family reunion. Total of 89 people attended. Many of them were the children and families of Archie and Grace Wycoff.

In January 1996, Bill and Ardis sold their McKenzie home and moved to Springfield.

WYCOFF RANCH---First Homesteaded by Peter Wycoff, the Ranch was taken over in 1882 by son, James, who married Emma Finn. Children, pictured, Etha, Adrian, Lester, Jessie and Chester, play in the rutted "toll" road. The toll gate is seen in the background.

CHAPTER 43

WALTERVILLE

Walterville -- named by George Millican for his son, Walter, the first white child born in Central Oregon, when he established the first post office in 1875 -- had its humble beginning much earlier.

The countryside was wild, heavily timbered. There were no roads, only Indian trails. Rivers had to be forded. Wild animals roamed freely. The town lies on a plain, extending to the mountains on the north. On the east, along a line following the power canal, and looking south, the land drops to a vast flood plain all the way to the McKenzie River.

Walling's *History of Lane County* said the area's first settlers of record were Ross Pollock and his brother, who in 1852 located on the banks of the McKenzie River. John C. Jamieson took up his abode on part of the same estate. The 1860 census for Camp Creek Precinct, which included Walterville, lists only a William M. Pollock, age 20, and a Marve Pollock, 16. An early-day map shows property owned by J. F. Pollock.

Other early settlers were the Storments and John Latta about 1852. George Millican, pioneer of 1854, said, after returning from the Idaho mines en route to California in 1862, he purchased land, apparently from Pollock. Caswell Hendricks established a ferry at the McKenzie River crossing in 1862. Latta sold to Robert Millican in 1864. The James Davis Fountains, pioneers of 1858, settled up on Buck Point in 1868.

An undated map, drawn and printed by the Douglas County Abstract Co., shows property owned by Latta, Storments and Fountains. However, Latta had sold to Robert Millican before the Fountains moved there. South of the Storments across the river was property of B. Nelson, W. H. Kanoff and J. B. Smitz. To the east was property of S. T. Coney, J, M, Coney, J. F. Strange and, south of the river, J. B. Bradley.

The map shows property lying west of that of Latta and Storment, north to south, as owned by A. L. Collins, Cyrus Long, J. C. Jamieson and J. B. Coney (possibly Couey), and far to the south, extending to the McKenzie River, were properties of J. McLean and W. L. Davidson, where Stephen Smeed about 1877 acquired holdings and grew hops.

The 1860 Camp Creek precinct census, which included Walterville and points east, lists a Cyrus Long, age 22, a farmer born in Iowa; Hal M. Long, age 13; Charles A., 5, and Efnia, 2. The 1870, census shows Cyrus Long, 32; wife, Nancy, 21, and children Fernando, 5, and Naomi, 3.

The 1870 census lists William L Davidson, 46, born in Ohio; wife, Mary, 36; Charles, 11; May, 9; Sherman, 5; Maggie, 8 months, and A. Pollie, 70, living in the household.

Properties west of Long and Jamieson, north to south, were owned by Wm. P. Coney (Couey), George Millican, A. L. Craig, W. Allen, J. F.

Pollock and J. W. McCormack. The M. D. Ritchey property lay west of the Coney and Craig properties. Due south of Ritchey's were J. W. Bogart, A. T. Schamp, Dave Stephens, Peter Key and S. C. Branton. Property to the north was owned by W. D. McLean. J. D. Dick's homestead lay further west in east Camp Creek, where the Goddards and Stephens later settled.

George Millican received his authority as postmaster under the administration of President Grant Feb. 24, 1875. The post office was located at the junction of what is now Millican Road and Camp Creek Road. Mail was first carried by pack horses weekly, later by stage.

Smeed Established Hop Yard

Stephen Smeed, born Dec. 2, 1842, in Peasmarsh, Sussex, England, to William and Letitia (Foster) Smeed, married Eliza Swaffer July 14, 1868. With daughter Annie, born Nov. 4, 1868, they sailed on the Cunard Steamship Java May 20, 1870, landing at Castle Garden, N. Y., June 5. They traveled on to Waukeshaw, Wisc., where Stephen worked on the hop yard of John Weaver whom he knew in England. A son, William, was born there Jan. 18, 1873. Stephen moved his family to Walterville in the late 1870's, bought property on the McKenzie River for a hop yard, and built a house in 1883, according to John Smeed of Eugene, a grandson.

The 1880 census listed Stephen, 37; Eliza, 34; Hanna (real name Annie), 11, and William, 7. Caroline (Carie), was born March 26, 1881, and a son, Herbert, Dec. 21, 1889, in Walterville. Annie died April 9, 1889.

Stephen's sister, Mary Jane Smeed, born in Peasmarsh April 5, 1833, married Thomas (Tom) Easton, July 23, 1852, in Playden, Sussex. Tom was born March 9, 1832, in Rye, Sussex. They came to the United States in 1883, settling on what is now Millican Lane in Walterville. They brought children Jessie, born Sept. 24, 1856; Richard William, June 1, 1861; Mary Ann, Jan. 21, 1871, and James Thomas, May 27, 1873. They also brought grandchildren Frances and Ned Morris, children of their daughter, Leticia. Frances Morris married Theron Thomson of Vida.

William (Will) Smeed married Mary Elizabeth Paine, known as Polly, July 3, 1893. A niece of Stephen Smeed, she was born Oct. 31, 1872, in Tenterden, Kent, England. Stephen brought her to the United States on one of his trips to England. Children were Charley, Elsie, Carie, Alice, Emily, Ethel, Rosy, Myra, Helen and Mary, all of whom attended Walterville schools. A son, Earl Thomas, born in 1912, died in 1914. Their home lay west of Stephen Smeed's house. William died July 3, 1927.

Caroline (Carie) Smeed, married Len L. Stevens, Eugene attorney, July 2, 1899, in the Eugene (Smeed) Hotel. He died Oct. 10, 1910. She then married Alan Tyson May 12, 1911. Born May 31, 1880, Tyson died May 13, 1953. Caroline died July 15, 1938. Their son, the Rev. Alfred Stephen Tyson, born Aug. 22, 1915, was Episcopal Church minister at Roseburg many years. He and his wife live at Elkton, where he served as mayor.

On March 2, 1885, Stephen acquired ownership of a newly completed hotel in Eugene. In 1884, Charles Baker (financed by Smeed) and George H. Parks contracted to build a three-story fireproof hotel which when completed cost $15,000. Smeed bought the building and rented it to Baker. It was called Baker's Hotel until 1892, when it was renamed the Eugene Hotel. Not until 1907 was it called the Hotel Smeede, the "e" added to give it a touch. In 1914 Smeed ordered the "e" painted out. The hotel remained in the Smeed family ownership until its closure in 1970. Stephen died Dec. 29, 1930. Eliza died Nov. 11 1924.

Eugene's other leading hotel, the St. Charles, was built by Dr. Alexander Renfrew in the 1850's. At the "luxurious" Smeede, Sunday dinners cost eighty-five cents. Choice rooms were two dollars a night.

Herbert Smeed married Ethel Beatrice Montgomery Nov. 19, 1912, at Springfield. She was born April 9, 1895. They operated the Stephen Smeed hop yard at Walterville from 1912 to 1921, moving then to Eugene.

Their children were Glenn Herbert, born Aug. 19, 1916, died June 15, 1988; Doris Beatrice, born July 11, 1920; John Stephen, Jan. 8, 1924; Ralph, April 18, 1926, and Dorothy, Feb. 23, 1932.

Ethel's parents were Alfred (Al), born at Cottage Grove Feb. 22, 1862, and Rosa Bell (Gaerte) Montgomery, born in Indiana Aug. 19, 1866. A son, Charles Frederick, was born Nov. 1, 1886. The Montgomerys operated the Minnesota Hotel in Eugene, 1897 to 1903, a stage stop at Vida on the McKenzie, then the Springfield Hotel at Third and Main streets, beginning in 1909. Al died April 14, 1929, and Rosa died Oct. 26, 1950.

In 1883, Billy Williams opened a store on Camp Creek road west of Walterville on property later occupied by the Schwering family. Ed Schwering married Mabel Easton, daughter of Jessie Easton.

The post office was moved by succeeding postmaster to property on Camp Creek Road, occupied years later by C. C. Polley and more recently by Clifford Crabtree, who died in 1994. It became the center of the community as several homes were built in the vicinity.

J. Bingle, who opened another store up town at the site of the old Woodman of the World building, was the next postmaster. He sold to C. H. Baker, who became postmaster, followed by Irene Brownson.

Schumates Buy Store

J. W. Schumate, born in St. Louis, Mo., came to Eugene in 1886. He clerked in G. Bettman's store for eight years. An opportunity arising, he bought Baker's general merchandise business about 1894. With the opening of the Blue River mines and establishment of logging camps on the McKenzie River, great impetus was given to trade. About 1900, Schumate erected a new store building near the present church. He specialized in loggers and miners supplies and outfits. Mrs. Schumate, as postmaster, moved the post office into the new store.

Early on, Walterville became a focal point for people traveling to mining operations on Gold Hill and to Belknap and Foley Springs, or traveling over the mountains to Central Oregon.

Martha Storment opened the first hotel north of the town center. The hotel, taken over by the Frank Post family, was operated as a stage stop until 1912. The property later became known as the Momb place.

A Mr. Brooks came in 1884. He ran a second hotel, located where the H. C. Page home was later built. The hotel was moved across the road. Anson Potter ran a livery stable. Pleasant Hartwig had a blacksmith shop. Mrs. Baker ran a millinery store. V. Dunton operated a pool hall and saloon. There was a shoe shop. The I.O.O.F. building was erected.

Logging, the main industry, gave employment to many men. "Walterville further offered attraction to summer visitors from its proximity to the beautiful McKenzie River, where the finest fishing in the country may be enjoyed," the *Eugene Morning Register* reported in 1903. "In the forests and foothills game of every description abounds, and excellent sports can be had within a distance of only a few miles."

During this period, the land was pretty well taken up and very little was offered for sale. Daily stages ran between Eugene and Walterville, a distance of 16 miles, with development of the Blue River mines and logging camps. Previously stages ran once a week, then twice and three times a week. Travel was limited by poor road conditions.

John and Bill Rennie in 1907 moved from Albany and bought the Walterville store. The Schumates built a home near Hendrick's Bridge in Cedar Flat and grew peaches. Bill Rennie ran the store, while John settled on a ranch east of Vida across the McKenzie from Bear Creek.

A major development in Walterville was construction of the Eugene Water and Electric Board power plant on Camp Creek Road and dredging of the five-mile-long power canal that feeds it. The canal work was begun in 1906. The project, completed in 1910, brought much activity to the community and electricity to the area.

The Rennies sold to Max Gebauer in 1912. John Rennie remained on his McKenzie ranch. Bill settled in Thurston. He had sons Ray, Ennis and Frank and daughter, Ada. Ray married Marjorie Phetteplace of Thurston. Ennis married Nettie Minney, daughter of the Kapp Minneys of Vida. Frank married Opal Taliaferro of Thurston. Ada married Eugene Goff, who became superintendent of the Leaburg fish hatchery.

Max and Myrtle Gebauer's children were Ted, Dorothy, Oma May and Harold. He sold to Ernest Hotaling in 1918. He moved to Medford, entered the candy business and built an apartment. He died Feb. 19, 1939.

Hotaling, superintendent of EWEB's Walterville power plant, operated the Walterville store with the assistance of his wife, Edith. Their children were Frances, Ray and Kathryn. About 1920, Hotaling was transferred by EWEB to its Eugene plant. He commuted until the mid-1920's, when he sold the store and moved to Eugene.

Edward Howells succeeded Hotaling as superintendent of the Walterville power plant. Howells continued in that position until EWEB's Leaburg plant was completed in 1928, when he took over operations there. He married Eva Hart of Cedar Flat. Eva, daughter of James and Mariah Carmen Hart, was born June 8, 1902, in Waynesburg, Ky. The Harts moved to Cedar Flat. Following Howells' death in 1971, Eva married George Easton, life-long area resident, March 27, 1974. She died Oct. 3, 1996. Survivors were her husband, George of Leaburg; a son, Gary Howells, and sisters, Lucy Peyton and Julia Gillespie.

George Marx bought Hotalings' store. The Marx children were George, Helen (Mrs. Sid Kastman) and Robert (Bob).

For a time the post office was located in the old I.O.O.F. Hall. Postmasters were Myrtle Farnham and Mr. Pember. The office finally was established in the store from 1930 to 1946 with Marx as postmaster.

The highway, relocated in 1930-31, bypassed two stores, a garage and warehouse. It cut diagonally through the north part of town. A new canal bridge was built. Marx purchased property from A. L. Vaughn, moved and remodeled his warehouse, and built two cottages and a campground. Merle Swearingen built a garage on land he purchased from Oscar Millican close to the crossroads that lead to Camp Creek.

In 1946, Georgia Christian, postmaster, moved the post office to a building east of the Van Arnam home. Only five families were receiving mail, the R.F.D. handling most of the patrons. Tommy Benson moved the post office into his store building at the time he took over as postmaster.

Walterville today has a modern shopping center, located where Marx moved his store. Cliff Christian acquired the land and erected a new building. His sons, Jeff and Andy, managed the store until selling to Larry and Jerry Swartz, who operate as Swartz Brothers Select Market. In 1996, the building was enlarged from 8,500 to 12,000 square feet to include a hot and cold dairy area, bakery, video stereo, new coolers and produce area. The brothers, long associated with the grocery business, worked in their family store as children, then were with Safeway ten years, becoming assistant managers. They operated stores in the Eugene area before acquiring the Walterville store.

The Walterville Feed and Tackle Store is owned by Carol Brooks. After her children finished school, she began with a small inventory. On Oct. 15, 1995, during remodeling, fire caused $120,000 damage. The building was repaired and the store observed its tenth anniversary in 1996. Walterville also has a modern restaurant, known as Tina's Lucky Logger. A video store adjoins. A new post office building and a beauty salon are included in the center.

Movement to organize a church was begun in 1901 through a Ladies Aid Society. Sunday school and Christian Endeavor were held in the school house. EWEB's canal construction cut off a corner of the Frank Post property. The Posts, who ran a hotel and stage stop, donated land lying south of the canal. In 1910, the church was formally organized, adopting the Presbyterian faith.

Walterville and Deerhorn residents prominent in the start of the church were Mr. and Mrs. H. C. Page, Mr. and Mrs. Frank Page, Mr. and Mrs. Joe H. Deavor, Mr. and Mrs. O. M. Stacy, Mr. and Mrs. Rennie Koozer, Marion and True Bigelow, Will and Lucy Irvin, Mr. and Mrs. John Rennie, Mr. and Mrs. George Willian, Mr. and Mrs. H. J. Wearin, William Morrow, Cora Wearin, Arthur Irvin and Mae Holmes. The Pages came to Walterville March 21, 1903. Frank Page married Edith Stacy.

Fire in 1932 destroyed the church buildings and I.O.O.F. Hall. The sanctuary was rebuilt that year. On Feb. 12, 1994, the new Fellowship hall was dedicated in the memory of the late Gloria Crawford.

Many Fond Memories

Walterville, the place of my birth and that of my sisters, Gladys and Violet, holds many fond memories. It was in Walterville, where my grandparents, James and Ella Belknap, in the 1890's sent their children to live to attend the eight-month school. It was there my parents, Clifton L. and Cora Belknap Inman, lived the first 20 years after their marriage (1903-1923); where my father operated sawmills on two occasions, where we children attended school and picked hops for the Smeeds.

Primarily a farming community, Walterville was laid out in a grid with two streets and an alley connecting with the road through town in anticipation of future growth. The road was graveled but unimproved until the early 1920's. The first road work of significance came after my sister, Gladys, and another girl of the community posted signs at two very large mudholes, "No Fishing allowed."

In the 1920's, there was a general store with a seed and feed warehouse across the street; an old pool hall, converted into a residence; an old livery stable, a blacksmith shop and garage owned by Pleasant (Ples) Hartwig, still doing horse shoeing; an Odd Fellows hall, where the post office at times was located; a Woodman of the World building, the ground floor used as a high school; a church, and a two-room grade school down the road which we children attended.

The Walterville store was the center of activity. About 200 people lived within a two-mile radius from the store -- east to Deerhorn, southwest to Hendricks Bridge, and west on Camp Creek Road to the EWEB power plant. Most of the people knew each other through school and church functions, lodge suppers, ball games and community picnics.

Among Walterville residents during the teens and early 1920's were: Lawrence and Verna Millican, the Fred and Katie Easton family, the Dave Fountains, the Carneys, Mr. and Mrs. Ezra Potter, whose son, Anson, had operated a livery stable. Next to the Potters were the Hays, whose daughter, Lena, drowned in the power canal, and the Hartley family. There were the H. C. Pages and their son, Frank and his wife, Edith, the Joe Deavors, son Claude and daughter, Cora.

Arthur and Debbie Day Campbell moved to Walterville about 1900 from Missouri. Their children were: Dolly (dec.); Martha Tanner, Springfield; Howard and Claude of Walterville. Howard, a Marine Corps veteran, died Nov. 17, 1995. Born Aug. 26, 1910, he married Alice Johnson April 29, 1945, in Seattle. They had two children, Glen of Springfield and Earl of Albany. Alice died May 7, 1992.

Northeast of town the Momb family lived on the former Frank Post farm. Then came the Lester Millican place. Due north was the Robert Millican homestead. The Osmer Stacys, Willians, John Wearins, and Storments lived further east. Ruby Wearin married Leland Shrode. Everett Wearin married Cora Deavor. The Fountains lived on Buck Point.

South from the Storments down a lane leading to Emmerick's Ferry were the McNutt, Berbaugh and Pepiot families. Across the river were five families who crossed by ferry boat to the Matt Emmerick place. Others were the Fred Russell and Louis Kanoff families; Alice Goff and her three boys, and a family named Dean. Mrs. Goff was the teacher at a one-room schoolhouse on the Emmerick place.

Emmerick children were Frank, Clara, Bertha, Matilda, who married Carl Dehne; Hilda, Mamie, who married Guy Lane, and Matt.

West from the town center, the Widers lived by Wider's Creek and Wider's Grove where we picnicked. South of town were the Herbert and Bill Smeed families. Further west was the grade school.

Beyond was Oscar Millican's ranch. Oscar expanded the George Millican holdings, farmed the land and raised Hereford cattle. He and his sister, Belle, lived there until their deaths in 1950. Part of the ranch, now owned by Cliff Christian, has been subdivided and new homes built.

Along what is now Millican Road were the Pete Ashleys, the Thomases and Jessie and Arthur Easton families. Down the Camp Creek road were the C. C. Polleys, Ed Schwerings, Drurys, Cash Meads, Charles and Hannah Jessens, the Smiths and the Jim Keys.

John Kickbush with wife, Bertha, and children Zula, Evelyn, John and Winnifred, moved in from Iowa in 1919 and settled down what today is known as Kickbush Lane, directly south of the power plant.

Camp Creek

Down Camp Creek Road beyond the power plant, high up on a plateau, was the Chaffee family, with children Nathan, Adna, Esther and Arthur "Bud". Later the Scott family occupied this property, still later the Hardy family. Further west on Camp Creek Road were the Stephens.

The Marion Chase family came in 1913 and lived south across the power canal tailrace. Ray Chase married Gladys Archer, a teacher at Walterville. Ranald Chase married Frances Hotaling.

The Fred Browns, early area settlers, had daughters Olive, born in 1875, and Frances. John Crabtree, who came in the 1870's, married Olive Brown. They moved to a 160-acre farm nearby. Olive died in 1913, at age 38, giving birth to her thirteenth child, leaving nine living children.

The oldest Crabtree child, Ruby, age 16, quit school to take care of the children at home, while their father worked as a logger to support them. Ruby late in life married Charles (Rusty) Meyer.

The Crabtree family story is told by the late Lola Marjorie (Crabtree) Lane in her book, *Missy Lane*, published in 1983. Born in January, 1903, Lola lived all her life in the area. She taught school, mostly at Camp Creek's School Districts 5 and 70.

Fred, the oldest son, married Gertrude Gum. They moved to Marcola. Next in line was Inza, "tall and "beautiful," as described by Lola. She was followed by Frank, who married Goldie Lynch. Their daughter, Juanita, married Maurice "Dick" Myers.

Lola married Jimmy Lane in 1935. His parents, the Creed Lanes, moved to Camp Creek in 1932. Other children were Bob, Jimmie and Jo. Lola and Jimmy lived in California six years, then returned and bought her father's farm. He lived with them until his death at age 95.

Other Crabtree family members were Lawrence, who married Helen Miller. Rachel married Everett Chase. They lived in Jasper. Their three children died when a fire destroyed their home.

Clifford Crabtree's wife, Renee, died. He married Jimmy Lane's widowed sister, Jo Washburn. Clifford died in 1994. Juanieta Crabtree married Ray Hotaling. Children were Phyllis, Kent, Carrol and Jimmie.

CHAPTER 44

Deerhorn and Leaburg

The community of Deerhorn was centered around the area of the present Norval J. Frank place, near where the basaltic cliffs rear above the highway and reach to the river below the road level, wrote the late Ethel Fountain in *Historic Leaburg*. Deerhorn sometimes was called Lower Leaburg.

At this location, known as Deerhorn Point and Deerhorn Grade before it was blasted away for a roadbed, a ferry boat crossed the river to a ranch owned by Major Forest. In 1904, N. L. FitzHenry, a Californian, bought the place and named it the Deerhorn Ranch.

In later years the ranch was owned by Barney Oldfield, still later by Dr. Lester Edbloom. It was subdivided. There now are two dozen houses, a golf course and a picnic area on the site.

Around the turn of the century, just east of the old Deerhorn Grade, the James O'Brien family ran a hotel, livery stable and the Deerhorn post office, started in 1908. The present house has been remodeled from the O'Brien Hotel at the west end of Holden Creek Lane. At one time the building was used as a sanitarium.

East of the O'Briens was the Charles Rossman place. The Rossmans, a six month old child and Mrs. Rossman's parents, Mr. and Mrs. Reuben Wickham, came west from Iowa in 1889 and bought eighty acres of land, all timbered except twelve acres which had been logged. They built a log house and cleared land for a garden and to pasture a couple of cows, according to the late Coy Lansbery, area resident.

In 1905, they sold the timber off the remainder of the land and built the house that is still standing. It remained in the Rossman family, owned and occupied by the late Fay Rossman's wife, Frances. Fay was the youngest of six children. The property has been subdivided into twenty-three parcels with twenty-two homes built.

Among early Deerhorn residents were Adam Taylor Morris and wife Charlotte (Stacey). With Morris' cousins, Philip Casebeer and Inez Eddy, brother and sister, they left Hay Springs, Neb., in 1889 by horses and covered wagons. The Morrises homesteaded on 80 acres of bench north of the present grade school at Deerhorn. Adam, a carpenter, built several houses -- the John Koozer, Odell and others.

Horace, one of six children, was six when they came to Oregon. Except for a year at Fresno, Cal., he lived on the place until his death in 1958. He married Carrie Grace Allen in 1908. They built a house above his parents' home. They had four children, Willis, of Eugene, Vesta Conklin of Walterville; Alma Mieze (dec.), and Evelyn Marcus of

Hermiston. They attended Deerhorn Grade School. After Horace, a logger, suffered an injury he worked on the power canal.

Willis and his wife purchased the old home and built a smaller home for his mother. After her death, Willis sold the place to his stepson, William Applewhite and wife, Wyola.

The Casebeers taught school at Blue River several years. Philip also drove the school bus. They lived near Vida.

Deerhorn residents living east of the Storments were the Harve Potters. On the hill north of the Potters was the Holmes place. John Holmes married May Irvin. Isaac Homes married Susan Irvin. Next came the Lew Flegal homestead, later known as the Nels Kaldore place. North of the highway was the Guy Lane place, later owned by Ross Bros., as identified by Coy Lansbery. Guy Lane married Mamie Emmerick. Rosa Lane married Dexter Sparks and Daisy Lane married Rube Montgomery.

Where the Ernest Watsons now live (former home of Joe and Alice Odell) was part of the Lane place. East of Flegals on the south side was the Gil Shirey homestead, later owned by Vern Hucka, who married Molly Potter. Arthur Irvin married Elsie Potter.

Next was the Deerhorn schoolhouse, then the Meyer family, the Sime Putmans, then the Ulery family, south of the highway, later owned by Koozer Bros. The Sam Goddard property was on the north side of the road, later owned by Dick Hart. Then came the Moore place where the Hart Bros. built a service station. Frank Moore married Emma Carter, daughter of Pleasant Carter of Leaburg. On the south side of the road was the Knuck Reams place, then the Walter Millican property, where the Emmit Rauch family later lived.

The Joe Gillispie place was just beyond. Joe married Ada O'Brien, sister of Joe Pepiot. The family included Victor, Vern, Vincent, Don, Darrel and Margaret. Vern married Julia Hart. He died in 1990. Vincent married Mary Fountain. He died in 1945.

The Thienes family lived just west of the old Deerhorn grade. Beyond the Rossman place was a family named White, where Stan McNutt now lives. Next came the Joe Pepiot, Dick Deadmond and Sherman Hickson families, then the Harrill Bros., where the Leaburg power plant is now located.

LEABURG

Leaburg, seven miles east of Walterville at mp. 20, was named for Leander Cruzan (1841- ?), who established the first post office Jan. 29, 1877. The 1880 census listed Leander, his wife, Caroline, and six children: Thomas, Andrew, Emma, William, James and Ida.

During the late 1800's and early 1900's Leaburg was locally known as "Jim Town," for James "Uncle Jim" and Emma (Fountain) "Aunt Emma" Kennerly, who owned the general store and hotel. "Jim Town" also was known as Upper Leaburg. It had two stores.

Booth-Kelly Lumber Co. in the late 1800's had a logging camp across the river, known as Donkeyville, with about 50 families. The camp was so named because it had the first donkey (steam-powered) logging engine on the river. A ferry on the Dale Carlson property in front of the schoolhouse led across the river to the camp.

Kennerly set up a portable sawmill in 1892 near the Frank Post place east of Walterville (*Oregon State Journal* June 23, 1892). The mill originally was operated by water power from the McKenzie river. Kennerly later purchased a steam engine from the Camp Creek shingle mill to run his mill as water power was insufficient.

Manena Schwering (1979) said the Kennerlys (her uncle and aunt) had the first automobile along the river in the early 1900's.

The post office name was changed to Deerhorn May 25, 1907, and included a change to a new location two miles to the west. After FitzHenry bought Major Forest's property, he killed a deer. He not only named his place Deerhorn Ranch but decided he would like the Leaburg community name changed to Deerhorn.

As the post office was located at Leaburg, changing the name required a petition to Washington. It was finally managed and it became Deerhorn. Jim Town residents salvaged the name Leaburg and applied it to their community. A new Leaburg post office was established Sept. 20, 1907. This name was used until the office was closed in September, 1913.

About fourteen houses in Leaburg were built by loggers who worked in the camp and crossed the river by ferry boat. They included the Bill Kennerly, Pleasant Carter, Henry Carter, Frank Moore, John and Mart Broom, Bill Campbell, Bill Slavens, Burt Scott and Walter Wheeler families. The Wheelers owned the two stores.

Next was the Johnson place. The Andy Hickson family lived in a logging camp north of where Gordon Vance now lives. Jack Doyle and Rowland Johnson were logging the timber off that place with horses. East of Johnsons was Jack Doyle, on the hill where the old road turned into the cemetery. Next was the Dutch Henry place, later owned by Wayne Yarnell, then the Seymour family, still later by Jim McKee of McKee's Bakery, Springfield. The VanProyens lived on the old John Cogswell farm. Then came the Albert Ward home, later known as the Currie place. Montgomery Bros. was just west of the present EWEB dam.

"Many changes took place," wrote Linnie Craft Beyerlin in *Historic Leaburg* (1987). "The local boarding house run by Uncle Jim and Aunt Emma Kennerly went out of business when they retired, as did Wheeler's store, and four others. Eventually Walter Millican's Store and Post Office became the shopping center. Outside, a staircase led up to a room where social gatherings were held. Earlier it was a dance hall.

"During these years," continued Mrs. Beyerlin, "Dr. Leiberg and his wife built an enormous house just east of the Leaburg school district boundary. It probably was the largest private home ever built on the McKenzie, with features adaptable for a hospital or nursing home."

Dr. Leiberg was a bacteriologist and his wife a physician and surgeon. After his death Mrs. Leiberg ran the place, doing the chores and keeping the vast lawns, beautiful flowers and a well-cared-for garden. She had brought many seeds and plants from her native Germany and from Africa where she had managed a hospital.

"These were hard times. Their only child, a son, was not heard from after World War I for several years. It was a joyous day when he returned cured of amnesia. They sold the place and moved to California. She came back twice and stayed with us for a week. It was a delightful time of long hikes and picking mushrooms.

"The place was sold again to R. G. Miller, a retired New York lawyer with a retinue of servants: chef, housekeeper, secretary and governess, plus a local crew of men to farm the 1,300 acres on both sides of the river. They became our good friends and neighbors for several years. They sold to the Barney Oldfields of Deerhorn.

"It was a shock when this fine mansion was destroyed by fire."

In the early 1920's, Leaburg was a small community along the Highway, serviced by a graveled road with a dozen houses near the store, owned then by Walter Millican, as the hub of the community.

Millican sold to the Clarks of Blodgett, Ore. Two years later they sold to Burrell and Elma Slavens. In 1927, electricity was brought into the community by EWEB, to supply construction of its new power facilities. With completion of the Leaburg Power Plant in 1930, nearly all the homes and buildings were lighted with electricity.

Most recent owners of the Leaburg store are Jacque and David Girard, who took over in early 1996, remodeled the building and changed the name to Leaburg Community Store.

Beyond Leaburg was the fish hatchery with Matt Ryckman as superintendent. Prior to building the dam at Leaburg Lake, fish racks were put in to catch the salmon going upstream. The racks were then moved to just above Hendricks Bridge near Walterville.

Eugene Goff, who began working at the hatchery just out of high school, became superintendent. Later he was named superintendent over all state hatcheries, headquartered in Portland. He and his wife, the former Ada Rennie, lived there the remainder of their lives.

Seymour's Chateau

A popular stopping place along the McKenzie from 1920 to 1960 was Seymours, near the fish hatchery. Begun by Darle Seymour as an ice cream and sandwich stand, it was taken over by his sister, Alberta.

In 1906, Henry and Nellie Bowen Seymour moved from South Haven, Mich., to Eugene, Ore. In 1915, they purchased the Dutch Henry place east of Leaburg on Greenwood Drive. Their children, Alberta, Darle and Virginia, attended Leaburg schools. Alberta and Darle were seniors that year, along with Veneta Fountain, Waldo Farnham, Myrtle Carter, Bessie Hickson and Jean Millican, the largest class on record.

Alberta worked at Log Cabin Inn at McKenzie Bridge, then at Foley Springs, later in Eugene for the Kor-I-Nor Candy Store. Darle established the very popular ice cream and sandwich stand in 1920.

In 1923, Alberta, visiting a cousin in Newport, Ore., met gillnet fisherman Henry Shermer. Married Aug. 2, 1924, in Eugene, they moved to the McKenzie to take over the business, as Darle had become owner of The Anchorage Cafe on the Millrace in Eugene, and later the popular Seymour's Cafe on Willamette Street.

The ice cream stand was located where EWEB was to start

construction on the power dam. The Shermers purchased land adjoining the trout hatchery from Mrs. Hendricks to build the Chateau in 1930 on the highway facing the lake front. The Chateau hosted many famous persons, including the production crew of the motion picture, "Abe Lincoln in Illinois," filmed in the area.

Alberta did all of the cooking. Shermer suffered an illness which made him an invalid. The place provided employment for many local girls, some housed in the Shermers' upstairs apartment. Among them were Rose, Rosalee and Roberta Fountain, Berniece and Dorothy Elston, Naomi Lansbery, Wynona Carter, Mae Wood, Margaret Montgomery, Clara Gravis, Mabel and Ellen Nestle and many others.

In 1946, the Shermers sold the restaurant to Ford Danner of Springfield, who operated under the name of McKenzie Chateau.

Alberta worked then at the trout hatchery, managed by Gene Goff and later his son, Bill. She and Henry moved to Eugene in 1953. Henry died in 1967. Alberta, born Aug. 7, 1898, in South Haven, Mich., died at age 95 on Feb. 8, 1994, at a Eugene care center. Darle retired in 1970.

The Chateau was closed in 1960. It burned Dec. 25, 1961, when no longer in operation -- "The passing of another McKenzie Landmark!" wrote the late Ruth Mills in Historic Leaburg (1987). This compiler was personally acquainted with the Shermers.

"Then we came to the famous Huckleberry Finn place, where the Baptist Church is now located just west of the old Finn house," wrote Lansbery. "Across the road was a cabin set back in the brush known as the Blazing Stump Blind Pig, owned by Herman Hartwig. Next was the Kapp Minney family where Albert's Lodge is now located."

COY LANSBERY

We have referred to the late Coy V. Lansbery, who came to Oregon in 1907 and settled in the Deerhorn-Leaburg area. His writings vividly portray life on the McKenzie after the turn of the century. Portions of his autobiography, completed in 1974 at age 88, appeared in Lane County Historian (Vol. XXVIII #3), reprinted in Historic Leaburg.

Born Aug. 29, 1885, he was the fourth son in a family of thirteen of William and Mary (Sankey) Lansbery. They lived on a 50-acre farm in Pennsylvania. His first recollections were when he was four years old and his father took him and the other boys to see the devastation of the Johnstown Flood.

On March 25, 1907, he and his brother, Bruce, left for Oregon. Their brother Ward had come west in 1904. Letters Ward wrote home about lots of work and good wages prompted them to make the trip. After a train ride of six days and nights from Clearfield, Pa., they arrived in Eugene March 31 and met Ward, who was working in a logging camp one mile east of Hendrick's Ferry. Four contractors were logging for Booth-Kelly in addition to the B-K camp.

"On April Fools Day we made the trip to the ferry by stage with Anson Potter, the only stage on the river at that time. It ran only from Eugene to Walterville, as the road was impassable in winter," he wrote. "All the natives on up the river would make a trip in the fall and lay in their winter supply and not go to town except by horseback in winter.

"We went to work where Ward was working. I started falling timber with Ward. Bruce was swamping road for the horse team, as most of the logging was done with horses and oxen then. We worked there until the job was finished about June 15," he said.

"Then Bruce and I went over to the Mohawk to see Rennie Koozer, his brother, Alfred, and uncle, George Shaw, and wife. They came west with Ward in 1904. They were working for Hammitt Bros. at Donna."

After a side trip by train to Newport, "Rennie and I took a contract falling and bucking for George Barnes, who was logging at Deerhorn back of where Dale Koozer now lives." Lansbery related an account of various logging jobs and hunting trips on the McKenzie.

"To begin with, I should say these were the horse and buggy days," he wrote. "The Bangs-McNutt Livery Stable in Eugene had the contract to carry the mail from Eugene to McKenzie Bridge and Foley Springs. They also had a stage line and ran freight and passengers, with a four-horse, three-seated coach both ways, six days a week, changing horses at Walterville, Vida and Blue River. The stages met at Vida for lunch, where Frank Minney and his wife ran a boarding house to accommodate the stage drivers and their passengers.

"And I may add the road was knee deep to a tall Indian in winter and dust in summer, even Main Street in Springfield, although Springfield was only four blocks wide and ten blocks long at that time. The only activity was a sawmill owned by Booth-Kelly Lumber Co. and a grist mill." (Springfield's streets were paved about 1910).

On March 14, 1911, he and Della Rossman were married in Eugene. They bought a house in Deerhorn. Their first child, Naomi Bernice, was born Dec. 23, 1911. A son Carroll William, was born Jan. 3, 1915.

Rennie Koozer married Ruby McNutt, daughter of John McNutt.

Lansbery told many accounts of logging, mostly for Booth-Kelly, working on the Walterville canal and hauling freight for Leaburg stores. After log drives on the McKenzie were closed down by the State Game Commission, Booth-Kelly shifted its logging to the Wendling area. He worked at different camps, sometimes hiking over the hill from Leaburg to camp sites. In 1919, they sold their house and moved into Eugene, where he clerked for Ax Billy's Department Store. His family didn't like town living. They returned to the McKenzie.

The Lansbery home burned in July 1932. They rebuilt. His wife died of heart trouble in 1961. He batched and began making wall plaques out of tin cans, which he sold, until 1968, when his eyesight began to fail. He sold his place and moved into Springfield near his daughter and her husband. For a pastime he began working on his family tree, going back to Pennsylvania to gather information. He celebrated his 90th birthday Aug. 29, 1975, and died March 30, 1979, at age 94.

This compiler has borrowed from Lansbery's writings as to places and names, most of which I can verify by my own personal knowledge from a lifelong association with Beautiful McKenzie.

CHAPTER 45

Gate Creek -- Vida

First settler of record in the Vida area was Nicholas Oliver, who in 1863, made his domicile on Gate Creek where Regis Pepiot located in 1868. Also in 1863, William Allen located across the river four miles east of Gate Creek on property acquired the following year by Thomas M. Martin. That property later became Thomson's Resort.

Fayette Thomson homesteaded in 1870 on what is now the Goodpasture farm on the south side of the river. The B. F. Finns came in 1871. A family named King was living and surveying in the area. Mrs. Thomson conducted school in her home. The first schoolhouse of record was the Blazing Stump School where Herman Hartwig later lived.

The Gate Creek Post Office was established Dec. 30, 1874, with Martin as postmaster. It was discontinued Sept. 30, 1880.

Regis Pepiot established the Gate Creek Ranch, hotel and stage stop, which he operated until his death Dec. 15, 1894.

The post office was reopened May 29, 1891, with Benjamin F. Finn, postmaster. The office, discontinued July 22, 1895, was again re-established Jan. 22, 1897. On Dec. 3, the name was changed to Ellston. The Ellston Post Office was later discontinued. (McArthur, 1982).

Reports show the post office was re-established April 12, 1898, under the name Vida, because the Gate Creek name was too similar to Gales Creek in Washington County. Postmaster Francis A. Pepiot selected Vida, the name of his oldest daughter.

Joanne (Joey) Garner, Vida postmaster until her announced retirement effective in January 1997, wrote in Historic Leaburg that subsequent Vida postmasters were: Herman F. Hartwig appointed March 23, 1900, and Charles Peek named on April 2, 1901.

The Minney Family

Benjamin Franklin "Ben" Minney (1861-1940), his wife, Rosa, (1863-1933) and son, John Franklin, moved to what became Vida in 1897. They purchased 30 acres of land and built a house on the hill above Gate Creek. Later they purchased the Gate Creek Ranch, hotel and stage stop from the Regis Pepiot heirs.

Frank Minney was superintendent for many years of the state Salmon Hatchery, on the south bank of Gate Creek. He started the hatchery on property he owned. The Oregon State Fish Commission took it over in 1902 as part of several such operations on the McKenzie designed to take fish eggs and sperm from adult spawning salmon. A flume ran from the creek above the pond to the hatching house

Frank married Mary Pearl Moore of Leaburg in 1905. Children

were: Arthur, born May 11, 1911, died July 30, 1986, at age 75; Harold; Gladys, died July 9, 1988; Thelma, born in 1917, and Shirley Jean, who lives in Tulsa, Okla. Thelma's first husband, Baker, died from multiple sclerosis. She is now married to Carrol Fountain. They live on Buck Point Road, two miles east of Walterville.

Frank and Pearl first lived in the hotel acquired from the Pepiots. The huge house he built on the property in 1907 became known as Minney Hall, the "Farm" or "Ranch." It served as a schoolhouse, resort and dance hall for many years, according to Mrs. Fountain. The place was a stage stop until 1913. The house stood as a landmark for 70 years until it was destroyed by fire Jan. 5, 1975.

"My granddad, Ben Minney, kept stage horses, and the stage from Eugene would change horses before proceeding on up to Belknap Springs," Mrs. Fountain said. "My dad built our home to take the overflow of tourists from the original hotel. The upstairs was the center of activity in our community. I can remember being told how people would come by wagon from miles around for the Saturday night dance. They would dance all night, have breakfast at the lodge then go home by light of day."

The late Art Minney, who worked at the fish hatchery, was quoted by Lisa Taylor in *Back Country Trader* as saying his grandfather and father, aided by family and friends "put together the hand-hewn timbers (for the barn in 1905-07). The walls and floor are mortised and pinned in the tradition of the true ax carpentry. . .Life at a stage coach stop was hard work for everyone.

"The women would get up at 5 a. m. to get the mid-day meal ready. And they wouldn't get to bed until 11 that night. It was two bits (25 cents) for a meal those days. I know those customers were fed good because I grew up on that food," Minney said.

At one time the McKenzie Highway passed right by the house. Stage coaches pulled into the nearby barn to change horses.

Another Attraction

Coy Lansbery said when he first came on the McKenzie in 1907 the store at Gate Creek was owned by a man named Clayton. Ben and Frank Minney owned a hotel, livery stable and dance hall. The place was very popular, as it was too far to go to Eugene for amusement.

"Another attraction at the Minney place was Huckleberry Finn, who lived a mile down the road," he said. "He used to visit the Minney place about noon and meet the stages when they stopped for lunch and spin some of his tall tales for which he was famous.

"I recall once I was going up the river on the stage, there was a stranger with us no one knew. Mr. Finn was sitting on the porch and while we waited for lunch he started to spin one of his yarns.

"He said he had been across the river and killed a four-point buck. After dressing it out and getting it on his back, on his way to the river, a forked horn jumped in front of him. He killed it, dressed it out, cut it up and stuffed the pieces in the four-point. At the river he had to wade. When he got across his hip boots were full of trout.

"About this time the stranger spoke up. 'Do you know who I am?' he asked. 'Don't know as I do,' said Finn. 'I'm the game warden,' said the stranger. 'Do you know who I am?' asked Finn. 'I'm the biggest damn liar on the McKenzie.'"

"When stage coaches were replaced with rubber tired vehicles, the dwindling stage coach stop business ended in 1913," said Art Minney. "It was quite a traumatic thing, I was told. The huge barn, designed for stage coaches and replacement horses, didn't stand empty. The Minneys remodeled the barn interior to accommodate dairy cows and of course the stage successor -- the automobile."

He said as many as 15 Booth-Kelly Lumber Co. workers, stationed at logging camps for the Wendling mill on the Mohawk drainage, stored their cars in the barn during the week. On weekends the men walked back over the mountain and reclaimed their cars for several days merrymaking in town. (Williams, 1991).

"I was born in the home in 1917," Thelma Fountain recalled. "By that time my family no longer operated the property as a hotel, after cars became commonplace. I can still remember people coming to the dance in our 'hall' upstairs, accessible by an outside stairway, as it was built with intent of becoming a community center.

"I can remember elections were held there. In the 1920's high school was held there for several years. The late Carey Thomson Jr., I remember having attended. After the addition was built onto the Vida school, the home was no longer needed for classes, but basketball was practiced in the hall. The floor was smaller than a regular court, but it offered a place to practice. Regular games were played in Thurston.

Lansbery said, in 1920, the old highway westbound went by the old red barn and stage stop, then over Gate Creek on a covered bridge. Next was an old, two-story building with F. E. Clayton, General Store, painted on the front. Clayton, confined to a wheel chair, lived on the second floor, accessed by a lift. He advertised for a wife. He was successful. They ran the store and post office for many years.

On a personal note, in the Teen years when this compiler was a pre-schooler, I had a Teddy Bear. Teddy went with me wherever I went. My mother, two sisters and I were on our way by stage from Walterville to visit Grandma Belknap. We stopped at the Clayton store. As we traveled on, I came to the realization I had left Teddy on the store porch. The next two weeks were fretful. Imagine my delight upon our return. There sat Teddy leaning against a store post, as big and strong as ever.

Road Supervisor

Ben Minney worked for many years as a Lane County Road supervisor and was well known in that capacity. From time to time he assisted at the fish hatchery, operated by his son.

He died Aug. 13, 1940. His wife, Rosa, died Feb. 5, 1933. Frank, preceded Ben in death Jan. 5, 1933. He was superintendent of the state salmon hatchery at the time.

Surviving Minneys sold the ranch to Richard Appling, who turned the run-down house and grounds into a showcase resort.

Appling renovated the house Frank Minney built in 1907, taking out the huge dance hall upstairs. Dancing was removed to the barn.

The Applings owned and operated the resort for 30 years. Their daughter, JoAnne (Appling) Larson, after her parents' deaths, sold the ranch to a group of businessmen who hoped to turn it into a house for mentally disturbed youths. When these plans failed to materialize the ranch was sold to Spencer Alpert of Eugene in 1974.

Before the renovation plans could be realized, the 70-year-old house burned to the ground Jan. 5, 1975, the anniversary of the date its builder, Frank Minney, died. The barn, built in 1905-07, still stands. Mrs. Larson repossessed the property. A portion of the barn was renovated as an office for her real estate business.

"It seems ironic the place should be destroyed by fire on the anniversary of my father's death, Jan. 5, 1933," commented Thelma Fountain. "We were still living in the home when he died. I have many fond memories of Vida and couldn't but feel heartsick when I was told by letter of our childhood home being destroyed."

JAMES KAPP MINNEY

Another Minney family at Vida was Ben's nephew, James Kapp Minney, son of Ben's sister. Kapp was born Jan. 19, 1872. His wife, Nettie Alice Kirk, was born Feb. 25, 1866, both in Urichsville, Ohio. They were married April 11, 1896. Their oldest daughter, Rose Anna, was born in Newport, Ohio, Feb. 13, 1899.

The Minneys brought their three sons and three daughters, Rose Anna, Lilly and Nettie, west from Newport, Ohio, arriving at the Stage Coach Hotel on Gate Creek at Vida Feb. 22, 1908. They first lived near the old Albert's Lodge, above Indian Creek, then moved into the Peter Finn home where the Baptist Church is now located.

They built a home where Leland and Betty Bloom now live. Kapp worked at the fish hatchery at Leaburg Dam. He died July 29, 1939. Mrs. Minney died May 27, 1947. Rose Minney married James Lee Fountain Dec. 26, 1919, in Eugene. They had daughters Rosalee and Roberta. Nettie Minney married Ennis Rennie of Thurston. She died in California.

Joanne (Joey) Garner reported the next postmaster after Clayton was Roy Payne, but no dates are found on his appointment or store ownership. The Post Office was located in Payne's store when purchased in 1937 by Weldon and Ruby Keller. Weldon was appointed postmaster that July. He built a new store behind the existing one in 1949 and was postmaster until his death Jan. 4, 1957.

Ruby Keller followed her husband as postmaster. She married Alvin Linquist in 1961. She sold the store, but two months after the sale the store and post office burned. Ruby erected a new building adjacent to the old store in 1961. She retired in 1972 and died Dec. 28, 1978.

Lois Dietz, Ruby's clerk, took over in 1972. She retired in 1978 and moved to Springfield. Joey Garner, daughter of Weldon and Ruby Keller, became postmaster April 7, 1979. In April 1996, she announced her retirement effective in February 1997. Buddy Crawford was appointed interim postmaster.

Hazelnut Production

Hazelnut production has become an important industry in Oregon. A goodly share of the volume is grown and harvested near Springfield and in the vicinity of Vida on the Goodpasture, Ennis and Elvin Nestle and Garry Rodakowski farms.

B. F. Goodpasture in 1924 purchased root stock from the Dorris ranch to start the first filbert orchard on the McKenzie near Vida. The Dorris Ranch is located south of Springfield along the east bank of the Willamette River just below the confluence of the Coast Fork.

Garry Rodakowski, owner of Rodakowski Farms, Vida, took over after the semi-retirement of his father who started the orchard about 1970. Garry grew up in Springfield, attended Thurston High School and Lane Community College. He has 60 acres of his own in filberts and another 155 under lease.

In the early days about 1907, three miles east of the Minneys' was Al Montgomery's home, built originally by Carey Thomson and now owned by the Nestle family. Across the highway was Thomson Lane leading down to the river ferry and on to Thomson's Resort. Carey and his sons were guides for hunters and fishermen.

Ben and Kay Dorris State Park

Ben and Kay Dorris State Park is located on the McKenzie Highway at mp. 29.1, about four miles east of Vida. The park land was donated to the state of Oregon July 7, 1942, by Ben and Klysta C. Dorris. A plaque within the park gives the date as 1943.

The park comprises 79 acres and offers an excellent view of Martin Rapids and the Rock House, located within the park boundaries. A public boat landing and 27 picnic sites are available.

Ben Dorris took over the Springfield ranch of his uncle, George Dorris, after the latter's death in 1935. He harvested filberts on the 250-acre parcel until about 1965. The Willamalane (Springfield) Park District which now owns the old Dorris Ranch is developing it as a "living history farm."

Returning to the early days, as described by Lansbery, a mile further east was Jimmy Redsides' homestead at the mouth of Martin Creek on the south side of the river. A bachelor, he was a cousin of Freeman Lansbery. The Tate place was just east of Bear Creek, and next were the Wycoff and Bare families, now known as Sheppard's Ranch.

In the 1930's, The Stockade was built at Finn Rock by the Millirons. The store went through several owners and alterations and became the Finn Rock Store. Most recent owners are Vaughn and Jill Clements, who took over Sept. 1, 1995. Both are originally from the Los Angeles area. Vaughn had worked for the U. S. Postal Service and Jill for the Children's Service Division. They were married after coming to Eugene and operated the Black Forest Tavern from 1986 to 1990. They plan to enlarge the building and offer new services, both indoor and outdoor. They said they want to become involved in the community. The store is near McKenzie High School.

Blue River

Sparks Ranch, a product of gold mining on Gold Hill, was half a mile west of Blue River. It was operated for many years by Dexter and Rosa Sparks. In the early days the Gruning family lived west of the bridge. Across the bridge into Blue River were two stores, a livery stable, hotel and a power plant that furnished electricity for the town and the Gold Hill mines. Next was the Scott. family, reported Lansbery.

Six miles east of Blue River across the McKenzie River was the Belknap Ranch, then the Sims place, where the Tokatee Golf Course is now located. On the south side of the river, east of the Belknaps on King Road was Andy King's homestead, then McKenzie Bridge. The O'Leary's store and livery stable had saddles and pack horses for hunters.

Log Cabin Inn, built originally by George Frissell in 1885, was under reconstruction following a destructive fire in 1906. The Frissells had turned the inn over to their step-daughter, Alice Croner, wife of Deputy Sheriff George Croner. The Croners had Belknap Springs leased and drove a two-seated, one-horse hack from the bridge to the springs each day to take care of the tourist trade.

Lansbery cut short a trip to Clear Lake, headwaters of the McKenzie, to join his cousin, Freeman Lansbery, in reconstructing the inn. The rustic building still stands today much as it was in 1907. The Lansberys also built a house for the Frissells.

Rosa Lane Sparks

The Inn was taken over in 1991 by new owners, Dave and Diane Rae, of Southern California

Foley Springs, four miles south of McKenzie Bridge on Horse Creek, was owned and operated by Ella Haflinger. Belknap Springs was seven miles east of McKenzie Bridge. The highway turned south one mile from the Springs, where the William Yale family later lived. It continued up White Branch and over the McKenzie Pass to Sisters.

Lansbery said, "In less than eight months I knew everyone from Walterville to Belknap Springs. They were the most friendly people, always had time to stop and visit, whether on horseback or in a wagon. They seemed like one big family, which they were, for I soon found they were almost all related in one way or another."

CHAPTER 46

Upper River -- Rainbow

The land lying immediately north across the McKenzie River from the homestead where James Belknap settled in 1869 is known today as Rainbow or Holiday Farm. John Whitlock and Dora (Belknap) Sims homesteaded up river in the mid-1870's.

Carey W. Thomson married Mary Isham in 1884. In 1885, they homesteaded on property opposite from where, in 1890, he built the Belknap Bridge to replace Belknap's ferry. About 1896, they moved down river and later established Thomson's Lodge.

John A. Isham (1845-?) and his wife, Catherine (1852-?), Mary's parents, were early-day settlers north of the Thomson homestead at Rainbow. The 1880 census listed five Isham children: Mary, Viola, Ira, Lorena and Stella. They attended the log schoolhouse adjoining the Sims property. John Isham was a justice of peace in 1890. In 1898, he and James Belknap were named by the Lane County Court as viewers of the McKenzie and Eastern Oregon road from Belknap Springs eastward. A viewer reviewed the purpose and feasibility of a project.

Isham Corral, where John Linn was murdered by Claude Branton and Courtney Green in 1898, was built by John and his son, Ira. It was 15 miles east of McKenzie Bridge and a mile down the mountain from Alder Springs. The Ishams apparently moved to Vida at a later date.

THE TROTTERS

Walden and Elva (Belknap) Trotter were married in 1904. Forest Service records show that, in 1908, Walden applied for homestead rights on property across the river from the Belknap Ranch.

Assistant District Forest Ranger Smith L. Taylor's report filed Oct. 31, 1910, on progress of improvement on the homestead prior to granting a patent, said Trotter had "two acres slashed but not burned. During the past year the claimant has built a woodshed and hen house, at present is getting out timber to build a large barn. The calaimant (sic) to my knolledge (sic) has resided on this land continuous for the last two years and is happy in the thought of making himself a home. He is a good citizen and rendered the Forest Service great aid in the past fire season."

About 1910, Walden built the large, two-story house, since remodeled and standing as Holiday Farm and Restaurant, at Rainbow. He was assisted by his brother-in-law, Richard Hileman, of Mabel, Ore. Bureau of Land Management records show a homestead patent for this property was granted in 1914. The house served as a stage stop until about 1917, when the Trotters separated and Elva moved to Eugene.

THE QUIMBYS AND RAINBOW

Lane County Courthouse records show Walden Trotter sold his property in 1922 to Lewis and Lyda Quimby, of Portland.

The Quimbys, frequent McKenzie visitors, were friends of Henry Westbrook, Portland attorney, and his wife, Lena, who bought the west 20 acres of the Belknap homestead about 1912. The Westbrooks and daughters, Gladys and Hyacinth (Honey), spent their summers there and were very much a part of the McKenzie scene.

Quimby built a store and restaurant on the river bank and established a post office July 1, 1924. The name Rainbow was selected at the suggestion of his wife, Lyda, because the McKenzie River is the home of the popular rainbow trout.

Lane County Planning Department records indicate several ponds, which served as a fish hatchery in days past, are located north of the house. This wasn't essentially a hatchery. Quimby put in these ponds by damming a stream, which ran through the back of the farm, and stocked them with Eastern brook trout. He specialized in trout dinners in his restaurant. Customers could catch the fish in the ponds themselves or could be supplied from a large fresh-water tank on the front porch of his store. Quimby netted the fish from the ponds and put them in the tank. A fish dinner cost $1.00 a pound, whether the diner caught the fish or was supplied from the tank.

As a teenager this writer, at Quimby's permission and request, used to fish in the ponds to help supply the fish tank. Some of the trout, up to 20 inches or more in length, were a menace to the smaller fish. My parents were living in the old Trotter house at the time. My father, Clifton L. Inman, built houses for Quimby in Rainbow's End Park. The Quimbys occupied the first house. My mother helped run their store.

INMAN BRIDGE

Inman Bridge, as shown on Metzger maps, was built about 1925 by Inman. It crosses the old meandered McKenzie River channel off McKenzie River Drive at Rainbow's End Park to a large island.

Floods over the years reshaped the river channel. Granddaddy of all floods occurred in 1861. A second major flood came in 1881. The river flows generally westerly through a well-defined channel, paralleling McKenzie River Drive (the old McKenzie Highway), to a point just below Rainbow. There it splits to form this large island and some smaller ones.

The old meandered channel at the time James Belknap settled in 1869 turned northerly on a more direct flow toward Crib Point. Over the years floods enlarged an old channel which cut through the westerly part of his homestead. Then it made a sweeping bend to the north, circling back to join the old channel at Crib Point, where Mill Creek empties into the McKenzie, and again flows westward. Only a small stream ran down the old meandered channel. In summer, it could be crossed easily by stepping from one rock to another.

For many years the bulk of the river followed this new channel. Ironically today, 130 years later, at least half of the river again flows through the old meandered channel. A massive flood in 1964 and another in 1977, have greatly altered the pattern.

In 1924, Clifton and Cora Inman purchased 18.5 acres of this island, a part of the original James Henry Belknap homestead, from James' widow, Ella Jane, and the Belknap estate. The northern portion was owned by the Boston-Oregon Timber Co. Inman acquired an easement from McKenzie River Drive across a narrow neck of land owned by Quimby and built the original bridge crossing the meandered stream. He cut a road and laid out 19 approximate acre-size lots

At the far west end of the property, the river again divided to form two small islands. One was sold to Chester Good, a Eugene garage owner, and the other to logger Dan Bowman. Other original purchasers were Bart Tate and Denzil Goddard, who worked in the area; Douglas and Dorothy Brown (Douglas was a Princeton University professor and Dorothy was Martha Belknap's twin sister); Louis Simpson, a Eugene car dealer, and Mrs. Cliff Cruzon, formerly Elva (Belknap) Trotter.

The Inmans retained the westerly three lots for their use.

DEARBORN ISLAND

The name Dearborn Island has been applied to the island Inman developed. Richard H. (Rick) and Julia Isabelle Dearborn were married in Eugene in 1903, the same year Clifton and Cora Inman were married. Dearborn was a professor of electrical engineering at Oregon Agricultural College, now Oregon State University, Corvallis. Mrs. Dearborn was the daughter of a Eugene doctor named Brown. They had daughters, Catherine and Isabelle.

The Dearborns acquired a long-term special use permit for a summer home on Forest Service land immediately east of Crib Point, bisected by Mill Creek, which empties into the McKenzie across the highway below Rainbow. They built a summer home and installed their own hydroelectric power plant by damming Mill Creek. Jerry Williams (1991) gives the time of the Dearborns' special use permit as from at least 1913 through Aug. 26, 1940. It was transferred to R. C. Taylor. Three years later it was transferred back to Mrs. Dearborn.

In the early 1930's, they purchased Dan Bowman's small island. About 1938 they bought the Inmans' three remaining lots.

The island today has about 15 families residing on it. At least one bridge has been built to replace the first bridge, and repairs have been required because of flood damage. Much of the old growth timber on the Island was cut and milled into lumber during the 1950's and 1960's.

HOLIDAY FARM

Holiday Farm and Restaurant today occupy the old Trotter place on McKenzie River Drive. The Rainbow post office was closed Aug. 31, 1937, with mail to Blue River, after Quimby sold to a man named Barrows. In the early 1940's the farm became the property of Bruce Forbes, Royal Forbes and Louis B. and Gertrude Forbes.

The Forbes had operated the original Holiday Farm, a mile east of Blue River on the McKenzie Highway. When the building on that property was destroyed by fire, the Forbes acquired the Quimby property and moved their Holiday Farm business there. They were joined by Isabelle Dearborn, who married Bruce Forbes May 8, 1943. Catherine Dearborn also had an interest in the resort.

The Forbes sold Holiday Farm in 1954 to Patrick C. and Vivienne Barnston Wright, current owners and operators of the resort. Court records show the Forbes filed notice of retirement from Holiday Farms Inc. Jan. 28, 1954. The Wrights filed articles of incorporation for the business June 11, 1954.

The Wrights remodeled the house, added a restaurant, bar and game room. Cottages are available for overnight accommodations.

CASCADE RESORT

One of the most ambitious private resort projects attempted on the upper McKenzie was Cascade Resort, located one and a half miles west of McKenzie Bridge on McKenzie River Drive.

It was built in the mid-1920's by Bart Sloan, who had managed Belknap Springs for several years, and Al Kuhn, and their wives. They built a restaurant and store, several cabins, a swimming pool, baseball diamond and other recreational facilities.

In the 1950's, the late Clarence Belknap and his son, Roy, took over the resort. They made several alterations, built the Patio Cafe and installed a trailer court. In the early 1960's the Patio, operated by Bob Rines, burned. Rines, who had the place six years, had just reopened following renovation. The Belknaps sold the property to Mr. and Mrs. Hal Boon of Eugene. A recreation vehicle park now occupies the site.

The Giddings

Charles and Lillian Mae Giddings, with children, Jaclyn and Charles, in October, 1936, moved from Los Angeles, Cal., to Oregon, which had been their dream for 20 years.

Married in Burbank, Cal., July 30, 1921, the Giddings discovered the McKenzie Valley on a vacation trip. They selected river frontage half a mile east of Rainbow at Belknap Bridge -- Carey Thomson's old homestead, occupied many years by Sandy Leach, packer and guide.

The Gidding's arrived on a cold, rainy day, fixed up an old deserted shack without lights or running water, but got by until they could build a house and include with it a store. They hired Forest Drury and his helper, Phil Begin, to do the carpentry work. Martha Belknap was their nearest neighbor and helped them become oriented.

They operated the store during the summer months, but there was little activity during the winter. They added a lunch counter, sold sandwiches, hamburgers, homemade pies and sometimes served meals to hungry, cold fishermen. They had four cabins, which they rented, wrote Mrs. Giddings in Historic Leaburg (March 1987).

The Giddings next moved to their Sun Ranch at Vida, purchased from the Ulla Brendells, where they and the Baldwins became pioneers as stockmen and tree farmers before moving to Springfield.

Charles Giddings died in 1964. Lillian, born Oct. 17, 1896, in Worthington, Minn., to Willis and Lillie Glass Guniston, died at Vida Dec. 19, 1995, at age 99. Survivors were daughter Jaclyn Giddings-Neilsen, and son Charles, both of Vida, and four grandchildren.

Jaclyn was graduated from McKenzie High School in 1942, and from Sacred Heart Hospital's School of Nursing in 1946. She was a registered nurse in the Air Force and as a civilian until she retired. She is now married to Robert Neilsen, a retired Navy man.

Jaclyn and Robert are both active in the Neighborhood Watch program, Jaclyn as an AARP Criminal Justice Services volunteer consultant, and Neilsen as an assistant AARP director. They are special deputies for the Lane County sheriff. At the Crime Prevention Association of Oregon conference in 1989 they received an award for their crime prevention service. They travel about 30,000 miles a year in connection with their work.

During the 1930's, Perry Williams and his wife operated a fox farm on land west of the old John Sims homestead. Joe Santelle, brother of Mrs. Williams, worked for them.

Phil's Phine Phoods

Phil's Phine Phoods, an historic landmark of more recent years on the upper McKenzie, was destroyed by fire of incendiary origin the night of June 26, 1993. Darin Harbick, manager and co-owner, who with his wife Kail and his parents, Dean and Margaret Harbick, had acquired the business two years earlier, estimated damage at $375,000.

The general store east of Rainbow, at 54879 McKenzie River Drive, was started as a restaurant in 1944 as a family affair by the late James and his wife Clara Phillips, and their two sons and their wives, Gene and Jeanne Beverly Phillips and Harold and Flossie Phillips. It evolved into a combination grocery store, hardware, lumber supplier and gift shop.

Clara Phillips was quoted in a *Eugene Register-Guard* news story, as saying the family had the restaurant until 1959, when "we got so busy, we decided we couldn't hack it any more. We turned it into a general store, and it just kind of grew and grew and grew." She said the business drew "a lot of highfalutin' people," including stripper Gypsy Rose Lee and movie star Clark Gable. "Herbert Hoover used to get his fishing license from us."

A large new metal frame building with four gas and diesel pumps was built along the McKenzie Highway at Mill Creek Road to replace the landmark structure. The expanded operation reopened for business in the summer of 1994 under the new name of Harbick's.

Jeanne Beverly Phillips died March 11, 1996, at age 75. Born Jan. 20, 1921, in Des Moines, Iowa, to Louis and Doris Sparks, she married Kenneth "Gene" Phillips in Eugene Aug. 26, 1949. She worked as a nurse and, for many years, with the family business, Phil's Phine Phoods. They moved to Springfield in 1991. Surviving were her husband; a son, Donald, Springfield; daughter, Peggy Osterbuhr, Blue River; three brothers and two grandchildren.

The Rustic Skillet Restaurant has been a welcome recent addition to the Rainbow community. The family-style restaurant, owned by Tom Siebers, specializes in home cooking. Siebers worked in the retail grocery trade from 1971 to 1990. Prior to his ownership the restaurant closed in the winter and didn't serve dinners. The nearby Tokatee Golf

Club was an economic influence in staying open year around and expanded hours. He has plans for expansion.

Nearby is the Sleepy Hollow Motel. A couple miles up the road toward McKenzie Bridge is the Tokatee Golf Course, built on a part of the old John and Dora Sims homestead. Developed by the Giustina family, it opened July 1, 1966, and has been rated by Golf Digest as one of America's top 25 public golf courses from 1984 through 1990.

The Drurys

"Maybe I would tell the truth, if I could remember what the hell it was."

That direct quote from Benjamin Franklin "Huck" Finn was recalled recently by James Drury of McKenzie Bridge. But that was a long time ago. James wasn't very old then. He was born in 1914. Finn died in 1919. "But," said James, better known as Jim, "I still remember the old man with his long white beard and white hair." Finn lived his last few years with his daughter, Ella Jane Belknap.

Jim Drury, age 82 at this writing, is one of the few life-long upper McKenzie residents. He is the sole survivor of the second generation Forest Drury family. With his wife, Mary Jane, he lives at McKenzie Bridge. Their son, Kenneth, lives on the King Road.

Forest Drury's father, William R. Drury, born in Adair County, Mo., March 12, 1851, came with his parents to Oregon with the Lost Wagon Train of 1853. They settled in Pleasant Hill. William Drury on March 11, 1876, married Margaret Riggs. She was born in Linn County Dec. 30, 1860. Children were William, Forest and Robert.

William's father was William B. Drury, born Oct. 11, 1811, in Norfolk County, Va. He was married in Macon County, Mo., in 1841 to Elizabeth Robinson, who was born in Amherst County, Va., in 1819. They settled on a farm in Pleasant Hill. William B. died Jan. 29, 1882.

Forest and his wife, Malva Buchanan Drury, in 1911, moved from Pleasant Hill to the McKenzie, settling on a homestead on the King Road, three miles up river from Belknap Bridge. With them were daughters, Veda, Eula and Wanda, all born at Pleasant Hill. Four sons, James, Robert, Max and Kenneth, were born after they moved to the McKenzie.

In the late 1920's, after the death of Ella Belknap (1924), the Drurys moved into Art Belknap's big house. Veda Drury married Art Clough, an artist and designer. They had five children. Eula Drury married Ross McClure. They had six children. Wanda Drury and her husband, Pat Brown, had two children, Fay and Forest.

Kenneth was killed in 1943 during World War II.

Max was shot and killed by a careless hunter in Alaska. He had two sons, both deceased. Veda, Eula and Wanda have also passed away.

Robert, born Sept. 20, 1918, in Goshen, attended McKenzie Bridge grade and Blue River High Schools. In 1936 he married Mary Hill. She died May 28, 1979. On Dec. 22, 1979, he married Vena Camelia Long-Moore in Reno, Nev. Robert died of a heart attack Dec. 10, 1994, at age 76. Survivors were his wife, Vena; married daughters, Marylan Uchytil of Santa Rosa, Cal., and Melva Donohoe of Blue River, two stepsons, John

Long of Springfield and Willis Long of Ely, Nev.; seven grandchildren and 10 great-grandchildren. Robert served in the U. S. Army in World War II. He operated his own logging company for many years.

The Drury homestead and property on King Road Jim and Robert acquired, including the McCann place, have been subdivided and sold.

Forest Drury worked many years for the Forest Service and later was assigned to the Civilian Conservation Corps when it was established at Camp Belknap, now the site of the McKenzie District ranger station. He engineered the first road from Belknap Springs to Clear Lake and the Santiam Highway. The road was graveled but not paved. A new highway, completed in 1965, now serves the area.

A recognized authority on places and names, James Drury worked for the U. S. Forest Service, beginning with the CCC in 1934, until retiring in 1970. After retiring, he became a member of the Lane County Electric Cooperative Board. He served until 1993, when he resigned. "I felt I had put in enough time," he commented.

During an interview in September 1991, Jim revealed many historical accounts of the McKenzie, some of which were told to him by Art Belknap, with whom he was associated from boyhood. Other knowledge he acquired from his years traveling trails and logging roads as a fire suppression officer with the McKenzie Ranger District.

BELKNAP COVERED BRIDGE was rebuilt in 1965 to replace the original bridge, erected in 1890, which was washed out by the flood of 1964. Arthur Belknap, Cora Belknap Inman and Mrs. Clarence (Martha) Belknap were at the dedication.

CHAPTER 47

South Fork -- McKenzie Bridge

For many years the Belknaps pretty well controlled access to the South Fork region. This famous fishing stream, now spanned by a massive dam which creates Cougar Reservoir, has its origin in the southern and western portions of the Three Sisters Wilderness. The river then enters a narrow and steep-walled canyon and follows along the base of towering Castle Rock, finally emptying into the McKenzie at river mile 59.7, two miles below Rainbow.

Early-day Indian trails led into the South Fork drainage from many directions. Later, trapper and hunting trails and, still later, Forest Service trails crisscrossed the area. Indians forded the McKenzie River about two miles east of Blue River, near a place for many years known as Redsides, into the South Fork bottoms.

The most logical entry into the South Fork country was through the Belknap Ranch across from Rainbow. James Belknap operated a ferry until 1889, when Carey Thomson built a toll bridge, half a mile upstream from the ferry points.

A crude road on the south side of the bridge forked. One fork ran easterly, known as the King Road, named for early settlers. The other fork ran west to the Belknap home, half a mile down river.

This road, followed the river, through a gate, then ran between the Belknap house and the river, through another gate into the barnyard. It turned south passed the barn and up a very steep hill to bench land. A trail continued on to the South Fork River. Later, an unimproved road was built three miles to the South Fork.

The Belknaps were not feudalistic, even though they had almost exclusive use of this vast timbered South Fork valley for hunting, fishing and trapping. Visitors were welcomed, so long as they closed the gates and did not cause property damage.

The drivers usually stopped to ask for directions or just to talk, then proceeded on to the barnyard. Sometimes it took several tries to reach the top. Art Belknap frequently towed cars up the hill with his team of horses when the road was slick from rains. Once on top the going was relatively easy, all the way to Strube camp.

This camp, just below the mouth of Cougar Creek, reportedly was named for Gustav Strube, who with his wife, Louise, came to Portland about 1865 and operated a butcher shop and slaughter house. He established a camp on the South Fork and his family came each summer from 1912-1915. In the early 1930's, the Forest Service built a shelter and other camp facilities there.

TERWILLIGER HOT SPRINGS

Terwilliger Hot Springs is located on Forest Service land on the ridge west of the South Fork of the McKenzie, on a tributary of Rider Creek, a quarter mile west of Cougar Reservoir. It is one of three hot, mineral springs on the upper McKenzie, along with Belknap and Foley. Terwilliger never was developed as a resort.

First used by Indians for ritual bathing, the springs was rediscovered in the late 1800's by Hiram (Hirem) Terwilliger, who came to the McKenzie to hunt with the Belknaps. Hiram Terwilliger (1840-1918), born in Vernon, Ohio, was the son of James and Sophronia Ann (Hurd) Terwilliger. The family was one of New York State's first settlers. His great-grandmother owned a large tract at the site of New York City.

James Terwilliger (1809-1892), Sophronia and five children headed for Oregon by wagon train in 1845. Sophronia died on the trip. James built the first house and established a blacksmith shop, the first business in Portland, in 1847. He then married Mrs. Palinda Green. They took a donation land claim in south Portland in 1850.

Hiram was five years old on the journey to Oregon. In 1862, he mined in Idaho but soon returned to Oregon and engaged in various business ventures. He married Mary Edwards in 1869. They had four children, James, Joseph, Charlotte and Virtue. (Joseph Gaston, *Portland: Its History and Building* 1911).

Willamette National Forest History files show that "on March 12, 1906, H. Terwilliger. . filed a lode claim to (the) well-known South Fork Springs, claiming to have a ledge of cinnabar. Rangers believe (the) claim is merely a subterfuge to service patent (title) to (the) hot springs for (a) summer resort." A 1912 Forest Service map of the old Cascade National Forest shows a Terwilliger mining claim was located at the springs. The claim was denied on the grounds the mineral claim was merely a ploy to open a resort like nearby Belknap and Foley Springs.

Larry Clemenson, a fire lookout on Indian Ridge, 1925-26, wrote, in 1972, that Smith Taylor knew about the springs and named them 'Terwilliger'."

In 1927, the Forest Service offered to let any qualified developer propose a sight development plan for the hot springs. The desired plan included a main hotel with lobby, dining room, kitchen and at least ten bedrooms; five cottages; a store with camp supplies; rest rooms for the general public, a concrete swimming pool; electric lighting plant; bridge; trail, and a public camp ground. From 1927-30, A. J. Jacobs, Dr. W. W. Elgin, R. C. Davis and A. C. Nelson of Terwilliger Hot Springs, Inc., held a Forest Service special use permit for a resort, near the springs, but it was not developed.

Art Clough, a designer and architect, who married Veda Drury, in the early 1930's showed this compiler an elaborate plan he had drafted for a resort in the picturesque, park-like area where Cougar Creek joined the South Fork River. Hot springs water would be piped in from Terwilliger. Depression years and a change in tourist travel and habits defeated any chance for development.

Trail access is located at mp. 7.5 on the Aufderheide Forest Drive (FR. 19). The trail follows Rider Creek about one-third mile. The springs, found a short distance north of the main creek, are comprised of three or four dammed pools of varying temperatures formed with lava rock. In recent years these springs though undeveloped have been very popular with counter-culturalists. Water pollution, trash and over use are major problems for managing the area by the Willamette National Forest. Their care was taken over by the Friends of the Springs Trust, a volunteer group formed in 1983, which works with the Forest Service. Terwilliger sometimes is referred to as Capra Hot Springs, Cougar Hot Springs, Rider Hot Springs or South Fork Hot Springs. (Williams, 1991).

The East Fork was another three miles upstream from Cougar. A Forest Service trail led up the East Fork to a "saddle" between Castle Rock and another mountain. At this saddle a trail branched off leading to the crest of Castle Rock. The main trail continued on, coming out onto the King Road, two miles east of Belknap Bridge.

JEFFRIES POINT

One of the more famous visitors to the South Fork was one-time heavyweight pugilistic champion James J. Jeffries. Art Belknap served as guide-packer for the Jeffries party of 10 into Rider Creek in 1906. Art is quoted as saying they were out 21 days and bagged 21 deer.

Jeffries Point, named for the boxer, is located along the east side of the South Fork 7.45 miles from the Belknap Bridge. Today the features remain submerged in Cougar Reservoir, except for the uppermost part, which is an island when the water is at full pool level. When the water is lowered during the fall and winter months all of the point are visible from Aufderheide Drive and may be viewed from the parking area of Terwilliger Hot Springs.

On Sept. 1, 1907, the *Oregon Journal* printed: "Champion James J. Jeffries and party from Los Angeles are expected to arrive in Eugene tomorrow and will leave Monday for the headwaters of the South Fork of the McKenzie in eastern Lane County, where they will spend three or four weeks hunting and fishing. Jeffries and a few friends were there last summer and were so struck with the excellence of the sport they decided to come again. C. P. Egnew, a noted chef, is already here and will cook for the party.

"The party will leave Eugene Monday morning in two large horse stages and expects to make the trip to their camping place on the South Fork in a day and a half. Already there has been sent to the camp a big wagon full of supplies weighing 3,000 pounds, and another supply will be sent up later. Six miles up the river from the camp a lodge will be established for the convenience of those who do not wish to return to camp while on their chase of bear and elk."

Jeffries, who won his championship from Robert Fitsimmons in 1899, remained undefeated until he came out of retirement to fight new champion Jack Johnson July 4, 1910, in Reno, Nev. Jeffries, who trained for his fight at his South Fork cabin, was knocked out in the twelfth round. Some Vida men, who went to Reno to witness the fight, later that summer visited his camp. They found one good reason why he didn't last long in the ring. The river was full of whiskey bottles used as targets during his training. (George L. Drake, forest Service retiree).

After Clarence Belknap built his sawmill on the bench land on the southern part of the Belknap homestead in 1923, he built a shorter access road to the mill from Belknap Bridge, eliminating the steep climb at the Belknap barn. This road was joined to the South Fork road south of the mill.

In the late 1920's, the Forest Service took up the road project with the intent of connecting it with the Willamette River drainage at Oakridge. By 1932 they had completed a crude roadway from Strube Camp to Dutch Oven Forest Camp, 16 miles up the South Fork.

The Civilian Conservation Corps (CCC), consisting of 211 men, which came into being in 1933 headquartered at Belknap Camp east of McKenzie Bridge, improved and finished the road by 1936. The completed roadway, referred to as the Box Canyon Road, a 55-mile forest drive, was renamed Aufderheide Forest Drive Sept. 10, 1982, to honor Robert Aufderheide (1909-1959).

Highly regarded, Aufderheide, a 1935 Oregon State University graduate in forestry, was employed by the USDA Forest Service as a forester on the Rogue River and Siuslaw National Forests and a forest supervisor on the Umpqua and Willamette National Forests. This writer, as a reporter for The News-Review at Roseburg, had the privilege of knowing Aufderheide while he was Umpqua National Forest supervisor headquartered at Roseburg in the mid-1950's. He died of cancer in 1959.

The road follows up the South Fork. About 12 miles out, at the upper end of Cougar Lake, was Hardy's Cabin. Eugene attorney Charles A. Hardy erected the log cabin about the turn of the century as a hunting and fishing lodge near the mouth of Hardy Creek. The cabin, creek and nearby Hardy Ridge were named for him. Hardy, born in Michigan in 1874 and a graduate of the University of Wisconsin in 1896, died in Portland Nov. 29, 1937. (McArthur's *Oregon Geographic Names*).

The road crosses the river at Frissell Crossing, mp. 21.8, where a bridge spans the river replacing an old ford, then continues on to its confluence with Roaring River. At this point the road follows uphill along Roaring River to the Box Canyon Guard Station, then downhill along the North Fork of the Willamette River to Oakridge.

The CCC built a number of roads, trails and campgrounds on the upper McKenzie, as well as fighting fires and other accomplishments.

At 3,808 feet elevation, Castle Rock, southwest of McKenzie Bridge and southeast of Rainbow, dominates the landscape. It was named for its resemblance to a fortress or castle as it overlooks much of the upper McKenzie and South Fork valleys. Several fire lookouts have occupied the mountain top since 1917. Among them, Manena (Sparks) Schwering spent two summers there during World War II. The lookout cabin was burned by vandals Oct. 31, 1974.

King Creek Road extends eastward from Belknap Bridge on the south side of the McKenzie River to Horse Creek Road. Martha Belknap said Mrs. Elizabeth King homesteaded in the area that became King Road in the 1880's. Andy and Rose King were her children. Rose later married into the Isham family. In 1910, Elizabeth King applied for a forest homestead (act of 1906) claim next to her son's property. She sold the claim to Charles Taylor.

Whereas King Road follows the hillside, the Delta Road built by the CCC follows the river and serves many summer homes built on leased Forest Service lands along the Horse Creek delta. However, two bridges washed out by the flood of 1964 were not replaced, so the road can be entered only at both ends.

Mysterious Death

Taylor Creek, which flows into Horse Creek near McKenzie Bridge, is named for the Charles Lincoln and Laura Wise Taylor family, who lived by the stream on the 160-acre homestead.

Taylor, born and reared on the Coquille River, as a young man, was lured to the northlands during the Klondike Gold Rush. He returned after twelve years to his mother and sisters, who had moved to Portland. To his surprise he met his old sweetheart, Laura May Wise. They were married at The Dalles about 1910, according to one-time District Forest Ranger Smith Taylor (no relation).

In the summer of 1910 the Taylors came up King Road from The Dalles, by way of the Deschutes River Valley and McKenzie Pass, with a team and covered wagon, containing all their possessions.

They bought Mrs. King's relinquishment rights and moved into a one-room log cabin on the property. District Ranger Taylor gave him work along with his team of horses on the road and putting out forest fires. A son, Jack (John) Edward, was born April 18, 1912. A daughter, Marion Elizabeth, was born Aug. 4, 1913.

In 1918, he sold his stock, team and wagon and went to Portland to work in the shipyards. He returned to the McKenzie in 1919. In July, while working as foreman of a road crew on the mountain side, he and Martin Clark, went to get "camp meat" (deer killed out of season).

Taylor did not come back. His body was found 14 days later with a deer on his back and a rifle bullet through his shoulder into his aorta. Clark was arrested, indicted and found guilty on trial of second degree murder, reduced to manslaughter on retrial. He served three years and died a few years later. No real motive was established for the killing. It was generally believed Clark sought Taylor's job as road foreman.

"That sad event ended our living up the McKenzie," wrote Marion (Taylor) Copping, the Taylor's daughter, in *Historic Leaburg* (1987). "It became necessary for my mother to teach in Lane County schools" to support her family. "Now I feel I have 'come home,' for I am located on Greenwood Drive on a beautiful bend of the river, which my family and I delight in calling Copping's Cove, east of Leaburg."

Mrs. Taylor's sister, Adeline, and her husband, Harry Hays, homesteaded the property in McKenzie Bridge where the Catholic Retreat and Church are now located. They ran the McKenzie Bridge store and post office many years. Harry also was a packer and guide.

After Harry's death, Mrs. Hays sold the store to the Willis Brewsters, who finally sold to Mario Lauers. After her husband's death Mrs. Lauers sold the store and post office but continued to live on the river and rented and maintained several cottages.

When the Blue McKenzie Turned White

A phenomenon peculiar to the McKenzie is no more.

For as long as I can remember -- almost eighty years and for centuries perhaps before that -- each morning during hot weather, the Blue McKenzie would turn from blue to white. How come?

High up on the slopes of the Middle Sister was a glacier, which fed a stream called White Branch. On hot days the glacier would slip just enough to disturb a white clay formation, causing the sediment to wash down the mountain side into White Branch.

This stream joins Lost Creek a short distance below where the latter gushes out of the ground at Lost Creek Ranch. Lost Creek drains Linton Lake via an underground conduit resulting from a lava flow that dammed the water forming the lake hundreds of years ago.

Lost Creek flows past Yale's Ranch and joins the McKenzie below Belknap Springs. The sediment washed down from the mountain side would turn the blue McKenzie white for a distance sometimes as far as Blue River. Other streams flowing into the McKenzie, like Horse Creek, the South Fork and Blue River, would dilute it sufficiently that it no longer appeared white.

The last few years changes in weather patterns have resulted in almost total disappearance of the glacier. In fact, White Branch sometimes now completely dries up in late summer. So the white clay formation is not disturbed.

Fishermen used to deplore the situation, saying the river was muddy and fishing poor. But it wasn't a dark brown, muddy color. It was white, and it was beautiful during the brief period when it happened. Perhaps some day the glacier will be restored and we can enjoy once again the phenomenon when the blue McKenzie turns white.

CHAPTER 48

Early-day Schools

In spite of the many hardships endured by pioneers who settled the vast empire of the west, schools were not overlooked.

Education was on the minds primarily of religious groups even before the great trek westward began. In 1834, Jason Lee with a small missionary party accompanied a trading expedition to the Pacific Coast. He established a mission school for Indian children near the present town of Salem. It was expanded, later was known as the Oregon Institute and eventually became Willamette University. A branch mission and a station were founded at The Dalles.

Although equally interested, the Catholic Church was a few years later in entering the Oregon mission field because of a lack of qualified priests. In 1838, Father Francis H. Blanchet and Father Modeste Demers journeyed across Canada to Ft. Vancouver and established a mission at St. Paul. Especially noted for his work among the Indians was Father P. J. DeSmet, known as the "Apostle of the Flatheads."

As settlements were established in the upper Willamette Valley, schools weren't far behind. Many were taught in private homes until public schools could be started.

Elijah Bristow donated land for a school, church and cemetery at Pleasant Hill. In 1850, he established Lane County's first school, District No. 1, in a log cabin. His son, William Wilshire, was the first teacher.

Eugene's first schools, called "select schools," were private. In 1850, Miss Sarah Ann Moore opened the first "select school" on a hill south of town in rattlesnake country. It flourished until a pupil was bitten by a rattlesnake in 1858. The first public school was built in 1856. Eugene became District No. 4, but select schools existed into the 1870's.

Columbia College, Eugene's first effort at higher education, closed after the first two buildings mysteriously burned and dissension arose when a third one was built. A move to establish a state university at Eugene was begun in 1872. The University of Oregon's first building, Deady Hall, was completed in 1875.

Camp Creek became District 5. A log cabin was built in 1854 on land donated by Joseph McLean in upper Camp Creek. The site, near the cemetery, later was occupied by the Presbyterian Church. In 1893, another school was built for lower Camp Creek District 70.

Springfield's first school was built in 1854 near the present-day Southern Pacific tracks at S. Seventh and B streets. Agnes Stewart, first teacher, lived with the Byron J. Pengras during the school term. Springfield became District 19.

John and Mary Cogswell lived briefly in Portland so their oldest daughter could attend school. In 1871, they moved back to the Thurston area. The children attended school in one of their father's tenant houses, taught by Emma Guthrie. He later built a one-room school.

Prior to 1865, a movement was started to establish a school at Walterville. Before that, children had to walk across the hill to the Camp Creek School. Martha Reasoner, age 16, was Walterville's first teacher. She boarded with friends and a year later married Frank Storment.

We have been unable to determine who were the children Martha taught, nor what happened to that first school, which was located where the late Clifford Crabtree lived (a mile west of the present town center). The official records of the district were burned in 1911.

Robert Millican Sr. is credited with building Walterville's first schoolhouse, consisting of upright planks and plank floor. He also built the desks and seats. The school became District 57.

In 1889, a new building was erected on land donated by George Millican. Miss Maggie Millican one of the early teachers, planted the maple trees east of the school. Sometime in the early 1900's, the building was enlarged to include a second room. Over the years the building was added to and enlarged again. It served until 1951, when the Walterville school was consolidated with adjoining districts. A new building was erected on a 10-acre site purchased from Dick Potter at Deerhorn. Classrooms have been added making it a 12-room school.

The first school for Deerhorn and Leaburg was built in 1870 on the Anderson Donation Land Claim, part of which was on the Emmit Rauch place, according to the late Mrs. Ethel Fountain. The schoolhouse, called the lower Leaburg school, was near the site where Dot's Cafe was destroyed by fire in 1983.

In 1884, a school was built where the Greenwood Cemetery is now located. (Edna Carter gave the date as 1887). Salinda Paxton, before her marriage to John Fountain, taught at this school, which was used until 1893, when a new school was built in Leaburg. Salinda lived with Jim and Emma Kennerly while teaching. The land for the Leaburg school (now the Leaburg Community Center) was donated by the Kennerlys.

Early teachers were Fannie Millican, Vernie Whetzell, Gertrude Dillon, Myrtle Stuart, Ina Millican, Maude Drury Rouse, Marie Horn, Alice Smith, Maggie Currie, Miss Meadows and Margaret Stuart.

In 1908, a two-story building was erected to house the high school upstairs and elementary grades downstairs. That building collapsed. It was torn down in 1923 by Elmer Pepiot, who used the lumber to build the house in which he and his wife, Lena, lived. She died in 1967 and he in 1970. The present school building replaced the former structure.

In 1948, Leaburg and Deerhorn schools were consolidated. In 1949, Leaburg District 126 consolidated with Springfield District 19.

First Vida School

At Vida, the Ben Finn children crossed the McKenzie in a boat with Fayette Thomson's children, joining the Pepiots to attend the first school, taught by Mrs. Thomson. The first schoolhouse was the Blazing

Stump School, built of logs in 1873 near Goodpasture Bridge, where a trailer court is now located, above McKenzie River Baptist Church.

The Nimrod school, located near the present Finn Rock Store, consisted of one room. However, this school was dismantled and moved to other locations on the McKenzie from time to time, depending on where the majority of children lived. The last teacher, Lucille Cook, lived at Sheppard's Ranch and drove a horse and buggy to and from school.

The first Blue River school was built in 1903. Alta Horne, 16, was first teacher. A high school was built in 1925.

Stories abound about various homes on the McKenzie which served as classrooms for children of their community. These included the John Sims home west of McKenzie Bridge, the Wycoff home, and the home built by Carey Thomson. The Frank Minney home at Vida was used as a high school and gym for several years.

The first upper McKenzie school was a small room built in 1885 of hewn logs on a land claim adjoining the John and Dora Sims place. Pupils were mostly Sims, Belknap, Isham and Thomson children.

The late Smith Taylor said Miss Evelyn Morgan was first teacher followed by Theo Roland, then Ora Babb, Minnie Evans and Anna Drury until 1902. After the O'Learys with eleven children moved into the district, the school was established in an unoccupied store at McKenzie Bridge. Mrs. Mike Cross and Nettie Cress, who became Mrs. Pennington, taught until 1904, when a one-room building was built on King Road, about one-half mile from its junction with the McKenzie Highway.

Later period teachers were Grace Brown, Haddy Stoyle, Will Brooks, Ann Jeske, Mrs. Beasely, March Dau, Martha (Andrews) Belknap, Gladys (Inman) Myers, Miss Beeson, Mr. and Mrs. Campbell, Florence Schults, Mr. Edwards, Beulah Thurman and Pat Steele.

A room was added in 1933 and children were bussed. The school in 1941 was consolidated with Vida and Blue River schools to form a combination grade and high school, District No. 68. A new building was constructed west of Blue River, about two miles east of Finn Rock. Students are bussed to the new McKenzie High School.

Around 1907 Alice Goff taught at a one-room schoolhouse on the Matt Emmerick place across the river east of Walterville. Twelve or thirteen children were of school age at that time.

MILLICAN MEMORIAL HALL

The George Millican Memorial Hall in Walterville was named for George, who donated the land and building for a school.

After the school closed due to consolidation, the Millican family -- Maggie and Walter -- donated the land to the Walterville Grange and the Welcome Rebekah Lodge on the condition it be maintained as a community center. The original old frame school house still serves the public, but is now the kitchen in the community hall.

Gerald Williams, in *McKenzie River Names*, 1989, quoting George Marx of Corvallis (whose father operated the Walterville Store for many years) wrote: "'I remember the huge maple trees, an enormous old tree we used to play under. I couldn't find the trees, but I found the stumps.'

"Marx can envision how things used to be when he attended the school in 1925: 'The location of a shed where the children used to play in foul weather, a familiar break in the fence behind the building, the nearby hills where we spent many happy hours hunting and fishing. It was heaven going to school there. A nine-year-old boy couldn't have asked for more,' he said.

"Lucile Hale (daughter of the late Lester and Ada Millican) has had an affinity with the building most of her life, both as a student (starting in 1921) and as a teacher years later. The experience of both attending and teaching in a two-room country school are memories she treasures. 'It was a good life. As a child you knew when the strawberries were ripe, because you walked to school every day. You became a lover of nature. The world has progressed so much, but it was a simpler life then,' she said." Her brother, Robert, and sister, Dorothy, also attended.

O'Brien Memorial Library

O'Brien Memorial Library is the name adopted in memory of Frances O'Brien who originated the Blue River library. She died Aug. 22, 1995. The library board in November that year changed the name in honor of Frances and her husband, Orel.

The saga of the library began in 1928. Mrs. O'Brien, who had taught school at Boulder Creek and Midland, near Klamath Falls, moved to the upper McKenzie and married Orel J. O'Brien. She became school district clerk and loaned books off her front porch.

River Reflections reported, "In the years to follow, O'Brien was ordering from fifty to one hundred different titles at a time from the state library system. By the 1950's, she let people know donations were welcome. The response was overwhelming. Soon books filled the nooks and crannies of her home, and space under her bed.

"Louis Elia, who owned the Forest Glen Restaurant, donated a three-room vacation cottage for use as a library. Other help came from Frank Wheeler, a logger, who built a foundation for a structure in O'Brien's back yard. Her husband, Orel, and Ron Doney helped move and renovate the old cottage. By 1971, it was ready for use by the public, with 3,700 books on the shelves."

"When construction of the South Fork and Blue River dams began in the 1950's, Frances kept the library open on a 24-hour-day basis. She ran it on the honor system -- allowing people to borrow books by simply signing them out and returning them whenever they wanted to."

Frances was the subject of national magazines write-ups. She was named citizen of the year for the McKenzie River in 1981, and Outstanding Volunteer for Lane County in 1984. The library was featured on Charles Kurault's television program "On the Road."

Because of vandalism, the building is no longer open at all hours, but the honor system remains. About 20 volunteers keep the doors open Monday through Saturday, as well as sorting and filing.

Leaburg Library

The first move to start a library at Leaburg came in 1972. When the Leaburg, Walterville, Thurston and Springfield schools were consolidated, the old school building at Leaburg was abandoned. The Leaburg-McKenzie Community Center was organized and the building leased from Springfield District 19.

The Community Center made extensive use of the building. The library was established and staffed by volunteers. It remained open for six years, then closed for lack of funds and volunteers.

However, volunteerism again made the Library possible. After much effort on the part of the late Ruth Mills and Rita Stadel, the library again became a reality Oct. 16, 1983.

Mrs. Mills and Mrs. Stadel scrubbed and cleaned the room, and Mrs. Stadel's husband built book shelves. In 1984, the McKenzie River Lions Club assumed maintenance of the building and responsibility for the electric bills. The Blue River Library, after which the Leaburg facility is patterned, donated some books. Today some 25 volunteers sort and catalogue more than 10,000 books. Volunteers staff the library Mondays through Fridays 1:30 to 4:30 p.m. with winter hours adjustment.

FIRST SCHOOL on the upper McKenzie River, Dist. 68, was conducted in a cabin built of hewn logs near the John and Dora Sims ranch. In photo taken about 1892 are, back row, Ervin Sims, Byrd Belknap, teacher Anna Drury, Ira Isham, Stella Isham; next row, Arthur Belknap, Alice Belknap, Dessie Bressler, Sadie Sims, Rena Isham, Laura Isham; front row, Theodoshia Isham, Effa Thomson, Robert Sims, Jessie Isham, Cora Belknap and Clara Belknap.

CHAPTER 49

Lumbering and Logging

The Oregon Country's first visitors were hunters, trappers and explorers. Early pioneers mostly were engaged in farming to support their families. They augmented their food supply with fish and wild game. Some sold pelts and supplied eating establishments with venison and fish as communities developed.

Elijah Bristow, Eugene Skinner and William Stevens were first to cut logs in Lane County to build cabins. However, the need for shelter in Oregon's rainy and often cold weather called for housing other than log cabins. Soon small lumber mills, mostly water-powered, came into existence. Harrison Stevens built a whip-saw, water-powered sawmill on the banks of the McKenzie near Coburg.

Springfield's first two mills, a grist and a sawmill, were erected by Isaac and Elias Briggs in 1853 and 1854 two blocks south of Main and Mill streets. A millrace the Briggs dug in 1852 supplied water power. None but the latest and most improved machinery of the time was used, at a cost of $10,000. The area became known as Millers' City.

Being close to the McKenzie River, which furnished both logs and waterpower, the Coburg community was the site of a sash sawmill, built by Jacob Spores and John Diamond in 1855. Felix Scott used a meander channel of the McKenzie River for a mill race to power a small sawmill near Hayden Bridge, also in 1855.

Spores and Diamond's sawmill was purchased in 1861 by Zack Pollard. Isaac VanDuyn bought Diamond's donation land claim and the sawmill from Pollard, but the mill was swept away by the massive flood of 1861-62. In 1865, the mill site was purchased by J. L. Brumley. A new mill was built with capacity of 15,000 board feet in 24 hours. In 1876, Brumley sold the mill to Horace Stone, who in turn sold to Hiram Smith. It was then sold to Coburg Milling.

Pengra Developer

In 1866, Byron J. Pengra, pioneer of 1853, moved to the site of present-day Springfield and, with partners Stratford and Underwood, bought the township. They developed flour mills and sawmills to promote the area. The old sawmill was torn down. The new one, considered the best in the county, operated two circular saws.

During the McKenzie and Mohawk rivers' log-drive period (1875-1912), large log booms extended into the McKenzie to catch the logs as they were floated down the river to Coburg. The upper limit of the log drives on the McKenzie was about two miles above Leaburg. Logging camps were established in the Leaburg and Deerhorn areas. Huge

Douglas fir and white fir trees, four to five feet in diameter, and other species were cut within 40 feet of the river and rolled into the water. Trees cut further up the mountain sides were flumed to the river and rafted downstream. Two trouble spots -- at Hayden Bridge and at Dutch Henry Rock -- were blasted in 1907.

Logs were diverted to the large sawmills near Coburg, including the J. C. Goodale and Booth-Kelly mills. Coburg probably was the leading sawmill city in the county until 1912, when river logging was ended by government authority.

Several small, two or three-man, sawmills operated along the river, like the mill of Charles Patterson near the McKenzie River ford at the mouth of Camp Creek. John Cogswell had a mill in the Thurston area. J. L Brumley built a sawmill in Eugene in 1875. B. F. Finn built a small mill at Vida in the 1880's and cut lumber for homes in the community.

Deerhorn Road had its beginning when W. H. Kanoff in 1886 petitioned Lane County for a road extending about five miles up from Hendricks Ferry along the south side of the river to John Bradley's barn. Kanoff and a cousin, who operated the Kanoff and Price sawmill, wanted the road for logging operations. In later years Booth-Kelly logged on the land, now owned by Weyerhaeuser.

During the late 1890's and early 1900's, Leaburg was known as "Jim Town," for James "Uncle Jim" and Emma "Aunt Emma" (Fountain) Kennerly, who owned the general store. Kennerly set up a portable sawmill in 1892 near the Frank Post place east of Walterville.

Felix Sparks' lumber mill at Blue River cut 500,000 board feet of lumber for the flume for mining operations on Gold Hill around 1900. He had nine men working full time to keep up with demand.

Booth-Kelly Lumber Co.

Booth-Kelly Lumber Co., by far the largest early-day employer on the McKenzie, had sawmills at Coburg, Springfield and Wendling and logging operations on the McKenzie and Mohawk drainages.

John Kelly, father of John F. and George H. Kelly, principals in B-K, came from Ireland to Canada at age nine years. In the early 1850's, he came to Oregon, went to Kansas, returning to Oregon in 1855. He packed supplies from Oregon City to the California gold mines for eight years. He and his wife, Elizabeth, each took up donation land claims in Douglas County. They moved to Springfield in 1866, then to Eugene around 1880. They had eight children. John died in 1910 and Elizabeth two years later.

Their oldest son, John F., one of the first students to enroll at the University of Oregon, attended one year, went to work at the Customs House in Portland, then entered the railway mail service as a mail clerk for four years. He went to southern Oregon and worked with H. X. Miller as railroad contractors, building tunnels between Roseburg and Grants Pass for the Oregon and California Railroad.

John bought a large timber tract around Grants Pass and established Sugar Pine Door and Lumber Co. sawmill. Eight years later he sold out and moved to Lane County to become an organizer of the Booth-Kelly Lumber Co. In 1905 he married Ida L. Patterson, who had two children by a previous marriage. John and Ida had four children. He sold his interest in B-K in 1913 and retired to Eugene. (Robert C. Clark, *History of The Willamette Valley*, Vol. 2, 1927).

The Booth-Kelly Lumber Co. was owned and operated by brothers Robert A. and Henry Booth, and brothers John F. and George Kelly. John Kelly was president; Robert Booth, vice president; George Kelly, secretary, and Henry Booth, treasurer.

H. J. Cox, who worked in the company office, described Robert Booth as "a stern man, a staunch Methodist and a foe of demon rum."

Booth-Kelly did extensive logging on the McKenzie, floating logs down river to Coburg. A logging camp across the river accessed by ferry was established in the late 1800's at Leaburg. The camp, called "Donkeyville" with about 50 families, was so named because it had the first donkey engine on the river.

Buys Timber Land

In 1898-99, B-K purchased 40,000 acres of O&C timber land in the Mohawk River drainage from the Southern Pacific Railroad Co., which had purchased it from the Oregon-California Railroad. This acquisition may have been of dubious legality, but it revolutionized the lumber industry in the upper Willamette Valley. The company also had timber land and a mill at Saginaw on the Coast Fork, north of Cottage Grove.

Because the Mohawk area was practically inaccessible, Booth-Kelly proposed that Southern Pacific build a branch line from Eugene to Isabel (now Marcola), B-K to supply right of way, furnish ties and provide 2,500 cars of freight annually beginning Sept. 4, 1899.

Wendling, a company logging town in the upper Mohawk Valley east of Marcola, was built in the late 1880's by Mr. Jordan and Mr. Holcomb, who sold to Mr. Whitbeck and Mr. Sterns. They sold to George X. Wendling, for whom the town was named, and Mr. Johnson. Booth-Kelly bought the logging operation and town in 1896.

The Wendling post office was established Dec. 20, 1899, with George Kelly as postmaster. By 1910, Wendling was at its peak with some 900 people. B-K built the 80-room hotel-boarding house, the bunk house, two churches, bakery, general store and post office, the homes and even the plank road and sidewalk. On Aug. 24, 1910, a forest fire, starting five miles to the east, destroyed everything except the sawmill and some houses. The town was rebuilt.

Booth-Kelly moved its logging camp down river from Leaburg across from Deerhorn about 1905. This camp, known as Deerhorn Camp or Kelly Camp, was a mile back from the river with a mile of log running shute. Logs were driven down river to B-K's mill at Coburg. The camp operated until 1912, when the fish and game commission stopped log drives on the McKenzie. The donkey engines were brought down the river, dismantled and hauled to Wendling on wagons.

Men from the McKenzie walked over the hills to logging camps in the Mohawk drainage that served the Wendling and Springfield mills. Booth-Kelly operations at Springfield and Wendling closed for about three years during the depression of the 1930's, then were reopened.

Long after the founders divested themselves of their ownerships, the Booth-Kelly name continued to play an important part in Springfield and vicinity for a half century.

Wendling survived until the mill burned Sept. 29, 1946. The post office was closed Dec. 22, 1952. The town, sold to Georgia-Pacific, is now owned by Weyerhaeuser. The last remaining building was sold in 1955, and the town remains today only a memory. The Springfield mill was purchased in 1959 by Georgia Pacific which expanded the operation.

Several small sawmills flourished on the McKenzie. Tom Willian and his son, George, owned and operated sawmills around Walterville, Cedar Flat and Camp Creek, starting around 1900 for many years.

Clifton L. Inman, bought the Willian mill and moved it onto the hillside north of Walterville about 1907, then sold it back to the Willians. The mill ownership passed through other hands, including Lester Millican. This was the first of two mills Inman operated at Walterville. He and Ray Chase of Camp Creek built another mill about 1920 at Walterville then moved it to the Seavey ranch north of Springfield.

The Willians continued in the sawmill business in the Camp Creek and Mohawk areas for many years. Melvin Douglas Zabrinskie, who lives on Millican Road, Walterville, later bought the mill. He had worked for the Willians prior to his purchase.

Clarence Belknap's McKenzie Lumber Co., located on the old Belknap homestead, was the major operation on the upper McKenzie during the 1920's, 30's and 40's. Other small mills operated on the Willamette, McKenzie, Mohawk and Camp Creek areas. William "Bill" Yale had a portable sawmill at McKenzie Bridge.

The coming of Rosboro Lumber Co. to Springfield from Arkansas in 1939 and the Springfield Plywood plant in 1940, later taken over by Georgia-Pacific in 1959, marked the beginning of a greatly expanded logging, lumbering and plywood era in the McKenzie valley. Logging camp sites were built at Vida and Finn Rock. After World War II, most logs were trucked to valley mills. The industry with Oregon's vast supply of Douglas-fir trees and other species grew over the years to rival agriculture as the state's principal industry.

The story of the lumberjack is legend -- sawing, cutting, felling trees, limbing and bucking logs, tree climbing, topping to provide spar poles, use of springboards and, in recent years, the chainsaw. In the past, mills were built close to the tree supply, logs were yarded by horses or rolled down hillsides, then came donkey engines, low lead and high lead logging. Today, with heavy loading equipment, it is easier to truck logs to valley mills than to take the mills to the trees.

However, restrictions resulting from recent environmental controversies over the effects of logging on endangered species, has greatly curtailed the timber supply from government lands. The industry is slowly giving way to tourism and electronic installations as dominant factors in the state's economy.

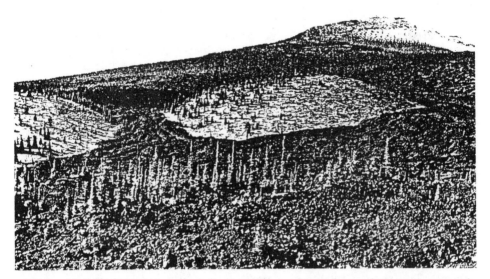

BELKNAP CRATER, seen from Dee Wright observatory, is impressive in stature, but is only a pile of cinders on the summit of a vast shield of recent lava. Forests in background grow upon old Belknap lava. Trees in foreground stand upon young lava from Yapoah Cone. Lava of intermediate age and position surrounds "islands" and issued from a subsidiary vent, Little Belknap. (Oregon Highway Department photo).

CHAPTER 50

Belknap Crater

"Belknap Crater, one of the important features of the Cascade Range, lies just north of the McKenzie Pass on the Deschutes and Linn counties' line. The crater and its enormous lava fields are easily seen from the McKenzie Highway and produce a spectacle that is awe inspiring to say the least. The crater has an elevation of 6,877 feet," reports Lewis McArthur in *Oregon Geographic Names*, 1984.

"It was named for James Henry Belknap, an early McKenzie River resident and son of Rollin Simeon Belknap, who developed Belknap Springs. James had an interest in the toll road that was built over the McKenzie Pass in the early 1870's." Arriving on the upper McKenzie from Southern Oregon in 1869, at age 21, he roamed over the mountains and valleys of the upper McKenzie and South Fork in search of game and fur-bearing animals to support a large family.

Belknap Crater lies northwest of the Dee Wright Observatory near the summit of the McKenzie Pass. The crater is a large cone remaining from a shield volcano, formed from overlapping flows of molten lava that erupt from a center hole, along with cinders, ash and lava bombs.

Professor Edwin T. Hodge (1925: 51) wrote, "The top of the mountain shows three distinct craters, all in a row, with the largest to the west." The estimated age of Belknap Crater is less than 3,000 years old. (Williams, 1991).

Little Belknap is a volcanic crater located near the crest of the Cascade Range, just northwest of the McKenzie Pass. It lies slightly east of Belknap Crater at an elevation of 6,305 feet.

Dr. Hodge wrote: ". . .no visitor to this region should fail to climb to the top of Little Belknap and see for himself the stalactites, the splatter cones and conduits through which the lava poured and other details of the marvelous crater. . .the effect of all (the violent volcanic action) was to flood all the previous valleys and bury them deep beneath a mantle of volcanic rock."

An extensive lava cave system adjoins the Crater.

Craig Skinner (*The Speleograph*, 1979: 109 Vol. 15, No. 9) wrote: "The Little Belknap system consists of a series of collapsed and intact sections of a single lava tube beginning just east of the Little Belknap summit. The system begins as a vertical conduit and lava tube complex and ends several hundred feet downslope, as the system, entirely collapsed at this point, is assimilated into other contemporary flow features."

The unique cave system is comprised of the following, as defined by Skinner.

LITTLE BELKNAP #1 is a locally named lava tube cave segment just east of the summit of Little Belknap. "This cave is without question the most interesting of the system. . .The entrance to the upper level is large and prominent and the well-worn floor attests to many visitors over the years. The short main passage of the upper level appears to be a continuation of a vertical conduit. It is partially roofed with splatter and is well ventilated by one large and one small skylight. Belknap Crater is fully framed in the west-facing entrance. . .A small sized tube dips sharply to the northeast and ends after about 45 feet in a lava seal. We named this the toilet tube because of the service it has provided for many trail weary hikers."

LITTLE BELKNAP #2 is a locally named lava tube cave segment just east of the summit of Little Belknap. About 100 feet downslope from the #1 cave is the upper entrance to Little Belknap #2. Only about 49 feet long, the floor is extensively covered with lava debris, though the lining is largely intact.

THE AMAZING COLOSSAL PIT is a local name for a lava cave part of and just east of the Little Belknap cave system. "This was named not for its cavernous and abysmal depths, but for its surprise value. The 24-foot pit is a most unexpected find and with a little imagination (especially for hikers who have no way of exploring it) it could be the beginning of a passage to wherever the imagination might take it. The pit, actually a vertical lava conduit, has a smooth lining and widens into a bell shape as it goes down. The pit absolutely requires a rope to negotiate. The overhang and smooth lining precludes any other method."

LOWER LEVEL is a locally named lava tube just east of the summit of Little Belknap. The Lower Level refers to the bottom pit segment of the Amazing Colossal Pit, one of several lava tube segments in the immediate area. "The room at the bottom of the pit is roughly triangular and contains snow throughout the year. The chamber also contains one of the more unusual lava features that I have run across in a lava cave -- a rope-like (spiral) lava cylinder nearly a yard in diameter." There are several turns and passages in the lower level.

COLLAPSED SEGMENTS is the local name for part of a single lava tube on the east slope of Little Belknap near the summit. "The collapsed segments of this system are easily distinguished as a prominent lava trench paralleling the trail that leads to the summit of Little Belknap and to the entrance to the main cave."

LOWER CAVES are locally named segments of the lava caves just east of the summit of Little Belknap. "There are several very short (less than 20 feet) segments downslope from the (Little Belknap) #1 and #2 caves. Typically these are low and mostly filled with breakdown and debris. The last intact segment occurs near the junction of the Oregon Skyline Trail (Pacific Crest National Scenic) with turn off to Little Belknap."

CLIMB TO BELKNAP CRATER

Climbing Belknap Crater has been one of this writer's life-long memories. Inman family members and friends, about eight in all, made the climb to the top of Belknap in 1926 -- the year after the highway over the McKenzie Pass was completed.

Our family was living that summer on The Island at Rainbow while my father worked in Clarence Belknap's sawmill. My older sister, Gladys, had invited teacher friends, Eva Phetteplace and her sister, Verna Luther of Thurston, sisters of Eugene doctor Carl Phetteplace, as guests. Grant Tate, a Forest Service fire patrolman, and logger Dan Bowman volunteered to serve as guides. Our party included my mother, Cora Edith, and sister, Violet.

There was no trail to Belknap Crater. It meant a 10 to 12-mile round-trip across the massive McKenzie Pass lava beds, which poured out of the crater some 3,000 years ago. We had heard tales of how the sharp lava could cut shoes to pieces, and a fall could be very bad indeed.

On Sunday we arose early and by daybreak were on mile-high McKenzie Pass, ready to begin our hike before the sun got too hot.

Belknap to the north, just over the Lane County line, is clearly visible from the McKenzie Pass. As we got out of our cars and stood viewing the sunlit peak off in the distance, we began to have misgivings. Walking across that massive lava flow, grim and foreboding, seemed a formidable task. But with firm resolve we determined not to give up.

Tate and Bowman surveyed what appeared to be the best route, across a river of lava to an island where lava had flowed around the elevated area, then across to a second island. This we negotiated. Then we were on our own to cross over the sharp and often treacherous lava beds any way possible. We couldn't get lost. Clearly visible surrounding mountains were ample guides.

We plodded along over steep lava flows, picking the easiest route. The trip was an arduous one. A false step on the unstable lava could prove disastrous.

At last we came to a cinder bed at the base of the crater. Up to that point there had been only moderate uphill climbing, but at the south side of the crater base it appeared straight up several hundred feet. We started our climb. Each step we mired almost to our knees in cinder ash. We moved cautiously, lest we slip back down to sharp lava below. We could see the summit. But when we reached the ridge, much to our surprise, we looked down into the crater depths.

The crater was awesome. The multiple colors of various rock formations, with the sun shining on them was a spectacle to behold. I was never good at estimating heights or depths, but my memory of almost seventy years ago is that the crater was about five hundred feet deep and a quarter mile across. The crater had partially filled from land slides. There was no water nor snow inside.

We climbed to the peak of the cinder-ash covered mountain. At the summit we felt like kings of all we surveyed.

We looked back to the south across the rugged lava beds to the ribbon of graveled highway over the McKenzie Pass, from whence we had come. Beyond were the Three Sisters complex of mountains, and Diamond Peak in the distance.

To the north Mt. Washington seemed but a stones throw away, then Three Fingered Jack, Mt. Jefferson and Mt. Hood. To the east was the Deschutes River Valley, and much further on was the High Desert of Central Oregon. We could look down into Little Belknap Crater directly to the east. Off to the north side of Little Belknap were too tiny craters like dimples. They appeared to have spouted ash only.

Few people had climbed Belknap Crater prior to that date, because of its inaccessibility and difficult climb across the lava beds. As evidence others had been there, a piece of paper under some rocks listed several names, so we added ours to it.

After eating our lunches, we began the long and tortuous hike back to the highway. We descended the east and longest slope. We made it without mishap, then launched out across the lava again. Though tired, we felt rewarded by our journey. The biggest problem was Mother's shoes were cut to ribbons by the sharp lava. She had to wrap her feet with every piece of cloth we could pungle up.

Today a well-defined trail, part of the Pacific Crest National Scenic Trail, makes a climb to Belknap Crater a relatively easy task.

DEE WRIGHT OBSERVATORY

Dee Wright Observatory was named in honor of Dee Wright, a U. S. Forest Service packer and later a Civilian Conservation Corps foreman. The monument is located near the summit of the McKenzie Pass.

Dee Wright's grandfather crossed the plains in 1844 and his grandmother in 1843. His father, Joseph, was born in 1847. Dee Wright, born in a log cabin north of Liberal, near Molalla in Oregon, was raised among the Molalla Indians.

"Until he went to school he could only talk Chinook and Scotch. He couldn't talk English, but he could talk Chinook, could jabber with the Indians like nobody's business," reported Ray Engles (1978).

He spent 24 years as a packer, trail foreman and construction supervisor. He knew the McKenzie and Three Sisters area. He helped locate and build sections of the Skyline Trail. He worked as foreman of the CCC crew which built the observatory at the summit of the McKenzie Pass. He died in 1934 before the work was completed. It was named the Dee Wright Observatory. As he had requested, his ashes were scattered across the summit of the Cascades.

Leaburg's Volcano

Leaburg has its own volcano, dating back to the Miocene age. Nearby Mt. Nebo, jutting 3,400 feet above sea level "is a dramatic reminder of a long-gone mid-McKenzie Volcano," to quote from *River Reflections* Sept. 28, 1984, reprinted in *Historic Leaburg.*

Some geologists believe the mountain may have approached Mt. Hood in size. Mt. Nebo is a granite formation left standing as water eroded surrounding material over the last 15 million years, according to Dr. Alexander McBirney of the University of Oregon Geology Department.

Volcanologists studying the Leaburg area have found other indications of a very large volcano near the community center. Rock formations are visible near Leaburg Dam and Goodpasture Bridge, where pale yellow or buff colored granite has been exposed, indicating molten intrusions very close to the surface, McBirney said.

Further inspection reveals tilting of the formations outward from the Leaburg-centered volcano's core. Current estimates are the volcano was active about fifteen million years ago over a million-year period. In the ensuing eons, rivers and rain have gradually removed softer material to reveal Mt. Nebo.

CHAPTER 51

Indians on the McKenzie

The history of Oregon Indians is too complex to delve into here. A bit on their movements may give a better understanding of their influence on early-day explorers and settlers in Lane County. Nothing reported here should be construed as racist in any sense but only to relate incidents that occurred.

Indians traveled around the state extensively in search of food or for pow wows and religious get-togethers. There was a certain amount of warring activity. The principal Oregon Indian tribes were the Chinook, Clatsop, Cree, Grand Ronde, Kalapuya, Klamath, Lower Chinook, Mohawk, Molalla, Nez Perce, Paiute, Rogue River (Takelma), Santiam Band, Warm Springs, Umpquas, Cow Creeks and the Snakes. Their trails often were followed by early-day explorers.

White settlers had some problems with the Indians and brief and bloody wars were fought -- the Modoc war in the Klamath Basin, the Rogue Indian War of 1855-56 and some skirmishes east of the Cascades. After that many Indians were placed on reservations. Willamette Valley tribes in general were friendly, even if minor problems often resulting from lack of understanding did arise.

Before the days of the Hudson Bay Co. ended in the upper valley, one of their hunters, an Englishman, named Spencer, lost his scalp to Indians on the butte south of Eugene which bears his name.

Eugene Skinner, his wife and baby were threatened one night by Chief Tyee Tom, resentful of palefaces in the cabin by Ya-po-ah. The sun was high before Chief Tom, admitted killer of Spencer, and the Old Settler smoked the pipe of peace.

Up on his "pleasant hill" Elijah Bristow fought and won two small wars, over stolen stock by brandishing anything at hand, from linchpin to rifle.

William Stevens reported there was a good-sized Indian settlement near the McKenzie north of Eugene. While not unfriendly, they often were a nuisance by being ever present and taking whatever was attractive. However, when he arrived Christmas day, 1847, with sons Alvin and Isaac and daughter, Sarah Jane, 13, three friendly Indians plunged into the deep, cold water and steadied the covered wagon drawn by oxen as they crossed the McKenzie River.

Jacob Spores of Coburg led a posse to trace down a band of Indians who had stolen his horses. He discovered a beautiful valley he named Mohawk because of its similarity to the Mohawk he had known in New

York. Further pursuing, the posse overtook the Indians, camped along a creek today known as Camp Creek. He retrieved his horses.

A party of seven men exploring a new route from Eastern Oregon into the Willamette Valley in 1852 were attacked east of the Bend area. John Diamond, J. Clark and William Macy were wounded. The others held off the Indians until they reached the Oregon Trail.

During the Rogue Indian War of 1856, a party was cut off in southern Lane County during a skirmish with the Indians, who stole their horses. After much hardship John T. Craig walked out. George Millican, John Latta and Walker Young went to their aid.

Felix Scott Sr., increasingly concerned over the possibility of Indian raids in the mid-1850's, was appointed a sub-agent of Indian Affairs for Southern Oregon. Scott, himself, and members of his party were killed by Indians in 1858 in northern California while bringing livestock to Oregon. The stock was scattered.

Indians turned back members of the McBride Party seeking the lost Blue Bucket Mine in Central Oregon. Robert Millican reported several skirmishes with Indians in Eastern Oregon about 1860.

Warm Springs Indians

The Warm Springs Indians made frequent forays into the McKenzie River Valley in the summer and fall to hunt, pick huckleberries and to fish, primarily for salmon, which they smoked or dried. In later years they came to pick hops around Walterville.

J. H. McClung, writing about a trip up the McKenzie in August, 1860, said the party followed an old Indian trail. He mentioned an Indian crossing of the McKenzie east of Blue River. Just before reaching the big prairie, known as Strawberry Prairie, later McKenzie Bridge, they found the prairie full of ponies. The men were hunting, the squaws drying meat. An old Indian handed them a paper which said, "These are good Indians," signed by the agent of Warm Springs.

Felix Scott Jr., on his historic trip over the high Cascades in 1862 with 900 head of cattle to supply gold miners in Idaho, traveled the main Indian trail over the mountain.

John Cogswell and John Diamond, traveling horse-back over the McKenzie Pass, became lost and wandered into an Indian camp. An old woman helped them off their horses and fed them stew made with meat, wild roots and vegetables, seasoned with wild onions.

Many problems, beside the rugged topography and changing weather, sometimes faced immigrants crossing the McKenzie Pass. The famous American poet Cincinnatus H. "Joaquin" Miller and wife were ambushed on the pass in 1864, en route to Canyon City.

Indians a Problem

James Belknap, in a 1905 letter to Franklin Belknap in Chicago, wrote, "When we came here (1869) the Indians were very bad." While the Indians may have posed problems by interference, curiosity and thieving, they did not appear threatening.

The late Manena Schwering of Blue River, wrote: "The first route across the McKenzie Pass was one used by the Warm Springs Indians in annual migrations to the McKenzie Valley. They came to hunt, pick huckleberries, take salmon for smoking and (in later years) to pick hops. The Hendricks Park location was their favorite camping spot. The salmon were plentiful there and they smoked quantities to use during the winter.

"The writer," she wrote, "can recall seeing them come in large bands of fifty to seventy-five prior to 1920. In later years they came, but in reduced numbers. I can remember them coming to the door and asking my father: 'You got any deer hides?'

"They sometimes asked for pasture for their stock and permission to camp overnight in a field. They sold beaded moccasins, gloves and other small buckskin items. My grandmother recalls an Indian man once came to the kitchen door looking for food. She gave him a freshly baked loaf of bread, she'd just taken from the oven. He picked it up, squeezed it into a small soggy ball, laid it down and said disgustedly, 'Bogus---no good,' and walked away.

"The Indians we saw were unfailingly friendly and polite. They traveled in a variety of vehicles -- covered wagons buckboards, buggies and saddle horses. Large numbers of extra saddle horses were driven by men and boys on horseback. Children were included, both riding and walking. Large numbers of lean, mongrel dogs dashed madly about, snarling and barking in the confusion. The women wore long, bright-colored cotton dresses. Both men and women usually wore their hair in braids and used bright blankets as shawls to wrap around themselves."

Indians Passing Through

Martha Belknap commented in *Seasons of Harvest*: "Oh, yes, they (Indians) were going up on Indian Ridge to pick huckleberries and down to Hendricks Bridge to dry salmon and pick hops. . .the Warm Springs tribe. They'd come to the door and ask for deer skins. Clarence (her husband) never hunted so he didn't have any. I didn't know how to get rid of them. Someone said to give them something, a box of matches, an old spoon, or something. Then they'd just get on their horses and go out. I never thought of being afraid of them."

She added, "When I taught at a little school at McKenzie Bridge (1914-1918), it was open in front. The Indians sometimes would camp there, and we would have to turn school out because it would smell pretty strong after drying a lot of fish."

For many years when Indians came to the McKenzie River to net and spear fish, hatchery employees gave them fish carcasses at the Leaburg hatchery and later at the Hendricks Bridge fish racks.

Cleo Carter, whose father, Walter, worked for the Fish and Game Commission as superintendent of the McKenzie Salmon Hatchery from 1921 until 1956, wrote in *Historic Leaburg* in 1987: "I have every reason to believe these Indians or their ancestors had been coming to this place to get fish long before any white men were in the area, because in a flat not far from the egg-taking area each time it was plowed arrow heads and flint came to the surface.

"The Indians came over every year (from the Warm Springs

Reservation) to dry salmon for their provisions," continued Mrs. Carter, who also worked for the commission. "They used every part of the salmon except the intestines. . .They only took what they had room to properly care for, the squaws doing most of the work with the fish while the men took care of the livestock and hunting. They would not take anything unless given to them."

This compiler remembers Indians coming into Walterville as late as the 1930's to take and dry salmon at Hendricks Bridge.

Indian Landmarks

The following information on early-day Indians is adapted mostly from Gerald W. Williams' McKenzie River Names:

INDIAN CAMP was located in the Three Sisters Wilderness, along the Pacific Crest Trail, west of the South Sister and south-east of The Husband. (Hodge, 1925 and Parker, 1922). The name was "given by (Fred W.) Cleator of the U. S. F. S. to an obsidian locality where Indians manufactured arrow heads and other implements."

INDIAN CREEK enters the McKenzie between Goodpasture Bridge and Vida. It crosses the McKenzie Highway at mp. 26 and enters the river from the north. "Indian Creek was named before my great grandparents settled there and they heard the story from early settlers," wrote Mildred Patch (*McKenzie Memories, 1959*: 12).

"The Indians were on their way back to the Warm Springs Indian Reservation from the valley. An old squaw became too old to go on. Her people left her to die under a tree on the banks of the creek. According to their custom, they left her belongings beside her to go with her in to the hereafter. The stoicism natural to the Indians made it possible for this parting, and the limitations of their transportation and mode of life made it necessary. My great-grandmother had in her possession a string of blue beads found where the old squaw so stoically died."

The Fayette Thomson family, later the Goodpastures owned about two acres of land near the mouth of Indian Creek.

Another Indian Creek flows from the north side of Browder Ridge and enters Hackleman Creek, which in turn flows into Fish Lake, near the Santiam Pass. The creek flows near an area once called Indian Prairie, now known as Tombstone Prairie.

A number of features bear the Indian name, which refers to the native Americans who once lived and freely traveled throughout the area. Indian Creek crosses Heart Lake Road. A fourth Indian Creek enters upper Quartz Creek near Indian Ridge.

INDIAN HOLES area is south of Sphinx Butte and southeast of Honey Lake in the Three Sisters area. Prince Helfrich (1961) reported Indian Holes, Squaw Holes, now referred to as The Potholes, and Lowder Mountain (elevation 4,800 feet) "must have been favorite (Indian) hunting camps. They had water and an abundance of grass, and they were in the heart of the summer range for deer and elk."

INDIAN RIDGE, elevation 5,405 feet, lies generally in a north-south direction, west of Cougar Reservoir. Former District Ranger Smith Taylor reported (1927), "Indian Ridge was named for an old Indian hunting trail that extended along the summit. The ridge is west of the South Fork River." (McArthur, 1982: 385).

There are conflicting accounts on the naming of Indian Ridge. In recent years, several old Indian habitation sites have been discovered and partially excavated by the University of Oregon Anthropology Department along the ridge. It is generally known Warm Springs Indians came there to hunt and pick huckleberries. Several Indian cairns have been found. The U. S. Forest Service maintained a fire lookout on the ridge for many years.

AVENUE CREEK is a tributary of Horse Creek near the old Foley Springs resort. The well-used Indian trail along the creek may account for the name. Manena Schwering remembered walking and riding the trail to Horsepasture Mountain and the Olallie Trail, an Indian and stock route. Indians often stripped bark from cedar trees to make baskets for storing huckleberries, abundant in the area.

CHUCKSNEY MOUNTAIN (an Indian name spelled variously), at 5,760-foot elevation, is located northwest of Box Canyon Guard Station. The name source is disputed, but it was supposed to be the site of a lost gold mine. When some Indians showed up at The Dalles with several gold nuggets, it caused quite a bit of excitement. A party was organized to return with the Indians, who agreed to show them the source of the gold. Along the way they met other Indians. After a pow wow, they refused to go further. Indians figured in other attempts to locate the mine, but all ended in failure.

HORSEPASTURE MOUNTAIN (5660 feet summit), south of Horse Creek, was named because of the excellent pasture on the south. Steve Schaefers (1978) related Indians had a horse racing track that encircled the mountain. They often were present in the high mountains during the summer for hunting and the berry season. Martha Belknap, the first woman lookout, served on Horsepasture the summers of 1917/1918.

THREE PICTURESQUE FALLS on the upper reaches of the McKenzie River in recent years were given Indian names -- Sahalie, the upper; Koosah, the middle, and Tamolich, the lower falls. Tamolich now is a part of the Eugene Water and Electric District Carmen-Smith hydroelectric system. The other falls can be reached from the Clear Lake Highway.

MOUNT MULTNOMAH was the name Dr. Edwin T. Hodge (1924) gave to the suspected mountain that once stood in the Three Sisters Wilderness ten million years ago. "Multnomah is an old Indian name for that part of the Willamette River between Oregon City and the Columbia River."

OBSIDIAN from Obsidian Cliff was used by native Americans in making various types of hunting and scraping implements. Often the Indians transported pieces of obsidian to their various hunting areas, where they transformed the natural glass into arrow points. Modern archaeological methods have been used to track the Indian use of obsidian from Obsidian Cliff to many parts of Western Oregon.

SQUAW CAMP was a favorite Indian site along the McKenzie River about six miles below McKenzie Bridge. "A noted (Indian) camping spot, it was so named for this reason." (Stobie, 1969: 30).

Jim Drury and Manena Schwering (1979) said Squaw Camp was near Slide Point at Aufderheide Forest Drive (FR. 19) junction with the McKenzie Highway. However, Martha Belknap remembered Squaw Camp was between Blue River and Finn Rock where a creek crosses the road. She said she and others picnicked there in the teens and 20's. John West (1980) said a person could smell the camp "for five miles down wind" when Indians were drying and smoking fish.

SQUAW CROSSING was a shallow McKenzie River ford crossing east of Blue River. Jim Drury said the crossing was near the mouth of the South Fork River below Bruckhart Bridge.

SQUAW MOUNTAIN (5,275 feet) lies west of Wildcat Mountain Natural Resource Area and north of Wolf Creek, near FR. 1348, on the divide between the McKenzie and South Santiam River drainages. Archie Knowles, forest ranger when the Cascadia Ranger District was formed in 1910, related this was great grazing country. Warm Springs Indians came every summer to graze 300 cattle and horses, hunt and fish and pick berries. They abandoned the site suddenly.

Knowles told the story that two Portland youths had a band of sheep there and decided to trick the Indians into leaving by playing on their superstitions. They rigged a balloon with head, arms and legs painted on it. Seeking council with the Indian chief, they explained they had word from the White Man's God that harm would come to all unless immediate action was taken.

They said the white men's "devil" was very dangerous, that he'd been seen recently, and if he came again he'd kill white men and Indians and all their horses and cattle. The boys said if anyone should see the white men's "devil" they should leave immediately if they intended to save their squaws, horses and cattle.

At dusk the balloon loomed overhead. The Indians needed no more warning. They left the area and never returned.

THREE FINGERED JACK, along the Pacific Crest trail north of the Santiam Pass, was called Little Khla-tee-wap-thee by Indians. The words mean "slide down and get stuck in the mud." That's what happened when people rode up the mountain in the spring -- the horses slid down and got stuck in the mud. Nearby Mt. Jefferson was Big Khla-tee-wap-thee.

CHAPTER 52

Fires on the McKenzie

Fire -- the friend of man, or the great destroyer?

Evidence of fires in virgin forests dating back far beyond the time of the first white men can be found in Oregon's wilderness areas. Lightning strikes probably caused many of these fires.

Indians frequently burned timber to provide grazing or hunting lands. These to a large extent were controlled but some got away. Some people today advocate controlled burns of underbrush on which wild fires feed. The Yellowstone fire of 1989 was allowed to burn itself out. Fires often rage uncontrolled in Alaska.

One of the worst fires of record on the McKenzie is said to have occurred in 1855, before any settlers arrived. J. H. McClung of Eugene, describing a trip he and six others made up the river in August 1860, said they passed through a heavily forested area, principally of Douglas Fir, east of Leaburg. Just before reaching Gate Creek they entered the "great burn" that destroyed billions of board feet of timber, the fire extending 15 miles up river and leaving hardly a green tree standing. Many trees, six to eight feet in diameter had fallen across the trail.

The late Manena Sparks Schwering, in *Lane County Historian,* described conditions before and after the U. S. Forest Service was established. On Sept. 28, 1893, President Cleveland authorized the creation of the Cascade Range Forest Service. This block of land included 4,883,588 acres, extending from the Columbia River almost to the California border, but it was not until much later that forest protection began. McKenzie Ranger District historical records show several men served as administrators between 1901 and 1908. Smith Taylor, appointed district ranger in 1908, served until 1934.

"The picture is greatly changed from that day in 1908 when Smith Taylor rode his horse up to a little log cabin that served as the first ranger station, with a wood stove and no plumbing, to begin management of almost 500,000 acres of forest," she wrote.

"Some forest fires of those years devastated large areas of forests, damaged watersheds and destroyed much game and forage and thousands of acres of prime old growth timber. The forest was roadless and the trail system was not a comprehensive one.

"Men went to fight fires walking with packs of personal effects and tools, such as axes, saws, pulaskis and other items. Pack teams were assembled and sent to the larger fires with food, bed rolls and other supplies. On larger fires requiring a long presence for control and 'moppin up,' mini-headquarters were set up, which included fire bases, time keepers, clerks, cooks, packers and other personnel. Local residents with suitable stock and equipment were hired to keep the supply lines functioning. The logistics of operating a fire camp in remote areas was a truly formidable responsibility. . . Major fires from 1912 through 1935 devastated more than 17,000 acres."

The late Martha (Andrews) Belknap, the first woman lookout, served on Horsepasture Mountain during World War I. She reported there were extensive fires in the South Fork region.

"The second summer (1918) the whole South Fork burned down," she said in an interview. "Seven or eight fires. It was dry with thunderstorms, and, of course, there wasn't anything but a trail out there. And the country was so covered with smoke. All we could do was send in men with shovels. That's why I like all these roads. You can go up to something and see the area that was burned. Fires, of course, just went to the ridge, but they lost beautiful stands of forest. Nature has a way of taking care of itself."

About 1920, a party, including this compiler, guided by Grant Tate, a forest service ranger, hiked over the ridge south of the Belknap Ranch to the headwaters of Cougar Creek. The upper area was virgin forest. Downstream, we passed through a burned area. There were several prairies in the South Fork bottoms where fires had burned off the timber leaving open areas. New growths had obliterated most signs of the conflagrations.

In 1935, a fire on Lookout Ridge was fought by the Forest Service and Civilian Conservation Corps crews from Camp Belknap. This compiler was working part time for the old *Eugene Morning News*, while maintaining a Portland *Oregonian* newspaper delivery route to Belknap Springs. The fire was clearly visible from the highway at McKenzie Bridge.

I observed fresh crews of young men leaving for the fire lines, and the tired, dirty men coming out of the mountains on long shift changes. They lacked the heavy equipment available today, but did an outstanding job controlling in four days this blaze, which swept up the mountainside in green, virgin timber, leaving blackened tree skeletons. I'd talk to District Ranger Smith Taylor at his office at McKenzie Bridge. On my return to Eugene I wrote news stories which ran under my by-line as Fireline Correspondent.

Many Landmarks Destroyed

Over the years fires destroyed many landmark buildings, homes and other property. Log Cabin Inn at McKenzie Bridge burned in 1906. A Blue River hotel burned in the early 1900's, and in 1983 the grand old hotel at Foley Springs went up in smoke.

The James Belknap home, the "big house," built about 1900 to replace his old log cabin, was destroyed by fire in 1910. Art Belknap's house on the King Road was destroyed in 1959, along with many heirlooms, including the much treasured family Bible and old guns.

Clarence Belknap's sawmill at Rainbow burned about 1935. The original Holiday Farm buildings, a mile east of Blue River, were destroyed by fire about 1940. Famed Thomson's lodge near Vida burned in April 1954. It was not replaced.

The long abandoned buildings at the Lucky Boy Mine on Gold Hill were destroyed by fire. John T. Craig's cabin on the McKenzie Pass burned down in 1909. In Walterville, the church, Odd Fellows hall and adjacent buildings were destroyed by fire in the 1930's.

Fire, Jan. 5, 1975, spelled finis to an historic old hotel at Vida Frank Minney built in 1907. Known as Minney Hall, it served as a hotel, school-house, and dance hall for many years.

Bill and Flora Yale's home at Yale Junction burned in 1950.

Seymour's Chateau, closed for a year, burned in 1961. A large restaurant at Blue River burned in the early 1990's. A smaller restaurant burned at Vida. The store housing the post office at Vida burned in 1961. Coy Lansbery's home burned in 1932. The Dr. Leiberg mansion east of Leaburg was destroyed by fire in the 1930's.

Phil's Phine Phoods

Phil's Phine Phoods, an historic landmark east of Rainbow on McKenzie River Drive, was destroyed by fire of incendiary origin June 26, 1993. Darin Harbick, co-owner, had acquired the store two years before from the Phillips family. A new building was constructed along the McKenzie Highway at Mill Creek Road. The store reopened for business in 1994 under the name of Harbick's.

In October 1995, fire caused an estimated $120,000 damage to the Walterville Feed Store. Firemen blamed the blaze on a roofing tar kettle placed too close to the side of the building.

Several fires caused major damage in the early days. The large sawmill at Springfield burned about 1881. The Booth-Kelly sawmill at Springfield, built in 1902, burned in 1910. The massive fire threatened the town. The mill was rebuilt in 1911. At Wendling on Aug. 24, 1910, a forest fire starting five miles to the east destroyed everything except the sawmill and some houses. The town was rebuilt and survived, until the mill itself burned Sept. 29, 1946.

Rural fire districts staffed with volunteers have been formed and have a good reputation for fire suppression. The Forest Service and county patrols maintain constant vigilance during the summer.

"With the early warning system, aerial patrols, helicopter crews, smoke jumpers and retardant drops, it is hoped that never again will the forests see the massive destruction of those years. Reforestation programs initiated by the Forest Service was prompted in part by the fire losses suffered in those early fires, as well as the need to maintain a productive forest to replace trees cut through sales of commercial timber," Mrs. Schwering concluded.

CHAPTER 53

Byways to Highways

A great amount of water has flowed over the dam, to use a trite cliché, since the first seafaring men viewed the majestic cliffs along the Oregon coast, and Capt. Robert Gray in 1792 entered the Great River of the West to open up a new world.

Then came the Lewis and Clark Expedition of 1804-1805 and the John Jacob Astor Pacific Fur Co. establishment at Ft. Astoria in 1811-1812. Out of this came Donald Mackenzie's discovery of the river which bears his name on a trip up the Willamette Valley. The great exodus of emigrants across the plains began in 1842.

Lane County's first pioneer settlers of 1846 were Elijah Bristow and William Dodson at Pleasant Hill, Eugene Skinners at what became Eugene City and Capt. Felix Scott, who settled on the McKenzie across from the Mohawk confluence. They were followed a year later by Jacob Spores, John Diamond, William Stevens, Mitchell Wilkins and George Armitage at Coburg and Willamette Forks. Isaac and Elias Briggs founded Springfield. B. J. Pengra later became an important player.

There were John Cogswell, the McNutts, John Latta, the Millicans, Storments and Fountains on the lower McKenzie River, and the Martins, Thomsons, Pepiots, Belknaps, Finns, Sims and Wycoffs who settled on the upper river from 1864 to 1874, blazing the way.

Life of the pioneer was not an easy one. Crossing the plains in ox or horse-drawn wagons was an ordeal. To come by way of the Isthmus of Panama was to brave disease-ridden tropical jungles, or the third alternative -- sailing around the Horn of South America -- meant facing the most turbulent seas known to seafaring men.

But men found a way and women and children for the most part went along. Many people died and countless livestock was lost. But those who survived found a new life in a land they grew to love.

Pioneers in general were adventurous peoples. Many did not stop their explorations once they had settled on the land. They were restless souls, many leaving their families and departing for California to seek gold or to go elsewhere.

Indian trails slowly became roads. Ferries provided means for crossing rivers until bridges, slow to come, could be built. Gradually settlers began to move out into the hinterlands as new areas were opened up to provide homesteads for the land-hungry setters.

Explorers, hunters and trappers made their way up the valley, and some cattle drives passed through the McKenzie Valley to and from Central Oregon. John Templeton Craig established a new route over the McKenzie Pass, after Felix Scott Jr.'s exploit of taking 900 head of cattle and freight over the old Scott Trail to Central Oregon in 1862. The McKenzie Toll Road was established in 1871.

It should be noted that the Martins in 1864, Pepiots in 1868, Thomsons in 1870 and Finns in 1871 were first to settle in the vicinity of Gate Creek, now Vida, about 25 miles east of Eugene. James Henry Belknap, at age 21 in 1869, homesteaded another 25 miles further up river -- a distance today of half an hour's driving time, but in pioneering days a two-to-three-day trip.

When James went up there, no one else was around, except for occasional hunters or explorers. John Craig knew the area well. Joseph Carter briefly operated a ferry east of Blue River. J. B. Alexander who established "squatter's rights" at what became Foley Springs sold to Dr. A. K. Foley in 1870.

James was the first permanent settler on the upper McKenzie. His father, Rollin, and family founded Belknap Springs in 1871. Then came John Whitlock Sims at the Springs and Philander Renfrew who homesteaded at McKenzie Bridge in 1874. The Peter Wycoffs and John Millers, Brownsville pioneers, moved to the McKenzie in the mid-1870's.

Illustrative of the isolation and loneliness of the area, James Belknap wrote in 1905, "When we came here the Indians were very bad and the mail was few and far between. We lost all track of kin fokes (sic.). Mother never heard from any of her fokes after (age) 55 or 58, and father did not seem inclined to write."

In spite of its relative isolation, it seemed everyone on the McKenzie River knew each other. And if the river could talk, surely it could reveal many tall tales, to top even those of B. F. Finn, about adventures and romances that took place in the fertile valley.

To illustrate, the Finn daughter, Ella, and young James Belknap got together and were married in 1873, within two years of Ella's arrival. Dora Belknap at 15, in 1874, married John Sims, who worked for her father, Rollin, at Belknap Springs. James Wycoff married Emma Finn. Many more young people got together, married and raised large families. My father, from Pennsylvania, drifted to the McKenzie, met and married my mother, Cora Belknap, in 1903.

Abolish Toll Road

John Craig built a bridge across the McKenzie at McKenzie Bridge in 1869, the first across a major stream in Lane County. It was replaced with one built by Carey Thomson in 1877. Washed out by the flood of 1881, it was again replaced.

With increased use of the road, brought on by mining activity on Gold Hill and travel to resorts and Central Oregon, there was increasing agitation from upper McKenzie residents to abolish the toll road and make it a public roadway, even though people could travel the road for six months of the year free. Indians, unwilling to submit to tolls, whenever possible made crossings at other locations.

Lane County Commissioners resolved the matter May 9, 1895, when they denied the petition of A. G. Hovey and George A. Dorris for a renewal of tolls, after declaring "the bridges are unsafe and the road in poor condition." In 1896 the road from Rock House to Belknap Springs was declared a county road. Two years later the entire road was taken over and renamed the McKenzie and Eastern Road. (*Eugene Register-Guard*, Feb. 22, 1959). Upkeep was paid by private subscription. State and county financing was authorized after 1900.

Caswell Hendricks continued operating his ferry crossing the McKenzie at Cedar Flat long after bridges had replaced ferries at Eugene, Springfield, Hayden Bridge and Coburg. Before his death in 1893, Caswell gave or sold the ferry to his youngest sons, Grant and Frank. By the summer of 1894, the ferry was operating at very low profits, so Grant gave his interest to Frank.

In January, 1895, Stephen Smeed and others petitioned Lane County to build a public (free) bridge across the McKenzie. But the county felt a wooden bridge would be inadequate, and a steel bridge too expensive (*Daily Eugene Guard*, Jan. 23, 1895). In the spring the commissioners purchased the ferry boat and fixtures from Hendricks for $80. They also arranged with a Mr. Whitrow to run the boat until the next term of court. The ferry continued operating as a public or free ferry with Sol Dodson and, later, Grant Hendricks as ferrymen until 1908 when it was replaced by a covered bridge.

Hendricks Bridge, named for Caswell Hendricks, today spans the McKenzie River east of Cedar Flat at mp. 11.4. The first bridge "was of two spans, 240 feet and 180 feet with 142 feet of approach on the north and 20 feet on the south. It had the distinction, I'm told, of having the longest wooden span in the nation at the time it was built. It was done for a total cost of $13,000," Carl Stephens said.

The covered bridge was removed by dynamite in about 1925 after being replaced with a steel bridge. This structure was replaced with the present bridge around 1963.

Carey Thomson, who built the McKenzie Bridge replacing Craig's crude bridge, also built the first Belknap Bridge across the McKenzie replacing Belknap's Ferry in 1890. He felled several large trees across the river to serve as stringers and covered them with an open, wooden deck. It was first called Thomson's Bridge, and he collected tolls.

The simple log Belknap Bridge was covered in 1894. The name apparently was changed to Campbell Bridge. Douglas County records show: "Commissioner's Court. . .now comes W. E. Brown, assignee of J. H. Belknap, and presents. . .by the claim of said Belknap for labor and siding the Campbell Bridge on McKenzie River, which said claim was duly examined and approved by the court. . . (and) ordered. . . full payment of such claim for the sum of. . .$100.00. (*Daily Eugene Guard*, March 16, 1894)." The name later became Belknap Bridge.

Promotions after the turn of the century continued to extol the health offerings of resorts at Belknap and Foley Springs, which brought many people to the upper McKenzie, in spite of poor road conditions. Glowing and enthusiastic reports of the scenic beauty of the high Cascades and the vast lava beds were received by early writers of McArthur's *Oregon Geographic Names*, who commented:

"Nowhere are there such remarkable evidences of comparatively recent volcanism as in central Oregon," these early reports said. "The writer is prepared to believe this, and is of the opinion the lava fields and flows of the McKenzie Pass present the most unusual aspect of nature he has ever seen. Fortunately, development of an excellent highway over the pass brought these lava flows within view of many people who knew little of them."

The McKenzie Pass was named for the river of that name "and besides being well known for its unusual lava flow it is historically interesting by reason of the construction by pioneer citizens of Oregon of a toll road over the Cascade Range at this point."

First Auto Stage

The first auto stage on the McKenzie River was established about 1910. A Forest Service file photo, showing the bus, passengers and a group of people in front of the Leaburg store, appearing in the *Springfield News* June 30, 1971, was captioned:

"FIRST AUTO STAGE ON THE McKENZIE attracted a great deal of attention when it stopped at the Leaburg store and post office more than 60 years ago. According to Mrs. Edna Carter of Leaburg, who spent her 80 years in the area, the bus went from Eugene to McKenzie Bridge. Those who wanted to continue on to the popular Belknap Springs had to go by horseback. Driver of the bus, with its chain drive, crank, solid rubber tires and open-air seating, was Frank Moore. Best known driver was Percy O'Brien, 45 years on the run."

After toll collecting was abandoned, the road over the summit languished. The road in many places was little more than wagon tracks, up over steep inclines, then down to stream beds, many of which had to be forded. The few bridges were crude affairs. There were many very sharp curves. One section of road was called "Old Honky Grade," because of a series of nine very sharp curves. Drivers customarily blew their car horns around each curve as a warning to oncoming cars.

Active reconstruction began in the 1920's. The old, tortuous road over the McKenzie Pass and its lava beds to Central and Eastern Oregon was relocated and widened. On Sept. 21, 1925, the highway project was completed between Blue River and Sisters, a distance of 50 miles. The highest point on the highway is 5,325 feet. It was a wonderful road, compared with the pioneer route built by John T. Craig. It was unpaved and had many sharp curves and switch backs. A 40-foot cut through lava beds, which can fill with blowing snow within hours during a blizzard, makes it impractical to keep it open during the winter months.

Before the McKenzie pass road was rebuilt, a series of wooden "ladders," or planking, was used to cross the lava beds. Cars had to be towed over some of these ladders.

Some improvements were made on the highway from Walterville to Belknap Springs in the 1920's, but it was not until the 1930's that any major reconstruction was done on this section of highway. Paving did not take place until after World War I. There were many detours and delays, and some very rough roads.

Around 1925, a new covering was built atop the original log Belknap Bridge by Clarence Belknap, son of James Henry. "It cost less than $1,000," according to Clarence's wife, Martha. In 1939, the roof caved in. The roof and floor were reconstructed, but the original log stringers still supported the bridge.

The entire bridge washed away during the Christmas flood of 1964. The present Lane County covered bridge, which connected King Road with McKenzie River Drive, was designed and built by the Oregon Bridge Co. of Springfield in 1965 at a cost of $87,000. Louvered arch windows were added in 1975 to the south side to give interior illumination. The bridge was listed in the National Register in 1979.

When the bridge was completed a ribbon cutting ceremony was held with Arthur Belknap and Mrs. Clarence (Martha) Belknap of Rainbow and Mrs. Cora (Belknap) Inman of Springfield taking part. A cutline with accompanying pictures stated:

"NEW BRIDGE---Mrs. Clarence Belknap Monday cut the ribbon and enjoyed the honor of being the first to drive across the new Belknap covered bridge which spans the McKenzie just east of Rainbow. Also participating in the ceremony were county commissioners Jess Hill and Kenneth Nielsen. Ernest Cullen Murphy, McKenzie resident, was master of ceremonies for the McKenzie River Chamber of Commerce which sponsored the affair."

The bridge replaced one that was destroyed in the December 1964 flood. It was the fourth structure to span the river at this point, the first having been built in 1890. Progress pictures showed the bridge under construction, as the first covered bridge to be built in Lane County in many years. Specially cut trusses were fabricated.

During the 1930's, Civilian Conservation Corp men from Camp Belknap at McKenzie Bridge built a road from Belknap Springs to Clear Lake and beyond to join the Santiam Highway. It was unpaved.

The McKenzie Pass Highway continued as the main route over the Cascades from Eugene until the late 1950's, when construction was begun on an alternate route. The new highway section, known as the Clear Lake Cutoff, routed most of the McKenzie Pass traffic above McKenzie Bridge to the Santiam Highway (U. S. 20) via scenic Clear Lake. When this alternate highway was completed in 1964, the old McKenzie route was renamed as a scenic highway and given the present Oregon route 242 designation. Today, the McKenzie Pass Highway is open from late June to early November, as snow fall blocks the highway during the winter months.

COUGAR DAM AND LAKE

The most recent and by far the major construction on the South Fork River is the massive 452-foot high Cougar Dam, a U. S. Army Corps of Engineers project authorized in 1950. Preliminary construction was begun in 1956. In 1960, an old river channel was found below the main dam site, which caused delays in construction by almost a year. The last load of rocks was finally placed on the dam in October, 1963. The project was dedicated in May 1964. Cougar, the highest rock-fill dam in Oregon, is 1,500 feet long and 452 feet high. At full pool level, the lake, or reservoir, is 10 miles long and covers about 1,260 acres.

Cougar is part of a three-dam flood control project: Cougar, Blue River and Gate Creek. These three dams were proposed for the McKenzie in lieu of a major dam near Horse Creek, a proposal which met with tremendous opposition in the 1940's. As part of the Cougar project, a regulating dam below Cougar, to be named Strube Dam, has been authorized but not yet built.

The dam is located along Aufderheide Drive at mp. 3.2. Bruckhart Bridge crosses the McKenzie River two miles west of Rainbow. King Road West follows the southern line of the Belknap Ranch and connects with Aufderheide Drive near the bridge. Wapiti Road (FR. 1993) crosses the dam and follows the East Fork to its junction with Horse Creek Road.

BLUE RIVER DAM

The second dam built under the supervision of the Army Corps of Engineers as part of a major flood control project for the McKenzie River was Blue River Dam and Lake.

The dam on Blue River is above the community of that name. The lake or reservoir is long and narrow with three arms: Quartz Creek, North Fork Quartz Creek and Scout Creek. Blue River and its companion Saddle Dam were completed in the fall of 1969. Blue River Reservoir was renamed Blue River Lake in 1972.

The dam is located 1.6 miles up the Blue River Dam Road (FR. 1620), which begins at the intersection of Blue River Drive (Old McKenzie Highway). An upper access road (FR. 15) to the lake and the east dam, Saddle Dam, begins at mpg. 43.9 on the McKenzie Highway. The high water surface covers 1,420 acres at an elevation of 1,357 feet. Other dam sites on the McKenzie have been studied.

Vida diversion dam is a name applied to a proposed hydroelectric project that would divert water from the McKenzie River to turn an electric generator. It would consist of a power house at river mile 40, connect to 6.5 miles of canal and a dam, located below Bear Creek. It would be five feet high and 170 feet long. The dam would divert water through the canal to the power house, producing 63 KV of electricity and costing $80 million. (*River Reflections,* 1980).

CARMEN-SMITH DAM

The Carmen-Smith project was designed by the Eugene Water and Electric Board for hydroelectric power generation on the upper McKenzie River. It includes Carmen Reservoir on the river above Tamolitch Falls; Carmen Diversion Tunnel, Smith River Reservoir, and Trail Creek Reservoir. Carmen Dam impounds the upper McKenzie water above Tamolitch at Beaver Marsh. The water is transferred from Carmen Reservoir via a diversion tunnel through the ridge, which is west of the reservoir, to the Smith River Reservoir. The reservoir covers some 30 acres at an elevation of 1,600 feet.

Planning was started in 1957, after Eugene voters rejected the Beaver Marsh Dam project. Construction, begun in 1960, was delayed near completion when cracks were found in the diversion tunnel. After repairs were made, the Carmen-Smith project was dedicated Sept. 9, 1963. Carmen-Smith is the third EWEB hydroelectric project on the McKenzie, the others being at Walterville, completed in 1910, and the Leaburg project, completed in 1927.

A migratory fish screen project, completed in 1983 below the Leaburg Dam in the power canal, was designed to enhance the salmon and steelhead runs in the river above the dam. The water board Municipal Park, located across the dam on the south side of the reservoir, has 120 picnic sites and several group picnic areas. Two boat landings are provided. Just below the dam is the Leaburg Trout Hatchery, one of two hatcheries on the McKenzie.

A modern highway now leads up the McKenzie River Valley. A four-lane section extends six miles east from downtown Springfield and several passing lanes have been built, although more are needed. A drive up the McKenzie now is an easy hour's trip.

A tourist information center has been established at the site of the old fish hatchery on the shores of Leaburg Lake. A highway widening project in the vicinity is under way.

Thus we return full circle from the byways of the past to the highways of today. Some people resent improvements to the McKenzie highway, saying it should remain a scenic route.

Sure, we all want the McKenzie to retain its scenic grandeur, but safety takes precedent in plans for the future. The McKenzie River Valley is becoming too settled to remain obscure. None of us want to see its pristine qualities lost in modern-day improvements. But we must face reality. Future construction should be with an eye to enhancing those aspects of beauty rather than detracting.

Modern improvements must come in order to control traffic. The McKenzie today is a major east-west thoroughfare leading to and from Central Oregon and points beyond. This fact cannot be denied. We can see a great future for the McKenzie as a residential paradise, without losing its recreational values.

We owe something to the brave and adventurous pioneers who sought out the McKenzie River Valley as a place to make their homes. Living in a modern-day society we must face change, but changes of which we can be proud while facing reality.

We salute you, McKenzie, and we salute the "Donald" who unknowingly gave you a name while he explored the West. We who love the McKenzie wish to be worthy of the trust in the preservation of its beauty and the security of its name.

THE END

McKenzie

By Clifton L. Inman

Oh, Grand McKenzie, fair of name,
  And rightful heir to rising fame,
Forgive, I pray, this bold acclaim.

If I should sing in boastful mood,
  Remember, if my song sounds crude,
I'm only one of Adam's brood.

In higher realm it should belong,
  So join me in the joyous throng,
And help the muses lift my song.

We sound our praises far and near,
  Such wealth and praises have we here.
What country can produce your peer?

A stream of virtues set with lure
  That purge our hearts and leave us pure,
When'ere we step within your door.

Oh, stream devine, whence comes this art
  That holds the key to every heart
And bids us stay, loth to depart?

With game abounding on your shore,
  Whence man has scarcely touched the store.
Could earthly mortal wish for more?

And fish that ever did beguile
  And call upon our best, the while
We pit our skills against their wile.

With giant trees on either shore,
  Their branches reaching far out o'er,
As if to hush your ceaseless roar.

The lurking redsides in the pool
  Entices us, with rod and spool,
At times to break from labor's gruel.

BEAUTIFUL McKENZIE

There, through the trees, we catch the gleam,
    Springs and branches countless teem
As feeders of the parent stream.

And as we view the restless scene,
    The river marks the line between
The sleeping hills of Douglas green.

With sources in everlasting snow
    And joining others as you flow
To enter lakes spread out below;

There pause awhile in restful sleep
    And gather strength to make the leap
That starts you onward to the deep.

In hesitation's seeming fear
    Upon the brink so high and sheer
Then plunging downward through the air.

Unguided by the rocks or shore,
    Your gladsome voice augments the roar,
As in the foam you disappear.

Thus over precipices fall,
    Obeying gravitation's call,
Sources to mouth no creep nor crawl.

Here rushing on with purling sound,
    There erstwhile, rock would fain impound,
Again escapes with leap and bound.

And as your pulses rise and sink,
    We kneel us down upon your brink
And pay due homage as we drink

Of sparkling water, nature's brew,
    With sources in never ending snow,
As onward, undefiled you flow.

If we but guard this treasure door,
    Return in need full much or more,
There is no limit to the store.

INDEX

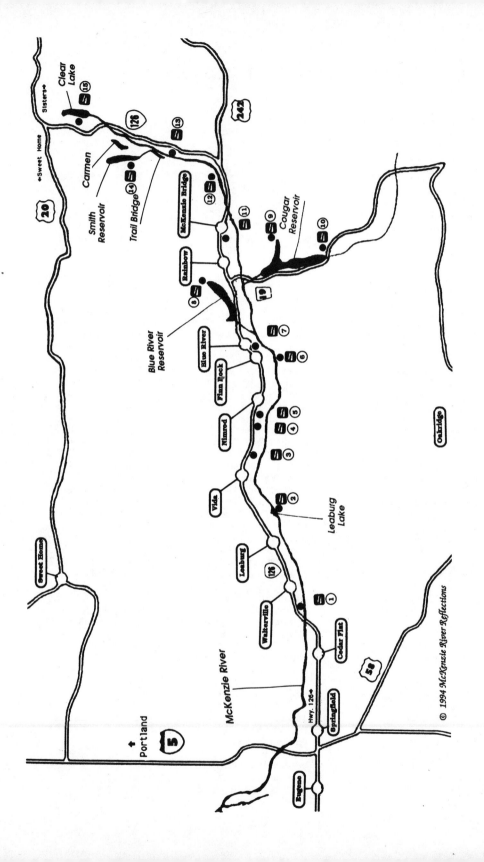

© 1994 McKenzie River Reflections